Advance praise for
The Power of Oral History Narratives: Lived Experiences of International Global Scholars and Artists in Their Native Country and After Their Immigration to the United States

This is an amazing book with a panorama of diverse and yet similar human life stories and a big inspiration for me. Most people, portrayed in this book have experienced tragedies in their homelands and some disillusionment when they have come to the country of their dreams, the United States. Yet, they have been strong enough to start building bridges between nations, races and ethnicities and their efforts have not been in vain. I have always seen building bridges, not walls, as my personal vocation, but my country's most recent policy and aggression has destroyed bridges that have existence for many centuries. As an ethnic Ukrainian but a Russian citizen I feel responsible for the pain that my country has inflicted upon the Ukrainian nation and the damage it has done to the future of its own children. But similarly, to the characters of this book, I am hopeful that my efforts to restore the destroyed bridges will not be in vain.

—**Elena Lenskaya**
Head, Education Policy Studies Center
Moscow School of Social and Economic Sciences Russia
Order of the British Empire (OBE) 2008

A rich collection of personal narratives that paints, in full color, the aspirations and anxieties of migration. The narratives in this absorbing book offer historical insights into the scholars' motives for migration from their home countries and recount the shocks that often awaited them in the United States. These are stories of belief and belonging, clutching the dream of the imagined land while searching for the soul of a straddled identity. As such, they portray the everyday dilemma of the migrant experience: the struggle between the rational argument for moving to a land of promise and the emotional attachment to the land of birth. The reflections and analyses of these distinguished scholars are perceptive and powerful, exploring the contradictions of their transcultural identities and documenting their efforts to challenge the marginalization experienced in their new homeland.

—**Graham Pike**
Honorary Research Associate
Faculty of Education
Vancouver Island University, Canada

The stories of intercultural learning, adaptability, and resilience told by the global scholars in this collection of history narratives are gripping in themselves. As a collection, they illustrate and illuminate the power and importance of oral history for the discovery of one's own voice, and in turn, one's connection to others. Such a book couldn't come at a more important time in our increasingly disjointed and difficult world—this is a must-read for all who value global learning.

—**Hilary Landorf**
Executive Director, Office of Global Learning Initiatives
Associate Professor, International & Intercultural Education
Florida International University

Toni Fuss-Kirkwood Tucker and Frans Doppen have endeavored to craft a volume of voices among global education leaders from an especially unique and significant vantage point: global scholars with global roots. Kirkwood-Tucker and Doppen—themselves prominent and long-standing members of the global education scholarly community with roots in Germany and The Netherlands, respectively—share this background and perspective. The power of this volume lies in making explicit the types of questions that we wonder about in our work and that of others; namely, what motivates them to be the scholar and teacher who they are? This is a simple yet profound question, one that all who work as scholars come to terms with to some degree. Here is an opportunity for academics, practitioners, indeed thinkers of all kinds, to learn from the elegant, timely narratives of others while engaging in self-reflection around motivations and purpose. The diverse collection of narratives demonstrates an ongoing and challenging dynamic for advocates of global learning; that these efforts are championed by immigrants and among those with "other" narratives. Perhaps that is an important inflection point for the field as well, to understand how the hybridity and migratory impulses that are increasingly normative are also verdant ground to grow the next generation of global education scholars. This is an important book that anticipates the next moment in global education in light of the people and pivotal events captured in this volume.

—**William Gaudelli**
Dean, Vice Provost, and Professor
Lehigh University
Bethlehem, PA

I salute the idea of this book and the immigrants who wrote it. I do so as someone who knows three of the participants and has engaged in oral history interviews with African immigrants, some of whom are professors.

—**Angene Wilson**
Professor of Social Studies Education and Global Education
University of Kentucky

The Power of
Oral History Narratives

REVIEW BOARD

After initial critical review by the editors, each chapter was rigorously peer reviewed by the individuals listed below. The editors of this book wish to acknowledge and thank the following members of the review board for their scholarly and unselfish service.

Barbara Bader, MA
Florida International University

Shatara Hanadi, PhD
University of Wisconsin-La Crosse

Jayme Harpring Pekins, PhD
Florida State University

Jennifer Hinkle, PhD
Athens City School District

Matt Hollstein, PhD
Kent State University

Mike Kopish, PhD
Ohio University-Athens

Ashley Lucas, PhD
Towson University

Carmen Morales-Jones, PhD
Florida Atlantic University

Nancy Patterson, PhD
Bowling Green State University

Graham Pike, PhD
Vancouver Island University

Keith Rivero, PhD
Florida Agricultural & Mechanical University (FAMU)

Frank de Varona, MA
Miami-Dade Public Schools

Clarence Walker, PhD
Barry University

Jacqueline Yahn, PhD
Ohio University-Eastern

The Power of Oral History Narratives

Lived Experiences of International Global Scholars and Artists in Their Native Country and After Immigrating to the United States

edited by

Toni Fuss Kirkwood-Tucker
Florida State University

Frans H. Doppen
Ohio University

INFORMATION AGE PUBLISHING, INC.
Charlotte, NC • www.infoagepub.com

Library of Congress Cataloging-in-Publication Data

A CIP record for this book is available from the Library of Congress
http://www.loc.gov

ISBN: 979-8-88730-297-3 (Paperback)
   979-8-88730-298-0 (Hardcover)
   979-8-88730-299-7 (E-Book)

Copyright © 2023 Information Age Publishing Inc.

All rights reserved. No part of this publication may be reproduced, stored in a retrieval system, or transmitted, in any form or by any means, electronic, mechanical, photocopying, microfilming, recording or otherwise, without written permission from the publisher.

Printed in the United States of America

This book is dedicated to

*All Educators of the World:
May You Teach About Global Awareness
and the Criticality of Equality, Equity, and Respect
for All People of this Earth.*

This book is equally dedicated to the

*Courageous People of Ukraine and Their Unequaled President
Volodymyr Zelensky in Their Struggle for Survival
Invaded by Russia on February 24, 2022*

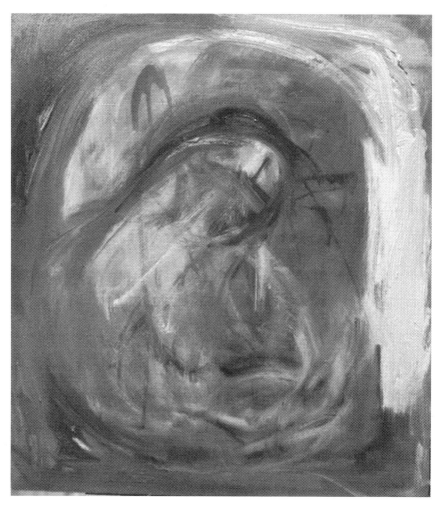

An Armenian Woman Longing for Peace for the Ukrainian People
by Varteni Mosdichian

CONTENTS

Acknowledgments xi
Genesis of Our Book xiii
Significance of Our Book xv
Methodology xvii
Outline of Narratives xix
Introduction xxix

SECTION I
AFRICA

1 Nigeria | Storied Narrative Across Time and Space:
   My Experiences Growing Up in Nigeria and Straddling
   Two Cultures in the United States 3
   Omiunota Nelly Ukpokodu

2 Zimbabwe | The Cultural Confluence of Ubuntu:
   A Journey from Zimbabwe to Global Educational Leader
   in the United States 35
   Josiah Tlou

SECTION II
ASIA

3 Japan | Repairing and Mending Broken Objects With Gold: The Story of a Global Citizen Coming-of-Age 57
Misato Yamaguchi

4 Nepal | Miseducation, Travels, and Contesting Racialized Worlds Within and Outside Academia 75
Binaya Subedi

5 People's Republic of China | Navigating Historical Currents: Reflections of a Chinese-Born Global Educator 87
Lin Lin

6 People's Republic of China | The "New Frontier" to the "New World": Stories of Surviving, Striving, and Thriving in China and the United States 115
Yali Zhao

7 People's Republic of China | Teaching for a Sustainable Future: Crafting a Pedagogy for Sustainability Education............. 135
Guichun Zong

SECTION III
CARIBBEAN

8 Cuba | Flight to Freedom: A Cuban Immigrant's Journey Through Education 157
Bárbara C. Cruz

SECTION IV
EURASIA

9 Ukraine/Russia | Tearing Human Minds to Pieces: The Power of Hypocrisy and the Hypocrisy of Power 179
Anatoli Rapoport

SECTION V
EUROPE

10 France | My Dream of Becoming a Contemporary Classical Composer Advocating for the Armenian Genocide 197
   Hayg Boyadjian

11 Germany | Nazism. Bordercrossing. Racism. All Lives Are of Equal Worth. 225
   Toni Fuss Kirkwood-Tucker

12 The Netherlands | On Crossing the Big Pond 261
   Frans H. Doppen

SECTION VI
MIDDLE EAST

13 Turkey | Fractured Visions of Remembrance 293
   Varteni Mosdichian

SECTION VII
SOUTH AMERICA

14 Argentina | From Buenos Aires to Buffalo to Books: The Politics of Populism 317
   Aixa Pérez-Prado

Epilogue 345
About the Editors 375
About the Contributors... 379
Index 387

ACKNOWLEDGMENTS

The editors are deeply indebted to the generous individuals who made this book a reality. First, we wish to thank the international global scholars and artists for their captivating and thought-provoking oral history narratives. We extend our deep appreciation to the authors for their trust and confidence in us as their editors. Second, and of equal importance, we wish to thank the distinguished members of the review board for their special efforts in appraising the content of chapters.

The editors also extend their very special thanks to Mr. George Johnson, president and CEO of Information Age Publishing, Inc., and to his staff, for their professionalism, civility, and warmth when responding to our many questions regarding our book. Our very special gratitude is extended to our now deceased parents, Antoon and Rikie Doppen from The Netherlands and Leonhard and Franziska Fuss from Germany, who from the very beginning of our border crossing to the United States have supported our academic dreams.

GENESIS OF OUR BOOK

The idea for a book of this nature was conceived by Dr. Frans H. Doppen, professor of social studies and global education, Ohio University Athens, in the United States. Dr. Doppen is a distinguished global scholar in his own right. He served as former president of the International Assembly, an associated group of the National Council for the Social Studies (NCSS), the largest professional organization for social studies educators in the United States. After reading an article on the power of oral history in teaching and learning by Dr. Toni Fuss Kirkwood-Tucker in which she portrays her lived experiences as a little girl during the Nazi era and the end of World War II, published in the *Journal of International Social Studies* (2010), Dr. Doppen contacted Toni about his idea of an entire book of that nature with which she wholeheartedly agreed. Consequently, we envisioned our book to be a collection of autobiographical oral history narratives of the personal and professional lives and work of international global scholars and artists sharing their challenges, joys, trauma, discrimination, disillusionment, and dreams they experienced in their native country and after immigrating to the United States. The participating authors enthusiastically endorsed the idea of the book and agreed to craft a chapter of their oral history narratives which you will find in these pages.

SIGNIFICANCE OF OUR BOOK

The significance of this book is its uniqueness. First, the book contains a collection of 14 chapters that capture the personal, professional, and historical experiences of international global scholars and artists to which they were subjected in their native country and after they immigrated to the United States. What makes this book project highly unusual in comparison to other publications is that these international global scholars and artists experienced historical events of trauma and joy in their native country and in their newly adopted country of the United States that lie deeply buried in their subconsciousness: that these memories are unforgettable and still painful for them, that these memories are a constant companion in their daily lives, and that the experienced historical events of trauma and joy have shaped their professional and personal lives to this very day. There exists a paucity in the global education literature of this far-reaching topic and, thus, has the potential to enhance and diversify the global education literature.

Second, the significance of this book lies in the pedagogical power of the oral history narrative tradition and its impact on students at the secondary and tertiary levels in education. When one's lived experiences of trauma or joy occur during a critical time in history, they rarely yield unforgettable memories and deeply held private knowledge that do not come to light without a storyteller. When firsthand accounts are shared publicly, they can bring powerful insights into past historic events to the very present. Thus, the pedagogical strength of this book contributes to *knowledge creation in the classroom* as oral histories move students from abstract textbook descriptions to concrete and compelling "lived" stories associated with historical happenings. This pedagogy leads students to become more critical of historical events of the past and develops in them a deeper understanding of the past. Consequently, oral history narratives enable teachers and teacher educators to enrich the abstract text of textbooks with the authentic voice of the individual.

A third significance of this book lies embedded in the rich historical perspective displayed by storytellers of non-native international global scholars and artists from around the world who portray their lived-through, firsthand experiences such as child labor, communism, hate, hunger, fascism, fear, intolerance, discrimination, prejudice, poverty, war, protest, and death. Finally, a major purpose of this book is to expose young learners from around the world to empowering non-native international role models in global education and the arts from nations in Africa, Asia, the Caribbean, Eurasia, Europe, the Middle East, and South America who build bridges—not walls—between peoples and nations.

METHODOLOGY

We would like to clarify the use of "international global scholar" in this book as there are disagreements among scholars as to the concept's definition. By international global scholar we mean that authors are born abroad and that their teaching strategies are transnational in scope.

The international global scholars selected for this book are distinguished educators, researchers, artists, and leaders-of-age in social studies and global international education from around the world and are senior faculty in departments of teacher education at universities across the United States. Their primary role in education is to train future elementary and secondary teachers in social studies and international global education and speakers of other languages (TESOL) in curriculum and instruction. Each scholar has made seminal research contributions to the field through scientific publications, distinguished lectures, and innovative teaching.

To complement and enhance our book, we added two artists of the humanities. Their compositions and paintings reflect the multiple layers of injustices permeating our world today, bringing to the moment audible and visual presence of the pain of universal suffering among nations that embrace the criticality of global mindedness, interconnectivity, and cross-cultural integrity.

The editors' decision to select non-native international global scholars for a chapter in this book comprised a complex journey as our three criteria for their selection met interesting challenges: First, authors had to have earned professional recognition as global international scholars as reflected in their teaching, research, and activities in the global education community; second, authors had to be immigrants to the United States; and third, authors had to originate from the major continents of the larger world.

In our random identification and selection of potential international global scholars and artists for our book, we started our project by systematically identifying scholars and artists by beginning alphabetically with the African continent and so forth until we covered the continents/regions of the world. Our intended research methodology required including participants equally from the continents/regions of Africa, Asia, Central America, Eurasia, Europe, the Caribbean, Middle East, and North and South America. Using peer recommendations and the internet, we randomly identified 30 scholars from 20 countries and contacted them via email as to their willingness to participate. When their response was in the affirmative, we requested the candidate's professional vita to confirm their eligibility being (a) a global scholar informed by their teaching, research, and academic work; and (b) an immigrant to the United States.

Of the 30 individuals we contacted 16 could not be selected for our book project due to the following reasons: Six candidates regretfully declined our request due to pressing professional obligations, one candidate changed his position from professor to administrator, one candidate was not an immigrant (born in the United States), and one candidate had to withdraw during the process due to illness—to our deep regret. In addition, one qualified candidate became nonresponsive, two potential candidates did not respond to our request, and four potential candidates did not qualify. We chose not to include a fourth candidate who, while having a promising global scholarship record, is in the early stages of her career.

Below you will find an outline of the oral history narratives of 14 international global scholars selected from across the world. In each section, they are listed in alphabetical order according to the country they once called their homeland before immigrating to the United States.

OUTLINE OF NARRATIVES

Chapter 1: Storied Narratives Across Time and Space: My Experiences Growing Up in Nigeria and Straddling Two Cultures in the United States

Omiunota Nelly Ukpokodu

In this chapter, I use the lens of storied case study research to share my experiences of growing up in my native homeland of Nigeria, immigrating to the United States, and straddling two different cultural worlds. Specifically, I reflect on and share distinct cultural and educational experiences that shaped my formative years and laid the foundation for my storied journey to a new continent. I will narrate and describe critical childhood experiences and events, such as the Biafran Nigerian Civil War in 1967 and its effect on my life, my family, community, and the nation. I was barely 12 years old when it happened, but I still remember the traumatic event as if it was yesterday—particularly the day my town was captured by the Biafran Army and how my mother was missing and mistakenly taken and detained because she was suspected of being from the enemy camp due to the tribal marks on her face and speaking the language of the enemy. I detail my unforgettable experiences of the political climate, school closure, air raids, bombings, gunshots, taking cover, terror, and witnessing the chilling hunting and killing of fugitives in the backyard of my compound and their effects. I narrate my immigration to the United States, and my experiences of racial innocence, racialization, and otherization due to my Africanity, my transnational identity, and agency. I conclude the chapter by highlighting critical lessons for restoring humanity in our currently troubled world.

The Power of Oral History Narratives, pages xix–xxviii
Copyright © 2023 by Information Age Publishing
www.infoagepub.com
All rights of reproduction in any form reserved.

Chapter 2: The Cultural Confluence of *Ubuntu*: A Journey from Zimbabwe to Global Educational Leader in the United States

Josiah Tlou

I was born and raised in the southwestern part of rural Zimbabwe, then named Southern Rhodesia. I belonged to an ethnic group called the Birwa, which is a branch of the Sotho-Tswana people who for generations settled at the confluence of the Shashi-Tuli and the Limpopo rivers. They belong to the Bantu African group who believe in the concept of *ubuntu*, commonly practiced in this part of the continent. When the British took control of this region of Africa by conquest, they made artificial boundaries that divided ethnic groups into separate entities. My primary education was influenced by the teachings of my parents and elders in the village and the Lutheran Church of Swedish Missionaries. The concepts and values that were taught by the missionaries in their classes and catechism lessons were complementary to those that emphasize the principles of *ubuntu* which include the capacity of the African culture to express compassion, reciprocity, dignity, harmony, and humanity in the interests of building and maintaining a community. In essence, the concept of *ubuntu* addresses the interconnectedness, the common humanity, and the responsibility one has to each other that flows from treating each other as fellow human beings. I innately used *ubuntu* ideals when relating to students in high school and with my colleagues at the teachers' college. The impact of colonial and imperial policies in my home country led to my emigration to the United States where I experienced interesting intercultural connections and disconnections of *ubuntu* during my education and when teaching in American schools and universities over the past 55 plus years.

Chapter 3: Repairing and Mending Broken Objects With Gold: The Story of a Global Citizen Coming-of-Age

Misato Yamaguchi

My oral history narrative presents the story of a Japanese woman who grew up in Yokohama City in the greater Tokyo area of Japan during the 1980s. Raised by forward-thinking parents, I gradually developed an awareness beyond my local community. At age eight, my first international trip was to China to visit the places where my grandfather was stationed during World War II. The experience triggered my thinking about the importance of multiple perspectives and peaceful coexistence. As a young woman, I became keenly aware of global events: the Tiananmen Square protests in

1989, the collapse of the Union of the Socialist Republics in 1991, and the British handover of Hong Kong to China in 1997. Wanting to learn English to better understand international relations, I departed to the United States at the age of 17 to attend high school. My first year in the United States became the turning point that connected me to the larger world, and vice versa. The United States I witnessed was not the melting pot I expected but a salad bowl with domestic and international diversity full of divisions, challenges, and potential. My perception was heightened by events such as the 9/11 attacks in 2001, the Obama presidency in 2009, and the Dream Act in 2012. During my higher education studies and career as an assistant professor, and after approximately 20 years living in different regions of the United States, I developed great pride as an international citizen in American society. At the age of 36, a medical emergency left me disabled and forced my return to Japan. I currently explore how global education addresses disability and how I can contribute to the discussion as a global citizen, in the hope that one day I will regain my full health again.

Chapter 4: Miseducation, Travels, and Contesting Racialized Worlds Within and Outside Academia

Binaya Subedi

I was born in Nepal and immigrated to the United States at a pivotal time in my life. My chapter addresses the challenges international faculty of color face in academia, particularly in dismantling Whiteness within higher education. By exploring the racial structures that have shaped academia, the chapter discusses how scholars considered to be "foreigners" are racialized in everyday higher education settings. By examining personal experiences, I critique the diversity, equity, and inclusion (DEI) efforts that place international scholars of color outside of diversity efforts within academia. Universities often appropriate social justice narratives by drawing on the language of diversity and equality. My chapter engages with stories of hope, loss, failures, and refusals. It seeks to explore how and if an alternative academic life can be crafted when one's disciplinary work is consistently separated from one's embodied identity and when one must constantly seek a sense of belonging in academia. It brings conversations about embodied knowledge about what it means to uncomfortably dwell within the racialized/neoliberal spaces of academia. It asks: "What politics enable such invisibility and marginalization?" I advocate for a counter storytelling approach to teaching, service, and research that critiques racist, White supremacist, and neocolonial influence within the context of higher education.

Chapter 5: Navigating Historical Currents: Reflections of a Chinese-Born Global Educator

Lin Lin

I was born and grew up in a Pacific coastal city in mainland China. I was blessed with a carefree childhood during the chaotic Cultural Revolution, at a time when young people were forced to labor in the countryside for "reeducation" by peasants to change their bourgeois ideology. Proud as a "red-scarf" young pioneer, I was never aware of the privileges and structural inequality in my socialist upbringing, which was soon dominated by intensive academic preparation after the national college entrance examination was restored in 1977. At the age of 17, I went to college and graduate school in Beijing, became a university professor, met my husband, established a family, and had my daughter as an "only child." Those years witnessed China's transformational changes under Deng Xiaoping's leadership, uplifting the nation from isolation with his undaunted conviction in economic reforms and opening to the outside world. My hopes for democracy were crushed despite having linked our arms to march for hours in vain to demand freedom of speech, justice, and a transparent press. My disillusion with the government's merciless crackdown on student-led democratic movements on Tiananmen Square and professional development opportunities abroad pushed me to go to the United States for a doctoral degree in the new millennium, and at the same time when China was admitted to the World Trade Organization (WTO) for even more rigorous economic growth yet dragging its feet on political reforms. As we survive and thrive in the United States as new immigrants, I find my family, including my U.S.-born son, in a continuous struggle for cultural, gender, and racial professional validation.

Chapter 6: From the New Frontier to the New World: Stories of Surviving, Striving, and Thriving in China and in the United States

Yali Zhao

Growing up as a poor girl next to the large Gobi Desert but enticingly diverse ethnic groups in northwest Xinjiang, China, during the Cultural Revolution, I never imagined in my wildest dreams that, one day, I would leave my sparsely populated hometown for college, pursue a decade of an academic career at two universities, and then move to the United States in the prime of my life to start a new journey as a student, professor, and mother of two children who are 16 years apart. In my 56 years of life, I have lived through the best and worst moments in China and the United

States, and I am forever grateful for these experiences. My oral history narrative describes my lived experiences and stories that, at once, frustrated and inspired me over the past 5 decades and shaped me into the person I am today. The memories in China include societal discrimination of my family during the turmoil of the Cultural Revolution, life with Muslims in my hometown, a rapidly changing society in the 1980s and 1990s, and the decision to cross the Pacific at age 35 to pursue a new life in the United States. My memories in the United States mainly include my trajectory as a professor who has passionately promoted global and multicultural education during the past 16 years, yet now feels bewildered by and frustrated with the worst political relationship between China and the United States, the accusation of human rights issues in my hometown Xinjiang, and the discrimination and violence against Asian Americans in the United States today. I offer teachers and students a unique, personal resource and perspective on different cultures, societal change, and unrest, as well as the impact on people who experienced it.

Chapter 7: Teaching for a Sustainable Future: Crafting a Pedagogy for Sustainability Education

Guichun Zong

In this chapter, I trace my own journey from a red-scarf girl growing up during the Mao era in China to becoming a senior faculty member who has served in three major universities in the United States. I describe and analyze how my past experiences in China, specifically my education, both at home and in the schools have shaped my work and commitment to global learning. My chapter focuses on my own observations and reflections on the Mao era's gender equality policies and the profound changes in Chinese society since Deng Xiaoping's reforms and opening initiatives. I explain how these transformations have shaped my consciousness about global diversity and commitment to making global and multicultural awareness and action a centerpiece of teacher education. I discuss how my pedagogy of global learning calls for examining how the educational legacy of imperialism has shaped mainstream academic knowledge and should incorporate the experiences, ideas, and knowledge of people who are usually omitted, marginalized, or misrepresented. In my chapter I explore three topics: teaching about globalization, teaching about global sustainability, and reconceptualizing teaching about Asia. I argue that to keep global education relevant in the shifting context of the 21st century, global education scholars must address globalization as an area of curricular inquiry and a site of sociopolitical and educational contestation.

Chapter 8: Flight to Freedom: A Cuban Immigrant's Journey Through Education

Bárbara C. Cruz

Immigrating to the United States from Cuba during the Freedom Flights exodus of the mid-1960s, my family and I were resettled in California. There, as an English learner, I started my education at a time when ESOL programs were not widespread, and teachers were ill-equipped to support non-native speakers in their classrooms. Although not all teachers were helpful or sympathetic, there were others who did invest in all their students' academic success. After a few years, I developed sufficient English language proficiency to excel in school. But challenges persisted—from teachers who did not understand my home culture, to college advisors who tried to squelch academic dreams, to the greater society where overt and microaggressions were an almost daily occurrence. These experiences resulted in a desire to promote change through teacher education and school reform efforts. As I progressed through college and university degrees, and later joined the professoriate, a focus on global and multicultural perspectives figured prominently. In academia, I embarked on research, scholarship, teaching, and professional service that I hoped would positively impact the field by challenging accepted practices and offering new approaches to ongoing issues.

Chapter 9: Tearing Human Minds To Pieces: The Power of Hypocrisy and the Hypocrisy of Power

Anatoli Rapoport

For more than 15 years, I have taught my social studies methods class at 7:30 in the morning. Readers can only imagine how "excited" my students are about hauling to class, particularly on dark freezing Indiana mornings in January. I, however, have found a trick to wake them up in the first minutes of our introductory class. When my students hear my accent and ask where I originally come from, I tell them I come from a country that no longer exists. I immediately see a change: Students' eyes, dreamy and half-closed a second ago, brighten up and take on the challenge. After initial suggestions of Ancient Rome, Yugoslavia, Spain, and Syria comes the correct answer: the Soviet Union. My chapter focuses on two very consequential issues that I and my peers faced in the Soviet Union and later in Russia: What it meant to be an excluded and vulnerable minority (I am a secular Jew) and how school functioned in the time of economic, ideological, and moral corruption when teachers had to lie to their students, who, in turn, knew they were lied to, and both sides learned how to play this game of deceit in order to survive. My experience has become an example of how these two seemingly parallel and unconnected trajectories, that is, being part of a semi-officially scapegoated community and the hierarchical cynicism of power, suddenly intersected, providing a context and background for a better understanding of authoritarian society and why so many people conformed and eventually succumbed to the evil of authoritarianism.

Chapter 10: My Dream of Becoming a Contemporary Classical Composer Advocating for the Armenian Genocide

Hayg Boyadjian

I am a classical contemporary composer. I am presently working on my third symphony in four movements and will compose my professional and personal history narrative in four movements also. The first movement will address my parents who were victims of the Armenian Genocide of 1915. They were forced to march through the desert of Deir ez Zor, today's Syria. My mother, Margarite, was the sole survivor of her family and was sent to an orphanage in Beirut, Lebanon. My second movement narrative takes place in Paris where I was born in 1938. We lived in a suburb of Paris. Surviving the Nazi occupation of France, continuous bombing, and the Allied invasion of World War II constitute horrifying memories when we were almost killed running for shelter. My third movement narrative will address our immigration to Argentina in 1948 where, as a little boy of 10, I sold stockings and other items at the market. I intensely listened to my Armenian friends playing classical music which was a critical time in my life as I realized that music was my calling. My fourth movement narrative begins with my immigration to the United States and my life-long dream to become a composer. I studied at the New England Conservatory and at Northwestern and Brandeis Universities. My present catalog is comprised of over 100 compositions ranging from single instrument, chamber music, to symphonies that demonstrate the internationality of my compositions which have been performed around the world. Their sounds incorporate the global mindedness of music reflecting the inner desires and longings of diverse cultures. The composition that gives me the most pride is "Time of Silence," a 1-hour oratorio on the Armenian Genocide referred to as "Esse Aeternam," accompanied with my own poem titled "Genocide" which premiered at Harvard's prestigious Sanders Theatre.

Chapter 11: Nazism. Border Crossing. Racism. All Lives Are of Equal Worth

Toni Fuss Kirkwood-Tucker

My oral history narrative tells of my life as a young German girl growing up in a Catholic farming village in the Bavarian Alps of southern Germany during the Nazi Era, the end of World War II, and the stories my father told me about the horrors of the Nazi Regime. My memories include racing home from school as shrieking bells announced imminent bombing attacks, the village priest taking down the hand-carved crucifix from the classroom wall replacing it with a framed portrait of Adolf Hitler, boy soldiers inducted into the *Wehrmacht* with mothers and siblings wailing as they departed, despair of villagers when death notices arrived informing them of sons and husbands killed in battle, bringing milk and bread to forced Polish and Russian laborers imprisoned near the sawmill, and the sabotage activities of my dissident father. I vividly remember my father and grandfather wobbling down our village street on their bicycles juggling on their shoulders wooden poles to which bed sheets were nailed to submit the village peacefully to the troops of General Patton's Third U.S. Army 10th Armored Division liberating us from the Nazi Regime. I will never forget how and Black and White soldiers on tanks rolling down our street throwing Hershey bars, oranges, and bananas foreign to us children-of-war. I immigrated to the Deep South of the United States at the age of 22. I intensely remember observing the profound racism and segregation of African Americans having to sit in the back of the bus, drinking from colored water fountains, civil rights demonstrators attacked by police and dogs, segregated schools, and much more. In my beloved world as a teacher in Miami's inner-city high schools and at two Florida public universities, I have integrated a global perspective into the social studies curriculum that emphasizes the equality, equity, and integrity of all human beings of the world, the historic shameful maltreatment of marginalized groups in American society, and my deep-seated abhorrence to war.

Chapter 12: On Crossing the Big Pond

Frans H. Doppen

In this chapter I explore my experiences growing up in Marienvelde, a small Catholic village in The Netherlands where I was born in 1957. I share stories that I was told about the Nazi occupation, and the impact of Solzhenitsyn's *Gulag Archipelago* on my global awareness which led to my decision to attend Utrecht University in 1975 to study history. I explore my student exchange experience at the University of Florida in 1980–1981 and discuss *Hollanditis*, the wave of pacifist neutralism that swept through The Netherlands in the first half of the 1980s. After immigrating to the United States in 1984, I taught in two rural schools in Florida where I encountered racist incidents against African Americans. When I taught in an urban ethnically diverse school, I had the opportunity to integrate African American history into my curriculum. Upon completing my doctorate at the University of Florida in 2003, I obtained a faculty position at Ohio University in Athens. Over the last 20 years, I have taught my courses from a global perspective and sought to make connections between local and global issues. As president of the International Assembly of the National Council of Social Studies, I had the opportunity to raise funds with my students to sponsor a potable water borehole project at an elementary school in Malawi. I also expand on my role as a Sending Site Coordinator for the Consortium for Overseas Student Teaching and its impact on the global mindedness of future teachers in the United States.

Chapter 13: Fractured Visions of Remembrance

Varteni Mosdichian

I was born in the unsophisticated lively town of Gedik-Pasha in the ancient section of Istanbul on the Sea of Marmara in Türkiye. The church; the elementary school which I attended for my primary education; the long curvy, old, and narrow stony streets with steps; the Armenian peasants from Eastern Anatolia and their colorful ceremonious lives—all these are deeply and strongly rooted within me. The protecting warmth of my grandparents, their traumatic experiences in the Armenian genocide, the poets in the family, my father's immense love for the sea, my mother's passion for freedom—all impregnated my soul towards a creative world. Moving to a relatively more cosmopolitan part of the city and my acceptance at the selective Sankt Georg Austrian Gymnasium where lectures were conducted in German, intensified the dialectical process of my early development for becoming a painter. One of my strongest memories is my departure in the autumn of 1969 to America to join my mother in Lynn, Massachusetts, where I attended high school. A foreigner in the United States and feeling alone, my consistent release of thoughts and feelings of my remote loved ones were expressed through drawing and painting. My early work reflects the multiple layers of injustice I have witnessed and lived through in the Old and New World. Whether it is the Armenian Genocide and continuous suffering of the Armenian people, the asylum seekers from the former Yugoslavia, or the political dissidents from the Middle East, the pain of this universal suffering is omnipresent in my artwork. My art screams in silence, slashing the apathy of emotions in the worlds of advertisement and entertainment. My life experiences and my inner world have shaped my work into a global mindedness of artistic expression that reflects the interconnectivity and cross-cultural integrity of the world's people.

Chapter 14: From Buenos Aires to Buffalo to Books
Aixa Pérez-Prado

In my chapter, I explore my experiences as a third culture child growing up between Buenos Aires, Argentina, and Buffalo, New York, in the United States. I share the stories of my grandmothers that created the rhythm of my childhood and provided a window into the challenges of distance and disruption. I recount my experiences during times of political unrest in Argentina and how these were interpreted and understood by the different cultural, ideological, and linguistic groups that surrounded me. I also share my experiences going to school in Buffalo in the United States and the racism, stereotyping, and labeling I received because of my unusual name, circumstances, and place of birth. I delve into the multidimensional aspects of being a female Latin American academic in the United States. My story is a story of many childhood immigrants, a story about never really belonging anywhere, yet being able to live anywhere. It is a story of balancing two cultures and languages that refuse to separate, yet also cannot be combined into one. It is a story of never quite finding oneself in books, or movies, yet always searching for kindred spirits everywhere. My personal story has led to a love of language, diversity, and discovery. It has led me to the field of Teaching English to Students of Other Languages (TESOL), to emigrating two more times, and later returning to the United States to pursue a doctorate in social science education and become a university professor. And most importantly, my journey has led me to a passion for writing and illustrating books for third culture children to find themselves.

INTRODUCTION

In 2012, then United Nations Secretary-General Ban Ki-moon, reminded us of the dire state of the world and called for collective ambition and action to rise to the pervasive turmoil, insecurity, inequality, and intolerance that characterize today's humanity (Ki-moon, 2012). Moreover, in the history of the world, humanity has been more interconnected than ever before. The immensity of advances in technology and transportation systems have rendered our world "flat" (Friedman, 2005) and the ubiquity of change in the dynamic of "connectivity" (Khanna, 2016) has resulted in an unprecedented global village. As these forces of globalization sweep relentlessly across the planet to the farthest corners of Earth, the impact of globalization on humanity necessitates a paradigm shift in how we educate our children for the 21st century and beyond. Deliberating on the *Zeitgeist* of our times, the integration of oral history narratives in social studies and international global education instruction at secondary and tertiary education levels offer a creative form of teaching that ignites student interests and the public, enhances the art of teaching, and elevates global education to higher levels of consciousness. The interconnectivity of humanity, however, is also exacerbated by the unexpected phenomenon of increasing international migrations of peoples across the globe of unprecedented proportions—leading to changing demographics of populations as individuals and entire families migrate for a better way of life, flee from human rights violations, persecutions, outright war, or voluntarily move to a predetermined country for a better life and professional advancement.

Among these migrants are the international global scholars and artists represented in this book. Having grown up in their native country experiencing tragic and joyous challenges during their childhood, youth, and adulthood at various stages of their lives, they were either forced to, or simply chose to immigrate to the United States in search of academic employment, intellectual advancement, or artistic fulfillment. Their oral history narratives are worthy of discussion leading to interesting perspectives on storytelling offered by Britzman (1994) and McCarthy (1998) on the dynamic influence of one's identity and the contexts of power on how experiences are seen and interpreted over time. These scholars argue that power undergirds the construction of identities and interpretations of experiences as these interactions are central to understanding how lived experiences create meaning in people's lives. It is in the telling of experiences, and in creating narratives of these experiences, who a person really is. When one's lived experiences of trauma or joy occur during a significant time in history, they yield rarely forgotten memories and deeply held, private knowledge that might never come to light without a storyteller. When shared publicly, these stories offer powerful insights into particular historic events otherwise unknown.

From a pedagogical perspective, oral history narratives can be a powerful force in the dynamics of knowledge creation in the classroom. Oral histories move students from abstract textbook descriptions to concrete and compelling experiential storied lives leading them to a deeper understanding of the past. Oral history narratives enable teachers and teacher educators to enrich historical facts with the voice of an individual who grew up during turbulent times in their nation's history. It may be used to enhance the study of topics such as China's Cultural Revolution; antisemitic pogroms in the former Soviet Union; women's struggle for equality in Argentina; the rise and fall of Nazism; genocides; resistance movements; or the impact of war on families, neighbors, and communities, among others. Educators can divide students into pairs, assign to each pair one of the lived experiences in the narrative, and have them dramatize the event before their peers. Or students might be asked to reflect on the documented oral history and write a letter or create a poem about the child or adolescent in the story. A concluding discussion can involve students' assessment of the value of oral history as compared to abstract textbook reading. It is with this mission and hope, that this book project originated and flourished.

REFERENCES

Britzman, D. P. (1994). Is there a problem with knowing thyself? Towards a poststructuralist view of teacher identity. In T. Shanahan (Ed.), *Teachers thinking,*

teachers knowing: Reflections on literacy and language education* (pp. 53–75). National Council of Teachers of English.
Du Bois, W. E. B. (1903). *The souls of Black folks*. A. C. McClurg.
Friedman, T. L. (2005). *The world is flat: A brief history of the twenty-first century*. Farrar, Straus, and Giroux.
Khanna, P. (2016). *Connectography: Mapping the future of global civilization*. Random House.
Ki-moon, B. (2012). *Global education first initiative: The UN secretary-general's global initiative on education*. Retrieved from https://www.un.org/millenniumgoals/pdf/The%20Global%20Education%20First%20Initiative.pdf
McCarthy, C. (1998). *The use of culture*. Routledge.

SECTION I

AFRICA

CHAPTER 1

NIGERIA

STORIED NARRATIVE ACROSS TIME AND SPACE

My Experiences Growing Up in Nigeria and Straddling Two Cultures in the United States

Omiunota Nelly Ukpokodu

In this chapter I describe memorable, significant lived experiences of growing up in Nigeria, my ancestral homeland, and then immigrating to the United States. Specifically, I narrate my critical childhood experiences that shaped my cultural identity, my educational aspirations, and major events such as the historic, devastating Nigerian civil war and its chilling, haunting impact on my life. Next, I narrate my border crossing to the United States and my transnational, transcultural, and trans-immigrant experiences in a *third space* as I straddle two cultural worlds confronting multiple racialized, ethnicized, immigrantized, and *linguicized* personal and professional identities. I conclude the chapter by highlighting critical lessons learned and a way forward to restoring humanity in our currently troubled world.

INTRODUCTION

At birth, my paternal grandmother named me *Omiunota*. As a child, and at the time, I did not fully comprehend the meaning of the name. When I had asked my grandmother about its meaning, she just chuckled and said, "You will know in time." Further, she said, "You are destined with talents, and you will have significant and life-changing experiences and stories to tell the world." As I grew older and reflected on my grandmother's predictions about my life and traverse across space and time and my academic discipline in the humanities, history, literature, and particularly, in my work as a teacher educator, I came to understand the prophetic and symbolic meaning of my name. My grandmother had significant lived experiences that were both traumatic and blessed. She suffered multiple miscarriages, birthed 17 children—seven of whom died—survived a house fire and lost everything, and was twice widowed and then, hope and dreams emerged. My grandmother was experienced, had wisdom that she readily shared with all. Traversing across time and space, I too, have had a similar life trajectory as my grandmother. Originally, my first name was Nelly, an Anglicized, Christian name, and my middle name, Omiunota. In 2002, as I processed my U.S. citizenship through immigration and naturalization, and in honor of my grandmother whose predictions about my life accomplishments had come to full fruition, I switched my first and middle names. Today, my official name identity is Omiunota Nelly Ukpokodu. As I contemplated writing this chapter, I was reminded of the meaning of my name, as well as Carolyn Clark's (1993) wisdom that, as we journey through life, we experience events that impact us and that we must exercise the privilege of looking back on such experiences and the effects they have had on our development and perhaps our course of action. I feel privileged to write this oral history of my lived experiences across time and space. I hope that it provides valuable, teachable, and learnable perspectives for understanding the commonality in the human experience and our social responsibility—individually and collectively—to educate for critical national and global citizenship needed to transform our currently troubled world to one that is more humane, humanizing, just, equitable, peaceful, and sustainable.

MY BIRTHPLACE

I was born and raised in Nigeria, Africa. Contemporary Nigeria is a multiethnic, democratic nation-state that is culturally, ethnically, geographically, linguistically, religiously, and socioeconomically diverse. As many as 300 ethnic groups exist, but the most dominant, powerful, and competing groups are the Hausa-Fulani in the north, the Yoruba in the southwest, and Igbo/Ibo in the southeast. Although Nigeria is diverse in ethnicity, language, food, religion, traditions, dress, music, lifestyle, and art, common beliefs, values, and practices can be identified. Nigerians tend to have a greater psychological identification with their ethnic groups than with their nation-state. Most often, they identify themselves as Northerners, Easterners, Midwesterners, and Westerners or more specifically, as Hausas/Fulani/Igbos/Ibos, Yorubas, and so forth. In Nigeria, I belonged to one of the most liberal, ethnic minority groups—the Edo people—located in the Midwest region. Its liberal character shaped my worldview premised on values of acceptance, open-mindedness, hospitality, and peaceful co-existence.

MY ANCESTRAL COMMUNITY

I was born into a large-sized community named Ikpe-Jattu, located in southern Nigeria. All I remember is that the town was the headquarters of what was known as the Uzairue Kingdom that comprised surrounding smaller communities. I remember my grandmother's storytelling about the myth surrounding the founding of the Uzairue Kingdom. The story was that the people of Ikpe-Jattu were part of the Benin Kingdom (one of the famous ancient West African kingdoms), who migrated to the northern part of the kingdom due to conflict and war. A distant relative, one of our town's great *griots* (storyteller) also posited that the founding of my town coincided with the coming of *Oyinbos* (Whites/Europeans) to Nigeria in the 15th century. What I remember fondly about the community was that it was close-knit, and everyone knew each other because of the shared participation in common basic human activities, such as the gathering at the community water source, the Ukheghi river, where everyone fetched their drinking water, bathed, swam, and washed their clothes. At the time, and for a long time, the town of about 65,000 people had no running water, and when it did, it had three public water pumps. Unfortunately, most of the year, especially during the dry season, the pumps did not work. The river became the connecting point. Families and children often walked five miles one way to get to the river to fetch water for household use. Going to the community river was often a fun but challenging activity as people raced down the river path with no weight on their heads but returned with a heavy bucket of water on their heads that they carried on a 10-mile walk. I often cried because of the weight and dumped my water before I could get home, which was humiliating and consequential. Cultural ceremonies and celebrations, such as the male and female rites of passage, and purity rituals were common occurrences at the river site. These shared experiences brought everyone, old and young, to the communal arena. The signature character of my community reflects the African proverb that it takes a village to raise the child.

MY ANCESTRAL FAMILY

I was socialized into my family's culture that was all-encompassing, all-pervasive, and all-powerful, and it touched and affected everything and everyone, both in the physical and the metaphysical realms (Ukpokodu, 2016). Prior to immigrating to the United States, I lived in a compound composed of a large extended family of a grandmother, six uncles, four aunts, their individual families, numerous cousins, and two adopted families with their own individual families. In the compound, each individual family had a room that was shared among their immediate family members of husband, wife/wives, and children. I lived in one bedroom with my mother and four siblings. The room was where we slept, kept our belongings, the drinking water pot, and kitchen utensils, food, and everything else. As a child, one of my chores was going to the community river to fetch water for cooking and drinking, which I did before and after school, each day.

The family is the most important institution in African societies. In the early days, during the agrarian society, and prior to colonial imperialism, the family was the primary unit of production and consumption. It was beneficial to have a large and strong family, and the family system was patriarchal. Children were very valued, first for their labor and then for the status of the man. The man was the master and father, and women occupied secondary roles. Gender traditional roles were strictly defined and enforced; girls helped with domestic chores while the boys helped fathers and other male relatives. Chores and obedience were cardinal virtues. The extended family was vibrant, compelling, close-knit, and profoundly impactful as each member was an integral part of the whole. I was socialized into the philosophical worldview of *ubuntu* that conveyed to me that, my humanity was intricately intertwined with other people's humanity, and the cardinal principle of "I am, because we are and because we are, therefore I am" (Mbiti, 1990, p. 106), and as in "I in you and you in me" (Battle, 2009, n.p.).

The twin values of respect and responsibility constituted the core of social morality and cultivating community membership, interpersonal relationships, caring, empathy, and full humanity. My family and community environments were designed and anchored in a strict and highly regimented network system. There was an unquestionable demand for absolute loyalty, reciprocity, obligations, reverence, and deference to elders and figures of authority, and family pride and honor. I internalized the belief that my behavior reflected on the family, both the living and the departed. Individualism was strongly discouraged because of the perceived destruction of the values that bind the family together or that gives essence and meaning to life. This instilled in me a strong sense of interconnectedness and group-orientedness, self-discipline, and self-regulatory behavior, which fostered my cultural, gender, national, and global citizenship identity, and social responsibility.

The most profound value I cultivated through my ancestral family was service to humanity. I learned early on what service to humanity meant. I did not know my paternal grandfather as he passed before I was born. I grew up with my grandmother who was the family matriarch and known and addressed as *Uwhewh*, a term of endearment. She was one of my three "sheroes" that I owe a debt of gratitude for shaping and influencing my life. She was highly revered by both my family members and my entire community. She was a community icon for her selfless community service and citizenship. She was a self-educated community midwife who delivered most of the babies in our community at a time when there were no hospitals. She built a baby birth space where expectant women from the community came to have their babies. It was a full-time, 24/7 service she provided. She nursed and nurtured the babies until 6 months of age when they graduated from her care. She did not charge for her service. Initially, each day, she woke up at dawn to visit each newborn she delivered and provided the traditional herbal bath, and the physical and moral training. But as she aged, in her late 80s, she was discouraged from going to people's homes, and instead people came to her—in our home. Overall, the significant impact of my ancestral family relates to my socialization to African cosmology and the values of humanism, collectivism, and communitarianism (not communism). These values shaped my worldview and habits of mind and heart for living and functioning competently in a globalized, interconnected, and interdependent world and with the agency to work individually and collectively toward a more humane, just, peaceful, and sustainable world.

MY HOMELAND EDUCATION, SCHOOLING, AND EXPERIENCES

Education in my homeland consisted of the informal, indigenous cultural education and the formal—Western education. The informal, indigenous education was fostered through communal socialization that began in the family circle that consisted of extended relatives, parents, grandparents, uncles, aunts, siblings, neighbors, and friends. I had a first-hand experience of the African concept that "it takes a village to raise the child." This concept is based on the African view that children are the most valuable possession on earth, as they are the means for perpetuating the chain of humanity and the continuity of the community. Most importantly, the view is that a child does not exclusively belong to the birth parent, family, or legal guardian but to the entire community. Therefore, because children are collectively owned, they must be collectively raised, which obliges everyone in the community or "village," regardless of relationship to the child, to partake in the proper raising of the child. Both my family and the entire community served as my teachers as they taught, modeled, enforced, and reinforced democratic and virtuous behaviors. Through strict discipline, discouragement of unacceptable, dishonoring, and shaming behaviors, my character and identity were fostered. The informal education consciously socialized me to the ideas and values of humanity, humility, respect, life's intrinsic value, personal and collective responsibility, integrity, honor, corporate existence (common and shared humanity and purpose), compassion, and cooperation. Although my family and community did not know or read John Dewey's work, they practiced Dewey's (1958) idea that "the best and the deepest moral training is that which one gets by having to enter into proper relations with others" (p. 431). Oral tradition/storytelling, proverbs, songs, music, communal ceremonies, and celebrations, and most importantly adult modeling through examples, were the primary means for cultural citizenship education. Oral tradition through storytelling, was the most common, and took place at nighttime. Growing up at a time when television was not in existence, storytelling served as the nightly social entertainment, but also intellectual and skill development. Most stories involved creation stories and explained the spirit of rivers, plants, mountains, as well as stories about virtues and vices, ethical behavior and dimensions of life, and stories that depict heroes/sheroes, evil and good, good and evil, greed and kindness, rich and poor, reward and punishment, among others.

My grandmother was the storyteller in my family. She knew a lot of stories and told them like no one else in our community did. In addition, she exposed me to the world of riddles, proverbs, and songs and quizzed us the next night for learning retention. Members of neighboring houses/families regularly came to our compound to join us during the nighttime storytelling, especially when the moon was up and bright. Storytelling time began with my grandmother singing a song. No one ever wanted to miss the start of the story. The singing meant everyone must hurry to complete the evening chores and to rush to the center of the theater. People often sat in a circle and crowded together. It was a natural, communal, and creative experience that taught both the old and young the cultural history, morals, values, and beliefs, which stimulated my intellectual development and growth. Unlike children in the United States, including my children, who grew up watching television and parents/families reading books to them, storytelling was all I had, and it made a difference in my life. I am forever grateful to my grandmother for her storytelling that nurtured my interest in the humanities, history, and literature, and consequently shaped my career path in social studies education. Proverbs were also a powerful way to teach and socialize the young to the fabric of society. As a child and young adult, my aunts and uncles often talked to me through proverbs; some were educative, others were convicting and condemning. For example, the proverb "A fowl (chicken) does not forget where it lays its eggs," conveys and reinforces the virtue of cultural rootedness, cultural identity, and that one never forgets where they came from. Most proverbs spoke to virtues of humanity, decency, self-discipline, work ethic, honesty, character, patriotism, kindness, generosity, empathy, compassion, thoughtfulness, perseverance, and humility.

Formal Schooling

My formal, Western education and schooling began at a missionary affiliated primary school—St. James Anglican School. I loved school right from day one and was excited to be in school and the classroom. I revered my teachers who were passionate and transformative practitioners and armed with agency to touch and transform my life. Our schools and classrooms were hugely under-resourced, yet, I had a quality, foundational education that allowed me to perform well on high stakes matriculating and scholastic examinations, and more importantly, laid the foundation for my future academic aspirations and success. My elementary school curriculum integrated both local and global learnings. Storytelling was a school subject that allowed students to tell stories, not from published books, but from stories learned at home, and to explain the moral values embedded in them. As children, we begged our grandmothers to tell us stories so that we had stories to tell at school. Early on in my schooling, I learned that Nigeria was a colony of Great Britain that came to be in 1914. In school, I learned about British history, its national anthem—*God Save the Queen*—which I sang and recited, each morning, along with other songs such as "London Bridge is falling down . . . My Fair Lady."

The most meaningful experience during my elementary school years was Nigeria's national Independence Day celebration. Nigeria gained its independence in 1960 and became a republic in 1963. What I remember most fondly about the Independence Day celebration was the whole school community cookout. Classes were often canceled. Students and teachers worked together to prepare the feast. All female students went to the Ukpeghi river to fetch water for the cookout and worked with the female teachers to prepare and cook the food. The male students went to the forest to gather the wood for the open flame fire for cooking and worked with the male teachers to build the tent and moved and arranged the chairs and tables under the big Iroko tree. It was the most exciting day in my and all students' lives. We performed traditional dances and songs we had practiced. Each student had a bowl of the food to take home to their family. The official national Independence Day holiday was celebrated on October 1st and people from far and near came to participate. There were parades, including school children marching; the Nigerian armed forces (the army, navy, etc.); the police force; World War veterans in their colorful, medaled, decorated uniforms; and local chiefs and kings, robed in their coronation costumes, and marching to the beats of bands and doing the salute as they marched past governmental dignitaries. It was an all-day event and featured traditional dances and performances that were judged and awarded prizes.

Another memorable experience of my formal education was my secondary school education (middle and high school). I attended an all-girls boarding school that was about 100 miles from my home. I was barely 12 years old, and I was homesick all the time. But the education was transforming and excellent. Although we read books by prominent African authors, such as Chinua Achebe's *Things Fall Apart* (1958), Ngugi Wa Thiong'o's *A Grain of Wheat* (1967)—to mention a few—my teachers also exposed me to global learning, whether it was in geography, history, or civics. For example, in literature, I read both Western and non-Western classics that broadened my knowledge and stimulated my imagination. I was exposed to classical books, such as William Shakespeare's *Julius Caesar* (2001); Charles Dickens's *A Tale of Two cities* (2021), *Great Expectations* (1944), and *Oliver Twist* (1992); Robert Louis Stevenson's *Treasure Island* (1902); Charlotte Bronte's *Jane Eyre* (1992); Jane Austen's *Pride and Prejudice* (1995); George Orwell's (1946) *Animal Farm;* Langston Hughes's *The Collected Poems of Langston Hughes* (1994); and many others. I learned about South Africa's apartheid and the struggle for freedom. The books I read were transforming, stirred my imagination, and helped me learn about the world in its complexity and dream of a world beyond my *Jattu-Ikpe* "village"—fostering my global citizen identity. To an extent, my formal education was culturally responsive. We brought items such as beans to class for counting. We were taken to the school garden where we counted ridges. We were taken to the community market to learn the English word for items. More importantly, my schooling experience introduced me to the vision of education as *the great equalizer*. All students, regardless of their cultural, socioeconomic backgrounds, had access to the same resources, achievement expectations, and were treated equitably (Ukpokodu, 2016).

Not So Good Experiences

In every society, and wherever we find ourselves, there are positive and negative experiences. Looking back to my homeland experiences, albeit appreciating the positives relative to my cultural citizenship education, I will be remiss not to unpack some not so good experiences: First, is my homeland's ideological cultural paradigm that privileges males over females. Fundamentally, my culture and family's structural system was patriarchal. The male-centric ideology was (and still is) deeply entrenched in the fabric of my socialization and consciousness and was oppressive and dehumanizing. I observed firsthand its dehumanizing violence that subordinates and relegates women to second-class status, irrespective of their educational and social status, and denies them opportunities for social advancement.

I was about 11 years old when patriarchy, sexism, and genderism raised their ugly heads in my life. I had successfully completed my primary education. I was ambitious and wanted to further my education. I dreamed of becoming an attorney. My mother aimed for me to be a nurse. I successfully completed the entrance examinations and had been admitted to a boarding secondary school. Then my hopes, dreams, and excitement were crushed when my family—except for my mother—decided that I could not further my education. At the time, while Nigeria had a Free Universal Primary Education, secondary education was not free. Due to the double promotions I received, my older brother and I were in the same grade level at the time we completed our primary education and matriculated. He, too, had received admission to secondary school. Due to tuition costs, my father could not support the two of us. Because of the male privilege in my culture, my father and the extended family decided that my brother would go on to further his education even though I was more academically inclined. I was told to go learn a trade (sewing) and then get married. Fortunately, my mother defied the decision and single-handedly supported and paid for my education, and I am forever indebted to her for her gift of life, advocacy, and sacrifice.

My mother's name was Beatrice, but we all called her "Mama" (Rest in Peace and Power!). She is my shero. She could be described in the proverbial sense as one who rose from rags to riches. She was not educated in the formal sense of Western education because she grew up at a time when formal, female education was highly discouraged—as educated women were viewed as lacking in character and virtue, and incapable of being a "perfect" wife and parent. My mother's mother died when my mother was very young, so she was raised by her father who ensured that she and her sisters were properly raised to be virtuous and marriageable. This meant that she and her sisters were not to attend school. My grandfather often took them to the forest to hide when missionaries came to the community to enroll children for school. However, my grandfather provided a woman tutor who taught them the skills, values, and attitudes of successful "homemaking." She was very talented, industrious, disciplined, self-empowered, and became a successful clothing and jewelry businesswoman, and one of our community's activists and icons. She was revered by all and called "Mamigold" (mother of gold). Because of her business, she came across women professionals such as teachers, nurses, doctors, lawyers, among others, and she was inspired by their knowledge and self-empowerment and became aware of the value and transformative power of education. As her first daughter, she wanted me to be educated and ensured that I would not be denied opportunities as she was denied. She encouraged my education and became my advocate and always told me that the sky was my limit. She taught and modeled for me the power of one to make a difference, and the values of humanity, humility, work ethic, and motherhood.

A component of the male-centric cultural paradigm was/is the application of a double standard in the treatment of men versus women. In my culture, a woman is expected to be subordinate, submissive, and disempowered and dependent. Being independent, self-empowered, assertive, and self-sufficient is not only discouraged but punishable. There is the saying that a man's money and property are his and his wife's money and property are his as well. Plainly, a woman is a man's property that he owns. For example, a year after coming to the United States, my family of four became financially stranded. I humbled myself and took on menial jobs to survive and provide for my family. My spouse did not. My marriage in-laws had expected that my spouse would send U.S. dollars in droves to enrich them. When they heard that my spouse was not working and that I was the one working and providing for the family, the response was quite revealing. It was: "It does not matter if you are not working; if your wife (me) is working, her money belongs to you, after all she is your wife." Similarly, my mother, an uneducated but successful businesswoman, had worked extremely hard and built the house that we lived in. My father, a police officer, and a polygamist with multiple wives and children, mismanaged his money and did not build a house. To save face, he claimed that he owned the house that my mother built, and his relatives agreed with him, saying a woman/wife does not own property in a marriage and that my mother did not bring the house from her family. Domestic abuse and violence were pervasive when I was growing up and continue to be. A husband would inflict abuse and violence on his spouse with no consequence and accountability, while a wife would be subjected to corporate punishment and community humiliation for the same behavior.

Another negative experience I had was school-related. My school system and structure were strict and highly regimented. The use of corporal punishment for infractions, such as tardiness, failing to curtsy or properly curtsy to figures of authority like teachers, failure to perform to standard, were everyday experiences. I was whipped if I missed one problem on an assignment. The use of corporal punishment was intensely worse when I was in middle school. Once I was punished by being required to wash the entire school's dinner dishes because I did not live up to an unrealistic, athletic performance expectation. I was barely 12 years old. I was in a boarding school, 100 miles away from my home and family. At the school, I had a cousin with the same last name, who was very athletic and the school's top track runner who had regularly won awards and trophies for her dormitory/residence hall during the all-school athletic sports competition. My dormitory/hall mistress felt that I had the same athletic talent as my cousin. But when I fell short, I was punished. My first punishment was to wash the entire school's dinner dishes for one night, which I did, from 7:00 p.m. until 5:00 a.m. the next day. The next day I was called out of class to run, thinking I had learned my lesson from the previous punishment and that I would perform better. Again, I fell short, and my punishment was to wash the entire school's dishes for three consecutive nights. My dormitory/hall mistress felt I was lazy and not living up to expectations. The truth was that I did not have the stamina and the talent. It was an incredibly, humiliating, and traumatic experience for an 11-year-old little girl.

POLITICAL CLIMATE IN NIGERIA AND CIVIL WAR

As I was entering my last year of primary (elementary) education, Nigeria was plunged into a series of unprecedented political turmoil. Historically, Nigeria has been a complex, multiethnic nation characterized by great diversity in ethnicity, culture, language, religion, and philosophical thought, although shared commonalities can be identified. These differences account for Nigerians' ethnic identifications and ethnocentrism known as "tribalism," which has been the root of decades-long geopolitical conflicts, tensions, military coup d'états; some bloody, and successive military regimes; and the most devastating political event in Nigeria's history, the Nigeria Civil War. At the time, Nigeria, which was divided into four major regions: the Northern region (composed of the Fulanis, Hausas, Kanuris, and other smaller ethnic groups), the Eastern region (mostly of the Igbo-speaking group), the Western region (the Yoruba-speaking group), and the Midwest (consisting of the Edos, Etsakos, Ishans, Itsekiris, Urhobos, Midwest Ibos, and others). It was redivided into 12 states, leading to the governor of the Eastern region to declare secession and establish the Republic of Biafra in May 1967. This affront was unacceptable to the federal government which pledged to keep Nigeria united. With no resolution, the federal government declared war against the Republic of Biafra. In July, full war, known as the Nigeria-Biafra War broke out between the Biafran army (the armed forces or the military of the secessionist state of Eastern Nigeria) and federal troops (the Nigerian federal government military forces).

The Nigerian Civil War (1967–1970)

I was barely 11 years old when the war began. Three weeks into the war, my town was captured, first by the Biafran army. It was one sobering early morning. My family and I were surprisingly awakened by army vehicles: jeeps, tanks, trailers, land rovers with many soldiers, many of whom looked very scary, standing at the back, front, top, and sides of the vehicles, and guns pointed in all directions, east, west, south, and north. I remember the fear and anxiety that gripped everyone in my family. I had never seen so many soldiers with guns pointing at people and ready to shoot. The Biafran soldiers shouted, "Hail Biafra"! They announced that they were not there to kill us (the Midwesterners), they only wanted the Northerners (Hausas), which meant that anyone who looked like a Hausa, had facial, tribal marks, and spoke the Hausa language was an enemy and in danger. At the time, I was too young to understand why my town was invaded. Initially, people thought that the war was between the Northerners and Easterners only, but as the war escalated, the course of the war expanded as both sides engaged in offensive attacks. The Midwest was the gateway to the east, west, and north. My town was located in the northern part of the Midwest and was a strategic position for the Biafran army's offensive attack.

This was the beginning of my nightmare. Moments after the Biafran army captured my town and the neighboring towns, roadblocks were erected at all entry points, and all transportation services were halted. Soldiers were stationed at each roadblock to check, screen, and question people. At these checkpoints, civilians were often manhandled, intimidated, and harassed. Lots of people were stranded, including my mother who had gone to her place of business earlier about 10 miles away. I was terrified and feared for her life as she might be mistaken for a Northerner because of her facial tribal marks and that she spoke Hausa, the language of the enemy. I cried bitterly and anxiously awaited her safe return, especially after learning that the Biafran army had raided the market where she had her shop and that lots of people had been arrested and detained. Indeed, my mother had been arrested and detained, but released after she was identified as a native of my town. What a relief when she arrived home!

The presence of the Biafran militia in our town made us vulnerable, especially my family. With the outbreak of the war, schools were immediately closed, and all school buildings were converted into army barracks. We could no longer attend school. Although this was the least of my worries, I was disheartened as it was my senior year in elementary school. The problem was that our house was adjacent to the school that had been converted into barracks for the Biafran army. This made the Nigerian army target our town. Air raids were frequent. Nigerian warplanes frequently flew over our compound and street, dropping bombs. With the war imminent, we received a crash course on how to protect ourselves and run to safety. Holes had been dug in the woods behind the family compound. We were to run and take cover in them when we heard or sighted airplanes. I now think that was less safe if a bomb would have dropped. There were some days we went to the underground shelter at least five times. The air raids were very terrifying. Once, I saw a bomb drop on the army barrack that set vehicles and a tent on fire. The air raids became part of our psyche to the extent that the sound of a burst tire sent us running for cover.

Biafran Fugitives

A few weeks into the Biafran army seizing our town, the federal army recaptured our town and liberated us. What a relief from all the air raids, bombings, and running for cover! But my nightmare was not yet over. The federal army settled in the same school building adjacent to my house, which the Biafran army had earlier converted into barracks and used during their siege. In no time, the federal soldiers were everywhere in the community. Like the Biafran army, they too started seeking, chasing, and killing Biafran fugitives. Unfortunately, some Biafran soldiers and civilians (the Igbos) did not get out before the federal army recaptured my town. The Igbos did not have distinguishing tribal marks, but they were easily identifiable by their fair complexion (skin color). This meant that individuals who had a light skin color, whether they were Igbos or non-Igbos, were in danger of being taken and killed. The federal soldiers could easily recognize the Biafran fugitives and often shot them on the spot. Sometimes, the town's people reported Biafran fugitives that were hiding in their compounds or nearby bushes to the federal soldiers. Sadly, fugitive chasing became a source of entertainment for many natives who could not engage in their normal, daily activities. Schools had been closed, so children could no longer go to school. Adults could neither go to the farms nor practice their trades.

One day the unimaginable happened. I was sitting with my grandmother when we were distracted by a sudden commotion, a small distance from where we sat. I heard loud chants, "Igbo! Igbo! Biafran! Biafran!" As I tried to run out to see what was happening, a young man ran through our hallway with federal soldiers chasing after him. I was stricken with fear. I had never been so close to soldiers with loaded guns. I thought they were going to shoot the fugitive right there in our hallway. The Biafran fugitive ran past the hallway and the federal soldiers followed. As he ran, he put his hands across his head, begged, and uttered, "Please, please, don't kill me, I surrender!" But the soldiers clasped their guns, pointed them, and cursed at him. The Biafran fugitive saw my grandmother, who was in her 80s, and ran toward her in a desperate attempt to save his life. The federal soldiers grabbed him and led him into the woods behind my compound. I thought that they were taking him to the barracks through a different route. Then I heard gunshots. I screamed and ran to my grandmother and said to her, "I heard the shot, the Biafran has been killed, oh, he is dead!" I fell on my grandmother, cried, and was gripped with fear. My grandmother tried to console me even as she tried to hide her own tears. Shortly, the soldiers returned. As they passed through our compound, they announced that children should not be allowed to go to the backyard until the body had been removed. What a sad and frightening day! For the rest of the day, and in the following days, I could not get the face of the shot Biafran fugitive out of my mind. I could still hear his plea, "Please, I surrender!" He was so young, and must have been about 16 years old, a child soldier. As I cried, several questions and thoughts flooded my head: "How would his mother feel when she finds out that her son had been killed?"; "Why did people have to go to war?"; "My grandmother was highly respected in my community. She was always able to stop our parents from hitting us, but why did the federal soldiers not respect her enough to spare the life of the Biafran fugitive?"

As the federal troops settled into our town and assured us that we were safe, life started to return to "normal" although the soldiers engaged in atrocious activities that included harassment of local people, confiscation of people's property, and sexual assault of young girls and married women. By the following year (1968), schools had reopened. I was able to attend interviews for admission into secondary school (seventh grade), including the one (a boarding school) that was 100 miles away from my town. My mother accompanied me to the interview given my age and the political climate and instability. Soldiers were still stationed at each entry point of towns, small or large. As the war continued, the Nigerian federal troops, due to its superior weaponry and soldiers, overpowered the under-resourced Biafran army. The Biafran army did not have a standard, formal army. At the outbreak of the war, people—male and female—were recruited, including children as young as 10 (child soldiers). By 1969, due to depleted resources, lack of outside assistance, increased starvation due to famine, and massive deaths, the Biafran army surrendered, and on January 15, 1970, the war was declared over. The Nigerian federal army won. The Republic of Biafra ceased to exist. The Nigerian Military Government achieved its goal to keep Nigeria ONE. The Nigerian civil war was bloody, fatal, and a catastrophe. Millions of Nigerians, mostly the Igbos, and children, died. It was a nightmare for me, my family, my community, and every Nigerian. The Nigerian

Civil War has been over for decades, but the vestiges and bitter memories of the war remain and continue to affect relations between and among the Igbos, Hausas, and the Yorubas. To date, whenever I see on television news about wars and conflicts, like the war in Bosnia, Chechnya, Rwanda, Senegal, Afghanistan, Israel, Palestine, Pakistan, India, Iraq, and Syria, and now Ukraine, my nightmares from the Nigerian Civil War come rushing down.

MY IMMIGRATION TO AMERICA

I immigrated to the United States in 1982 to join my spouse and to further my education. My spouse had come to the United States to pursue his PhD at the University of Kansas. I could be described as a voluntary African immigrant who came to the United States to pursue my aspirations and better opportunities. I did not experience any problem with the immigration process. I came on a spousal visa even though I had been admitted to the university and was eligible for the F-1 Visa. Two weeks after my arrival, I enrolled at the University of Kansas, in Lawrence, Kansas. Within a span of 9 years, I earned four degrees: BEd in 1983, my MA in 1984, MSEd in 1991, and my PhD in 1991. Upon completing my educational programs, I chose to remain in the United States because life had become difficult in Nigeria due to the economic crisis that made it impossible to send funds overseas. More importantly, I had lost my mother who was my bedrock and shero. She was an incredible support system and I felt lost and vulnerable with her not being alive in Nigeria. My children were young and had lived the American comfortable life. I did not want to uproot them from a good life to one that was uncertain, unstable, and economically challenging. Additionally, my spouse who had completed his degree program and had returned to Nigeria to teach had come back to the United States to join us. We decided to seek employment and remain in the United States. Through institutional support, we processed our permanent residency (green card) and 4 years later, our U.S. citizenship through immigration and naturalization.

The process of attaining the permanent residency was difficult, at best harrowing. Although our application for the permanent residency had been approved, we were required to leave the United States and go back to Nigeria to wait for the green card due to the H-1B Visa status we held at the time. My family and I were terrified because of the risk of being stuck in Nigeria for years or denied the permanent residency altogether, which, at the time, was happening frequently. Through divine intervention and legal assistance, we successfully received our green card. Four years later, I received my U.S. citizenship, which was a profound, transformative, life-changing experience for me. I had desired to be a U.S. citizen especially after I joined the U.S. academe where I was subjected to daily, overt, and subtle "otherizing," microaggressive experiences such as microinvalidation (Sue et al., 2007). I was taunted and stigmatized as the "forever foreigner." More importantly, as a social studies educator and scholar, I had desired to have the full legal status of U.S. citizenship as it guarantees my right to participate in a democracy and influence change. But, also, to legitimize my identity and "voice" as an American, and my qualification to teach about American democracy and social studies. Fortunately, at the time I applied for U.S. citizenship, Nigeria had provided for dual citizenship.

Life in the United States

My life in the United States has been a bittersweet experience! Upon arriving in 1982, I did not imagine, let alone dream of, the numerous U.S. opportunities and possibilities that I have been fortunate to experience, including successfully raising two Black males, the degrees I earned, and becoming an accomplished faculty and professor in the academe. I came to the United States with the goal of earning a bachelor's degree and returning to Nigeria in 3 years, which was the typical time expectation for anyone who had gone abroad. This goal and reality changed quickly as I immersed myself into the American society and institutions that opened my eyes to a whole new world. The opportunity for successful high-level education, earning a PhD degree, becoming a faculty and professor, and attaining U.S. permanent residency and citizenship, surpassed my wildest dream. I have been able to plant roots in America.

Along the way, I met some wonderful, kind, and lovely individuals and families that made a difference in my life. Meeting the Erb family that adopted and became our host family made a whole lot of difference in my acculturation. It gave my children a taste of an extended family they never had. The family introduced me and my family to some of America's cultural celebrations, like the local Renaissance festival that displayed events, such as entertainment, games, rides, foods, historical reenactment, and more. It was at this festival that I was introduced to some of America's foods like sandwiches, pickles, and, especially, grilled turkey drumsticks. I immediately fell in love with grilled turkey, which has remained one of my favorites to date. We also spent Thanksgiving together and celebrated our children's birthdays in each other's homes. My host "mother" Karen (Rest in Peace and Power) and I cultivated a loving relationship that transcended to a sisterly relationship. I also had two other families, like the Gordons and Cobbs who gave me and my family our first restaurant experience. I always remember the Gordons who took my children and me to a Holiday Inn restaurant, which was our first experience. My 2- and 4-year-olds could barely contain themselves in the environment as they played peekaboo under the dining table. It was also during my early years that I met my best African American friend, Debra Doyle (I call my sister-friend) who is a gem and has been a ram in the bush support system I could ever ask for.

Challenges in Being an African Nigerian-Born American

However, amid these memorable and cherished, rich experiences, my lived reality as an African Nigerian-born American has been one of unwelcomeness and outsider treatment due to my racialization, colorization, and Africanness. Am I integrated or assimilated into U.S. democratic multicultural society? I would say that I am neither integrated nor assimilated into multicultural America. I will say I am more of a transnational, transcultural, trans-immigrant. I see myself as a hybrid, and I live in the third space (Bhabha, 1994), sort of, an in-between and straddling two cultures. Living in the third space in multicultural America where race, racism, colorization, White supremacy and social dominance, xenophobia, anti-immigrant sentiment, and ethnocentrism are perpetual and pervasive, has been harrowing, painful, and hard. I have U.S. citizenship which grants me rights and protection, but I am subjected to the life of a second-class citizen.

As a foreign-born African American, I experience double racialization and microaggressions that are vertical racism (with Whites) and horizontal racism and ethnocentrism (with native-born Blacks/African Americans; Ukpokodu, 2013, 2022). By vertical racism, I experience the harrowing effects of White supremacy, social dominance, and racism that affect all Black, Indigenous and people of color (BIPOC)—such as exclusion, stereotyping, discrimination, prejudice, bias, linguicism, and xenophobia. I face the constant micro-invalidation microaggression that questions and interrogates my place and belongingness in America such as "Where are you from?"; "When are you going back home?"; and "Go back to where you came from" (your sh...hole country). Horizontally, I experience exclusion, hostility, and adversarial relationships from native-born Blacks/Black Americans who question and interrogate my choice and preference to identify as an African American. While it is hard and challenging to live and be a BIPOC in America, it is doubly challenging and hard to live and be an African-born BIPOC in America.

Personal Challenges

I came to the United States with my two children who were 2 years old and 3 months old at the time. My children and I have benefitted from the vast opportunities—educational and occupational success that otherwise would have been difficult to impossible to achieve had we not come to the United States. However, there have been challenges, many of them harrowing. As I previously described, life in America has been challenging due to my racialization, colorization, and racial microaggressions that include, micro assault, micro insult, and micro invalidation (Sue et al., 2007). My personal challenge began the moment I arrived in the United States. Two weeks after my arrival, I enrolled at the university and began juggling parenting, spousing, and schooling. As a young mother of a toddler and infant, and less than 2 years into marriage, it was challenging juggling multiple roles and responsibilities and acclimating and acculturating to a new culture and navigating culture shock and clash with no support system.

In 1983, the year after I came to the United States, Nigeria suffered a devastating economic crisis that impacted our sponsoring institution. We had come to the United States under the sponsorship of my spouse's institution. My spouse was a lecturer at the University of Benin who was approved for study abroad to pursue his PhD degree. Per the sponsorship, we were to receive allowances, including health insurance benefits for each member of my family. With the economic crisis, we no longer had the financial assistance to survive. This created financial constraints on my family and pushed me into taking menial jobs as an aide in nursing homes. Prior to my immigrating, I was a teacher, and had lived a middle-class life. Because I needed to survive and to provide for my young children who did not choose to come to the United States, I humbled myself to do what was necessary. It was the first time I had been outside the university environment, and it was a rude awakening as I was called the "N" word, a monkey, and a slave. It was dehumanizing, to say the least. Two years later, my spouse completed his degree program and returned to Nigeria, leaving me behind in the United States to raise our two toddlers. I found myself a single parent juggling multiple responsibilities as parent, worker, and student. I struggled with financial difficulties as I had to pay my bills, buy food and supplies, and pay for my tuition.

I must note that through all these difficult times, as I mentioned above, I came across a few American families who became my support system and family. I also was fortunate to receive scholarships from organizations such as the Philanthropic Educational Organization International (PEO International). PEO International is a U.S.-based nonprofit organization by women and dedicated to promoting educational opportunities for women through a variety of scholarships on a competitive basis. I received the competitive PEO for 3 consecutive years. As part of the organization's culture, I was sponsored by a local PEO International chapter in Kansas. The chapter members adopted me and made me a part of their life and provided not only financial assistance but also a support system for me and my children. At the time of my scholarship award, the chapter president was an

85-year-old woman who personally adopted me and my children. She became my children's "adopted grandma." That was the closest my children got to knowing and having a foster grandmother in their childhood lives since their biological grandmothers were in Nigeria. My children and I always looked forward to her visit because of the "goodies" she brought to us. She organized funds and supplies such as money, clothes, stamps, stationary, canned foods which she brought to me. She passed away (May she Rest in Peace and Power) while I was in Nigeria for my mother's funeral in 1986. I was devastated when I heard the news. I had made her a Nigerian attire and other gifts that I was looking forward to presenting her and watching the smile on her face. Losing her at the same time that my mother also passed away was excruciating and psychologically traumatic.

Another major challenge of mine relates to the difficulty of straddling two cultures that could not be more oppositional. I was socialized and grounded in the African/Nigerian cosmological worldview that places a premium on collectivism and corporate existence compared to the American worldview of individualism. The clash between the African sense of cultural collectivism, human sociality, and relationality, with emphasis on human dignity, reverence, and deference to age and figures of authority, reciprocity, interdependence, corporate existence, and the American individualism that places premium on the individual, self-sufficiency, supremacy, competition, exceptionalism, and equality and freedom has been consequential and difficult to navigate and negotiate. Like me, my children have grown up straddling two cultures, the African culture in the home and the mainstream American "culture" through their education and schooling. The clash of cultures has been most blatant and harrowing as my children became exposed to the all-powerful and pervasive values of individualism. I grew up learning to hold my peace (silence) when my parents or elders spoke, but my two sons quickly learned the American "back-talk" and "sense of entitlement" that they readily display, which I have struggled to cope with—especially with the absence of the extended family that disciplined and corrected unacceptable behavior.

My Identity as an American Citizen

The most harrowing and relentless challenge I have faced and continue to face relates to my identity as an American citizen. What am I in America? How do I define and live my identity in America? Can I define and identify myself without being challenged? According to the U.S. governmental racial classification my racial identity falls within the Black/African American category. Upon attaining my citizenship, I chose to identify myself as African American, which I believed appropriately reflected who or what I am; African and American. My children, who are a generation and a half African immigrant, have only known America and have the American experience. They have grown up and constructed for themselves the African American identity until middle and high school when they were blatantly challenged by native-born African American peers that they were not African Americans. One day my 15-year-old son came from school, disoriented and distraught because he had been told by a native-born African American peer that he could not join the school's African American activity because he was African and not African American. He experienced what Adrienne Rich (1986) refers to as "a moment of psychic disequilibrium." I felt his pain and anguish. Both my sons frequently experienced micro invalidation in school as they were always barraged with questions as to when they would be going back home, signaling that they did not belong or were not Americans.

As an adult, I also have had the unsettling disorientation when native-born African American colleagues have challenged me about identifying myself as African American. Once I encountered a native-born African American colleague at a conference where I presented a paper on African-born conceptualizations of American identity. The colleague took issue with my presentation and asserted her "rightness" and audacity, telling me to identify as Nigerian American and not as African American. I have periodically experienced the same exclusion by native-born African American colleagues at my institution who see me as not one of "them." Elsewhere, I have begged the questions: "In contemporary United States society, who is an African American?" I am unapologetic identifying myself as African American or my children and other African-born Americans identifying themselves as African American. I was born in Africa, and I am an American citizen. Rightly, I can and should identify myself as African American. After all, I am African and American. Arthur (2010) perceptively provokes this reality that contemporary African diasporans find themselves in and must confront their racialized transnational or transcultural spaces, regardless of their status, voluntary or involuntary (Ogbu, 1978).

PROFESSIONAL SUCCESSES AND CHALLENGES IN THE ACADEME

Twenty-nine years ago, soon after obtaining my PhD, I embarked on my professorial journey in teacher education, teaching courses in social studies, multicultural education, global education, among others. First, I taught at Northwest Missouri State University, Maryville, Missouri, and after 5 years, relocated to the University of Missouri-Kansas City, Missouri. Since entering the U.S. academe, I have successfully risen through the ranks. Today, I am a tenured, full professor at the University of Missouri-Kansas City, Missouri.

In my role as a faculty, I have made accomplishments in the areas of teaching, research, and service. I have developed and taught several courses both at the undergraduate and graduate levels. I have initiated and led groundbreaking projects, such as the Diversity Curriculum Infusion program that has helped faculty to transform their curricula and pedagogies. I have also distinguished myself in the areas of research having developed a robust, cutting-edge, innovative research agenda that addresses various teacher education programs and issues, global perspectives in education, and those that disproportionately affect minoritized populations at the local, national, and international level. I have published several books, book chapters, refereed journal articles, monographs, and I have made hundreds of local, national, and international conference presentations that have contributed to research, scholarship, and advanced conversations on critical issues and pedagogies. Some of my books, include *Erasing Invisibility, Inequities, and Social Justice of African Immigrants in the Diaspora and the Continent* (Cambridge Scholars Publishing, 2017), *Contemporary Voices from the Margin: African Educators on African and American Education* (Information Age Publishing, 2012), and *You Can't Teach Us if You Don't Know Us and Care About Us: Becoming an Ubuntu, Responsive and Responsive Urban Teacher* (Peter Lang, 2016). I have served on the boards of several major professional organizations including the National Association for Multicultural Education, the International Assembly of the National Council for the Social Studies, the International Association of African Educators (which I founded). I was a founding member of World Coalition for Equity and Diversity in Education (WCEDE), a global network of organizations and associations advocating for multicultural and global education, educational equity, and justice around the world.

I have served on several journal editorial boards, including *Multicultural Perspectives*; *Social Studies Research and Practice*; *African Journal of Teacher Education*; *Journal of Urban Teaching, Learning, and Research*; among others. My leadership and advocacy in the fields of multicultural education, diversity, social studies, global education, and immigrant education, are well-documented. I have hosted and co-chaired annual conferences at national, international, regional, state, and local levels. I have and continue to serve on reputable national and international journal editorial boards. My works and accomplishments have not only been recognized, but also rewarded such as receiving the Social Studies Excellence in Service Award (2021), from the International Assembly (IA) of the National Council for the Social Studies (NCSS); the Chancellor's Award for Embracing and Promoting Diversity (2019); the Multicultural/Multiethnic Carlos J. Vallejo Memorial Award for Lifetime Scholarship (2019) from my university; the Social Studies Research Outstanding Contributions Award to the Field of Social Studies (2019); the American Educational Research Association Award (2019); the

National Association for Multicultural Education Equity and Social Justice Advocacy Award (2011); the Fulbright-Hays Seminar Abroad Award (2007); the University of Missouri South African Exchange Program Scholar Award (2020); and more.

My Field of Study and Contribution

My field of study is teacher education with focus on social studies education and multicultural and global education. I have loved teaching and teacher education since I got into teaching, although it was accidental. I was inspired by my homeland teachers who were transformative practitioners and agents of change, because of how they were committed to their job and touched my life and those of my peers. My grandmother was instrumental in my choice of teaching content or discipline of social studies as she introduced me to oral history/storytelling that piqued my interest, motivation, and inclination to pursue the humanities, history, and literature. I taught history and literature in my homeland before immigrating to the United States. The values of the African concept of ubuntu of humanism, collectivism, and my personal experiences of internationalism, immigration, transnationalism, colonial education, cultural and gender oppression fostered my passion and commitment toward diversity, equity, social justice, and global and citizenship education.

Since entering higher education, particularly teacher education, I have approached my work from critical, transformative multicultural and global perspectives pedagogy. I have developed and taught courses in social studies, and coordinated the social studies program, the master's multicultural education, and the interdisciplinary PhD programs. As a social studies teacher educator and scholar, I have aimed to prepare teachers to cultivate the critical knowledge, skills and dispositions for cultural and global competence and global perspectives pedagogy. Specifically, I utilize an interdisciplinary/multidisciplinary pedagogical approach that explicitly, intentionally, and systematically integrates multicultural and global perspectives into curricular content and discourse. Understandably, given my national origin and international orientation, global education and global perspectives pedagogy have been my teaching, research, and service passion. I always emphasize the reality of our increasingly interdependent and interconnected world and how we must be teaching toward a commitment to our shared humanity through internationalizing curriculum and global education, and global citizenship education. In my teaching, I have always integrated global perspectives and issues into my courses. In 2016, I proposed and taught a social science curriculum seminar course that integrated global content and perspectives such as the United Nations, human rights, and discussion boards on nationalism and globalism, and more. Like many teacher education programs, the social studies methods comprise the only, singular course that preservice teachers complete for their degree and teacher licensure. And because the social science and humanities courses students complete before entering the teacher education program is often inadequate, as it focuses on technical competence such as writing lesson plans and engagement in teaching strategies, I advocated, proposed, developed, and taught the social science curriculum seminar course to strengthen their knowledge base. This allowed me to foster their awareness and consciousness of global education and global citizenship education.

Over the years, I have contributed to the scholarship on social studies education and global education through my publications that include, "Marginalization of Social Studies Teacher Preparation for Global Competence and Global Perspectives Pedagogy: A Call for Change" (Ukpokodu, 2020); "Fostering National and Global Citizenship: An Example from South Africa" (Ukpokodu, 2008); "Fostering Preservice Teachers' Transformative Learning in a Social Studies Methods Course" (Ukpokodu, 2008); "The Challenges of Teaching a Social Studies Methods Course from a Transformative and Social Reconstructionist Framework" (Ukpokodu, 2010b); "The Effects of 9/11 Tragedy on Preservice Teachers' Perspectives and Disposition Toward Global Concerns" (Ukpokodu, 2006); among others. The article, "Multiculturalism vs. Globalism" (Ukpokodu, 1999), is a cutting-edge work that has been well received and referenced as it illuminates for researchers and practitioners the synergy between multicultural education and global education. I have made conference presentations that examined teacher and preservice teachers' global awareness and consciousness.

My membership and participation in the IA of the NCSS began in 1994. Twenty-seven years later, I remain committed to the goals of IA, making important contributions to the scholarship on global education and intercultural education. I have supported, mentored, and collaborated with colleagues from around the world, especially the continent of Africa. I continue to attend and present at the IA annual conferences. I also have collaborated and encouraged colleagues from other parts of the world to participate in IA conferences. I have published extensively and contributed to social studies journals, including *Social Education, Social Studies Research and Practices, Social Studies and the Young Learner*, and the *International Journal of Social Studies*. I recently guest-edited a special issue of *Social Studies Research and Practice* on global education and pedagogy in PK–12 schools and teacher education for the 21st Century.

As vice chair, program chair, and chair of the IA from 2000 to 2004, I led the organization to democratize its practice, first by creating the bylaws and holding elections for the board. Prior to this, the male leaders of IA handpicked individuals to serve on the IA board. As vice chair and program chair, I was privileged to invite internationally renowned, globally minded humanitarians and activists such as Dr. Shall Sinha (known as the Modern-Day Mahatma Gandhi) and Ms. Nane Annan (spouse of the late UN Secretary General of the United Nations, Kofi Anan) for the Jan L. Tucker Memorial Lecture. My service activities in social studies, especially IA, contributed to my receiving the IA Excellence in Service award in 2021. Through my Fulbright-Hays Seminar Scholarship Award to South Africa (2007), I visited South Africa and developed a comprehensive curriculum project entitled *South Africa in the World*, which, per Fulbright-Hayes' award conditions, was uploaded to its website. In 2020, I was again privileged to receive the University of Missouri-South African Exchange Program (UM-SAEP) scholarship to the University of Western Cape (UWC) where I served as a visiting scholar and collaborated with colleagues on curriculum projects and research study. While the field of social studies provided me ample opportunities to promote global education and global issues and pedagogy, I also promoted them in other professional organizations in which I was affiliated. For example, in my role as a board member of the National Association for Multicultural Education (NAME), I advocated for the integration of a global perspectives strand in the annual conference program, and the formation of the Global Issues Committee, which I organized and chaired.

Professional Challenges

I will always appreciate the privilege to achieve success in my professional journey in the U.S. academe. However, these achievements and successes have materialized amid harrowing difficulties and challenges. Since my immigration to the U.S. in 1982 and embarking on my professorial journey in U.S. academe in 1993, I have worked at two predominantly White institutions (PWI) where I have faced challenges that include unwelcomeness, hostility, differential, and discriminatory treatment, and blatant environmental microaggressions. Being African-born faculty (ABF) and as a BIFOC, I have faced unsettling challenges that include isolation, tokenism, devaluation, and dehumanization. At both institutions I have worked at, some colleagues felt I was unqualified and incompetent and believed that I was hired for affirmative action. This has caused me enormous pressure to work harder to prove that I am qualified, competent, and that I deserved my position. Even as I work in teacher education where issues of diversity, equity, inclusion, and social justice are core of our mission statement, I experience dehumanization as my accent and communication style are mocked and belittled both by my students, colleagues, and staff. I am ascribed low intelligence irrespective of my accomplishment and productivity. I am not expected to perform superbly. Elsewhere (Ukpokodu, 2010a, 2022), I mentioned how an administrator once questioned whether I had written a piece that he found impressive. He asked, "Did you write this? It is so good"! I have engaged most of my scholarly activities singularly and with no opportunities for collaborative endeavors because of the low expectations my colleagues have for me and their disinclination to collaborate with me.

The most debilitating of the challenges I have faced is that of resistance. Student resistance and incivility have been the most harrowing. While I have had some great students, I also have frequently encountered students who displayed rudeness and disrespect that I never experienced when I taught in my homeland. Being African and linguistically different, students often have low expectations of me and consequently expect me to hold them to a low standard to submit low quality work and expecting a palatable grade no less than an "A." Another student resistance is that of micro invalidation. Students perceive me to be the "forever foreigner" who does not belong and should not be teaching them. In every class I teach and have taught, I am "othered" and "otherized." My accent gives me away the moment I encounter my students, whether they are majority, European Americans, or students of color. An example: I recently had a weekend class in our school building. I came across a student I believed was enrolled in my course and was looking for the room. I offered to assist her and asked if I could help her, rightly, she was looking for my class. I told her to follow me and that I was heading that way. Immediately, the predictable, and "forever foreigner" screening, happened. The student asked, "Where are you from? Are you from Jamaica or Africa?" As a social studies teacher educator, students have questioned my identity and even written in my course evaluations that I am an alien/foreigner and should not be teaching social studies simply because I utilized a transformative pedagogical approach that challenges dominant narratives and causes them cognitive dissonance that they find uncomfortable. Once I voted during the presidential election and had the "I voted" button on my dress. My students had the audacity to question why I voted in an American election, stating that foreigners should not vote in our election. Even when I told them that I am an American citizen and I had exercised my constitutional right, they were upset and insisted that foreigners should not vote in an American democratic election. But that was not the end of it. Some students drafted what sounded like a preamble to the United States of America constitution that declared the United States for "sons and daughters of the soil only." Even though I have lived in the United States and been a U.S. citizen longer than all my students, I am forever a foreigner who does not belong. I have students also challenge me that I should not use "our country" when I speak and that I am not an American.

Similarly, I have faced resistance from my faculty and colleagues (Ukpokodu, 2010b, 2022). While I have had some few faculty colleagues who have supported me, I have struggled with strong resistance from my department, unit, and colleagues. This ranges from voting down programs and course proposals I was encouraged to develop, sidelining my courses, and deactivating the programs I have coordinated for decades, including the secondary (middle and high school social studies and multicultural education), and denying me opportunities for leadership advancement. I have been in one department for almost 24 years, and for an extended period, as the only Black faculty of color. During this entire period, all the departmental leadership has been White. Even when I had been nominated for a departmental chairship by a well-meaning and good-hearted White colleague, I was not even given a hearing. At meetings, I have occasionally and jokingly introduced myself as the "orphan" of my department. As one whose commitment is toward critical diversity, equity, social justice, and quality preparation of teachers who are culturally and globally competent, empowered, and agents of change, I have taken on the lone burden of challenging, interrogating, and disrupting the status quo practice in our teacher education, which makes me vulnerable to attacks and alienation. I have served as the lone voice of diversity for transformative teacher education. A colleague, from another department, once shared with me about plots to push me out of the university because of my "big voice" and yet I have felt ignored, overlooked, dismissed, and disregarded when I shared perspectives or questioned some policies and issues. These experiences have been emotionally tasking and traumatic, contributing to and exacerbating my physical and mental health. Many times, I have said to myself, "I love teaching, but I am so sick and tired of climbing the hill of diversity, equity, inclusion, and racial battle fatigue and African-born faculty fatigue.

Lessons Learned Across Time and Space

Being immigrant, bicultural, transnational, transcultural and trans immigrant, and an American BIPOC is a paradoxical phenomenon that I must constantly navigate and negotiate. I have learned that I am caught in the inextricable web of confusion and duality and life in a third space, an in-between. I am proud of my African identity and its values that have grounded and served me well and, yet, I find that I can no longer go back home to Nigeria and enjoy the comfort and support system it once offered. On the other hand, as an American, I appreciate the opportunities, successes, and relative privileges I have and, yet, resent the effects of dehumanizing social dominance, White supremacy privilege, and "otherization" that relegate me to second-class citizen status. Apraku (1991), in the preface to *African Emigres in the United States*, poignantly captures my dilemma as an African Nigerian American, when he writes:

> The African emigrant in America, like a child of two worlds, is torn between America and Africa. On the one hand, he[she] loves the political freedoms, the civil liberties, and the economic prosperity he[she] enjoys in the United States, although he[she] does feel a sense of alienation and discrimination. He[she] also feels ignored, underutilized, unrecognized, and unfulfilled. On the other hand, he[she] loves his[her] country, his[her] family, his[her] friends, and the culture that he[she] left behind him. However, he[she] resents political dictatorship and abuse, corruption, economic mismanagement, tribalism, and civil wars that are pervasive in Africa today. (p. xvi)

As an African-born who was deeply rooted in the African cosmological reality, I cannot sever the umbilical cord that ties me to my homeland even if I wanted to. I will always be Black and African, and I am proud and privileged to have been born and experienced the life I had in Nigeria. I cannot lose who I am and I cannot transplant and impose my African way of life on the American way of life, to be comfortable. I cannot control situations that are beyond me. Then I must adapt and renegotiate my identity in order to survive and thrive even though it is a terrible way of "unbecoming" in order to "become" without losing the African essence and my American reality. Another important lesson I have learned regarding the challenges of my border crossing is that I must be strong and look back to my roots and values for survival. Activist Gloria Anzaldua (1987) reminds me of the strength of my rootedness when she tells me that my "lineage is ancient and that my roots like those of the mesquite" (a Spanish/Mexican word for tree) are firmly planted (p. 234). I must note that no one society is perfect. Each society has its positives and negatives. Although, I did not experience the blatant discrimination and microaggressions in Nigeria that I have experienced in America, Nigeria also is fraught with its own cultural paradigm and ideologies that dehumanize and oppress those on the margins, be it ethnicity, gender, and religion.

DREAMS AND HOPES

More than ever, our world has become more diverse, interconnected, and interdependent and yet so troubled as we face unprecedented challenges that require both individual and collective, national, and global responsibility for resolution and sustainability. Some of these challenges, include racial injustice, xenophobia, anti-globalism, environmental and ecological degradation, devastating effects of climate change, poverty and economic disparity, sexism, genderism, racial and religious tensions and conflicts, political turmoil, migrant and refugee crises, epidemic and pandemic viruses and diseases, natural disasters, terrorism/cyberterrorism, among others. My dream for a world is that it is more inclusive, humanizing, equitable and just, peaceful, hospitable, and sustainable. As we celebrated the 2022 July 4th Independence Day in the United States, I reflected on how far we have come and yet remain exclusive. I am reminded of Frederick Douglass's (1852) pain of this exclusion, that he so poignantly articulated:

> I am not included within the pale of this glorious anniversary! Your high independence only reveals the immeasurable distance between us. The blessings in which you, this day, rejoice, are not enjoyed in common. The rich inheritance of justice, liberty, prosperity, and independence bequeathed by your fathers, not by me.... (para. 4)

I hope for a world that embraces the concept and value of ubuntu, the South African/African notion that denotes humanism and humanity. The late Nobel Peace Prize awardee and former South African Archbishop, Desmond Tutu, aptly articulated and called for a world that embraces ubuntu in which each person's " humanity is caught up [and] is inextricably bound up in yours" (Tutu, 1999, p. 1). To live our full humanity means valuing, validating, and affirming each person's humanity. Tutu (1999) explains that when we validate the humanity of others, we, in essence, validate our humanity; but when we invalidate, diminish, and disaffirm another person's humanity, we in essence devalue, diminish, disaffirm our own humanity. Therefore, I dream and hope and call for a world class education that provides critical citizenship education for cultivating the young's national and global identity and empowerment and agency to promote a more humane, just, harmonious, equitable, and sustainable world.

PURPOSE OF MY NARRATIVE

Connelly and Clandinin (2006) write that through stories and experiences a person enters the world, engages the world, and interprets the world for personal meaning making. A person's story is a window to other lands and other people's lives that illuminates for others' perspectives and knowledge that otherwise would not be available. Others' stories allow us to learn about people's experiences that illuminate the commonalities in the human experience. For example, telling story about my experience of the Nigerian–Biafran war, will resonate with children around the world who have and/or currently are experiencing the tragedies of war like the children in the Ukraine today, and how we must work individually and collectively to interrogate, disrupt, and eradicate conditions and behaviors that predispose us to conflict and wars and dehumanization. How we treat each other in this world can either bring about healing, peace, development, and sustainability or destruction of our world. Former UN Secretary General Ban Ki-moon

(2012) reminded us of the dire state of the world and planet. He called for collective ambition and action to rise to the pervasive turmoil, insecurity, inequality, and intolerance that characterize today's human family (n. p.). I echo his call to all educators of the world to embrace an ubuntu-oriented education and pedagogy that educates the new generation and develops their knowledge, skills, and attitudes and values for living and functioning in an increasingly interdependent and interconnected world challenged by concerns and issues that defy national singular resolution. More than anything, the ongoing COVID-19 pandemic was a rude reminder about how events in one nation/region of the world affects all others. This calls for the need to prepare all students for critical global citizenship education that allows them to cultivate the global competence and identity for collective social responsibility toward humanity and world. We must aim for a world that is more humane, peaceful, just, hospitable, prosperous, humanizing, more sustainable.

REFERENCES

Achebe, C. (1958). *Things for apart*. Penguin Press.
Anzaldua, G. (1987). *Borderlands/la frontera: The new mestiza*. Spinsters/Aunt Lute.
Apraku, K. K. (1991). *African emigres in the United States: The missing link in Africa's social and economic development*. Praeger.
Arthur, J. (2010). *African diaspora identities: Negotiating culture in transnational migration*. Lexington Books.
Austen, J. (1995). *Pride and prejudice*. Modern Library.
Battle, M. (2009). *Ubuntu, I in you and you in me*. Seabury Books.
Bhabha, H. K. (1994). *The location of culture*. Routledge.
Bronte, C. (1992). *Jane Eyre*. Wordsworth Editions.
Clark, M. C. (1993). Transformational learning. New *Directions for Adult and Continuing Education, 57*, 47–56.
Connelly, F. M., & Clandinin, D. J. (2006). Narrative inquiry. In J. Green, G. Camilli, & P. Elmore (Eds.), *Handbook of complementary methods in education research* (pp. 375–385). Lawrence Erlbaum.
Dewey, J. (1958). *Education and experience*. Macmillan.
Dickens, C. (1944) *Great expectations*. International Collections Library.
Dickens, C. (1992). *Oliver Twist*. Wordsworth Editions.
Dickens, C. (2021). *A tale of two cities*. Chartwell Books.
Douglass, F. (1852). *What to the slave is the 4th of July?* Retrieved from https://www.ushistory.org/declaration/more/douglass.html
Hughes, L. (1994). *The collected poems of Langston Hughes*. Random House.
Ki-moon, B. (2012). *Global education first initiative: The UN secretary-general's global initiative on education*. Retrieved from https://www.un.org/millenniumgoals/pdf/The%20Global%20Education%20First%20Initiative.pdf

Mbiti, J. (1990). *African religions and philosophy*. Doubleday Anchor.
Ngugi Wa Thiong'o. (1967). *A grain of wheat*. Heinemann.
Ogbu, J. (1978). *Minority education and caste: The American system in cross-cultural perspective*. Academic Press.
Orwell, G. (1946). *Animal farm*. Harcourt, Brace and Company.
Rich, A. (1986). *Blood, bread, and poetry: Selected prose, 1979–1985*. Norton.
Shakespeare, W. (2001). *Julius Caesar*. Oxford University Press.
Sue, D. W., Capodilupo, C. M., Torino, G. C., Bucceri, J. M., Holder, A. M. B., Nadal, K. L., & Esquilin, M. (2007). Racial microaggressions in everyday life: Implications for clinical practice. *American Psychologist, 62*, 271–286. https://doi.org/10.1037/0003-066X.62.4.271
Stevenson, R. (1902). *Treasure island*. Macmillan.
Tutu, D. (1999). *No future without forgiveness*. Doubleday.
Ukpokodu, N. (1999). Multiculturalism vs. globalism. *Social Education, 63*(5), 298–300. https://eric.ed.gov/?id=EJ612181
Ukpokodu, N. O. (2002). Breaking through preservice teachers' defensive attitudes in a multicultural education course. *Multicultural Education Magazine, 9*(5), 25–33. https://eric.ed.gov/?id=EJ646525
Ukpokodu, O. N. (2003). Teaching multicultural education from a critical perspective: Challenges and dilemmas. *Multicultural Perspectives, 5*(4), 17–23. https://doi.org/10.1207/S15327892MCP0504_4
Ukpokodu, O. N. (2006). The effect of 9/11 on preservice teachers' perspectives and dispositions toward global concerns. *Social Studies Research and Practice, 1*(2), 179–200. https://doi.org/10.1108/SSRP-02-2006-B0003
Ukpokodu, O. N. (2007). Fostering preservice teachers' transformative learning in a social studies methods course: A reflection on transformative pedagogy. *Social Studies Research and Practice, 2*(3), 315–340. https://doi.org/10.1108/SSRP-03-2007-B0002
Ukpokodu, O. N. (2008). Fostering national and global citizenship: An example from South Africa. *Social Studies and the Young Learner, 21*(1), 15–18. https://www.socialstudies.org/social-studies-and-young-learner/21/1/fostering-national-and-global-citizenship-example-south
Ukpokodu, O. N. (2010a, December). Engagement in social justice and institutional change: Promises and paradoxes. *International Journal of Critical Pedagogy, 3*(2), 104–126. https://libjournal.uncg.edu/ijcp/article/view/132/107
Ukpokodu, O. N. (2010b). The challenges of teaching a social studies methods course from a transformative and social reconstructionist framework. *The Social Studies, 94*(2), 75–80. https://doi.org/10.1080/00377990309600186
Ukpokodu, O. N. (2013). A synthesis of scholarship on African-born teacher educators in the U.S. colleges and schools of education. In I. Harushimana., C. Ikpeze., & S. Mthethwa-Sommers (Eds.), *Reprocessing race, language and ability: African-born educators and students in transnational America* (pp. 13–34). Peter Lang.
Ukpokodu, O. N. (2016). *You can't teach us if you don't know us: Becoming an Ubuntu, responsive and responsible urban teacher*. Peter Lang.
Ukpokodu, O. N. (2020). Marginalization of social studies teacher preparation for global competence and global perspectives pedagogy: A call for change.

Journal of International Social Studies, 10(1), 3–34. https://www.iajiss.org/index.php/iajiss/article/view/433

Ukpokodu, O. N. (2022). My lived reality and CSOE values of diversity, equity, and inclusion: Interrogating the disconnect (special issue). *Journal of Multicultural Teaching and Learning, 17*(1), 59–89.

CHAPTER 2

ZIMBABWE

THE CULTURAL CONFLUENCE OF *UBUNTU*

A Journey from Zimbabwe to Global Educational Leader in the United States

Josiah Tlou

I was born and raised in the southwestern part of rural Zimbabwe to an ethnic group called the Birwa (see Figure 2.1). A branch of the Sotho-Tswana people and part of the Bantu African group, the Birwa settled at the confluence of the Shashi-Tuli and the Limpopo rivers for generations. Widely practiced in the region, the *ubuntu* philosophy informed my upbringing and was a core principle in my family and community.

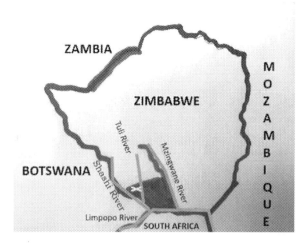

Figure 2.1 Map showing location of Dr. Tlou's birthplace in former Rhodesia.

When the British took control of this region of Africa by conquest, they made artificial boundaries and divided ethnic groups into separate entities. My primary education was thus influenced by both the teachings of my parents and elders in the village and the Lutheran Church via Swedish missionaries. The concepts and values taught in our classes and catechism lessons were complimentary to those emphasized in ubuntu. Nussbaum (2003) defines ubuntu as the "capacity to express compassion, reciprocity, dignity, harmony, and humanity in the interest of building and maintaining community" (p. 21). Like the confluence of the Shashi-Tuli and the Limpopo rivers, I saw the cultural confluence of ubuntu in both my native community and the Lutheran faith. Colonial and imperial policies in my home country later led me to the United States, where I experienced similar intercultural connections and disconnections of ubuntu throughout my education, teaching career, and social justice work. As I moved through my personal and professional life, I continued to live with ubuntu ideals. Today, it still informs my interactions with students, colleagues, and family. Like Mandela (1994), my life and work has been rooted in the ubuntu philosophy that "respects and enhances the freedom of others" (p. 544).

This chapter narrates my tumultuous journey from Zimbabwe to the United States. It will emphasize the nexus of global education and ubuntu as it weaves together discussions of the conscious application of ubuntu in global education. It also weaves together the train-the-trainer model for capacity building in teacher education projects in Botswana and Malawi and in other projects in which I have been involved.

THE AFRICAN CONCEPT OF UBUNTU

The African concept of ubuntu embraces notions of cohesion and mutual understanding with the goal of fostering peace among people. It promotes a common link between fellow human beings that leads us to discover our own humanity (Manda, 2009). The concept is expressed in different ways, across African languages. In southern Africa, for example, the Sothos from Lesotho say, *"Motho ke Motho ka Batho"* while the Zulus say, *"Umuntu Ngumuntu Ngabantu."* In Zambia, the Leya say, *"Muntu muntu kambokabantunyina,"* which means a person is a person through other persons. In other words, people affirm their humanity when they acknowledge the humanity of others.

Ubuntu acknowledges both our interconnectedness and the shared responsibility that flows from that connection. Like my own, Nelson Mandela's story is grounded in ubuntu. Even as he was incarcerated on Robben Island for 27 years, Mandela maintained faith in human goodness despite his circumstances. He cultivated a culture of peace that extended beyond hatred and vengeance—the essential spirit of ubuntu. In an expression of our mutual interconnectedness, Mandela (1994) reflected:

> It was during those long and lonely years that my hunger for freedom of my own people became a hunger for the freedom of all people, White and Black. I knew as well as I knew anything that the oppressor must be liberated just as surely as the oppressed. A man who takes away another man's freedom is a prisoner of hatred; he is locked behind the bars of prejudice and narrow mindedness. I am not truly free if I am taking someone else's freedom, just as surely as I am not truly free when my freedom is taken from me.
>
> The oppressed and the oppressor alike are robbed of their humanity. When I walked out of prison it was my mission to liberate the oppressed and the oppressor both. Some say that has now been achieved. But I know that that is not the case... We have not taken the final step of our journey but the first step on a longer and even more difficult road. For to be free is not merely to cast off one's chains, but to live in a way that respects and enhances the freedom of others. The true test of our devotion to freedom is just beginning. (p. 544)

Historical Context of Rhodesia and Zimbabwe

My native land, which was ruled by King Lobengula of the Matebele Nation, was renamed Rhodesia in honor of Cecil John Rhodes—a deceptive colonist who used missionaries to spread British influence and occupation. With knowledge of the communal African culture, Rhodes likened the land to a cow and claimed he only sought permission to milk the cow—not own it. In other words, he told the king that he was only interested in digging for minerals, not gaining political power and control. Rhodes assured the king that he would continue to rule his country without interference from White settlers (Tlou, 1969). In exchange for mining rights, Rhodes promised King Lobengula 100 pounds of sterling a month, 1,000 rifles with 100 rounds of ammunition, and a steamboat to sail on the Zambezi River (Hole, 2018). However, in 1893, Rhodes and the British settlers broke the treaty and drove the king off his land. After the conquest of King Lobengula and the Matebele Nation, the British settlers renamed the country "Rhodesia." The broken agreement became a sore point among Africans cheated by White missionaries and their settler compatriots. From this incident and similar acts of exploitation grew an adage:

> When the Europeans came to Africa, they had their Bibles in their armpits, and we had the land. They taught us to pray by closing our eyes. At the word AMEN, lo and behold, we had the Bibles, and they had our land! (Tlou, 2018, p. 217)

Across Africa, land was similarly stolen from indigenous populations. Southern Rhodesia was under British control from 1923 to 1980. White settlers were allowed to own land, while Africans were not. At the same time, missionaries of various denominations promoted their religion and provided education. Settlers governed the region; Africans were denied the right to civic participation. Indeed, the settler regime adopted and enforced the policies of racial segregation practiced in South Africa as apartheid. All privileges were reserved for European settlers, much like the Jim Crow laws in the American South of the United States. Africans who opposed the government were locked up in prisons or internment camps. Some teachers I knew as a youngster were rounded up and sent to the Gonakudzingwa internment camp in the heart of a wildlife sanctuary full of lions, elephants, hyenas, leopards, and far away from human habitation. The country was a police state if you were a Black person. I contributed a chapter to Edward Berman's (1975) edited collection, *African Reactions to Missionary Education*. Although the contributors to the book had never met and were all from different denominations in Africa, our stories nevertheless revealed that missionaries emphasized the spread of Western civilization and minimized African values—particularly ubuntu.

MY FORMATIVE YEARS AND EARLY EDUCATION

Manama Central Primary Boarding School

My journey as a global international educator can be best understood with the ethnic, educational, historical, and political approach of the

Manama Central Primary Boarding School where I was educated. I learned many important lessons there, and I had my first White teacher. Another startling first occurred when I met the school superintendent in (the equivalent of) third grade. I was absolutely amazed when the White teacher began speaking to me in Sesotho—my mother tongue. I did not think any Europeans knew how to speak my language! As a missionary, this man had learned the local languages well. That impressed me and my friends.

Our classes at Manama Central Primary Boarding School started sharply at 5:00 a.m. We gathered for morning assembly at the chapel, with prayers and scripture led by the principal or a teacher. Religious instruction was always first, followed by arithmetic, English, and other subjects. In addition to academic subjects, we received instruction in gardening, building, carpentry, leatherwork, and home economics. Students were ready for bed each weeknight, when the dormitory lanterns were turned off at 9:00 p.m. Saturdays began with morning assembly, after which the students tidied up around the school compound. In the afternoon, students played football (American soccer) or studied. Sunday was exclusively devoted to religious activities. We marched to the chapel, singing such songs as "Onward Christian Soldiers" and other hymns. Although we were free after lunch, we were very limited in what we could do. Creative activities and things like fishing were prohibited. However, a lot of students kept busy playing games. At this faith-based primary school, it was difficult to differentiate between the religious and secular concerns. The primary interest of the Church of Sweden Lutheran Mission was in converting as many Africans as possible to Christianity by way of prayer and the self-help described in the Bible.

Since it was a British Colony, the missionaries from Sweden propagated the gospel only. Politics and other worldly pursuits had no role in the salvation of people. They left politics to the government. Indeed, the missionaries were careful to protect themselves against government sanctions resulting from political activity. Political participation was never discussed because missionaries and locals were not allowed to discuss politics. This was severely frowned upon which was against the ideals and practice of ubuntu, as ubuntu teaches freedom of expression and the treatment of people humanely.

Goromonzi Government High School

It was not until after World War II in 1945 that the Rhodesian colonial government became interested in opening secondary schools for Africans. Before the end of World War II, education for Africans was taken up by missionaries. While European children were supported by public funds,

African children paid fees for both primary and secondary education once it became available to them.

Established in 1949, Goromonzi Government High School was the first government-funded high school in the country to admit African students. In 1952, I joined the school's fourth cohort representing the top 5% of students from across Rhodesia. Since Goromonzi Government High School was a government school under colonial British rule, the Anglican Church was the predominant religious organization responsible for the school's spiritual needs. School protocol restricted African staff members at the school from taking political positions. When I attended the school, only two African teachers worked at the school. Even so, it was at Goromonzi Government High School that many African students became politically conscious.

One morning in 1953, the school principal made demeaning remarks during assembly about the uncivilized, barbarous, and unchristian acts of those individuals involved in the Mau-Mau uprising in Kenya, thus implying that all Africans were the same. Students responded immediately and booed him roundly. The European teachers were very quiet, while the only two African teachers left the assembly hall in anger. Like all the African students, staff, and teachers, I felt demeaned and insulted. Nobody had ever said that to us before. A former military officer, the principal was infuriated at our behavior and ordered all students to participate in a rigorous military drill. He paraded the students to the yard and conducted the drill, armed with a cane. As a further threat, the school alerted the Air Force in nearby Salisbury which sent several planes flying over the school grounds while we were in the yard. This rash and extreme reaction to such minor rebellion only further angered the African students and staff, including me. For a few days, the atmosphere at the school was tense but the tempers eventually cooled. However, for some students, it was the first time we witnessed a spontaneous political response by African students. For us, the collective action and swift response held important implications for the future.

While I saw the promise of the future, the Federation of Rhodesia and Nyasaland was formed. The federation's conception of partnership with Africans was that of a horse and a rider wherein the Africans were regarded as horses and Europeans as riders. In response to these attitudes, many students became increasingly politically conscious. Like my experience at Manama Central Primary Boarding School, the instructional activities at Goromonzi Government High School were largely unfriendly to the concept of ubuntu.

Morgenster Mission Dutch Reformed Teacher Training College

After graduating from the high school in 1955, I was enrolled as a teacher exchange student at Morgenster Mission, a Dutch Reformed teacher training college in the southeastern part of Rhodesia. Its philosophy was based on the apartheid system of South Africa which strongly emphasized African subservience to White people. There were regular Bible study sessions multiple times a week where this ideology was emphasized. For example, one of our Afrikaner instructors continually quoted his favorite passage for "our benefit." He recited Paul's letter to the Ephesians, Chapter 6:5–9: "Slaves, be obedient to those who are your earthly masters, with fear and trembling, in singleness of heart, as to Christ." The carefully chosen passage resonated clearly with apartheid meaning "apartness," a policy that governed relations between South Africa's White minority and non-White majority for much of the latter half of the 20th century, sanctioning racial segregation and political and economic discrimination against non-White Africans.

The rules at Morgenster Mission were strict, rigid, and discriminatory and entirely antithetical to ubuntu. The physical structure of the church was divided into European and African sections. The two sections were under the same roof and shared a common pulpit divided by pillars. However, on the African side, there was no ceiling, and the seats consisted of moveable planks and boards. The European side had comfortable pews, chairs, and a ceiling to cover the rafters.

Arriving Late to Church

On one occasion, a Lutheran friend and I arrived late to church service. The African section was full, so many people were seated outside listening on loudspeakers. The European section had many empty seats. Instead of sitting outside, we found seats on the European pews. All eyes—European and African—were on us. We pretended not to notice and offered rapt attention to the service. The preacher was the chairman (bishop) of the entire Dutch Reformed teacher training colleges in Rhodesia. His sermon that day dealt with how the devil comes to people in different ways and forms. Among those ways, he noted, was assuming positions and seats that were reserved for a person. As he made these remarks, all eyes in the congregation were focused on my Lutheran friend and me. We were cast as strangers, indeed devils, who sat on the wrong side of the church—even if it was half empty. Our cheeks burned and we were very uneasy throughout the service.

After the service, the bishop invited us to the vestry to explain ourselves. He informed us that we would be reported to our parish pastors for appropriate disciplinary punishment. When we told him that we were exchange students from the Lutheran denomination, he changed his demeanor and apologized. He knew that while the Dutch Reformed Church in Rhodesia propagated the same apartheid White supremacy segregationist policies practiced in South Africa, the Lutheran Church was under the auspices of the Church of Sweden, and they were not discriminatory in their religious practices. Changing his tune, he asked us to understand and cooperate with the way things were organized in his denomination. In an act of courage, my friend asked the chairman on which side Christ would sit if He entered the church while the service was in progress. Uneasy, the chairman changed the subject and sent us on our way without answering my friend's question. In closing, though, he offered some advice: "When in Rome," he warned, "do as the Romans do."

Principal of Lutheran Boarding School

I graduated from the Dutch Reformed teacher training college in 1957 and started working at an upper primary school at the Gungwe Mission (Figure 2.2). There, I met a young woman named Litha Ndebele. We fell in love and got married in 1959. The following year, the Lutheran Church sent us to the Masase Mission, a Lutheran boarding school for girls, where I became principal. As the first African to assume the role, I found myself performing functions formerly reserved for European missionaries. In this elevated role, I was thrown into continual contact with missionaries from Sweden and other European countries. My experiences with the missionaries harkened me back to the day when the superintendent of the Central Primary Boarding School addressed me in Sesotho, my mother tongue. Instead of seeing them simply as "Europeans" or White people, I came to know them as individuals and friends.

At the Masase Mission School, most of the staff members were Africans and a few Europeans who lived at the mission station. This was much different than the Morgenster Teacher Training College, where most of the

Figure 2.2 1957 Graduating class at Morgenster Teacher Training College, Masvingo, Zimbabwe. The author is the 4th person in the center of the second row.

academic staff were White South Africans who followed the apartheid system of government. The concept of ubuntu was not practiced at Morgenster. The whole idea was regarded by missionaries as backward thinking, and hence, there lies the dilemma of the church. At the Masase Mission School, however, the African students, staff, teachers, and the local community worked collaboratively in accordance with the philosophy of ubuntu. There was a committee that was set up to ensure that there was collaboration with the local community.

The Dilemma of Christian Missionaries in Africa

Many Christian missionaries who lived in South Africa and Southern Rhodesia witnessed the legalized violence and brutality of government regimes against Africans. Some practiced brutality themselves. In the face of this physical and spiritual violence, many Christian denominations remained silent. While many would like to be absolved of their role in this violence, the missionaries' silence served as a vote of support for spiritual oppression wherever patterns of discrimination and injustice prevailed.

Spiritual violence is as distasteful as physical violence. Actions that stultify and damage the spirit are injurious to the total person. Discrimination and physical violence violate the spirit of a person. According to Christ's teachings, this must be rejected. Physical or spiritual coercion contradicts the message of the gospel. In fact, it is doubly noxious and doubly injurious. Not only does coercion breed injustice and thwart the person's normal development, but it also contradicts the teachings of Christ as indicated in the Bible. Even so, the use of such coercive tactics was rife in both South Africa and Southern Rhodesia.

LEAVING RHODESIA

For 6 years, I served as the first African principal of Masase Mission Boarding School. As I grew into school leadership, I became an active member of the Rhodesian African Teachers Association (RATA), an organization that openly opposed the policies and practices of segregation in Zimbabwe. Little did I know that my participation in RATA made me a target for arrest. To continue my education, the Lutheran World Federation had agreed to fund my study in the United States at Luther College in Iowa. My decision to transition from being a principal to study in the United States, did not bode well with the government of the day. At the same time, Rhodesian Prime Minister Ian Smith was preparing to launch a Unilateral Declaration of Independence (UDI) from Britain in November 1965. The UDI enabled

Smith to declare a state of emergency, prohibiting any African from leaving or entering the country, and allowing arbitrary imprisonment of anyone who opposed the government.

Just prior to my arrest, some friends in the security services alerted me and helped me escape to the United States. My wife and children were not so lucky and remained trapped in Rhodesia. My wife was subjected to several interrogations about my departure and my studies in the United States. Always calm, Litha answered them wisely, suggesting that since I was issued a passport by the government, they must already know the answer to that question. The year-and-a-half-long separation was a trying time for my family. Under the terms of my educational scholarship, my family could not join me in the United States until I proved that I could meet the university academic expectations.

Reunion With Family in the United States

Through the help of the Lutheran World Federation, my wife, Litha, and our three children, Lehlohonolo (Lee, age 5), Lehlaseli (Hla, age 3), and Joy (Bonolo, age 2) were reunited with me in Decorah, Iowa, in 1966 where I attended Luther College. As one would imagine, it was quite a transition for my family. We were the first Black African family to live in Decorah. While I had initial concerns for my children, they were welcomed in the community and in the schools. It was the period of President Lyndon Johnson's "Great Society," and many communities showed their liberal inclinations. I graduated with a bachelor's degree with a major in history focusing on European imperialism. After graduating from Luther College, I attended Illinois State University in Normal, Illinois, to pursue my master's degree. My thesis was titled, *British Policy and Cecil John Rhodes in the Occupation of Mashonaland and Matebeleland: 1888–1897* (Tlou, 1969). The topic of my thesis was driven by my desire to understand the motives behind the inhuman treatment of Africans by European settlers—an approach that ran counter to the ubuntu philosophy I had learned as a child.

It became clear that to maintain such a cruel policy of apartheid, settler regimes in both Rhodesia and South Africa had to create similarly inhuman laws and enforce them through physical violence, unwarranted arrests, imprisonment, and financial extortion. Furthermore, they expected European missionaries to enact a kind of spiritual violence to soften the hearts and minds of Africans and discourage rebellion. Had the churches insisted on the teachings of the Bible and rejected pernicious White supremacy, apartheid laws might never have been promulgated. To my mind, all Christians have a responsibility to denounce the misuse of the Bible to justify doctrines antithetical to the central teachings of Christ. Upon my graduation from Illinois State University, my family and I returned to Luther College where I taught history and social studies for 3 years (1969–1972). While I was teaching at Luther College, I enrolled at the University of Wisconsin as a commuter student in the African Studies program for 3 years.

Teaching in Public Schools in the United States

I obtained my doctorate in curriculum and instruction with emphasis in social studies and civic education from the University of Illinois. After graduation, I taught eighth grade social studies and civic education for 2 years (1976–1978) in the Glencoe Public Schools. The students were bright and curious and stretched the boundaries of classroom décor to the limit. Glencoe is a "bedroom" community of Chicago. Residents were upper middle class and well to do. At their homes, the majority had nannies, often recruited from the Caribbean area, especially Jamaica. The community was cordial and welcoming, and my children had the benefit of attending some of the best schools in the country. While teaching there, I arranged visits to all my students' homes which greatly impacted the students' cooperation in class. This strategy was motivated by my belief in the concept of ubuntu. The parents volunteered to do class projects with their children. We embraced the mantra, "It takes a village to raise a child." My early experiences in American public schools were invaluable to my understanding of its education system.

Becoming a Working Ceramic Artist

My scholarship from the Lutheran World Federation to study in the United States was only for undergraduate studies. I did not have funding for graduate studies. Therefore, I had to look for funds to support my graduate studies as well as my family. As an undergraduate student at Luther, I met an extraordinary professor, Dean Schwarz. He greatly inspired me, became a friend, and helped me in my struggles as a ceramic artist. Professor Schwarz studied with the world-renowned Marguerite Wildenhain, a student at the Bauhaus in Weimar, Germany. Wildenhain herself studied with such giants as Gerhard Marcks, Max Krehan, Walter Gropius, Otto Lindig, and Frans Wildenhain among others. When Wildenhain visited Luther College's art department, I was a student in Professor Schwarz's class. A distinctive characteristic of my pots were African motifs, grounded in my experiences and perspective as a rural Rhodesian. The world-renowned German Bauhaus artist offered me a full scholarship, enabling me to take my family with me to study at her Pond Farm studios in California during the Summer of

Figure 2.3 Examples of Dr. Tlou's pottery.

1967. Many great artists, including my mentor and friend, Dean Schwarz, had also studied under her. When I returned to Decorah, I opened my own studio to create ceramic pots, the sale of which contributed significantly to the cost of my graduate studies (Figure 2.3).

I was honored to contribute a chapter to a book titled, *Marguerite Wildenhain and the Bauhaus: An Eyewitness Anthology*, edited by Dean and Geraldine Schwarz (2007). In the book, students share insights and memories of working with and learning from the famous Bauhaus artist. In her book, *Pottery Form and Expression*, Wildenhain (1962) states:

> When more men and women are willing to live with one basic idea in mind...and the unity of life is based on ethical convictions...then we shall have a chance for a valid human civilization. (p. 21)

This comment touched me deeply, as it expressed an ubuntu ideal for which all of us should strive as human beings. Wildenhain's genius greatly enriched me. It was the chance of a lifetime for a financially struggling African student studying in the United States.

FROM PUBLIC SCHOOL TO HIGHER EDUCATION

After teaching for 2 years in Glencoe Schools in Illinois, I was offered a position in the College of Education at the Virginia Polytechnic Institute and

State University, known colloquially as Virginia Tech in 1978. At that time there existed no global or international program in the College of Education. Working at Virginia Tech over the next 30 years, I worked diligently to foster international and global education in the College of Education and contributed significantly to the program not only at the university but in African nations. One incident will always remain in my memory. When I invited Professor Geneva Gay from Purdue University, a national specialist on multicultural education, to Virginia Tech, to give a seminar for faculty and students on the merits of global and multicultural education, only my students attended. I was deeply disappointed and became acutely aware of the struggles ahead in the Department of Teacher Education.

At the same time, I was submitting my case for promotion and tenure to the university. In my dossier, I emphasized the importance of teaching, community engagement, and cross-cultural understanding in my research. The committee delivered a split decision on my promotion and tenure. I was tenured but not promoted. The argument made against my promotion was that the College of Education was focused on K–12 programs in Virginia, not international or multicultural education. I was disappointed, discouraged, and demoralized. The rationale seemed weak and unconvincing to me, as I understood the value of international education through my lived experiences. Furthermore, I felt the decision was discriminatory as, at that time, the university was actively encouraging colleges and departments to internationalize curricula. Despite my deep frustration, I continued my efforts to bring international global education to the university as I had been highly influenced by the scholarship of James Becker, a leading scholar in global education at Indiana University.

Global Education

In 1981, I organized a conference that engaged representatives from the State Department of Social Studies Education from both public and private sectors in different industries in the Commonwealth of Virginia. Titled "Virginia's Role in Economic Activities and International Trade," the conference was a great success. Becker's work provided a model for the conference in the integration of global education in curriculum and instruction. The conference led to published proceedings and articles including, "Virginia's Role in World Trade," "Global Interdependence: Arkansas and the World," and "Teaching International Trade of Strategic Minerals: Dependence and Interdependence" (Tlou, 2018, p. 228). My deep interest, inspiration, and commitment to international global education over the years can be attributed to the following scholars in the international global education community who excelled in the field in the 20th century and beyond: Lee and Charlotte

Anderson, James Banks, James Barth, Jim Becker, Dan Fleming, Geneva Gay, Carole Hahn, John Jarolomak, Willard Kniep, Toni Fuss Kirkwood-Tucker, Margit McGuire, Howard D. Mehlinger, Merry Merryfield, Peter Muyanda Mutebi, Anna Ochoa, Andrew Smith, James Shaver, Robert Stahl, Jan Tucker, Ralph Tyler, Angene Wilson, and others.

Ubuntu in International Global Projects

My life-long dream has always been to come to the United States for advanced education and then to return to Rhodesia to reform its education system. It became a futile objective, however. The war in Rhodesia (1969–1978) for liberation from a regime that murdered my brother and brother-in-law, and was hunting for another brother and me, did not make my dream a reality. My brother and I were targets of arrest and, thus, I decided to remain in the United States and become deeply involved in the development of international global education and civic projects in African nations.

In Botswana, I worked on international projects to establish degree programs for teacher educators at the University of Botswana (Tlou, 2018). In Malawi at the Domasi College (Tlou, 2018), I introduced a train-the-trainer model sponsored by the United States Agency for International Development (USAID). I also developed a social studies curriculum that incorporated civic education for all primary schools' standards for Grades 1–8 (Tlou, 2018). Additionally, I assisted in the implementation of *civitas* chapters in Malawi and Kenya, sponsored by the Center for Civic Education in the United States. Furthermore, I was instrumental for the International Assembly (IA) of the National Council for Social Studies (NCSS) in the United States to adopt the Mwanje Primary School in Malawi, a self-help community-built school. Initially, the IA provided backpacks for each student at the school, followed by the IA raising money for a water borehole to provide clean water for the school and community (Doppen & Tesar, 2012). These projects reflect my commitment to global education and the application of ubuntu extensively practiced in many African nations. Figure 2.4 highlights the multiple interdisciplinary global education projects implemented in African nations by Virginia Polytechnic Institute and State University under my leadership.

As shown in Figure 2.4, Virginia Tech partnered with Kenyatta University in Kenya to arrange a citizen exchange program with the United States, referred to as "responsible governance" in service-learning engagements for different communities. In Malawi and Zambia, we created Global Health Exchange programs on healthcare serving 28 Malawians and Zambians that included 17 professionals in the United States. In Zambia, we partnered with the University of Zambia to train four doctoral candidates to start a new Department

The Cultural Confluence of *Ubuntu* ▪ **49**

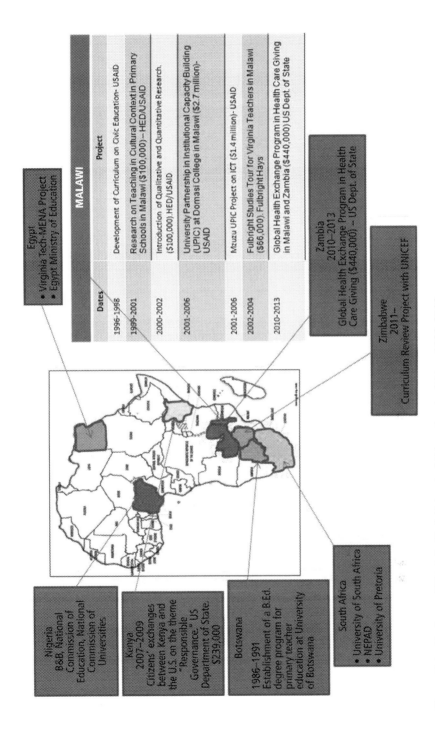

Figure 2.4 Projects of Virginia Tech School of Education in Africa, 1986–2016.

of Vocational and Technical Education at their university. In Nigeria, we invited 120 leaders from 95 universities to participate in workshops on the use of instructional technology and management of tertiary institutions. Further examples are highlighted in Figure 2.4. In Malawi, the USAID sponsored the program, "University Partnership in Institutional Collaboration" (UPIC, 2001–2006), using the successful train-the-trainer model I had deployed in Botswana. I served as the coordinator and director of this project. The projects in Botswana and Malawi were based on ubuntu. When the UPIC project started, we recruited six PhD students and 24 master's students. Five first-time students were recruited for the Master of Arts in instructional technology (MAIT). The program was posted at Mzuzu University to establish the distance online program. The other UPIC graduates developed and established degree programs and were posted in all the following six teacher training colleges: Blantyre Teachers College, Lilongwe Teacher College, Karonga Teachers College, Kasungu Teachers College, and St. Joseph Teachers College. Some graduates were absorbed by the Ministry of Education, the universities in Malawi, and nongovernmental organizations. In less than 10 years, graduates of the UPIC project effectively replaced volunteers from other countries.

By 2020 of the 35 UPIC graduates who started the "University Partnership in Institutional Collaboration" program, 11 upgraded themselves to the PhD levels from different institutions such as the University of Pretoria, University of Cape Town, and Virginia Tech. Some went to Japan, Kenya, Australia, and the United Kingdom. The graduates were either teaching or serving at the administration level in higher education institutions in Malawi. One PhD graduate became the Minister of Education of Malawi. Unfortunately, of the original cohort, five graduates passed away from vehicle accidents or natural causes. About 500 of their students from Domasi College were awarded BEd degrees and were deployed in the teacher training colleges replacing the expatriates.

As I look back, I have come to realize the importance of cultural influences and the transfer of societal values that occur through global education. As the world is becoming more interconnected, global education programs have the potential to enable students to (a) respect cultural diversity, (b) appreciate the humanity of all people, and (c) accept divergent worldviews. To this end, I feel that the pedagogy of global education could benefit greatly from incorporating the humanistic concept of ubuntu, one of Africa's philosophical frameworks underlying the definition of humanness.

REFLECTIONS

I chose to approach this chapter by acknowledging that since the Universal Declaration of Human Rights of the United Nations is reflected in the ideals of both global education and ubuntu, global education teachers can also design projects for students that incorporate the African concept of ubuntu in advancing world peace. The concept clearly addresses our interconnectedness, our common humanity, and the responsibility to each other that flows from our connections. Clearly, ubuntu has much to contribute to the well-being of the world (Mukuni & Tlou, 2018, 2021). However, the question remains: "Will ubuntu be universally applied across all African cultures and all societies?"

In my view, African nations are poised to apply this concept universally. In fact, ubuntu has been applied, for example, as a solution to the problem of disunity and lack of justice in South Africa's Truth and Reconciliation Commission ([TRC], 2017). The use of restorative justice was more effective than the retributive method that was applied during the Nuremberg Trials (Moyers, 1999). The aim of the process was to seek healing and forgiveness between the victims and the oppressors. In South Africa, many who abhorred apartheid perceived the TRC as an effective way to highlight the truth about the many evils of apartheid. This augurs well with the ubuntu egalitarian concept. Indeed, the caste system of apartheid is undermined by the TRC and it levels the playing field in the social structure and relationships promoting egalitarian principles.

It is important to point out here that in Botswana the concept of *kgotla* is another effective deployment of ubuntu as a mechanism for restorative justice, community-building, and positive peace-building. Focused on the importance of making peace and resolving conflicts, local communities come together to solve their differences and minimize misunderstandings (Moumakwa, 2010; Tlou, 2021). Kgotla promotes local citizens working together to resolve social conflicts and encourage partnerships and collaborative strategies. Traditionally, Botswana has used a combination of four principles to produce the national philosophy of *kagisano* (social harmony) which embraces social justice, unity, interdependence, and mutual assistance (Botswana National Commission on Education, 1977).

Admittedly, this capacity to apply ubuntu to society's problems in African societies has not always been adequately employed. For instance, Zimbabwe and Rwanda failed to apply ubuntu to resolve conflicts and differences among their people. As a result, many nationals were killed and some have sought refuge outside their countries. In Zimbabwe, shortly after independence, between 1983–1987, the followers of Joshua Nkomo, the leader of the Zimbabwe African People's Union (ZAPU) opposition party, were massacred by Robert Mugabe's Zimbabwe African National Union ([ZANU]; Coltart, 2016). In Rwanda, the Hutus carried out a genocidal mass slaughter of the Tutsis, estimated at 500,000–1,000,000 deaths over 100 days between April and July of 1994. By the end of this massacre, over 2,000,000 Rwandans were displaced and became refugees (United Nations, 1994).

While they had the capacity to apply ubuntu, Zimbabwe and Rwanda (and other countries) failed to implement it. I argue that if all nations of the world embraced the tenets of ubuntu in their application of human rights, the United Nations' goal of peace and prosperity would be achieved.

CONCLUSION

In this chapter, I have mapped the journey of my long career and reflected on the factors influencing my worldview as a global international educator. Most importantly, my cultural heritage as a person who was raised among the Sotho-Tswana people of Southern Rhodesia (present day Zimbabwe) who are deeply rooted in the philosophy of ubuntu, influenced my worldview. My lived experiences as an African living in a racially segregated British colony earlier in life, as an under-resourced adult student in a foreign country, raising a family in a culturally different setting, and my 30-year global international work at Virginia Polytechnic Institute and State University shaped my ever-increasing worldview. Against this background, I have discussed my life's experiences and the application of the African concept of ubuntu in global international education using the train-the-trainer model as a vehicle for capacity building in teacher education in African nations to build a more harmonious world.

REFERENCES

Berman, E. H. (1975). *African reactions to missionary education.* Teachers College Press.
Botswana National Commission on Education. (1977). *Kagisana ka thuto* [Education for Kagisano]. https://eric.ed.gov/?id=ED154521
Coltart, D. (2016). *The struggle continues: 50 years of tyranny in Zimbabwe.* Jacana Media.
Doppen, F. H., & Tesar, J. (2012). The Mwanje project: Engaging preservice teachers in global service learning. *Journal of International Social Studies, 2*(2), 52–65. https://www.iajiss.org/index.php/iajiss/article/view/62/65
Hole, H. M. (2018). The Rudd concession. In *The making of Rhodesia* (pp. 64–75). Routledge.
Manda, D. S. (2009). *Ubuntu philosophy as an African philosophy for peace.* https://www.benkhumalo-seegelken.de/wp-content/uploads/unconditional-humanness.pdf
Mandela, N. (1994). *Long walk to freedom: The autobiography of Nelson Mandela.* Little, Brown & Company.
Moumakwa, P. C. (2010). *The Botswana kgotla system: A mechanism for traditional conflict resolution in modern Botswana: Case study of the Kanye Kgotla* [Unpublished

master's thesis]. University of Tromsø. https://munin.uit.no/bitstream/handle/10037/3211/thesis.pdf?sequence=1

Moyers, B. (1999). *Facing the truth with Bill Moyers*. PBS. https://billmoyers.com/series/facing-truth/

Mukuni, J., & Tlou, J. (2018). The place of *ubuntu* in global education. In P. Talbot, B. Bizzell, & R. Kahila (Eds.), *Cases on global competencies for educational diplomacy in international settings* (pp. 223–248). IGI Global.

Mukuni, J., & Tlou, J. (Eds.). (2021). *Understanding Ubuntu for enhancing intercultural communications*. IGI Global.

Nussbaum, B. (2003). Ubuntu: Reflections of a South African on our common humanity. *Reflections, 4*(4), 21–26. http://dx.doi.org/10.1162/152417303322004175

Schwarz, D., & Schwarz, G. (Eds.). (2007). *Marguerite Wildenhain and the Bauhaus: An eyewitness anthology*. South Bear Press.

Tlou, J. S. (1969). *British policy and Cecil John Rhodes in the occupation of Mashonaland and Matebeleland: 1888–1897* [Unpublished master's thesis]. Virginia Polytechnic Institute and State University.

Tlou, J. (1984). Teaching international trade of strategic minerals: Dependence and interdependence. *The Social Studies, 75*(5), 193–199. https://doi.org/10.1080/00377996.1984.10114447

Tlou, J. (2018). My journey in global education through the decades. In T. F. Kirkwood Tucker (Ed.), *The global education movement: Narratives of distinguished global scholars* (pp. 215–258). Information Age Publishers.

Tlou, J. S. (2021). Ubuntu as reflected in the kgotla system of the government in Botswana. In J. Mukuni & J. Tlou (Eds.), *Understanding ubuntu for enhancing intercultural communications* (pp. 68–75). IGI Global.

Truth and Reconciliation Commission. (2017). *Promotion of national unity and reconciliation act 34 of 1995*. https://www.justice.gov.za/legislation/acts/1995-034.pdf

United Nations. (1994). *Demographic yearbook: 1992 (44th issue)*. United Nations Statistical Division. https://digitallibrary.un.org/record/166679?ln=en

Wildenhain, M. (1962). *Pottery form and expression*. Reinhold Book Corporation.

SECTION II

ASIA

CHAPTER 3

JAPAN

REPAIRING AND MENDING BROKEN OBJECTS WITH GOLD

The Story of a Global Citizen Coming-of-Age

Misato Yamaguchi

This chapter addresses a Japanese girl dreaming of becoming a global citizen. The international encounters in my childhood motivated me to pursue education and work experiences in the United States where I saw a microcosm of the world. After 20 years of first-handedly exploring the world, I resettled in Japan nurturing my *Kintsugi* life.

My Birthplace

I was born and grew up in the 1980s in the historic port city of Yokohama in the greater Tokyo area of Japan. The port of Yokohama has historical significance as it opened for the U.S.–Japan Treaty Amity and Commerce in 1858 after feudal Japan had closed the country for 200 years. Following the Meiji Restoration in 1868, Japan rapidly modernized herself, adopting Western ideas and methods. Yokohama became a formal residential area for foreigners, and many elements such as the steam trains, gas lamps, telephones, ice cream, and beer were spread from Yokohama throughout Japan. The city, a suburb of Tokyo, has continued to grow and flourish to this day with a population of approximately 3.8 million and a strong economy undergirded by the presence of a striving industrial zone. My immediate community is located only 10 minutes by train southwest of the ever-growing Japanese capital of Tokyo. I felt the remnants of the good old days of tight-knit communities that raised children in multigenerational families. However, I also witnessed the community rapidly transforming into a growing urban residence area where large apartment complexes were constructed which resulted in high population mobility and fewer connections with neighbors.

My grandparents were referred to as the war generation, tossed around by general poverty and limited education. Work opportunities were largely war opportunities due to the Sino-Japanese War (1937–1945), World War II (1939–1945), especially with the Pacific War beginning in 1941. The war generation was an outstandingly hardworking group of people who reconstructed postwar defeated Japan, fought for a simple standard of living and struggled for educational opportunities for their children. My grandfathers, and my grandmothers alike, joined the workforce when many women were housewives. My parents are part of the post-World War II baby boom generation who grew up during the Japanese economic miracle from 1955 to 1972. They witnessed historic events such as the 1968 Tokyo Summer Olympics, the first Olympics held in Asia. On the other hand, there was a pervasive nervous international and domestic political atmosphere that built from opposition to the Vietnam War and the Japan–U.S. Security Treaty during the 1960s to 1970s, the reversion of Okinawa to Japan in 1972, student movements and protests during the 1960s to 1970s against the Japanese government and related institutions and organizations over a wide variety of political debates about educational policies, administration and fees at the high school and university level. Despite the blue-collar family background, my parents managed to earn graduate degrees and held professional careers.

I grew up as the second daughter of a forward-thinking, young, educated professional couple in the 1980s. My parents' goal was to raise their daughters to be international personalities. From a young age, my elder sister and I were taught the importance of not only speaking English but to do something professional using the language and becoming financially independent. They foresaw the potential benefit of having my elder sister and I work and live in a Western country where women's rights were better established. I lived my childhood in a hustle-bustle big city environment amidst the economic bubble boom from 1986 to 1991 that led to high inflation and high consumption. Things were increasingly competitive and demanding even for children and youth, including the so-called *Jyuken Senso*, a fiercely competitive school entrance examination preparation war, especially for upper-mobile families. I had extremely limited time with my family and spent most of my waking hours separate from my working parents and school days with extended hours Monday through Saturday starting before I was even 2 years old.

My upbringing was relatively rare as most of my friends had homestay mothers. The experience brought me loneliness and self-imposed pressure to be accepted by others, even my family, out of fear and uncertainty, and unconsciously training myself to prioritize what I should do instead of what I wanted to do. On the positive note, I grew up quickly and became an independent little girl who was aware of her surroundings. Despite being a tomboy full of life, I had a long-term hospitalization, starting 1989, and was bedridden for a time. I missed the majority of fourth grade and was forced to adapt to a quiet indoor lifestyle.

As a positive distraction, I started watching daily news religiously and continued to do so well into my teenage years. One of my childhood memories is the Chernobyl disaster in the Soviet Union in 1986. It triggered within me the memories of how my maternal grandmother spent her birthday, the day the atomic bomb was dropped on Hiroshima. In her mourning, she

Figure 3.1 At a daycare sport festival with my maternal grandmother at age 3.

taught me about the destructive power of radiation, including about how many lives were lost and how the surviving victims continued to suffer.

Another memory is the Tiananmen Square protests and massacre in China in 1989. I connected with how my paternal grandfather fought a war in Beijing and our family trip to China visiting Tiananmen Square in 1987, and it definitely led to my interest in world affairs. I also vividly recall watching live news and becoming keenly interested in learning about global events: (a) the fall of the Berlin Wall in 1989, (b) the invasion of Kuwait by Iraq in 1990, (c) the Gulf War from 1991 to 2000, (d) the collapse of the Soviet Union in 1991 and the end of the Cold War, (e) the wars in Yugoslavia from 1991 to 2001, and (f) Nelson Mandela becoming the president of South Africa and the official abolition of Apartheid in 1994. Regarding the United States of America, many Japanese—who do not have legal gun ownership excepting special cases—developed the perception that the United States is a dangerous place after events such as (a) the Los Angeles riots of 1992, (b) the shooting death of a 16-year-old Japanese high school exchange student in Louisiana in 1992, (c) the 1993 World Trade Center bombing, and (d) the Centennial Olympic Park bombing in 1996. Domestically, the bursting of the bubble economy from 1991 to 1993 impacted Japanese society. The larger community faced a challenge in handling large numbers of undocumented migrant workers who lost their jobs with the burst of the bubble economy, which resulted in forced deportation administrated by the Japanese government. Watching the news and feeling overwhelming social uncertainty triggered my interest in understanding the background of different cultures, societal and world systems, the issues at the table, and causes behind them.

My and My Family's Impactful Experiences

My father's family took the first international family trip to China when I was 8 years old in second grade. Visiting the place where my paternal grandfather was stationed during World War II was an awakening experience that stands out. This childhood experience certainly directed my interest in global education in later life. With great interest we visited the Great Wall of China, the Forbidden City, Tiananmen Square, the Yellow River, and many other sites. The most important purpose, however, was visiting the temple where my paternal grandfather was stationed as a telegram operator in active service for a few years in the Beijing area. When we visited the site, the temple was no longer there but grandfather shared his stories including how warm many local Chinese were. He always wanted to thank them for their kindness and apologize for the hardships caused by the war and enacted his hope after all these years. It taught me that while countries

Figure 3.2 At a traditional Japanese rite with my paternal grandfather at age 7.

might have been at war against each other, in some cases people could form friendships. This China trip also taught me about how my paternal grandfather became a prisoner of war, captured by the Soviet Union after the war ended along with 561,000 Japanese for several years. Grandfather had been spending decades searching for his military troop friends' families to give them mementos of the missing and fallen soldiers. My grandparents had brothers who were sent to and died in detention camps in Siberia along with 53,000 Japanese. My paternal grandparents had also been following news of the annual group trips organized by the Japanese government from 1981 to 1999 for Japanese orphans left behind in China after World War II to look for Japanese families of origin. The war directly had a major impact on my grandparents, particularly my paternal grandfather, and it indirectly influenced me to see how interconnected the world is.

MY TRAUMATIC AND MEANINGFUL EDUCATIONAL EXPERIENCES IN THE UNITED STATES

My childhood educational experiences highlighting international travels and international family friendships motivated me to choose the educational path. I also have a vivid memory of being inspired by a newspaper article about a powerful speech by Severn Suzuki, a Canadian preteen environmentalist, addressed at the United Nations Earth Summit in Rio de Janeiro, Brazil in 1992. As I aspired to be like her, I became eager to go beyond memorization and test score-driven Japanese school education. I had to learn English to better understand cross-cultural and global issues and joined a yearlong high school exchange program of Youth for

Understanding (YFU) at age 17 in the United States. I moved to Houston, Texas, in 1996 and attended Bellaire High School, a prestigious national public school. The school had capped enrollment with approximately 3,500 students: 1,500 White, 900 Hispanic, 700 Black, 400 Asian, and others. There were students from wealthier families as well as students from low economic families, including large numbers of recent immigrant English speakers of other languages (ESOL) students. The intense racial and social dichotomy within the school was beyond my imagination. I enrolled in classes for ESOL for low-achieving students and enjoyed working with caring teachers who cared about my academic needs and also personal wellness in and outside of school. That was my initial version of the American school experience.

Among the many significant school and educational experiences, Mr. Lawrence's American History class stands out. More than half of the students in his class were recent immigrants. Many of these recent immigrant students' countries of origin were involved in World War II, and they received school education about it. Mr. Lawrence cared about and respected what recent immigrant students had learned about the historical events covered in the class and incorporated it to provide a holistic approach to the lesson. Mr. Lawrence and I had multiple meetings discussing how to approach a lesson about the atomic bomb. I shared my personal memories of how the topic emphasized human suffering, employing oral history and personal narrative in addition to transmission of factual information. I also shared that August 6, the day the atomic bomb was dropped on Hiroshima, was my maternal grandmother's birthday, an event that had a significant impact on her life. In the delivery of the actual class, Mr. Lawrence first introduced the atom bomb dropping on Hiroshima and Nagasaki as America's strategy to minimize American soldier casualties and end the war against Japan sooner. He then also introduced how the Japanese understand the events based on what I shared with him. Even before he opened the class for discussion, many non-Japanese students, even American students, strongly criticized the American decision to drop the atomic bomb as overly inhumane attacks on an unarmed general public. I was also taken off guard when my classmates countered me out of compassion when I explained how this lesson helped me to objectively approach Harry Truman's decision and the American side of the story for the first time. The class session was totally controlled chaos and gave me many unforgettable ah-ha moments. My first year in the United States was very rough but became a significant turning point expanding my mind and connecting to the world. I rapidly got to know and feel at ease among many people from all walks of life and from different countries across the world beyond my expectation.

Figure 3.3 High school prom with friends from eight countries of origin.

With an interest in becoming a diplomat, I joined the international relations bachelor's program in St. Mary's University in San Antonio, Texas, and later the Chaminade University in Honolulu, Hawaii. I could not forget the terrible class discussion and the shocking view of U.S. Navy ships lined up right off the coast of beautiful Waikiki. At the same time when Japan attacked Pearl Harbor, I was also inspired by witnessing the 4-day-long reconciliation event held in December 2001 in Waikiki, Hawaii, where American and Japanese Pacific War veterans gathered to meet and shake hands with old adversaries, including those directly involved in the attack on Pearl Harbor on December 7, 1941. This effort motivated me further to explore how I could take part in bettering the world, resulting in interning in the United Nations World Food Program (WFP). My assigned project at WFP, in the Japan office, was developing an educational curriculum and teaching materials about WFP as well as delivering workshops focused on food for education, food for gender equality, and women's empowerment.

I was fascinated with the power of education, so I chose the field of education for my graduate degrees. I joined the International Training and Education Program (ITEP), a master's program at American University in Washington, DC. I focused on international education with emphasis on educational development and cross-cultural understanding as many of my classmates were former Peace Corps volunteers. During this time, I interned at a worldwide cultural exchange organization, Youth For Understanding. I also worked onboard for an educational global voyage program,

Peace Boat, organized by an international nongovernmental organization and was intrigued by the field of intercultural communication and global education as well as teaching and curriculum evaluation. In 2006, I joined the Social Studies and Global Education PhD program at The Ohio State University [OSU] in Columbus, Ohio, and became Dr. Merry Merryfield's advisee whose literature provoked my interest in global education. The internationally diverse program at OSU was designed to allow additional cognate areas, which for me were multicultural education, teaching English as a second or foreign language (TESOL/TEFL), and qualitative research apprenticeship. The PhD program became a life changing, eye-opening period, meaningfully and effectively connecting my interests and strengths in a supportive environment. When the personal interest, academic and professional interests and lived experience are well-aligned, they become a genuine life passion and philosophy.

My Immigration Journeys and Experiences in the United States

Being educated in the United States became the best antidote for me to the rote school experiences in Japan, while leaving hope for possible future success. I held a J-1, F-1, H-1 visa, and permanent residency green card during my time in the United States. It was consuming and nerve-racking at times, but I knew I would get the permission as I had the luxury of working with legal professionals. My first challenge with immigration was not obtaining a F-1 student visa for attending a university but maintaining my full-time student status by passing a minimum of 12 credit hours for the undergraduate program and 9 credit hours for the graduate program per semester due to my limited English. After each academic degree, there was a time I considered returning to Japan. However, I never felt done with my American life and always felt America was where I should be. The second major immigration challenge occurred after my first year of working as an assistant professor in the phase of changing my optional practical training (OPT) status, which is permitted to F-1 visa holders, to H-1 visa, then applying for the United State permanent residency, commonly known as "green card."

I successfully obtained an H-1 visa through my employment at Augusta University in Augusta, Georgia. The major issue raised as I was applying for a green card emerged when my lawyer informed me that the application would be denied due to the mismatch between the position description in the job announcement and the actual classes I had been teaching. The university officially ran a national search with a different job description and appointed me for the new position. I found the green card related immigration process problematic and even traumatic. At the same time, earning a green card based on my own professional ability was rewarding and one of the proudest moments of my life.

My Experiences With Assimilation and Double Consciousness in the United States

I never imagined that a description of me would change drastically based on how different societies and its people perceive me. I was a respected student from a good family in Japan one day, but I was a social outcast the next day, a lost isolated new immigrant Asian young woman without English and American cultural knowledge or family support. The feeling of being invisible frightened me and my long fight to be seen began. Even in the racially and culturally diverse American schools I had attended in the United States, the culture of othering was more or less always present. For instance, in the public high school I witnessed how the massive cafeteria seating was strictly divided by race. I walked in and immediately walked out of the cafeteria in great shock, trying to process what I was seeing. I ate lunch in a hallway alone for days screaming and crying out in my heart, "What is this? No one told me this!" Not only the racial majority but various minorities also called and treated me as an oriental, yellow monkey, Jap, "fresh off of the boat"—referring to recent refugees with no status, "Banana"—referring to an Asian who acts White, "Yellow Cab"—referring to Asian females seeking American men for status or a green card. I was unaware of the hidden meaning behind the labeling at first, but once I became culturally conscious, my double-consciousness became a way of life and a survival skill. I also conformed with the Asian model minority notion of appearing easygoing, even when I had strong disagreements. Among five states in which I lived across the United States, only Hawaii made me blend in enough to find comfort in my own skin and be at ease. I was only able to put my finger on and name what I had been experiencing living in the United States after learning critical race theory in my doctoral program. The difficulties I faced taught me a process of self-searching, self-discovery, and self-confirming.

My Personal Successes in the United States

The major personal success I had while living in the United States was forming international friendships, especially during my student years. While there were people I did not see eye to eye with, there were also people with whom I agreed. In my first year in the United States attending a diverse local public high school, I saw my future in a microcosm of the world; that is in the United States. My personal experiences in the United States lived up to my expectations. I was always surrounded by an internationally diverse group of friends that consisted of international and immigrant friends as well as their families in the United States, or even abroad. I became increasingly connected to and interested in who they were and the kind of culture they were from. They eventually became my chosen family, actually witnessing my struggles and effort to make my American dream come true. My personal life in the United States existed in a global village rather than an American community. Regardless, I was also blessed to have a few but extremely special American friends. In retrospect, I am amazed by their one-on-one careful attention and tremendous patience, empathy and passion in helping me plant roots in American society. They were my bible to learn the A to Z of American life and American school, and to unfold American mysteries.

Another personal success is my worldwide traveling, volunteering, and working experiences as a result of the international friendships I formed while living in the United States. Throughout my student years in the United States, I saved up my paychecks working at the university cafeteria or interning to travel across the United States and abroad. I enjoyed shorter domestic travels and longer annual backpacking trips, mainly in Europe and in a few countries in Central America and South America. The occasions to stay with friends I met in the United States were priceless. I also had the privilege to volunteer a winter in an HIV orphanage in Peru and to work for the educational global cruise ship for 8 months, organizing onboard lecture sessions with experts and conducting educational programs at about 25 ports of call.

I saw the faces and cultures of my friends in many places as I went around the world, and that helped me to be less biased, more tolerant, and more connected to the world. My wide international friendship experience in the United States greatly helped and enriched my world adventures. The first-hand experience in about 40 countries was always humbling. It was also a self-confidence building experience that encouraged me to nurture my identity as a global citizen.

Figure 3.4 Volunteering in Peru.

ACADEMIC AND PROFESSIONAL SUCCESSES AND CHALLENGES IN THE UNITED STATES

Academic and Professional Successes

As an assistant professor at Augusta University in Augusta, Georgia, between 2011 and 2015, I taught graduate classes in multicultural education, global education, and teaching English to speakers of other languages (TESOL) focusing on culture and ethics, incorporating discussions on how teachers could positively impact student life using my own case as a successful example. My academic and professional success I had while living in the United States—particularly in a regional city in the Deep South—was the effective use of outsider status in classroom teaching to introduce the culturally sensitive topics people were often taught not to talk about—such as race, ethnicity, religion, language, sexuality, gender, socioeconomic status, and politics. I would often take a neutral or third person approach inviting all students to the table as important contributors in creating opportunities to speak and be heard, valuing various perspectives, examples, and firsthand experiences; we all are in it together and have a unique role to play. I also employed inquiry-based teaching. I focused on facilitating meaningful discussions using phrases such as, "Help me to understand"; "Please tell me more about..."; and "I wonder if...What do you think?" I believe creating a safe and engaging learning community environment with an effective facilitation instead of a top–down teacher-student learning environment was meaningful in developing rapport with the class, especially for a young professor with limited experience.

Another academic and professional success I had while living in the United States was being a cross-cultural mediator on academic content. I found a role in effectively bridging the United States and Japan, especially on controversial historical events such as World War II, including the attack on Pearl Harbor in 1941, Japanese internment camps from 1942 to 1946, and the atomic bombing of Hiroshima and Nagasaki in 1945. I gained cultural and academic understanding on how events are addressed and perceived differently in each country and analyzed effective ways to convey messages and provoke thoughts in a culturally sensitive yet affirming manner as a cultural bridge. My research strength involved resources and data in Japanese or American–Japanese international comparative study and resulted in publications and conference presentations. As a cultural bridge, I also proudly designed and delivered a Japan study abroad course, the first study abroad to Asia from Augusta University. It was my ultimate dream come true, and I poured in decades of my knowledge and experience engaging in the fields of international relations, study abroad administration, social studies, and multicultural, intercultural, international, and global education in order to authentically introduce the country, culture, school education, and other aspects in a way that was meaningful and thought-provoking for American students. Interestingly, the study abroad Facebook page has remained active 6 years later. Out of 20 students, two students returned to Japan to teach English in Japanese public schools, one came back to visit, and four are in touch with me planning future trips to Japan.

Academic and Professional Challenges

The development of academic or professional English language fluency is the hardest academic and professional challenge I faced while living in the United States and continue to face, particularly even more so after returning to Japan. The more I try, the more I notice my non-fluent English. My English dramatically improved during my first year living and attending a high school in the United States. Disappointingly, I gradually realized my English would not be like the native speakers' English in the undergraduate program. My academic English language use has definitely improved over decades. It never got easy, however, as I pursued a higher academic degree and began a professional career in academia that raised the expectation level of academic English sophistication. My English verbal communication and reading skills improved to acceptable levels with training but not my writing skills. I always had help from native English speakers editing my writing. Continued effort working on writing is a must for me but also accepting my limits and seeking help is an acceptable option. It is important for me to know my English language weaknesses and how to manage them.

Another professional challenge I faced while living in the United States was not having scholars I can resonate with and have steps to follow in my working environment. There were two factors that caused this challenge. The first factor was me teaching in a teacher education program without a formal kindergarten to 12th grade (K–12) classroom teaching experience in neither Japan nor the United States. My teaching experience was limited to nonformal education. The second factor was that I started working in a university department with few international or minority professors and no other non-native English-speaking professors. I was used to the universities where there are established international and minority professors and how they are respected regardless of their nationality and minority status by colleagues and students. I believe many first-time professors have to go through a learning curve and put effort into proving themselves and earn respect. I personally feel the process was challenging and bumpy, perhaps due to a lack of confidence in my ability as an academic as well as in my interpersonal and intrapersonal skills, but perhaps due to my status as an international and minority scholar as well. Successfully demonstrating my legitimacy for the position while building rapport with colleagues and students was a long intense experience. It heightened my double-consciousness, requiring a balancing act of being respectful and humble while at the same time being firm and confident.

MY DREAMS AND HOPES FOR EDUCATION

Dreams and Hopes for the Larger World

I wish for the world to strive for a better life for all in terms of health, sustainability, and happiness as a whole. I agree with Nelson Mandela when he asserted, "Education is the most powerful weapon which you can use to change the world" (GBH News, 2013). I hope educators in the larger world would ideally all employ global education, preparing people to live effectively and responsibly as an agent of change in a global society by developing global perspectives and world-mindedness (see, e.g., Case, 1993; Kirkwood-Tucker, 2001). It may be necessary to contextualize global education how to best nurture global citizens, an education based on a cultural and environmental understanding that equal input does not lead to equal outcome. To make solutions global, make them also local by taking a "glocal" (global + local) approach.

Dreams and Hopes for Education in the United States

I find that the challenge and asset of American society and American education are its immense domestic and international diversities. The diversities create intense disagreements but also tremendous opportunities for awareness about the challenges people can overcome to advance further as a better society. Not all countries have the degree of diversity among its people, therefore there exists a unique opportunity in American society to first-handedly learn how to agree to disagree or witness mutual respect and co-existence. I strongly agree with authors Liz Fosslien and Mollie West Duffy who state, "*Diversity* is having a seat at the table, *inclusion* is having a voice, and *belonging* is having that voice be heard" (Boshernitsan, 2019, para. 10, emphasis in original). I hope the United States and its educational system continue to further embrace what the country offers. One of my most memorable moments in the United States was attending the Barack Obama 2008 presidential campaign at The Ohio State University campus with Somali refugees whom I taught English at a settlement center as a part of TESOL course. I, a legal alien international student, was spontaneously rewording the presidential candidate's speech into simple

English, mediating to Somali refugees who were studying for the citizenship exam. The sense of enthusiasm and unity despite varying backgrounds was unforgettable; "Yes, we can!" That is my version of the United States of America. I strongly hope the United States remains a microcosm of the world, importantly and uniquely offering a special place where domestic and international diversities gather and continue to develop and evolve as a leading global community.

Dreams and Hopes for Education in Japan

The Japanese school education I experienced emphasized transmission of content knowledge, and I agree with the importance of having a content base to build on. But I also agree with Albert Einstein's belief that "education is not the learning of facts, but the training of the mind to think," and I believe in the benefit of cultivating thinking skills such as *The Framework for 21st Century Learning* (Partnership for 21st Century Skills, 2009) introduced by an organization, The Partnership for 21st Century Skills, with a holistic, global view. Education must not be limited to memorization and school education but should be approached as a commitment to critical reflection throughout a lifelong journey. Since I moved back to Japan, I came across the United Nations Sustainable Development Goals (SDGs; United Nations Department of Economic and Social Affairs, 2015), the 17 goals to achieve a better and more sustainable future for all, which was introduced by the United Nations General Assembly and adopted by 193 countries, and are intended to be achieved between 2016 and 2030. There are many Japanese, especially public figures wearing SGDs pins and public transportation decorations dedicated to SGDs. There is a variety of media, even occasional cartoons and family quiz television programs dedicated to SDGs, encouraging viewers to actively think and develop a global perspective (United Nations, 2000a). The SDGs succeeded the Millennium Development Goals (MDGs) following the adoption of the United Nations Millennium Declaration in 2000 (United Nations, 2000b), which all 191 United Nations member nations committed to achieve by 2015. Unfortunately, the MDGs were barely known to the Japanese public, so this is a positive shift. I hope people have better awareness about the interconnected world and ownership in examining the individual's role as an active global citizen. As Japan needs to explore outwardly, Japan also needs to explore inwardly. Japan has been facing a rapid population decrease. Continuous increase in the elderly population and decrease in the working population is particularly concerning. As Japan seeks an increased number of working immigrants, a development that must be accompanied by effective support not only by the Japanese government but also the general public. Here, I believe, Japan can learn from the example of the United States, a country of immigrant and multicultural nations.

AN UNEXPECTED CHALLENGE AND CHANGE

My Immigration Crisis

My great immigration crisis, maintaining my United States permanent residency green card, occurred only a year after finally receiving it. In 2015, I had just led a Japan study abroad and had taken a few days off to spend time with my family and friends. On the way to the airport returning to the United States, I had a major stroke of cerebral hemorrhage due to a rare cerebrovascular disease called Moyamoya, which is an innate condition I was not aware of. I was hospitalized for a total of a year for multiple brain surgeries and acute rehabilitation, followed with outpatient rehabilitation that continues to this day. I used to assume once I had a green card everything would be all right. That was far from reality.

I have been in Japan for 6 years now; however, the original plan was to spend less than a month in Japan for the study abroad. I naturally had not applied for a permit for a green card holder to be away from American territory for a year or longer, which one must apply for physically in the United States prior to departure. It had not been relevant at the time. Not having the permit, I flew to Guam, the closest American territory, to make my entry to the United States to keep my green card status in 2016, right before the 1-year mark. Through the exchanges with immigration officers in Guam, the United States Embassy in Tokyo, as well as Japanese and American immigrant lawyers in Tokyo, I learned that my green card was practically out-of-status. To regain the status, I needed to apply for a visa for an out-of-status green card holder to enter the United States as a permanent resident while in Japan. If I were granted the visa, I would need to travel to the United States and start the process of applying through the United States Citizenship and Immigration Service (USCIS) under Special Situations for Extensions considering a special situation that prevented a planned and timely return due to extraordinary circumstances beyond my control. Both applications can be denied. The process in the United States could take longer than 3 months and being away from my Japanese medical and rehabilitation teams raised concerns for me and many others in my life. If I were to regain active green card status, I was also advised to enter the United States every half year. For various reasons, I was aware that this was an unrealistic commitment. It was at that time that I suffered the emotional trauma of losing my life in the United States overnight due to a cause beyond my control.

My Experience Returning to Japan

The onset of Moyamoya caused my unexpected and nonvoluntary reentry to Japan, which ripped away my professional but also a large part of my personal and cultural identity. My experience living in the United States in my teens, 20s, and 30s transformed my identity as a Japanese into a first-generation Japanese immigrant in the United States or a global citizen. I have been going through reverse culture shock in addition to digesting my new identity as a disabled person and facing isolation at my own native home as an estranged returnee. I now exist in cultural limbo after 6 years of rest and recovery in Japan, and continue to terribly miss the United States, the lifestyle, my friends, and myself being in my element. On a positive note, the stroke has opened a door to the field of rehabilitation, which I have been blessed to be involved with for the last 6 years.

I have seen similarities in practice between quality classroom teachers and the occupational, physical, and speech therapists who employ care-centered, one-on-one, mastery-based training with tremendous empathy and patience. Speech therapy to manage broca aphasia has been most frustrating to me; the damage in the language center in the brain cannot be reversed, and time and rehabilitation may or may not improve my condition. When I get discouraged, I remember how I worked on my English even though I would not be a native speaker. My resilience and ability to turn a weakness into a strength has been critical in this challenging process. My disabilities caused me to leave Augusta University in the United States, but my disabilities and prior experiences with academia also brought new opportunities. I have presented at the Japanese Association of Speech-Language-Hearing

Figure 3.5 Occupational therapy and rehabilitation.

Therapist annual conference, taken part in participatory action research in occupational therapy, and worked with organizations on developing disability-friendly products and services. I am in a new chapter in my life, working with different versions of double-consciousness, embracing valuable experiential knowledge to explore a new version of my "self" in the best way possible.

My Dreams and Hopes Moving Forward

The United Nations World Health Organization (WHO) reports that about 15% of the world's population lives with some form of disability as of 2021. My academic and professional background in multicultural and global education makes me think about how these fields do or do not address the topic of disability. I hope to find a way to contribute with my insider view by engaging in dialogue. As a start, I took an intense training course and became a registered facilitator of the internationally recognized Disability Equality Training (DET) in which only individuals with disabilities are granted a role in the organization. DET was incorporated in the Tokyo 2020 Olympic and Paralympic volunteer training program, promoting diversity and inclusion. In the future, I dream of incorporating my firsthand experience into DET training, especially the challenges that come with aphasia, informing the public that aphasia affects a person's language but not their intellect. Individuals are often misunderstood and do not receive the support needed as many have difficulties communicating effectively with others, and the disability is hard to see. I dream of conducting DET worship in both English and Japanese, in person or online, incorporating elements of multicultural and global education, such as diversity and inclusion. I hope my limited-but-determined speaking fluency creates an opportunity for participants to have a meaningful firsthand experience with a person with aphasia. I hope my experience promotes value for a wider perspective, multicultural awareness, and empathy with action-taking.

Today, I am a stroke survivor learning to live with right-side paralysis and chronic fatigue, an aphasia warrior fighting against and living with broca aphasia. The sudden loss of lifestyle and self-identity helped me gain profound respect for people who gracefully and resiliently cope with challenges beyond one's control without recognition by others, and who still choose to shine even after all the health and other crises they may have gone through. My current motto is the philosophy of *Kintsugi*, the ancient Japanese art of repairing and mending broken objects with gold. Treasuring the flaws of a piece creates a unique history, which is now considered more beautiful and not at all broken. I dream of embracing the Kintsugi life and embodying Mother Teresa's teaching, "It's not how much you do but how much love you put in" (The Nobel Prize, 1979). Developing this autobiographical self-narrative is a meaningful actualization of the motto.

REFERENCES

Boshernitsan, R. (2019, April 26). These two millennial authors want you to acknowledge your feelings at work. *Forbes.* https://www.forbes.com/sites/rimma boshernitsan/2019/04/26/these-two-millennial-authors-want-you-to-acknowledge-your-feelings-at-work/?sh=78641ecd17b6

Case, R. (1993). Key elements of a global perspective. *Social Education, 57*(6), 318–325. https://eric.ed.gov/?id=EJ476723

GBH News. (2013, December 7). *Raw Video: Nelson Mandela visits Madison Park HS in Roxbury in 1990* [Video]. Youtube. https://www.youtube.com/watch?v=b66c6OkMZGw

Kirkwood-Tucker, T. (2001). Our global age requires global education: Clarifying definitional ambiguities. *The Social Studies, 92*(1), 10–15. https://doi.org/10.1080/00377990109603969

Partnership for 21st Century Skills. (2009). *P21 Framework definition.* https://files.eric.ed.gov/fulltext/ED519462.pdf

The Nobel Prize. (1979). *Mother Teresa Nobel lecture.* https://www.nobelprize.org/prizes/peace/1979/teresa/lecture/

United Nations. (2000a). *We can end poverty: Millennium development goals and beyond.* https://www.un.org/millenniumgoals/bkgd.shtml

United Nations. (2000b). *United Nations Millennium Declaration.* Resolution adopted by the General Assembly (September 18, 2000), A/RES/55/2. https://www.un.org/en/development/desa/population/migration/generalassembly/docs/globalcompact/A_RES_55_2.pdf

United Nations Department of Economic and Social Affairs. (2015). *Sustainable development: The 17 goals.* https://sdgs.un.org/goals

CHAPTER 4

NEPAL

MISEDUCATION, TRAVELS, AND CONTESTING RACIALIZED WORLDS WITHIN AND OUTSIDE ACADEMIA

Binaya Subedi

I grew up in the city of Kathmandu (Nepal), an urban area that included multiethnic and multilingual communities. I was privileged since I was raised in a middle-class family setting and came from a "higher" caste background. Similar to the U.S. racial caste formations, in Nepal, caste identities have been socially constructed along ethnic hierarchies and have reproduced inequities within schooling, employment, healthcare, housing—and so forth—spheres. My schooling in the city of Kathmandu is intimately connected to the larger politics of education, both in the local and the global contexts. To ensure that I would receive a meaningful education, my parents enrolled me into a Jesuit school. Both of my parents did not complete high school and saw to it that I would receive an education that would provide access to college education: an option my parents did not have because of the lack of financial resources.

Akin to the Jesuit schools that have historically been established over centuries in the Americas, Africa, and Asia, the Jesuit school that I attended was deeply connected to neo/colonial politics. Even as the school aimed to promote social justice causes based on liberation theology (the belief that Christianity-based missionary work uplifts economically underprivileged people), it served the purpose of educating youth who came from mostly elite families. This (mis) education often led, as my experiences illustrate, to being disconnected from local experiences, local histories, and local concerns/needs. Through the formal curriculum of the school, which often used standard English language, we became more familiar with global events (in Europe/North America) than within our own cities and communities. This did not mean that we were not versed in our local languages and cultures, but that formal schooling became increasingly disconnected from our family and community experiences.

What we were studying in our school was somewhat akin to what students were learning in privileged schools in New York, New Delhi, Seoul, or in Johannesburg. The (global) standardization of curriculum (math, science, English, etc.) is connected to neoliberal education model that seeks to teach standardized curriculum without considering community experiences or local needs. Even during my adolescence, expenses related to private schooling were beyond the financial means of under-resourced families who could not afford the excessive fees that private schools demanded. Within the last 2 decades, the growth of private schools has been exorbitant, and private schools often market themselves as having "higher" or "selective" status by claiming to be English medium, "more" rigorous, and as meeting international curriculum standards. Similarly, by requiring entrance exams to enroll and by often raising tuition/fees, schools often seek to claim the (false) aura of having or maintaining academic excellence. The rise of private schools, as witnessed in my childhood, has reproduced social class (and caste) status in society where privileged families maintain the power structure over generations. Indeed, such models of schooling are aligned with global capitalism; and private, competition-based model of schooling supports state and corporate interests, where schooling is seen only as a preparation for a certain kind of workforce. As in many places around the world, in Nepal public schooling continues to be perceived as being less prestigious even when public school teaching and learning practices are on the same level as private schools. I have observed that formal education, especially through the privileged schooling path, has given many people in places like Nepal options regarding social mobility: especially traveling for work or education within Asia and globally. This has indeed been my experience that privileged formal schooling provided, especially an all too familiar Jesuit brand name of the school that played a role in securing my admission to a U.S. higher education institution.

In college, I found the math and science curriculum somewhat manageable yet found what Freire (2000) terms the banking approach to teaching a major impediment to progressing towards my desired academic field of study: engineering. Faculty-centered teaching and the lack of academic support systems in math/science courses became a barrier to studying my area of interest: the kind of engineering that I imagined would serve the purpose of social change. Since childhood, I was interested in studying how tunnels or bridges could be built across or through hills in rural Nepal where people spent days walking from one hill region to another, without having access to bridges. I had observed people finding it impossible to cross rivers by foot during the rainy monsoon season, considering there were no bridges at certain locations. In college, a bigger challenge I faced was in areas of the humanities and social sciences that focused on dominant Western European (English speaking) or European American experiences. I had a difficult time being intellectually present and being engaged in foundational courses in psychology, English literature, history, communications, and so forth. The courses rarely had any meaningful material that spoke of the experiences of non-White people in the United States or from the Global South. Similarly, the language courses available to study were only in areas of French, German, or Latin. A major assignment in the first-year writing course was on observing and writing about the campus architecture and the landscape. I could not find much meaning in the assignment and struggled to even write a paragraph. This was my introduction to creative writing experiences that privileged Euro-American aesthetics and art/architecture. When the instructor in the required speech/communication course mentioned that I needed to work on my accent, I lost all faith in higher education. In many of the courses in humanities and social sciences, I struggled to approach the dominant curriculum and wondered, "Why, precisely, was I sitting in this classroom?" (Coates, 2015, p. 26).

Over the years, I have benefited from having access to standard English language: a language that continues to be privileged in the sphere of international higher education and in the world of international commerce/politics. Like my childhood, most children in the city of Kathmandu today grow up speaking three (or more) languages. First, Nepali (the most commonly spoken language) is widely spoken in cities but not in rural areas where communities speak languages that are more commonly practiced within specific ethnic communities. Secondly, like Nepali, English is a required language in schools, and both languages are assessed within high school exams. Since my childhood, the language requirements have been a major impediment for school success for youth in rural areas where students (and their parents) have limited access to formal instruction in Nepali and in English. Also, similar to my experiences, youth today grow up being familiar with Hindi, the language that is widely spoken in India. It is through the Hindi language that youth gain access to the (globalized) Indian popular culture and the film industry known as Bollywood. We can interpret this cross-national exchange within the context of cultural forms of globalization, and it is through consuming movies and songs that Nepali youth participate within the larger South Asian (and global) popular culture.

My adolescent years in Kathmandu were near the end of what is known as the Cold War, the protracted tension between the United States and the Union of Soviet Socialist Republics (USSR). It is within the Cold War contexts that I remember the presence of various public, international cultural centers (Russian, Chinese, U.S., French, Polish, etc.) in the city. As a nonaligned nation-state (meaning that Nepal did not formally support either the Soviet Union or the United States), it allowed various international embassies to open centers, which essentially served to showcase specific (inter)national cultures. The political showcase (and the public relations) included offering free books or posters of leaders such as Mao Tse-Tung or from movements such as the Bolshevik Revolution or the everyday (seemingly calm) life of people in the United States. The centers housed libraries, offered language courses and, most of all, showed popular movies and documentaries for free-of-charge. This active dissemination of films/documentaries was not innocent since it sought to promote certain representation of the nation-state, often aligning with a particular state ideology. Clearly, the books or the subsidized language courses were designed to influence the local audience, especially the youth. I remember neighbors, who were informally associated with the centers, showing films in public spaces in our neighborhood and the feelings of "global" we felt. The films included subtitled old Soviet or Polish movies (via 16 mm movie projectors) that spoke of the value of socialist revolutions and ways people overcame the hardship during World War II. The United States, French, and British cultural centers often showed popular movies that spoke of the benefits of capitalism, and the everyday lives that were seemingly untouched by racism or class or gender inequities. Never did we ever see people of color in such films that had noteworthy roles. Clearly, we were captivated by the films, but we knew that it was a form of propaganda; and we selectively consumed what was disseminated. The cultural centers also offered scholarships for youth to study in Russia, China, and so forth. During the mid-1960s, my father was one of the recipients of a scholarship to study leather production techniques in China. This was the time of Mao Tse-Tung's

Cultural Revolution, and my father recalls his mobility being restricted and being under surveillance during his 2 years of training in Shanghai.

Similarly, Whiteness (as an ideology) arrived in the city through various mediums: European and U.S.-based comic books, formal curriculum in schools (English novels, etc.), prevalence of "whitening" cosmetics and skin care products in stores, White missionaries, Hollywood movies, and so forth. We often cheered watching the performance of White actors (Harrison Ford, etc.) in movies not knowing that the joke was on us. It was indeed difficult to develop a critique during the adolescent years, the ways we were (as Third World subjects) being misrepresented as exotic, ignorant, and being infantilized. Only later in college did I realize that the (mis)representations were broadly about power and were about producing (and disseminating) knowledge about the Other. During this period, a prominent public narrative was around "development," which essentially meant that the nation-state (and people) needed to modernize/develop to conform to Western political, social, and economic standards and norms (Escobar, 1999). The narrative of "development" was a way of incorporating Nepal into the predatory global economy where the rules were already benefiting wealthy entities in the world.

The development policies also had a deep psychological impact on youth like me who had yet to understand local-global politics. The institutionalization of development or market-based modernization policies meant being dependent on loans from the likes of the IMF (International Monetary Fund) and the World Bank. I remember reading various world rankings (poverty, formal education, health, etc.) that placed Nepal on the bottom tier, along with many South Asian and African nation-states. Signing loan agreements with the IMF and the World Bank meant that such agencies would regulate and dictate the economic and political policies within the country. National elites were eager to sign such agreements since it benefited them also: the predatory partnership between national and international elites. It is not that we did not need more schools or hospitals in rural or urban areas, but that the development policies relied on external frameworks to understand/solve complex local issues, and how local/cultural ways of knowing became devalued. I remember hearing the word "dependency" during my adolescent years regarding Nepal's relation to the world. Later in graduate school, I would realize that the culture of dependency was connected to power and was about controlling social life within communities.

The Function of Racial Stereotypes

Since my arrival in the United States, at the age of 18 to attend college, my cultural and political identity has gone through transformation, mostly in response to my experiences and also in relation to how people read my racial identity. Hall (1997) writes on how identity is about being who we are and is also about becoming, in the sense of negotiating new identities in relation to new encounters or experiences. Hall explains how the "becoming" element creates new possibilities to craft political and cultural solidarities, particularly when one migrates to different geographical and/or cultural spaces. As an immigrant from the Caribbean, Hall writes about reclaiming Black identity and further politicizing Black identity in Britain during the 1950s, particularly in response to institutionalized racism. My identity has also evolved because of migration: I did not identify as Asian in everyday life or as a South Asian when living in Nepal. The political aspect of Asian or South Asian (and immigrant) identity evolved in response to how people identified me and how I came to re-identify myself in relation to the various "racial formations" (Omi & Winant, 1986) in the United States.

Since my college years, because of my racial identity, I have realized that I am both invisible and visible to dominant people in U.S. society. I am invisible in the sense that people of Asian descent are seen as perpetual foreigners and not having any sort of legitimacy in the United States. Over the years, I have been told that Asians are "good" minorities or "good" immigrants. I have also been told that I am fortunate to be "here" as if I have been "saved" by being in the United States. These references may seem "positive" but they are indeed racialized stereotypes which are often used to discipline people of Asian descent or people of color in general. As I have encountered in my academic life, like many faculty of Asian descent, I am often not included within discussions of diversity. Faculty of color face hurdles in being taken seriously as scholars in academia: an institution that consistently rewards White mediocrity (Patton & Haynes, 2020). Mitchell (2018) writes how, for Black faculty, "noticing white mediocrity is a form of self-care" (p. 254) since, too often, "white mediocrity is treated as a merit" (p. 254). Unfortunately, I become visible (to my colleagues) when I speak out against what may make my colleagues uncomfortable, whether the topics are U.S. military involvement in the world or the racial injustices in the United States.

Over the years, especially after 9/11 and the U.S. occupation of Iraq and Afghanistan, people of South Asian, Arab, and Muslim people have become more visible or hyper visible, often being perceived as the enemy Other. What this means in classroom contexts is that faculty who look like the Other must negotiate their identities differently, often to protect the self from harm. This is because of student (or White faculty) resistance to critical curriculum or because of the social surveillance of their writings or community activism. Student resistance to curriculum, especially around questions of race and U.S. military presence in the world, has been more common in my classes. Most students have difficulties in recognizing how

U.S. military interventions or U.S. funded wars violently damage impacted communities, often for generations. Students who are socialized to think about concepts such as freedom and rights only think through narrow, hyper patriotic lenses. Too often, the prevailing belief is that U.S. foreign policies are innocent or are formulated to "protect our way of life." Similarly, because of students' socialization, it is also difficult for many students to recognize that Muslims in the United States have lived a life of fear and violence in the aftermath of 9/11 events (Maira, 2009). Islamophobia is prevalent in U.S. schools and society, and Muslim youth and their families continue to be racialized in everyday lives, including in schools. Because of my embodied experiences and social justice commitments, I have felt the responsibility to address global events through a critical lens in the courses I teach. And I also feel the responsibility to address how local/national policies impact global events (U.S. wars, predatory economic policies, etc.), knowing well that the discussion may make students uncomfortable. However, as Kumashiro (2015) writes, it is through being vulnerable and being open to new knowledge that students can (un)learn racism and other forms of oppression.

Consider the following three lived experiences that I have been part of: (a) I am walking home from a public event with my family, and I hear a group of youth yelling: "You fuc*%#@ Mexican. Go back to where you came from"; (b) my father is walking in a suburban area and a White family calls the police claiming that a suspicious person was walking in the neighborhood; and (c) my son mentions: "Dad, I don't know if I told you this, but my friends often call me a "bomber." For me, over the years, a more challenging part of everyday living has been when family members are publicly harassed. I have often wondered how I could respond to such racial humiliations. Or what might be the consequences (more violence, etc.) if a person like me is to create a response. The racial profanity that I encountered speaks of the anti-Mexican or anti-immigrant sentiment in the country. It illustrates how people, who feel they are entitled, have the license to racially harass people of color in public spaces. My initial instinct was to correct the mis(identification) but I felt at-ease being a "Mexican" at that particular moment. I have come to realize that "we" are the same to dominant people even when we embody complex ethnic, racial, linguistic, or gender identities. My father's experience also illustrates how non-White people become hyper visible in spaces that are under constant surveillance. Hong (2020) writes about the conflicting (and traumatic) emotions youth experience when witnessing the physical or the verbal violence that family members encounter in everyday lives. Hong speaks about witnessing the physical violence that her grandmother endured in front of her, when White teenagers openly mocked her grandmother in public, and one girl kicked her grandmother on her back. Unlike what Black people often endure, my dad was not physically harmed by the police, but he was emotionally and psychologically traumatized over what had taken place. The police questioned him and eventually he was released to us. Over the years, because of the public/racial humiliation, he has refused to speak about the incident. The bomber reference that my son speaks about illustrates the prevalence of Islamophobia in society, and how U.S. wars and military occupations in the Middle East and West Asia (and globally) continue to represent Muslim (and people in the Third World) as the enemy Other. For me, these experiences further illustrate how local/global events are interconnected and overlap in everyday experiences. Immigrants and people of color, in general, are often told that they don't belong "here" and are reminded of being a perpetual racial Other in everyday life.

ACADEMIA AND CONTESTING LOCAL–GLOBAL FRAMEWORKS

My higher education experiences have been within predominantly White institutions in the United States, which has limited the curricular options or the intellectual experiences that I could have been part of elsewhere. It was in graduate school that I felt that I began to learn the critical language and the tools to decolonize what I had learned in various formal learning spaces. The graduate school experience included being in affirming spaces of mentoring, provided by Black faculty, and also having Black faculty members as instructors in courses. The experience also included working with White faculty members who understood how (and why) Whiteness needed to be decentered and who worked to dismantle Whiteness in academia. I remember reading Edward Said's (1979) book *Orientalism* in graduate school, which provided me with the theoretical language to interpret the world in a critical/liberatory way. I began to take the initial steps to un/learn the role colonialism and imperialism had played in the making of the modern world. This included critically reflecting on the politics that shaped what was included/excluded as legitimate knowledge to be learned in schools. Said's work is not without criticism: for example, the absence of gender analysis or the minimization of feminist scholarship in theorizing colonial discourses. Reading Said's call for the urgent need to reclaim Palestinian sovereignty helped me recognize the value of engaging in public scholarship, and it reminded me that being in academia was a political project. And, it was also through reading writings by bell hooks, Angela Davis, Sara Ahmed, and Chandra T. Mohanty that I began to think through the different positionalities we inhabit and the critical ways we can read (and respond to) dominant discourses within academia. I began to think through questions such as: "Who is valued and not valued in academia and why the politics of devaluation?" and "What does it mean to engage in transformative writing at the contemporary moment?"

Along with unlearning gender, patriarchy, cis-gender privilege, my work also included unlearning settler colonialism. As an immigrant, I have benefited from my settler status and have felt the obligation to work against settler colonial violence (Patel, 2016). It was Linda Tuhiwai Smith's (1999) writings, especially *Decolonizing Methodologies*, that enabled me spaces to read local and global aspects of indigenous history and experiences that are deeply connected to racism and neo/colonialism. I write and teach/research themes that interconnect local-global experiences and how ethical and decolonial notions of citizenship can be reclaimed and practiced in school and in society. Smith's work created spaces for me to recognize how indigenous experiences can offer critical ways to read local/global histories and contemporary world politics, especially around cultural appropriations, land rights, sovereignty, and so forth.

Yet, as I have experienced, the broader field of education is often not receptive to engaging with scholarship on transformative and decolonizing theories in international contexts (McCarthy, 1998). Within many subfields of the discipline, scholars who are engaged in international, social justice dimensions of scholarship face methodological roadblocks, where the history of colonialism and neocolonialism is not considered as being relevant or being intellectually valuable within the field. I have come to learn that, too often, in teacher preparation programs nationally, including in doctoral programs, serious inclusion of critical global-themed coursework is an afterthought. Not surprisingly, these practices reinforce U.S. exceptionalism: as if U.S. role, policies, and presence are not to be interrogated.

The identities, experiences, and social commitments of an educator matter since it shapes the ways in which an educator may develop curriculum and engage with learners. Over the years, I have felt uneasiness in working with faculty members who follow a status-quo, dominant approach to global pedagogy (see Subreenduth, 2010). Status-quo approaches focus more on "neutral" ways of interpreting world events rather than engaging with questions of social change in society. Clearly, the neutral path reinforces deficit frameworks: the belief that we only seek to understand and not make political commitments. As we know: Being neutral or not making a political stand is itself a political position. Deficit frameworks treat communities in the Global South as "problems" and as communities without agency: people who are unable to "progress" in cultural, social, political, and economic spheres. This approach fails to question the policies and practices developed in the Global North that further marginalize people in places like Nepal. In essence, deficit ways of conceptualizing the world reinforces dominant paradigms on theorizing local–global relationships. Too often, I have found that (some) faculty members view my role to be (only as) a "native informer" so that I can "help" the scholars accomplish their goals (research, etc.). Clearly, our embodied experiences, our research, and ways in which faculty of color see the world is often not viewed as legitimate or intellectually rigorous in academia.

I have learned to inhabit spaces that can be affirming in academia. This is not to suggest that all or most of the work has led to transformative pathways but that the journey itself, often exhausting, has helped me better understand (and critique) U.S. society and academia. Over the years, I have been part of supportive writing groups, affirming teaching support communities, and critical social networks which have enabled me to survive academia. Most of all, I have found community work, especially the work with working-class immigrant and refugee communities, as a constant un/learning space—a path that continues to guide my work towards a decolonized world.

REFERENCES

Coates, T. (2015). *Between the world and me*. Spiegel & Grau.
Escobar, A. (1999). *Encountering development: The making and the unmaking of the Third World*. Princeton University Press.
Freire, P. (2000). *Pedagogy of the oppressed* (30th anniversary ed.). Continuum.
Hall, S. (1997). Old and new identities, old and new ethnicities. In A. D. King (Ed.), *Culture, globalization, and world-system: Contemporary conditions for the representations of identity* (pp. 41–68). University of Minnesota.
Hong, C. P. (2020). *Minor feelings: An Asian American reckoning*. One World.
Kumashiro, K. K. (2015). *Against common sense: Teaching and learning toward social justice* (3rd ed.). Routledge.
Maira, S. M. (2009). *Missing: Youth, citizenship, and empire after 9/11*. Duke University Press.
McCarthy, C. (1998). *The uses of culture: Education and the limits of ethnic affiliation*. Routledge.
Mitchell, K. (2018). Identifying White mediocrity and know-your-place aggression: A form of self-care. *African American Review*, 51(4), 253–262. https://doi.org/10.1353/afa.2018.0045
Omi, M., & Winant, H. (1986). *Racial formations in the United States*. Routledge.
Patel, L. (2016). *Decolonizing educational research: From ownership to answerability*. Routledge.
Patton, L. D., & Haynes, C. (2020) Dear White people: Reimagining Whiteness in the struggle for racial equity. *Change: The Magazine of Higher Learning*, 52(2), 41–45. https://doi.org/10.1080/00091383.2020.1732775
Said, E. (1979). *Orientalism*. Vintage Books.

Smith, L. T. (1999). *Decolonizing methodologies: Research and indigenous peoples.* Zed Books.
Subreenduth, S. (2010). Travel dialogues of/to the other: Complicating identities and global pedagogy. In B. Subedi (Ed.), *Critical global perspectives: Rethinking knowledge about global societies* (pp. 199–222). Information Age Publishing.

CHAPTER 5

PEOPLE'S REPUBLIC OF CHINA

NAVIGATING HISTORICAL CURRENTS

Reflections of a Chinese-Born Global Educator

Lin Lin

In this chapter I will share the lived experiences of my professional and personal journey between East and West as I have traveled thousands of miles over decades between China and the United States. I will share my stories chronologically by applying the basic concept of sociology that our position in our social structure and historical currents create visible and invisible forces that push us towards our career paths, worldviews, and interactions with people in our lives. Factors such as gender, race, ethnicity, class, age, religion, residential locations, family background, and nationality, together with other aspects of our identity, blend together in shaping who we are as we navigate historical currents.

I have been living in the United States since 2000. I was born in Qingdao, a beautiful eastern city on the Pacific coast in Shandong Province in the People's Republic of China, where my mother still lives. My husband and our daughter Hannah were born in China and became citizens of the United States through naturalization. Our son Daniel was born in the United States and became a United States citizen by birth. I remain a Chinese citizen living in the United States as a permanent resident simply because my Chinese citizenship enables me to travel more freely between the two countries. During the pandemic, I became the only one in my family who could return to China without having to apply for a Chinese visa when visas had been suspended by the Chinese government for United States citizens except for emergency and special humanitarian reasons.

My decision to remain a Chinese citizen has an indelible impact on my identity as a global educator. I firmly believe that the world we live in is intricately connected and that countries with distinct territorial borders are interdependent. Just look at the COVID-19 pandemic which continues its ruthless grip on the world into the year of 2022. What links us with the rest of the world also includes the imminent danger of wars and other forms of violence, concerns for deteriorating environments, and prevalent injustices due to biases and bigotries. In Spring 2022, snow was falling relentlessly in central New York even after the spring equinox as I was sitting inside my house overwhelmed by anger as Russia just invaded Ukraine. On top of that, China abstained from a vote in the emergency meeting of the United Nations General Assembly to denounce the Russian invasion. A few days earlier, I was overjoyed at the news from the Winter Olympics about gold medals won by athletes from all around the world, including China and the United States. I cheered for the United States, and I cheered for China.

China's Achievements vis-à-vis Suppression of Diverse Voices

During the last few days of the Winter Olympics (February 4–20, 2022) as the world watched the precarious situation in Ukraine, I was praying for world peace. Then, a video went viral on the Internet about a chained woman in China (Cao & Feng, 2022). It revealed that human trafficking is a common and prevailing issue in my home country that boasts its glorious achievements as a soaring superpower in the world. Messages about the "chained woman" posted on WeChat, a social media platform widely used by 1.2 billion people around the world, were eliminated within seconds as they could have stirred up grievances against the government. Now, some Internet users in China together with the government seem to be siding with Russia, whose leader has threatened to use nuclear warheads or chemical weapons to subdue Ukraine.

I cannot help making connections with the first and only Summer Olympics held in China in 2008. During the Chinese New Year month of 2008, I stopped in Beijing on my return trip to the United States. I was on a research leave that semester and spent the Chinese New Year in Qingdao with my mother and grandmother. It was the first Chinese New Year, also known as the Spring Festival, after my father passed away in 2007. In this 1,000-year-old city of Beijing, my college roommate drove me past the Bird's Nest, the stadium that would host the opening ceremony of the 28th Summer Olympics. At that time, China had gained an opportunity to show itself off to the world.

But just as the eyes of the world focused on China, Beijing expelled its own citizens, the migrant workers, who came to Beijing from central and southwestern provinces, to make space for the more "important" people, such as foreign athletes, celebrities, journalists, and spectators. The housemaid hired to take care of my aunt had to leave Beijing for her hometown in Sichuan, a province in Southwest China, Moreover, an earthquake in Wenchuan, close to the housemaid's hometown in Sichuan, alarmed the nation and the world about a large number of casualties of children due to shoddy school construction and a chemical melamine that can cause kidney stones discovered in Chinese infant formula. These scandals were covered up until the Summer Olympics were over. If 2008 had witnessed enough incidents to warn the world of the potential undemocratic road undertaken by the Chinese government, should we be alarmed now with China's strategies to contain COVID-19?

The cover-up strategy by the Chinese government was not anything novel. It suppressed the accurate and timely reporting of the first case of SARS in late 2002 and, therefore, missed the best window of time to keep the epidemic effectively controlled. The severity of the epidemic ended up infecting thousands, and hundreds of people died of SARS in 2003. Unfortunately, the COVID-19 crisis in Wuhan in 2020 followed a similar pattern. As I was writing this chapter, Shanghai started a city-wide quarantine measure to achieve the goal of "zero case," but the 5-day lockdown evolved into a 70-day lockdown, affecting the lives of more than 25 million people. My mother, living in a city far away from Shanghai, has just completed her 18th mandatory COVID-19 test within 2 months. Posts complaining about such situations on social media have been promptly censored.

My Continued Concerns for China

China, undoubtedly, has been making huge progress with its miraculous economic development. The economic miracle has transformed the lives of many people in China, including my family. At the level of material wealth, buildings, highways, bridges, airports, residential complexes, public parks, supermarkets, railroads, cars, and so forth. China can rival the counterparts in the most advanced countries in the world. My family moved from a tiny matchbox-sized brick house into today's seaside deluxe three-bedroom apartment overlooking the beach. But has China really been transformative in its political reforms since then? Obviously, this year's nationalistic, self-congratulatory propaganda for the 2022 Winter Olympics has been successful until the chained woman in Feng County in Jiangsu Province revealed that competition at the sports games is a sham without fairness and freedom. Born in China and having lived there for 34 years, I am concerned about the future of my motherland.

I have lived in times when truth prevailed and when lies were considered truth. I have also lived in times when human lives were compromised for ideological differences and class struggles. My life started with the Cultural Revolution, a turbulent time in the history of modern China when people were persecuted, incarcerated, or lost their lives when they told the truth. I benefited from the ending of the Cultural Revolution and China's opening up to the outside world, starting in 1978 as I came of age. As economic and naked profit seemed to have gripped China, how long could the Chinese government gloss over the ideological gap that separated it from the world's democracies and continue its dream of globalization. I ask myself, "When will China stop celebrating extravagance and ostentation, and promote fairness and justice for its grassroots citizens instead?"

My Birth and Childhood Branded by the Cultural Revolution

On a January morning in 1967, just as dawn began to break in the east, the powerful loudspeaker on the roof of the Qingdao Municipal Women and Children's Hospital sprang to life waking up my mother. "The East Is Red" blasted over the loudspeaker and continued with "the East is red, the sun rises, China sends forth a Mao Zedong." This most popular hymn probably woke up everyone in this beautiful northeastern city on the Pacific coast in Shandong Province, China.

Such details were never lost in my mother's numerous retellings of my birth story. She was in constant pain from contractions the night before but was left unattended in her hospital bed as the doctors and nurses were at a political study session to learn Maoist thoughts, and my mother was told to "suck up" her pain in early labor. That morning, as I entered the world, the same song, played by an army band, burst out on the airwaves accompanied by an infant's piercing wail. That song appeared to have made its way into the heads of my parents, because when they were urged to have a name for their newborn child at the hospital, they named me Red. Red is pronounced "Hong" and means socialist-minded and ideologically conscious. "Being red" signifies taking the right ideological and political stance. This meaning of my name was extremely important to my mother who was denied membership in the Communist Youth League because of her "bourgeois" family background. People like her had to go through "socialist remolding," which aimed to make sure that her kind of "people" would not depart from the socialist path and turn to the capitalist path. Many children born during the Cultural Revolution had names with political, ideological, and historical meanings. It was not unusual that many adults changed their names on purpose in that era, taking the "right" side with the political and ideological camps.

I was born into a 10-year chaotic decade when one's family background mattered more than anything else. The booming shipping company owned by my mother's grandparents made her forever stained with a bourgeois family background that rendered her ineligible for membership in the Youth League or the Communist Party. My father, on the contrary, was from a peasant's family, and his loyalty to the Communist Party was never suspected. In his old age, my father always bragged that when he chose to marry my mother, he was asked to either give up his relationship with my mother or give up his prospect of joining the Party, but he did not cave in when pressured.

A year and half later after my birth, my younger brother was born. My earliest memories of Qingdao always include my brother, Peng Peng, named after my father's hometown, Penglai, a city in Shandong Province. A family of four, we lived in a small brick house with three tiny rooms, sharing one outdoor water faucet and an outhouse as a bathroom with 13 other families of teachers and staff members working at the same high school where my parents taught. In wintertime, one could slip and fall on the frozen platform where the water faucet was installed. We had to bring a kettle of boiling water to thaw the water hose before getting any tap water. The bathroom situation was far worse. A total number of 14 families, with an average of four people in each family, shared the two bathrooms, one for males and the other for females.

Although it was a time of severe scarcity in China, we were never in short supply of books and the joy that came with reading books. The library at my parents' school was open to all the children of teachers and staff. The palm-sized black-and-white picture books opened the door of literacy to us. Our lives in the 1970s were miserable in many ways, but as children, we were free from any pressure for the cut-throat academic competition. We had the freedom all day long to go on adventures in the gardens and play games around the pond of my parents' school. If we were not in school, we were picking unripe fig fruits on Northridge Mountain, collecting fallen leaves to sew them into long trains of leaves to drag across the street, scavenging for colorful glass shards, with which we viewed the sun, and roasting cicadas on a fire as our most favorite snack. We jumped rope, individually or in teams, for competition; played marbles; collected candy wrappers and stamps to fold into home-made albums; played house by assigning roles to every child in our mix; and we played hide-and-seek until dark.

President Nixon Visits China

We were too young to notice that, as we jumped rope for fun in 1972, something happened on the international stage that would forever change the relationship between China and the United States. This event would have long-term impacts on the lives of many Chinese as well as American people more than we could fathom. The impacts are still felt today. On February 21, 1972, Richard Nixon became the first sitting U.S. president to set foot in the People's Republic of China (Neal, 2022). This year, 2022, marks the 50th anniversary of Nixon's 1972 trip. While, in the minds of the Chinese, Nixon was always one of the most favored presidents due to his initial trip to China, most Chinese did not know that other Western countries had begun even before Nixon's trip to placate Beijing and improve relationships. Neither did many Chinese care about Nixon's wrongdoing in the Watergate incident.

In September 1973, as I started elementary school, I chanted rhythms with derogatory words against Confucius and the Confucianist traditions. Mao's anti-Confucius initiative was meant to counteract more pragmatic elements in the Communist Party. Soon, this initiative was combined with a denunciation of Lin Biao, a Communist leader next to Mao and a military marshal, who died in a plane crash in 1971 trying to defect to the Soviet Union. Caricatures ridiculing Confucius and Lin Biao appeared on the exterior walls of my parents' school and the bulletin boards of my elementary school. My parents told me to be quiet when I asked them who Confucius and Lin Biao were. Before long, another name, Deng Xiaoping, was added to the collection of derogatory images in public spaces when Mao distrusted and demoted Deng from a leadership position in the Communist Party.

Death of Premier Zhou Enlai

I was in third grade when a series of events took place in China. The death of Premier Zhou Enlai on January 8, 1976, put everyone into deep grief. I cried with my parents, as they read news headlines about tens of thousands of residents lining the streets of Beijing to bid farewell as the hearse drove to the crematorium. The following month, Hua Guofeng was appointed acting premier instead of Deng Xiaoping, who was clearly in disfavor. Hua's promotion resulted from his neutral position between the radical left and moderates in the party. On April 4, the day before Qingming Festival, a holiday when loved ones were traditionally mourned, people gathered on Tiananmen Square with their poems and wreaths and demonstrated their pent-up resentment against the radical left, which was represented by the Gang of Four, a Maoist political faction composed of four Communist Party officials coming to prominence during the Cultural Revolution. To prevent further demonstrations, the government removed the poems and wreaths overnight. Angry civilians attacked the police and many were arrested.

Back in Qingdao, my parents heard on the radio that a "counterrevolutionary incident" had taken place in Tiananmen Square and that Deng Xiaoping was accused of being behind it. My parents were certainly on the side of the demonstrators, and they were outraged that the demonstrations had been so ruthlessly suppressed. I remember my father repeatedly uttered under his breath, "lies, lies, and lies"! In 1989, 13 years later, I was directly involved in another demonstration on Tiananmen Square when the Communist Party took a similar approach toward the democracy movement, a nonviolent challenge to the party, which used its ruthless force to crack down on human lives and human liberty.

Mao Zedong passed away on September 9, 1976. Within a few weeks, the newly appointed premier Hua Guofeng arrested the ultra-left Gang of Four, which included Mao's widow and her three confidants in the Party. With the fall of the Gang of Four, Mao's Cultural Revolution was officially over. We became teenagers in the new hopeful era after the "counterrevolutionary incident" in Tiananmen Square in April 1976 was reversed, and the Cultural Revolution Mao launched was repudiated. We were also the generation that no longer was sent to "the rural areas to get reeducated by the peasants." The college entrance examination, *Gaokao*, was resumed in 1977 as the nation was on its path to Deng Xiaoping's four modernizations in industry, agriculture, defense, and science. That same year, a movement began brewing in Beijing that called for a fifth modernization: democracy. Represented by Wei Jingsheng, an electrician turned thinker and writer in his late 20s, a group of people proposed to modernize the political system first before proceeding to the four modernizations.

Thanks to the Shanghai Communiqué, the agreement that resulted from President Nixon's visit in 1972, President Carter's administration now had a clear pathway to normalizing relations with China in 1979. That same year, Deng Xiaoping visited the United States for the first time as a top leader of the Communist Party. That same year also, my family finally owned a

9-inch made-in-Japan black-and-white TV, and we watched Deng Xiaoping hugging Carter as he was watching American elementary students singing *I Love Beijing Tiananmen* at the Kennedy Center in Washington DC.

SEEDS OF GLOBAL EDUCATION EMERGE AT THE UNIVERSITY

One of the most significant changes that impacted me was the restoration of the National College Entrance Examination in 1977. While many young people forever lost the opportunity to pursue higher education, particularly those who were already settled down in the countryside during the Cultural Revolution, high school graduates now felt hopeful. The idea of a college visit was unheard of at that time, but my mother had the vision of taking me to see universities in Beijing. My mother was a first-generation college graduate as Grandma raised her as a single mother who was widowed at the age of 29 after her husband died in a Japanese prison camp during World War II. My father was also the first-generation college student in his family. His elder sister advised him to major in physics rather than his dream major in legal studies as she knew too well that a lawyer might not navigate well in China where one political campaign was staged after another since 1949.

In 1984, I was accepted by Beijing Foreign Studies University (BFSU) to major in English language and literature. It was at BFSU where seeds of global education were planted for me to orient my teaching and scholarly work towards international and cross-cultural global education. As China opened its door to the world, I became engrossed in foreign movies. Making it into BFSU, I knew I was one step closer to my dream at a university where more than 70 foreign languages are taught and that specializes in training ambassadors and foreign service officers who represent China around the world, and where university professors train teacher candidates and foreign service staff. At BFSU, I met classmates from all provinces in China as well as foreign students from North Korea and Cambodia. Native speakers of English from Great Britain, the United States, Australia, and New Zealand became our English teachers and teachers of world geography, world history, and global cultures. I realized that, while I did not have the privilege of growing up in top cities, I had access to opportunities and resources that were denied to many classmates from rural areas. Excitement, anxiety, ambition, and insecurity made my heart burst with ideas and emotions. I loathed when city people made fun of rural people. I felt overjoyed when I made progress in listening and reading comprehension. Voice of America and BBC news started to make sense to me, and I was slowly on my way to acquiring English proficiency.

In the tiny college dormitory that I shared with four other young women, we dictated lyrics from songs by John Denver, Karen Carpenter, Michael Jackson, ABBA, the Judds, Simon & Garfunkel, and Stevie Wonder using pirated copies by listening to them again and again on battery-powered tape recorders. We devoured every word in *The Thorn Birds* (2004) overnight as there was a long line of readers waiting to read the only copy in the library. We read with a flashlight under our quilts. We watched English movies to learn how native speakers speak English and what their cultures were like. We never missed any dance parties in cafeterias transformed into dance halls, drinking sodas, and stepping on each other's toes. We studied hard to pass exams and felt proud that we could now speak English to communicate with people from around the world.

THE 1989 TIANANMEN SQUARE PEACEFUL PROTESTS

I was in my first year in the American studies program in the graduate school of BFSU when turmoil broke out in Spring 1989. It all started when Hu Yaobang, former secretary general of the Chinese Communist Party, passed away from a heart attack on April 15, 1989. His death triggered a power struggle between top leaders in the party who favored political reform and those who tolerated only economic reform. I was one of the thousands of university students marching to Tiananmen Square to mourn Hu. At BFSU, graduate students quickly formed a committee to lead the students and their activities. One of our classmates became the leader and asked me to be a receptionist in a make-shift office answering phone calls. I also helped with printing flyers. This was a time before photocopying. I engraved words on a steel plate and others made copies on a mimeograph. After the government issued the "April 26 Editorial" to call the student movement a "riot," we marched for 16 hours in Beijing and returned to campus with hoarse voices and tired legs.

Such marches quickly escalated into nation-wide demonstrations demanding the government to address inflation, unemployment, and corruption, and increase media transparency and freedom of the press. A group of university students began a hunger strike in mid-May on the Tiananmen Square, and 400 other cities responded with support. The students in Beijing asked for a dialogue with the government, but the hardliners in the Party decided to crush the demonstrations by force. Martial law was declared in late May as 300,000 troops were deployed in Beijing. None of us thought that our government would use force against nonviolent student demonstrations. But it did on June 4, 1989.

My brother Peng escaped just in time from Tiananmen Square the night before as the government issued an ultimatum to the hunger strikers to leave the square by midnight. For days the government-controlled media rolled out coverage of the "riots" in Beijing. My parents believed that the students' peaceful demonstration was hijacked by the few people who wanted to dethrone the Communist Party. In my heart, the legitimacy of the government crumbled to dust.

As we returned to campus in the Fall of 1989, we were corralled to meet weekly for a "brainwashing" session to conclude that the government did everything right to crack down on the riots. Professors who had supported the student demonstrations were suspended from teaching, and students who had participated in hunger strikes and demonstrations were required to confess their wrongdoings. Our team leader had walked with us as we marched to Tiannanmen Square in May. Consequently she neither conducted those brainwashing sessions seriously nor endlessly. We usually just took turns reading the newspaper editorials and quickly moved on to other topics. Thus, we could say that our brains had been washed "clean." Young people in China today do not have any knowledge of the students' peaceful protests in Tiananmen Square in 1989. The history textbooks they read make no mention of or give voice to the people who witnessed what really happened. Recently, a memorial to this 1989 incident on the campus of a university in Hong Kong was smashed to the ground. Who will continue sharing the witness narratives of the past? Who dares to forget what really happened? I will never forget.

BECOMING A FEMINIST SCHOLAR

Marching in the students' demonstrations as a graduate student in the American Studies program at BFSU, I met Fan, my future husband, a graduate student in the British/American literature program at the same university. At that time, a few graduate students had decided to study in the United States and other countries. Some of them had relatives as sponsors in the United States. Some left for the United States with their partners in STEM fields. All of them paid a hefty amount of money, known as "training fees," to the institution they graduated from or worked for, a government measure to discourage the "brain drain." We decided to stay put and start a family first as we could not afford the training fees. After we graduated with our master's degrees in 1991, we got married. Upon graduation, I was hired as a lecturer to teach English in the same department where I had studied for six and a half years as an undergraduate and graduate student and was subsequently promoted to assistant and associate professor. My husband went to work as an interpreter in the Office of International Affairs at the China Law Society in the Ministry of Justice.

At that time, China's economy had grown by leaps and bounds. Higher education was among the major areas that the Chinese government recognized as a leading field to champion the reforms and bridge the country to the outside world. Opportunities unfolded as I served as an interpreter for nongovernment organizations such as the Ford Foundation and the Canadian International Development Association when the government sponsored representatives to attend the Nordic Women's Regional Conference in Finland and Sweden in 1994 and the Preparatory Conference for the Fourth United National's Women's Conference in New York City in 1995. Representing a women's youth organization in Beijing, I served as one of the volunteer interpreters at the Fourth Women's Conference of the United Nations, which convened in Beijing in 1995. I was beyond excited to hear former Senator Hilary Clinton speak in person. In Helsinki, on my first trip abroad in 1994, I was asked if I was Japanese. When I said "No," I was asked whether I was from Hong Kong or Taiwan. They were surprised to learn that I was from Mainland China as very few Chinese women traveled abroad then. At a United Nations (UN) event in New York City in 1995, I was asked whether China had electricity. With frustration, I responded that we "did not have electricity—as a joke—but that we did have nuclear power." Many years later, the dearth of knowledge of my students about certain parts of the world always reminded me of my unfriendly reference to nuclear power at the UN event.

My involvement with women's studies in China in the 1990s led me to international women's activities. Supported by the Ford Foundation, I was one of the translators at the convention for the Chinese version of the United Nations Declaration on the Elimination of All Forms of Discrimination Against Women after it was adopted in 1993. I was also one of the authors who translated the seminal book, *Our Bodies, Ourselves* (1976), into Mandarin Chinese to Chinese readers and feminists. Through this book, published by the Boston Women's Health Book Collective in 1970, I learned about women's health, sexuality, and sexual orientation for the first time, and realized how much China lagged behind in the field of feminist studies. Based on my experiences visiting women's organizations in Finland, Sweden, and the United States, in 1996 I contributed a chapter to *Reflections & Resonance*, a bilingual book compiled by Yuen Ling Wong, a Hong-Kong-based journalist, and Bohong Liu, one of the leading feminist scholars in China (Wong, 1995). To describe and reflect upon my first encounter with the European feminists' fight for gender equality, in my chapter I shared four letters I wrote to my mother during my trip to the Nordic Women's Conference in Finland.

In May of 1996, I strapped my newborn daughter on my back and attended the news conference of the book launch with other contributing authors in Beijing. Who could have imagined that my baby girl in 2015, 20 years later, would work as an intern for the Roosevelt Institute in New York City that invited Senator Hilary Clinton to speak at a commemoration event for the 20th anniversary of the 1995 United Nations Women's Conference that was held in Beijing? At the same event, Hannah, my daughter, called home and asked whether I knew Bohong Liu, another keynote speaker from China. Bohong was pleasantly surprised and overjoyed that she met Hannah, the baby girl who had attended her book launch 20 years ago. In 2015, to commemorate the 20th anniversary of the United Nations Fourth Conference on Women, Bohong and her co-editors published a sequel to the first edition of *Reflections & Resonance*, edited by Wong Yuen Ling in 1995. The new sequel's title is *Reflections and Resonance of Women—Sequel"* with *"Accelerating the Realization of Gender Equality and the Empowerment of Women"* as its subtitle (Liu et al., 2015). I was again invited to contribute a chapter to summarize my growth as a feminist, educator, and scholar in the last twenty years.

OPPORTUNITY TO STUDY IN THE UNITED STATES

After I returned from my maternity leave in 1996 to teaching at BFSU, I applied for a 1-year Chinese language scholar position in the Chinese Language and Culture Department at Reed College in Portland, Oregon. Working with Dr. Charles Wu, an BFSU alumni and the founding faculty member of the Asian languages and studies program at Reed College, was a precious opportunity whose significance to my professional life I did not realize until later. With the support of my parents and my husband, I left for the United States in 1997. The year at Reed College between 1997 and 1998 opened my eyes to a new way of teaching and learning history. No longer were students forced to regurgitate disconnected facts from history textbooks. Instead, I learned history as an interpretive process that depends heavily on primary and secondary sources created by people from their unique perspectives. As primary sources can be incomplete and problematic, historians gather, use, and interpret multiple sources as evidence for their conclusions and make ethical decisions about what goes into school textbooks and, subsequently, into the minds of children. Such a way of learning history was unfamiliar to me, and it made me curious about the ways of teaching history and historiography in the United States. This 1-year visiting scholarship helped me decide to return to the United States in 2000 as a doctoral student at the University of Georgia.

In 2000, my husband and I decided to study in the United States. He wanted to study law and I wanted to major in social studies education. At that time, my university made it clear to its young faculty that a doctoral degree would soon become a standard requirement for promotion. With encouragement of Dr. Strother and his wife, Fan's American professor and his wife, who are alumni of the University of Georgia (UGA), I applied to the doctoral program in social science education at UGA. What I failed to know was that Dr. John Hoge, the graduate coordinator and department chair at that time, tried his best to persuade the Graduate School Admissions Office at UGA to accept me and another Chinese applicant with a full graduate assistantship without which I would not have been able to obtain a visa to come to the United States. Dr. Hoge did not share his behind-the-scenes efforts until last year. Again, I failed to appreciate at that time the invisible forces that enabled me to enter the doctoral program. I feel ashamed of my "soclexia," a word coined by James Loewen (2018) to describe his students at the University of Vermont who failed to understand the basic concepts of sociology. I thought that my own merits led to my admission to the University of Georgia. I will be forever grateful to Dr. Hoge and the Graduate School.

Our Daughter Hannah

In Athens, Georgia, our daughter Hannah, who was born in China, started in a lottery-sponsored pre-K classroom. Her teacher, Lisa, made Hannah feel comfortable as a 4-year-old who did not speak a single word of English. Lisa asked the whole class to locate "China" on a map and encouraged children to help Hannah. It took Hannah about 6 months to go through the "silent" stage, typical for many English language learners. She thrived in the immersive language experience and quickly felt confident enough to participate in classroom discussions. One day, she raised her hand to respond to a question. When she did, Lisa later shared with me, all the eyes of the children were on Hannah as her classmates must have thought she was dumb, mute, or both.

The second year at UGA, we moved into a graduate student housing apartment where international students from Asia, Africa, and Latin America created a diverse neighborhood. Hannah thrived in this inclusive environment and made friends with playmates from Argentina, China, Egypt, India, Japan, Pakistan, and South Korea. I still remember Aurora, a girl from Argentina at Barrow Elementary School, with whom my daughter made friends. Aurora's mother was a doctoral student in the linguistics program at UGA. She wanted Hannah to teach Aurora Mandarin Chinese and Aurora to teach Spanish to Hannah. Aurora's mother envisioned that when "speaking these three languages, Spanish, Chinese, and English, one ends up pretty much speaking to everyone in the world." Today, my daughter's linguistic competence is close to this aspiration. With her native language proficiency in English, high competence in Chinese, and conversational fluency in Spanish, Hannah's multilingual skills have helped her find jobs in Hong Kong and Mexico City.

In 2004, my last year in the doctoral program at the University of Georgia in Athens, I survived a back surgery to fix a ruptured disc when I was 8 months pregnant with my second child, Daniel, our bonus child, and the first United States citizen in my family. We had Hannah under the one-child policy in China and, until we came to the United States, we would not have been able to have a second child. We named him "Ruoyan" in Chinese, meaning "like a rock" as he survived with me in that high-risk back surgery. Hannah also attended my successful dissertation defense, while I was seated in a wheelchair, and the commencement during which I received my PhD in social science education and a certificate in qualitative research. At age 8, she was too young to understand that I would not have achieved this personal milestone had it not been for the tremendous mentorship from Dr. Hoge, my doctoral advisor, and the most supportive dissertation committee at UGA.

After I graduated from UGA in 2004, since Fan, my husband, was still in law school at SUNY, I moved to Buffalo, New York, where I made lifelong friends with young mothers just like me as I stayed home while recuperating from my back surgery. I offered to teach them English using Rick Warren's (2002) book, *The Purpose-Driven Life*, during a weekly luncheon, and they shared with me invaluable tips to take care of my newborn. Even though our journey in Buffalo was less than a year, we made lifelong friendships with Chinese scientists, lab technicians, doctors, nurses, public school teachers, grocery supply chain managers, church pastors, and stay-at-home mothers.

Accepting a Position at the State University of New York (SUNY)

When the invitation for an interview at the State University of New York (SUNY) at Cortland arrived, my husband drove our whole family to Cortland for the interview. In 2005, I accepted the job offer and we moved to Cortland. Since then, I have witnessed my children grow up in a predominantly White college town. Their struggles for identity, experiences as Asian American children in the only high school in town, have shaped their worldviews, interactions with friends, and made them unique.

BEING AN ASIAN MINORITY IN THE UNITED STATES

At school, both my children fit into, and at the same time, defied the "model minority" stereotype. Being two of the very few Asian students at school, they were noticeable at concerts, award ceremonies, commencements, and community-based service projects. They always had to navigate between their home culture and their school culture. Their presence posed continuous challenges for their public school teachers to teach them as culturally and linguistically diverse students. Many of their teachers supported their students unconditionally to help them reach their potential and kept challenging them. My children thrived at school. A few teachers, however, seemed apathetic and indifferent. They rewarded mediocrity by inflating grades and discouraging excellence at school.

In the United States, as a mother, I am acutely aware of our family's minority status and that we must be "tiger moms" to expect our children to achieve academic excellence so that they will have a competitive edge in a society that sees us as "minority." In my family, ever since their childhood, we have expected two things from our children without compromise: (a) to follow a daily Mandarin Chinese curriculum at home and (b) to practice playing a musical instrument of their choice. Every day, after the children returned from school, we made sure that they read in Chinese and practiced Chinese characters. Believing that literacy is not real literacy without reading and writing, we subscribed to television programs in Mandarin Chinese, ordered books and magazines in Chinese, and at home spoke our native language as much as possible. We hosted every Chinese visiting scholar and international student from China or Taiwan at SUNY Cortland. As these visitors appreciated our assistance, our children enjoyed learning from people who spoke Chinese. As English majors in college, my husband and I understand that language connects closely with one's culture. If the language is lost, the culture will be lost as well.

Another aspect we did not compromise on with our children was to learn to play a musical instrument. At school, they were encouraged to select a musical instrument as early as fourth grade in order to join band or orchestra. Both of my children play the piano and the violin. They also played the trumpet and trombone in the school band and at homecoming rallies. Since music is a universal language, as children they connected with other children at school while, as adults, they connected with community members. We are forever grateful for our fantastic music teachers. As top-class musicians in our tiny college town, they are models of passion and perseverance.

Asian Representation in Books and School Curriculum

In 2005, as we settled in an apartment close to an elementary school in Cortland, I was alarmed to find out that Hannah, my fourth grade daughter, disliked reading. "Why don't you read a book, Hannah?" was my daily suggestion, which was always ignored. "There is no one like me in those books," Hannah responded. Such conversations bounced back and forth between us again and again and usually ended with me sighing and continuing to ignore her complaint and resistance. As a first-year tenure-track assistant professor with two young children, I was struggling every day to get the next day's lectures prepared for two new courses. My motherly duties became more challenging due to my husband's perpetual "absence" as he worked in New York City. After graduating from law school, as a Chinese national, my husband was dispatched to work in the Beijing office of an American law firm since he had qualifications to practice law in both the United States and China. In 2008, the economic depression caused his firm to go bankrupt and my husband had to look for another job in China to pay off his hefty law school tuition debt.

One day, I "met" Dr. Rudine Sims Bishop during my literature review for a research project. Dr. Bishop (1990) called for teachers and parents to diversify their selection of children's books and find books as mirrors and windows. Mirror books help children see who they are. Window books open the world for children to see the lives and experiences of people in a new world. Hannah's frustration now made sense to me: She needed change in her school curriculum that lacked stories about Asians and Asian Americans. She demanded to be validated for her culture and identity. I decided to take action. Since then, Hannah has buried herself in public library books that represent the diverse reality of Americans. While our local library does not have a diverse collection of books, we have benefited from the interlibrary loan system, which brings books to our local library. Books written by Asian Americans about Asian Americans and Asia have enriched her understanding of the world and our cultural roots. The books she read captivated her imagination. Many characters in the books mirrored her bicultural and bilingual identity and strengthened her self-esteem and confidence as she overcame challenges and growing pains. More books serve as windows for her to see the struggles of others and experiences of those characters as they deal with challenges. One of those books was the autobiography of Supreme Court Justice Sonia Sotomayor. Many years later, on her college campus, she met Supreme Court Justice Ruth Bader Ginsberg. These distant but real models of female leaders have inspired Hannah to pursue her own dream and reach her potential.

Daniel, my son, was slower in building up his confidence and self-esteem. When he was in seventh grade, I was frustrated with his newly acquired habit of going to the mall with his friends every weekend. I was honest by sharing my personal biases with him against spending too much time in the mall. Instead, I encouraged Daniel to walk to the nature center close to our house, to play tennis outdoors, and to read inspiring books. He knew that we went to the mall only to shop for something we needed. So, he began to lie about his trips to the mall with friends as he knew all too well that I would always support his collaborative projects that required teamwork.

Daniel wrote me a note in which he fumed, "Why can't I have parents who think like Americans? Why can't I be an American?" He referred to the values of his friends who wanted to hang out at the mall on weekends, and at the same time, he was aware that this value did not resonate with us as we preferred that he engage himself in something more productive and meaningful than squandering his time at the mall. What he did not realize was that not all Americans share the value of going to the mall on weekends either. Many Americans do not go to the mall unless necessary. One thing that was evident to us was that, as a junior high student, Daniel struggled with his identity as an Asian American. He bleached his hair covering his forehead. He asked us not to speak Mandarin Chinese in the presence of his friends. He did not want his friends to know that his grandmothers stayed in our house for the entire summer and might stay for a longer period of time. He did not want his friends to know that we eat some "exotic" foods at home. He missed his father who worked in China most of the year. Now that he is a high school senior, Daniel laughs about his immature behaviors and time of insecurity. Such experiences hopefully will make him stronger for his future college life.

THE STATUS OF ASIAN AMERICANS IN UNITED STATES SOCIETY

Hate Crimes on the Rise

Cortland, New York, the college town we have lived in since 2005, remains predominantly White, and its Asian population stays at 0.2%, including members who have ethnic origins in the east, west, and south of Asia. They work as nail salon and spa owners and workers, postal office staff, restaurant owners and waiters, engineers, computer programmers, doctors, nurses, teachers, and college professors. The residents of Cortland are generally kind, understanding, and respectful. While incidents of anti-Asian hate crimes are usually not reported in the newspaper, they do happen in Cortland. In 2008, some pickup truck drivers rolled down their window and yelled at one of my Asian colleagues "You, Asians, go back to where you belong" more than once. Hurtful experiences such as this weighed so heavily on my colleague that he eventually decided to move to a larger urban community where he hoped to find support, solace, and resilience.

Today, Asian Americans are the fastest growing ethnic category in the United States (Budiman & Ruiz, 2021). However, the lack of representation of Asians and Asian Americans in the school curriculum and instructional materials continues to be a concern (Stechyson, 2019). After President Trump's multiple references to China during his campaign debates in 2016, children on the school bus made faces at my son by slanting down the corners of their eyes and telling him to "Go back to China" and 'You, Chinese people, have taken our jobs." As parents, we must encourage our children to be strong, but how much can we encourage them to survive by dealing with such hurtful slurs? One strategy is to stay together in our tiny Asian community, which exists in our tangible reality, and in the larger Asian community which exists in our world of virtual and social media. Another strategy must be to form solidarity with other people of color and marginalized groups in our town.

The rising tide of hate violence against Asians and Asian Americans has rippled through our community as well. In 2020, an Asian American student reported that a high school girl, emboldened by her peers, poured hot coffee on her face on the downtown sidewalk and walked away laughing. During the pandemic, I stepped up to become the faculty advisor for the newly established Asian American Pacific Islander Student Union (AAPISU) at my college. I was heartbroken each time college students shared their personal experiences at our biweekly meetings. One Vietnamese American student reported she was pushed off the bus as she went home for spring break in 2021. The passenger who pushed her thought she was Chinese and screamed at her blaming her for bringing the virus to New York City. Another young man said he felt lonely and excluded on campus since everyone in his dorm avoided him as if he was the virus.

We all know that in the United States, historically, the color line has been drawn between Blacks and Whites. As the nation confronts systemic racism, which is built into its history, we must realize that the land has never been inhabited by only those two groups. As the pandemic cast a shadow over the entire world in 2020, the death of George Floyd precipitated Black Lives Matter demonstrations in our village, city, county, and state, as well as around the world. During the demonstrations, I was proud of Daniel, who, as an Asian American, marched in solidarity, which offers hope to the battle against racism. Unfortunately, many Asian Americans do not see "Black Lives Matter" as an Asian American issue. They fail to understand that we are in this together and that Asian American lives matter as much as Black lives matter. For decades, Asian Americans have only acted in solidarity in moments of crisis. For example, the killing of Vincent Chin in June 1982 and the Atlanta spa shootings that left eight people dead in March 2021. Such crises always remind me that I live in a nation where people speak different languages, worship different religions, are politically divided, are diverse, have the largest wealth gap, and experience rampant gun violence.

The community of Asian Americans has always had competing threads. At one end, there is a conservative camp that leans into the "I want what's mine" mentality, and cares less about a larger collective. This group aligned itself with White conservatives in a recent legal suit against Ivy League universities to end affirmative action. This group always calls for greater policing presence in the wake of anti-Asian violence. At the other end, there is a more progressive camp that sides with Black Americans and other minority groups and sees White supremacy as the root cause of social evils.

Model Minority Myth

Pulitzer Prize winner Viet Thanh Nguyen points out that socially constructed racism makes us focus on physical differences rather than our common humanity. He reminds us that having Asian Americans as a model minority creates inequality not just for Asian Americans, but for everyone. The model minority myth works against Asian Americans such that they are expected to be tough, self-sufficient, and self-reliant. In fact, Asian Americans who come from diverse cultural, religious, and linguistic backgrounds need resources just as any other marginalized groups in the United States. Children, like Daniel, need mental health services just as much as other children in school. The support Daniel's teachers and counselors have given him are just as important as the content knowledge he has learned from any academic curriculum.

The model minority myth, which is socially constructed, posits Asian Americans as more successful than other ethnic minorities because of their hard work, dedication to education, and inherently law-abiding nature. Here we must apply the basic concept of sociology again to explain the achievements of Asian Americans since the 1960s. Racial progress was not the result of hard work alone, but also of the same systemic racism that held others down. The advancement of Asian Americans resulted from the Immigration and Naturalization Act of 1965, which abolished the anti-Asian immigration laws and prioritized skilled workers which characterizes most Asian Americans who have immigrated to the United States since then. As I read books on the history of Asian Americans, I always asked Daniel who, at the time of this writing, is a high school senior, whether his teachers bring up such topics in classroom discussions. He always reminds me that no one cares about the history of Asian Americans at his school, and that none of his teachers have included such topics in their Advanced Placement (AP) courses in English, U.S. History, World History, U.S. Government & Politics, or Macroeconomics and Microeconomics. Like many Asian Americans, my children did not learn much about the history of Asian Americans in their school curriculum. They did not know that such immigration policy changes reflected the United States strategy to expand its Asian interests to counter the Civil Rights Movement and curb the expansion of communism during the Cold War (Lee, 2015).

As we survive and thrive in the United States as first-generation immigrants, I find my family, including my USA-born son, in a continuous struggle for racial, gender, cultural, and professional validation. We must be the hardest workers, the brightest students, the biggest achievers if we want to belong here. We cannot just be human beings who mean no harm. We cannot look for jobs as office secretaries or managers as Asians since our campus hires predominately White secretaries and office managers. We could be the first to lose our jobs, for example, if we teach Mandarin Chinese when funding for foreign languages teaching dwindles.

Faculty and Student Diversity

The teacher education program at SUNY at Cortland has a predominantly White faculty and student population. In recent years, the campus has put in tremendous efforts to diversify its community. How can we recruit more faculty of color? How can we recruit more students of color to educate children from increasingly diverse backgrounds in our K–12 public schools? In our entire School of Education, plus at four dozen of various education programs across our entire campus, faculty of color remain a tiny fraction. The number of students of color I have taught since 2005 does not exceed 20 among at least the 1,000 students I have taught over the past 17 years. While increasing the number of teacher candidates of color is a commendable goal, educating teacher candidates regardless of their racial or ethnic backgrounds seems to be a more viable approach. After all, many teachers in our public schools today face the challenge of teaching children who are culturally and linguistically diverse from them.

Last year, a diversity, equity, and inclusivity program was put in place to recruit and keep more faculty in the entire SUNY system. While I applaud this new program that aims to increase faculty diversity, I also notice that among potential candidates, Asian Americans have not been listed as a subcategory. The model minority stereotype is working against Asians once again. It implies that Asian achievements demonstrate that they can "pull themselves up by their bootstraps," thereby totally ignoring the diversity of the Asian American community.

Social Studies: Core Subject of School Curriculum

As a short-listed candidate in 2005 at SUNY Cortland, during the campus interview, I was asked the question why I should be hired instead of an American-born citizen for the assistant professor position to teach social studies. Without much thought, I promised that I could offer a unique perspective to look at historical and current issues. Since then, I have kept that promise as I have been teaching elementary social studies pedagogical courses and other courses to undergraduate and graduate students. In my teaching and scholarly work, I explore multiple perspectives to learn about the history of the United States and world. I always believe that I have "the most important job" in town. Since social studies has as its primary purpose to prepare justice-minded citizens who can "make informed and reasoned decisions for the public good as citizens of a culturally diverse, democratic society in an interdependent world" (NCSS, 1994, p. 3), whose job can beat mine? I learned, however, from research study after research study, from observations my teacher candidates have made in local schools, and my own research that social studies has seldom been a school subject as important as reading and math.

One school principal told our teacher candidates almost every semester during the orientation for preservice teachers at his school that his in-service teachers could skip social studies when they had little time to prepare students for state tests in language arts and math. When I shared my observations with my ailing father in Qingdao in 2007, he reminded me of Haim Ginott's remarks about preparing future citizens with humanity and a strong sense of social justice. As a Holocaust survivor, Ginott was suspicious of education and warned all teachers against equipping students' minds only with knowledge without any discussion about ethical decisions they will have to make as responsible citizens. My father and mother, high school chemistry and physics teachers for 33 years in China, espoused their philosophy of teaching by inspiring their students with the wonders of science and a sense of justice.

When my father's remains were interned in a public cemetery in Qingdao, I felt that part of me left with him. I always wonder what my father would have said if he knew that the Constitution of China in 2018 removed the two-term limit on the presidency. Why did the National People's Congress approve this change to the constitution at its annual session? Why out of 2,964 votes, did only two delegates vote against the change and three delegates abstain?

I am certain that my father would have been very happy to know that I earned the Excellence in Teaching Award as a tenure-track assistant professor in 2010. In 2013, the SUNY Cortland chapter of the National Society of Leadership and Success selected me and another colleague as Excellent Teacher of the Year. I have no doubt that my father would have been so honored to learn that I am also a recipient of this year's Rozanne Brooks Dedicated Teaching Award, the most prestigious and competitive teaching award on campus. Honor and humility overwhelm me and motivate me to work hard and strive to be the best teacher my students deserve.

PROFESSIONAL GROWTH IN THE UNITED STATES

Earning tenure and promotion to the rank of associate professor at SUNY in 2010 meant that I would have the opportunity to disseminate knowledge with freedom. For me, having tenure also brings a modicum of job security, which my immigration status heavily hinged upon. In fact, my whole family's immigration status depended on my tenure. I also saw it as a new responsibility. Now I had the power to use my professional capital to call out and document obvious discrimination within my ranks. I have served on multiple committees to review professional portfolios, nominate candidates for SUNY Chancellor's Awards for Excellence in Teaching and Scholarship, reviewed students' scholarship applications, and chaired search committees. I heard a colleague argue against hiring more qualified faculty with international backgrounds simply because our department at that time "had already had the largest number of international faculty members." Being tokenized, I realized that my tenure had become a potential block for other candidates with international backgrounds.

A few years after I started teaching at Cortland, my Chinese colleagues recommended that I join the Empire Interpreting Services (EIS), a language service company in New York State that provides multiple language interpretation and translation services in settings including schools, courts, and medical centers. Interpreters coordinate with EIS to meet the needs for interpretation services in nearby cities and counties. Being part of this service company, I am well aware that not all immigrants from China have a background in higher education. In fact, they come from all walks of life and offer their services to their communities in multiple professions and careers. My service as an interface or bridge for them makes me proud.

Cross-Cultural Global Citizens

As I have benefited from my cross-cultural and global experiences, I encourage my students, future teachers, to expand their experiences. I recommended my colleagues and students to teach in a summer English academy in Shanghai. Collaborating with the South Asia Area Studies Program at Cornell University, I am thankful that I have twice been awarded the Global Education Learning Fellowship. In January 2017, I traveled with an anthropologist from Cornell to conduct school visits in Sri Lanka as the country went through post-civil-war reconstruction. With two colleagues, we led a team of 29 undergraduate students on a 2-week service-learning trip to Costa Rica before the pandemic. In my methods courses, I have brought in numerous global children's literature books to help my teacher candidates learn about how people in other parts of the world respond to global issues such as cultural identity, global epidemics, climate change, and social justice.

I have encouraged my own children to be global citizens as well. In the Summer of 2015, my daughter took a summer course in Middle Eastern studies and traveled widely from the refugee camps in eastern Turkey to adjoining war-torn areas in northern Syria, from Jordan's huge Syrian refugee camps to the no-man's land on its northern border. Subsequently, she wrote up her analysis of U.S. foreign aid and its impact on nation building in the Middle East. I was concerned about her safety, and at the same time, amazed by her courage and passion for the situations of refugees. I think back to my grandmother and my mother, when they escaped from their hometown to settle down in Qingdao in 1945. I imagine the dilemmas they faced and the choices they made. A sense of belonging is central to one's identity. Through music, my son has explored the world by playing in orchestras at various local events, and by playing the violin during a Red Tour of five European countries in the Summer of 2019.

Navigating Historical Currents

My personal and professional experiences across the world are tightly linked to the fates of countless people I have never known. Writing this chapter has provided me the opportunity to share with others what's in my heart. The day after Election Day in 2000, we asked our professor who taught the educational assessment course whether he voted for Bush or Gore. He explained to us, his foreign students, that the ballot he cast was his privacy as a voter. When the Supreme Court ordered a recount of votes in Florida, "hanging chads" became a new term in my vocabulary. Another strong recollection I have is September 11, 2001. Our professor showed up late to class, shocked and scared, and dismissed us so that we could go home and watch the news on television. The war on terrorism in Afghanistan and Iraq that unfolded afterwards has changed the relationship of the United States with the rest of the world. Such changes have greatly impacted immigrants in this country. Throughout history, America has had its dark periods of intolerance towards those who were believed to pose an imminent threat to the country. Because of ignorance, bigotry, and a fear of the unfamiliar, an ill-informed and gullible public has made foreigners and new immigrants easy scapegoats for society's ills. Many of the same fears and prejudices are alive and well today.

As immigrants are blamed for taking jobs, eroding values, spreading the COVID-19 virus, breeding crime, and bleeding the welfare system dry, I remind my children of our Chinese cultural values that highly elevate the importance of education. We continue to pursue academic excellence.

As I share my grandmother's tragic experiences with my children, my parents' tribulations during the Cultural Revolution and their higher education experiences, I hope these stories become lighthouses in their journey through life. Despite the uncertain and invisible currents in history, I am thankful for my academic development in China and in the United States. Any success would have been impossible without the support of my family, colleagues, students, personal perseverance and determination, and some streaks of luck. I encourage my students to become critical thinkers, expand their reading about the larger world and its people, and develop awareness of global events and issues. I wonder how the relationship between China and the United States will shape the experiences of the Chinese Americans in the years to come. I hope future teachers are more reflective about the existing anti-Asian sentiments in the United States and will work on ways to eliminate hate and value each human life as equally worthwhile as that of any other. After all, we are all one human family.

The epidemic of mass shootings continues to plague the United States as simultaneously the depressing news about the escalating Russian invasion of Ukraine unfolds every day. Such tragedies alarm us that human lives have not been valued in our turbulent world. I believe in the power of justice-oriented young people to bring about changes in gun control laws, end wars, bridge the political divide, and call for transformative changes in our social relations, educational structures, and cultural values. When will the day come when it will be safe to go into our schools, grocery stores, and places of worship? I am ready to navigate historical currents with them in an exceptional America where, I hope, one day we can tell the story of a diverse democracy where no one population group has the majority, and all groups have equal access to opportunity.

REFLECTIONS

It has never been easy to live so far away from China where my family and friends live. I did not intend to immigrate when I came as a doctoral student. At UGA, unlike some of my peers, who completed extra courses or degrees to make themselves marketable in the United States, I never took more than nine credits each semester, hoping that I could meet the minimum requirement of credits to earn my doctoral degree and then return to my teaching position in China. When I graduated in 2004, Fan, my husband, was still studying in law school for his Juris Doctor degree at SUNY at Buffalo. We were deep in debt as he paid his own law school tuition by borrowing money from relatives and family in China without having received any scholarship or student loan from the United States. I had to find a job to support my family until he graduated. At that time, Hannah, my daughter, was finishing up third grade, feeling confident in speaking English. Returning to China would have put her behind linguistically and academically. Taking care of my newborn son and my third grade daughter as a stay-at-home mother seemed to be easier here in the United States than in China. After Fan graduated, we seriously considered moving back to China as my father was battling cancer in 2007. But we found out that we must pay a heavy fine for registering our second child as a Beijing resident under the one-child policy. The possibility of returning to my previous teaching position, if we were to return from China, was also impossible as my doctoral position became a threat to peers who saw me as a potential rival for administration leadership.

Four additional reasons affected our decision to remain living and working in the United States. First, as a college professor, I enjoy working in a higher education community with less bureaucracy where nothing else matters except for my teaching, scholarly work, and services. While relationships with colleagues are important everywhere, I do not have to gain favors from anyone for my professional growth. Neither do I have to compete for limited positions in the ranks of professorship in a university. Promotion to a higher rank depends solely on my achievements, solid credentials, and professional collaboration with colleagues. Second, I enjoy the open and free access to information such as books and research resources on the internet, in my university library, and in the public libraries in my community. China keeps Google, YouTube, and other web-based sites out of its virtual reality. Here in the United States, an interlibrary loan can get me any books I want to read for my research and teaching. Librarians are always so helpful and supportive. The professionally trained librarians demonstrate their best dispositions to help readers locate necessary resources. I never take for granted my privilege as a faculty to access books for almost unlimited time.

Third, no matter where we live in the United States, we live in communities where people profess a multitude of faiths, and some profess agnosticism or atheism, and where people speak countless different languages. I would like my children to grow up in a place where the forebears of people came to this land at different times and in profoundly different ways, some with bullwhips, some in chains. Some of us are females, others male, still others neither or both; some are gay, others straight, and still others in between or beyond. This is the land where people can embrace a wide range of ideologies and viewpoints.

Finally, I would like my children to grow up without having to go through cutthroat competition in an overly crowded community in China, where people exhaust their efforts to access the limited medical and educational resources and where one needs wealth or social power to gain more resources. After my survival of two major surgeries and my children's experiences of going to top universities in the United States, even my mother, who never intends to immigrate to the United States, has become impressed by the equal opportunities that citizens can have in a hospital or a school here. Inequities undeniably exist, and so does the anti-Asian hate. Our decision to stay means that we can contribute to our shared community as responsible and justice-minded citizens in an interdependent, interconnected, democratic, and culturally diverse world.

Thanks to the Internet, wireless communication, and modern transportation, I never really left China. Every year before the pandemic, I was able to travel between China and the United States for the purpose of family visits and scholarly activities. Parents living across the Pacific Ocean are only a click away. Communicating with them daily is an integral part of my life. I also find it challenging to balance our cultural and linguistic differences with the demands of my teaching job. It is very hard for me, our children in particular, to try to fit in a society where they are invariably considered racial minorities even though they are U.S. citizens. I remind myself and my children that people share more similarities than differences, and our quality of life depends heavily on the quality of our thoughts.

Such thoughts are based on our understanding of Asian Americans and their history in this country. Last year, Americans went to the streets to protest anti-Asian violence after the spa shootings in Atlanta. I believe it is important to discuss with all children, particularly Asian American children, the ways in which the Asian American community has been impacted by such violence which became exacerbated since the beginning of the pandemic when many people lashed out against Asian Americans. It is also important to help our children understand that they are among the 23 million Americans who trace their ethnic roots to more than 20 countries in East, South, and Southeast Asia (Budiman & Ruiz, 2021). While most people, including Asian Americans, know little about these diverse communities and their impacts on American history and cultures (An, 2016; Rodríguez, 2017; Takaki, 1998) we, global educators, must include and highlight Asian American history in the school curriculum. It is our shared responsibility to increase the representation of diverse Asian Americans' stories and voices (An, 2016; Rodríguez, 2017; Venkatraman, 2021). While the representation and visibility of Asian Americans in the school curriculum and books children read is important, it is not enough just to read diverse books or books about Asian Americans (Yi, 2022). Yi challenges teachers and parents to confront the racialization of Asian Americans and interrogate the power structure of the communities Asian Americans live in. Asian Americans in the United States can challenge the stereotypical and monolithic images of Asian Americans with their unique voices and stories.

Such voices and stories can be found in diverse communities in the United States. In my work at SUNY Cortland in central New York, I interact with colleagues and students from other world regions. Sometimes I come across some Americans who have outdated information or are ignorant about cultures, countries, or even the continent we live on. To promote the unity and diversity of a community, Asian Americans must organize and participate in more community-based activities beyond keeping our own native languages, cultures, and personal advancement.

The seeds of global education that were planted at BFSU have been growing well. The university offers more than 70 foreign languages, including graduate programs in cultural studies and translation programs. It was at BFSU where I had teachers from the United States, New Zealand, Great Britain, and fellow students from various countries. Global education is an essential component of its curriculum and guides its graduates to develop cross-cultural competence and become foreign service professionals who can collaborate with officials from all over the world to tackle global issues. After spending 17 years at the university, global education is in my veins. It has inspired me to promote the importance of cross-cultural understanding, the interconnectedness of cultures and the commonalities and differences that bind us together into one humanity. In the United States, global scholars such as Ngugi wa Thiong'o (1986, 1993) calls for a conscious "moving the center" from a curriculum centered on American and European worldviews to a curriculum that is inclusive of worldviews of the majority of the world's peoples. Such a mission is still relevant today, and I am grateful that I am one of the global educators who are continuously inspired by these committed global scholars.

REFERENCES

An, S. (2016). Asian Americans in American history: An AsianCrit perspective on Asian American inclusion in state U.S. History curriculum standards. *Theory & Research in Social Education, 44*(2), 244–276. https://doi.org/10.1080/00933104.2016.1170646

Bishop, R. S. (1990). Mirrors, windows, and sliding glass doors. *Perspectives: Choosing and using books for the classroom 6*(3). https://scenicregional.org/wp-content/uploads/2017/08/Mirrors-Windows-and-Sliding-Glass-Doors.pdf

Budiman, A., & Ruiz, N. G. (2021, April 9). *Asian Americans are the fastest-growing racial or ethnic group in the U.S.* Pew Research Center. https://www.pewresearch.org/fact-tank/2021/04/09/asian-americans-are-the-fastest-growing-racial-or-ethnic-group-in-the-u-s/

Cao, A., & Feng, E. (2022, February 17). *The mystery of the chained woman in China.* NPR. https://www.npr.org/sections/goatsandsoda/2022/02/17/1080115082/the-mystery-of-the-chained-woman-in-china

Lee, E. (2015). *The making of Asian America: A history.* Simon & Schuster.

Liu B., Xie, L., & Wu, H. (2015). *Reflections and resonance of women sequel: To commemorate the 20th anniversary of UN Fourth Conference on Women* [Chinese ed.]. Contemporary China Publishing House.

Loewen, J. (2018). *Teaching what really happened: How to avoid the tyranny of textbooks and get students excited about doing history* (2nd ed.). Teachers College Press.

McCullough, C. (2004). *The thorn birds* (25th ed.). HarperCollins.

National Council for the Social Studies. (1994). *Expectations of excellence: Curriculum standards for social studies.* https://www.socialstudies.org/standards/national-curriculum-standards-social-studies

Neal, J. (2022, February 17). *When Nixon went to China: On the 50th anniversary of President Nixon's trip, China experts William Alford and Mark Wu discuss that history-making journey.* Harvard Law Today. https://today.law.harvard.edu/when-nixon-went-to-china/

Rodríguez, N. N. (2017). "But they didn't do nothing 'wrong!'" Teaching about Japanese American incarceration. *Social Studies and the Young Learner, 30*(2), 17–23.

Stechyson, N. (2019, July 3). Kids' books still have a lack-of-diversity problem, powerful image shows. *The Huffington Post.* https://www.huffingtonpost.ca/entry/diversity-kids-books-statistics_ca_5d0bb0f8e4b0859fc3db38c3

Takaki, R. (1998). *Strangers from a different shore: A history of Asian Americans.* Back Bay Books.

The Boston Women's Health Book Collective. (1976). *Our bodies, ourselves: A book by and for women.* Simon and Schuster.

Venkatraman, S. (2021, October 25). *Anti-Asian hate crimes rose 73% last year, updated FBI data says: Corrected FBI numbers show a disproportionate increase in hate crimes against Asian Americans.* NBC News. https://www.nbcnews.com/news/asian-america/anti-asian-hate-crimes-rose-73-last-year-updated-fbi-data-says-rcna3741

wa Thiong'o, N. (1986). *Decolonizing the mind.* Heinemann.

wa Thiong'o, N. (1993). *Moving the center: The struggle for cultural freedom.* James Currey Ltd.

Warren, R. (2002). *The purpose-driven life: What on earth am I here for?* Zondervan.

Wong, Y. (1995). *Reflections & resonance: Stories of Chinese women involved in the international preparatory activities for the 1995 NGO forum on women.* Ford Foundation International Club.

Yi, J. (2022). Reading diverse books is not enough: Challenging racist assumptions using Asian American children's literature. *Social Studies and the Young Learner, 34*(3), 8–13. https://www.socialstudies.org/social-studies-and-young-learner/34/3/reading-diverse-books-not-enough-challenging-racist

CHAPTER 6

PEOPLE'S REPUBLIC OF CHINA

THE "NEW FRONTIER" TO THE "NEW WORLD"

Stories of Surviving, Striving, and Thriving in China and the United States

Yali Zhao

Growing up as a poor girl next to the large Gobi Desert but close to enticingly diverse ethnic groups in far northwest Xinjiang China during the Cultural Revolution, I had never imagined in my wildest dream that one day I would leave my scarcely populated hometown for college, pursue a decade of an academic career in two universities, and then move to the United States at the prime of my life to start a new journey as a student, professor, and mother of two kids who are 16 years apart. In my 57 years, I have lived through the best and worst moments in China and the United States, and I am forever grateful for these experiences. This oral history will describe my lived experiences and stories that at once frustrated and inspired me over the past 5 decades and shaped who I am today. My memories in China include many important events: societal discrimination against my family during the turmoil of the Cultural Revolution, the exotic yet amusing life with Muslim people in my hometown, the rapidly changing society in the 1980s and 1990s related to my life, and the decision to cross the Pacific at age 35 to pursue a new life in the United States. My stories in the United States mainly focus on my immigration experience and professional work. I am proud to work in promoting global and multicultural education over the past 2 decades. Meanwhile, I feel bewildered and frustrated with the current intense relationship between China and the United States, the accusation of human rights issues in my hometown, Xinjiang, and the discrimination and violence against Asian Americans due to the pandemic. This oral history will offer readers of oral histories a unique, personal resource and perspective about different cultures, social changes, and the impact on people who lived through them.

MY HOMETOWN XINJIANG: THE NEW FRONTIER OF CHINA

My hometown Xinjiang (new frontier) in the Xinjiang Uygur Autonomous Region (XUAR) is located in Northwest China and borders eight countries: Afghanistan, Kazakhstan, Kyrgyzstan, India, Mongolia, Pakistan, Russia, and Tajikistan. Xinjiang used to be an essential passage on the ancient Silk Road in history, and today it still has close trade and economic connections with these bordering countries. Its location and cultural and ethnic diversity make it unique and exceptionally important to China's border security. It is home to 47 ethnic groups, including 13 major ethnic groups that the Chinese government officially recognizes: Daurs, Han, Hui, Kazaks, Kyrgyz, Manchu, Mongolians, Russians, Tatars, Tajiks, Uyghurs, Uzbeks, and Xibes. While the Han comprise 92% of the Chinese population, in Xinjiang, only 42.24% of residents are of Han origin. The other ethnic groups include 57.76% of the people, with the Uyghur accounting for 44.96% of Xinjiang's population of 25.85 million (Bureau of Statistics of Xinjiang Uyghur Autonomous Region, 2021). The Uyghurs and other ethnic groups are predominantly Muslim and speak Uyghur and other languages strikingly different from the Chinese language spoken by Han people.

Culturally Diverse Han and Uyghur Community

My parents were born Han Chinese and grew up in Henan province, in the central part of China. They spoke the Henan dialect. We kids were born

Han Chinese in Xinjiang and used to speak the dialect at home and Mandarin at school. They migrated from Henan to Xinjiang in 1965 and 1960 respectively in response to the central government's call for young people to move to Xinjiang to build and defend the frontier. They met and married in Xinjiang. Millions of young people voluntarily or involuntarily left their hometown provinces in inland China and resettled in scarcely populated areas with different ethnic groups who had lived there for generations. Most of them joined one of the Xinjiang Production and Construction Corps (XPCC) as the first generation of state-owned farm workers. XPCC was founded by the Central Government in 1954 as a unique administrative and economic organization in Xinjiang and played a significant role in developing the local economy, strengthening unity among diverse ethnic groups, maintaining social stability, consolidating border defense, and promoting the unification of China for decades (Xinhua News Agency, 2003). The total population of the XPCC currently is 3.48 million, with 82.8% Han and 17.2% other ethnic groups (Jiang, 2022). XPCC, mainly composed of Han people, has played a crucial role in developing the local economy, strengthening unity among diverse ethnic groups, maintaining social stability, consolidating border defense, and promoting the unification of China for decades (Xinhua News Agency, 2003).

I was born in 1965 and lived with my parents and two siblings in one of these XPCC settlements located in a remote and small oasis in southwestern Xinjiang, surrounded by the endless Gobi Desert. The nearest city was 60 miles away, and there was no public transportation to get there at that time. Life was simple, poor, and challenging. Watching a night movie occasionally in the open air was heaven. We had to keep waving our arms repelling the numerous annoying mosquitos in summer, and stomping our feet to keep them from freezing in winter. Almost all families lived in adobe houses lined up like barracks with no trees or plants around. Drinking water had to be collected from a waterlogging dam and conserved at home in a large water tank made of cement. To this day, I still remember the icy cold and scorching heat, the dust storms, the thirst for water, and the hunger for food during my childhood years. To this day, I still remember the rare but precious new clothes and shoes handmade by my mother for the Chinese New Year and the small, simple, and easy-to-satisfy happiness we shared with families and friends. Of course, the situation is different now. My hometown has improved substantially over the past few decades, thanks to the economic reforms that started in the early 1980s.

Most of our neighbors were Han people who came to Xinjiang from different provinces and regions of China after the New China (the People's Republic of China) was founded by the Chinese Communist Party in 1949. The year 1949 is a dividing line in modern Chinese history. The term "New China" is commonly used by the Chinese government and people to refer to the new communist-led country and distinguish it from the old China before 1949. As each family spoke its own home dialect, we could understand or even talk a few dialects at a young age. We all celebrated national holidays such as the Chinese Lunar New Year and Mid-Autumn Festival, but each family also observed holidays according to its own traditions. With little schoolwork in those days, we girls would often sit together on the dirt floor sharing stories and folktales passed on by our parents, and boys would play all kinds of games our parents' generation used to play when they were young. Although we were familiar with old stories of our parents' hometowns, as second-generation XCPP immigrants, few of us had an opportunity to visit our parents' hometowns. For some reason, our parents were only allowed to visit their hometowns once every 4 years. Most importantly, Xinjiang was too far away from any other province or region, and most families were too poor to afford travel for the whole family to visit their parents' hometown.

Residing in the primarily Han Chinese community did not isolate us from other ethnic groups we often encountered on the street. Living in a Uyghur-dominated area inevitably strongly influenced our way of life. While we enjoyed Han culture, we all loved the Uyghur food, lively music and dances, and the colorful and beautiful dresses and artwork. The love for my hometown's cultural and ethnic diversity and beauty was engraved in my heart early on and has always inspired me to seek the beauty of such cultural integration in my later life. It was indeed a regret that we did not get to interact as much as I wished I had with these ethnic minority groups due to language barriers, cultural differences, and religious concerns. The Han Chinese in Xinjiang are primarily atheist, while most other ethnic groups in Xinjiang are Muslim. Biracial marriage was rare and ethnic bias and conflicts did exist in those days, but in general, we lived in peace with each other. Being a majority Han member in the nation but an ethnic minority member in Uyghur-dominated Southwestern Xinjiang taught us early that getting along well with cultural and ethnic groups was crucial to Xinjiang's border security and social stability. Parents and teachers kept telling us to be mindful and respectful of religious practices and lifestyles of ethnic minority groups and to avoid any ethnic conflicts or clashes (Zhao, 2013).

School and Labor

I started school at the age of eight and experienced the chaotic period of the Chinese Cultural Revolution (1966–1976). During this time, society paid little attention to education, and there was no college admission and academic pressure. Physical labor was a typical theme of school life, especially in my hometown, where there was a severe labor force shortage.

Adults were busy in the fields or at factories all year round. Large rice and cotton fields required much labor during farming and harvest time; thus, all students would skip school and work for days or weeks. Just like the adults, we did all kinds of physical work. We plowed and planted in spring, harvested rice with sickles under the scorching sun in summer, handpicked cotton in chilly fall, collected livestock manure everywhere and dug deep drains for alkali drainage in freezingly cold winter. These physical tasks were heavy and dull, and we often compared the blisters and calluses on our hands with each other. I still vividly remember the extremely sore waist after bending over a long time to cut the waist-deep rice and the dying thirst for water under the scorching sun. We were child laborers, but we never questioned this because it was mandatory to work and part of the school curriculum. We believed that our labor helped alleviate the labor shortage, and we were proud to be part of the community in bettering the future of our homeland. To this day, I am still grateful for having had this labor experience while growing up because it truly made me stronger and more resilient to any hardships in my later life. It also taught me to be more empathetic and appreciative of physical workers.

THE CULTURAL REVOLUTION IN CHINA

I grew up during the Chinese Cultural Revolution in the 1960s and 1970s, when traditional customs were abandoned, knowledge and teachers were belittled, and all citizens were intentionally divided into different social classes. Soon after 1949, the central government launched the Agrarian Reform across China to sort people into different sociopolitical categories. The purpose was to redistribute land and give land ownership to the farmers. Later, local governments further divided people into "Seven Black Categories" and "Five Red Categories." The Red Categories referred to those from politically preferable backgrounds: workers, poor farmers, revolutionary leaders, and soldiers. The Seven Black Categories included those from unfavorable class backgrounds, such as capitalists, landlords, wealthy farmers, reactionaries, and even intellectuals. People in the black or wrong categories were socio-politically discriminated against, punished, and excluded from many privileges such as better jobs, the honor of joining the army and the Communist Party, promotion at work, and more advanced education.

Unfortunately, my parents were in the "bad category" even though they were about 10 years old in 1949, and my father lost his parents when he was only three. My sister, brother, and I were naturalized "landlords," an inferior identity we had to carry for many years. We dreaded whenever we had to write down our class identity on school registration forms at the start of every school year. We were embarrassed to see propaganda slogans or posters

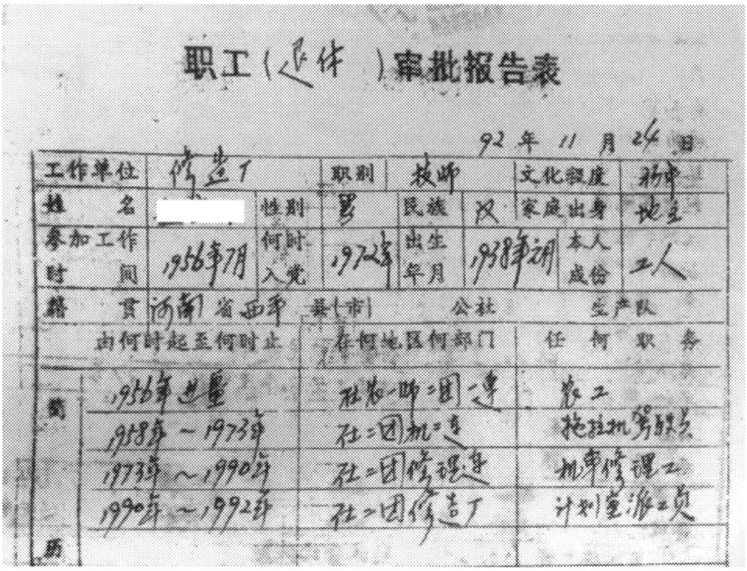

Figure 5.1 My father's retirement approval.

hanging around school or in public spaces denouncing the black category of people. We felt uneasy reading school texts about how poor people were bullied and mercilessly exploited by landlords and wealthy farmers in the old days. While it made no sense to me why my parents and we young children had to carry this humiliating burden of our ancestors, I dared not discuss or question this with anyone outside of my family for fear of bringing trouble to us. Like my parents and many people in the wrong category, we had to accept our fate, keep a low profile, and work harder to protect ourselves and try to earn approval from other people. I loved my family, school, and friends and treated everyone with deep respect. My school recognized me as an outstanding and hardworking student. The humiliated social status affected my family in many negative ways. Still, I'm glad my parents and some teachers did care about me and always encouraged me to bravely face challenges and work hard to better myself in any circumstances. Figure 5.1 is an image of my father's retirement approval document issued by his work unit in 1992, with clear information of his family class as "地主 (landlord) and his identity as "工人" (worker) at the right side of the form.

Life Changes After the Cultural Revolution

To our great surprise and happiness, a series of historical events occurred during the late 1970s that brought total change to China. The

10-year Cultural Revolution was over in 1976, the national college entrance examination was resumed in 1977, and the practice of labeling people into social class and discrimination based on birth origin was eliminated in 1979. This fundamental policy change allowed thousands of young people in the "wrong" categories to be eligible for college entrance examinations even though the competition was fierce and the prospect of admission was poor. In the early 1980s, my sister, brother, and I became the first generation of college students in my family, both in Xinjiang and in my parent's hometown in central China. Our persistence and hard work finally paid off, and we were overjoyed! I'm forever grateful to Deng Xiaoping for our life change. Deng Xiaoping was persecuted during the Cultural Revolution but survived and stood out as an insightful and powerful leader after Chairman Mao died in 1976. His administration moved China out of 2 decades of chaos and into a new inspiring chapter of opening China up to the world and economic reform which substantially changed the country for the better.

To this day, I still wonder but tend to believe that our inferior social status was both a curse and a blessing. It was a curse because it brought me years of humiliation and pain growing up. It was a blessing because it made me humble, kind, self-reflective, and more appreciative and respectful of anyone of less privileged status. It taught me to be strong, patient, and optimistic in difficult times. All my childhood experiences, whether it was the hard physical work or lower social status, have become valuable assets in my life. The dedication to hard work and confidence my parents and teachers have instilled in me has shaped who I am. I know I could never have gone so far without their support.

My experience of living in a poor but culturally diverse area in Xinjiang for 18 years taught me a lot. I am proud to be a part of the Han cultural heritage that boasts 5,000 years of history and civilization. I also feel lucky and grateful to have grown up in Xinjiang with its fantastic and rich ethnic, cultural, and geographic diversity, a place most Chinese know about but have never visited even today. In retrospect, I realize my life in Xinjiang has better prepared me and inspired me to be more willing to welcome and embrace different cultures and people than my friends and colleagues who may have grown up in a more isolated and monocultural environment, both in China and the United States.

MY STUDIES AND WORK AT XI'AN NORMAL UNIVERSITY AND BEIJING UNIVERSITY OF SCIENCE AND TECHNOLOGY

In mid-September 1983, at age 18, I left Xinjiang for the first time in my life to attend Shaanxi Normal University, a prestigious teacher's university in

Xi'an. I specialized in English language and literature. This university admitted students from different parts of China, but most students came from the northwest, including Qinghai province, Gansu province, Ningxia Hui Autonomous Region (also an ethnic minority area), Shaanxi province, and Xinjiang Uygur Autonomous Region. With a delayed college acceptance letter and eight days of truck and train travel, I finally arrived at the beautiful ancient city Xi'an and college campus during the rainy season, starting a new chapter of my life. For the first time in my life, I saw a big city full of interesting people and life. I soon discovered that most of my college mates knew little about Xinjiang. To them, Xinjiang was far removed and seemed mysterious and exotic as a distant country. My classmates felt strange that I did not look, act, speak, and dress like the Uyghurs and other ethnic minorities they saw in movies although I had a typical Han Chinese name. They had no idea that Han people had resided in Xinjiang for generations and that millions of young people had migrated from inland China to Xinjiang in recent Chinese history. They assumed we all lived nomadic lives on the pastures, in the mountains, or in the Gobi Desert. It dawned on me that both Han and ethnic minority groups in remote areas could be misrepresented, misunderstood, marginalized, and isolated from the dominant Han culture because of cultural differences and psychological geographical distance. This awareness pushed me to learn more about Xinjiang and its rich culture from books and personal visits later in life. It was great to see the world of my classmates in Xi'an and use myself as a new window for them to see and learn about the world in my hometown Xinjiang.

The 1980s was the most eye-opening, exciting, inspiring, and dynamic period in China's recent history. At that time, China had just gotten over the damage of the Cultural Revolution and began to open up to the outside world. Deng Xiaoping launched economic reforms in hopes of improving people's life and catching up with the Western world. The whole society was blooming with new thoughts and ideas from the world of the West. Knowledge was highly valued, and college students were respected and proud to be "on top of the world," a commonly used term to describe the highly admired status of young college students. The great atmosphere of academic freedom and respect for knowledge and intellectuals inspired many to create numerous outstanding works in the arts, literature, and social science.

I truly enjoyed my 4-year college life (1983–1987) in Xi'an, a beautiful ancient city with 3,100 years of history. I worked hard to develop my knowledge of Western history, culture, philosophy, and literature through books, movies, and lectures. We were full of dreams and expected a brighter future for us and China even though we only had a vague idea of where to go upon graduation. From 1977 to the mid-1990s, college was free, and the college and government assigned all graduates with the basic policy of "returning to where you are from." This policy meant that I would have to return to Xinjiang after graduation in 1987, even though I longed to pursue a more exciting life in an inland city. Regardless, I worked extremely hard, spending most of my time in the classroom and library. I earned excellent grades for my college degree and passed the graduate program entrance examination from a university in south China. To my happy surprise, based on my grades and 4-year performance, my department hired me as a full-time faculty member to teach English classes. Being hired to work in Xi'an was a life-changing turning point for me. Growing up in a very poor, remote, and scarcely populated area, I had never seen any city before. It's hard to imagine that someday I could live in a big city, become a young university professor, and have many unknown dreams and opportunities ahead of me. Attending 4 years of college and teaching in Xi'an for 2 years were significant periods in my early life. There, I gained a profound knowledge of both Chinese and world history and culture. It was there that I realized we could start small and dream big. It was there that I began to build my self-esteem and confidence. There, I married my husband and together we moved forward to pursue new dreams.

The 1980s were a dynamic, exciting, and most memorable period for millions of college students, who experienced the radical changes after the Cultural Revolution, embraced the Western ideology of democracy and expected the government and officials to be more democratic and freer from political and economic corruption. From mid-April to early June of 1989, hundreds of thousands of college students across China took to the street to mourn the death of then-president Hu Yaobang and marched for a more democratic society and political change. Tiananmen Square protests were the highlight of this student movement, and the government crackdown occurred in early June. At that time, I was still in Xi'an and did not participate in the protests in Beijing. For 3 decades, the Tiananmen Square protests of 1989 have become a sensitive and forbidden topic in China. Many young people today have no idea about the Tiananmen Square protests of 1989.

At that time, the Chinese government vehemently accused the Western world of misleading Chinese students; vice versa, the Western world criticized the Chinese government for the crackdown. The relationship between China and the West was at its lowest for a few years until, in 1993, Deng Xiaoping started to emphasize economic reform and more global trade which stimulated rapid economic growth in China and benefited the outside world.

In the Fall of 1989, I moved to Beijing to join my husband and pursue graduate studies. I lived in Beijing for 11 years, first as a graduate student and then as a faculty member teaching English and conducting research at the same university. In 1991, we had a beautiful daughter and named

Figure 5.2 My family at Beijing University of Science and Technology.

her Wei Lai (魏来) with the expectation that she would have a "bright future." In those days, it was popular to name kids with meaningful words or phrases, so we named our daughter Wei (family name) Lai (given name), which is literally pronounced as "未来" (wei lai), a Chinese phrase meaning "future." Like most Chinese people who experienced the chaos of the Cultural Revolution, we were content with our lives in the 1990s and continued to work hard to educate students and achieve success in our academic work.

With further economic reforms in the 1990s, profound socioeconomic changes took place in every sector of China. The decades-long state-planned economy began to transform into a market economy which motivated millions to test the business waters, seeking new business opportunities and economic gains. Living in Beijing, the political, economic, educational, and cultural center of China, I was able to witness and experience many changes in Chinese society over a short period of time. I was proud to be a part of this change and excited about China's economic development and the betterment of people's lives, including that of my family in Beijing and Xinjiang. Of course, I was also aware of the financial gap between different groups of people, urban and rural areas, and between the eastern and western parts of China. Overall, 1990–2000 is a decade of social change and economic success. Thousands and millions of people across China were moved out of poverty and started to have a much better life.

CROSSING BORDERS TO THE UNITED STATES

Having taught English and social sciences subjects at Beijing University of Science and Technology for 10 years, I decided to go to the United States and pursue more advanced studies. I felt the need to improve my academic career and see the outside world I had learned much about but never set foot in. It was not an easy decision because I was already a tenured associate professor and had to give up my job, leave my family behind, and start all over as a student in a new country. My husband strongly supported me because he also believed that we needed to expand our knowledge and experience in the most advanced country in the world. Due to my educational background and interest in social science, I applied to the social science education doctoral program at the University of Georgia in Athens. Very luckily and gratefully, I was not only accepted into the program but also offered a full-time graduate research assistantship. On August 8, 2000, at age 35, I left China for the United States, adventuring into a new field and new life in a strikingly different cultural and language environment. I didn't know what challenges and opportunities I might have, but I was confident that I would work hard and survive well, just as I did in the long past.

I did not experience much of a language barrier and cultural shock thanks to my English teaching and learning experience, but still, many things surprised me. As much as I knew about cultural diversity in Xinjiang and Inland China, I was in awe at the level of diversity in the American population in terms of race, ethnicity, nationality, language, culture, and religion. I was shocked to have to fill out all kinds of forms and documents with names and gender, race, ethnicity, and even color of eyes and hair. That was the first time I had to think hard about my identity and what it means to my fellows and me. It dawned on me that when I checked Asian or Pacific Islander, or alien resident, I would represent a much larger population. I came to realize that my words and deeds may affect people's attitudes and behavior towards whoever may look like me. Suddenly I felt that I had changed into a brand-new person, a person representing not just the Chinese but also all Asian populations, and a global citizen carrying more and broader roles and responsibilities. This awareness excited me and motivated me to learn more and explore different cultural diversity topics and issues in the United States, my home country, and the broader world. Cultural diversity became the topic of much of my coursework and, later, my research interest.

For my doctoral program, I specialized in social science education at the University of Georgia. Franky, when I applied for the PhD program in social studies, I thought I would mainly learn social science knowledge. I was determined to return to China after finishing my degree to continue teaching college students. I was disappointed that the program focused on K–12 social studies education. Still, gradually, I realized how critical social studies is in shaping young people's minds and actions about people and the whole world and developed a sincere love for this major. The 4 years of program study were truly eye-opening and enlightening for me. I met and appreciated people from all walks of life with different ethnic and cultural backgrounds. I learned profoundly from books, coursework, lectures, discussions, and interactions with professors, fellow students, and new friends. It allowed me to know more about multicultural and global education, which are critical and impartial components of American education and the whole society. I was moved and inspired by scholars and activists in their efforts to promote multicultural and global education in the United States and worldwide. During this time, I decided to dedicate my life to building cultural bridges and working for the common good and world peace. My upbringing in multiethnic and multicultural Xinjiang and my cross-cultural experience in the United States have strengthened my determination and commitment to multicultural and global education.

A New Career at Georgia State University

In May 2004, after 4 years of hard work, I graduated with a doctoral degree in social science education from the University of Georgia. At the same time, I was offered a tenure-track faculty position in social studies education at Georgia State University. I was as thrilled as I was in 1987 when I graduated from college in Xi'an and started a new and different life. Growing up in Xinjiang during the Cultural Revolution, I never imagined in my wildest dream that one day I would live in a big and beautiful city, pursue a decade of an academic career at two Chinese universities, and then move to the United States in the prime of my life. My cultural-linguistic background, educational and professional experience in China and the United States, and knowledge of Eastern and Western culture and education has benefited my students and me in the past 18 years of my academic life in the United States. I am able to share my life stories and immigrant experience with my students. I am able to teach from cross-cultural, comparative, and multiple perspectives. Through my research and service, I help promote cross-cultural awareness and global knowledge in my class, community, and profession. For many years, I have directed Study Abroad and international education exchange programs, which have enabled many faculty and students to have an intensive teaching and learning immersion experience in China. For the past 3 years, during the COVID-19 global pandemic, I have engaged my classes in meaningful virtual exchanges with international students in different countries and regions.

For a couple of reasons, I did not return to teaching in China. At the time, my husband and my daughter had already joined me in the United States. My husband was working on his PhD, and my daughter was attending eighth grade. I realized that remaining in the United States would put me in a better position to freely conduct teaching and research from a more objective and cross-cultural perspective. I saw myself as a cultural ambassador between East and West, between different ethnic and cultural groups in the United States. I enjoyed living in a multicultural environment and was motivated to work with my colleagues and students to build a better society in this increasingly diverse and rapidly changing world.

Green Card Challenges

Of course, I have witnessed many changes and faced challenges in my 22 years of life in the United States. My green card application posed a unique challenge in my early academic career in the United States. The application process was long, tiring, costly, and painful for complicated bureaucratic reasons. For more than 6 years, we struggled to obtain a green card that would allow us to stay legally. For 10 years after I first came to the United States, I was afraid to go back to China to visit my family for fear of getting denied re-entry to the United States because in 1999 my visa application was rejected twice before I was allowed to come to the United States for academic studies in 2000. It was not rare for Chinese students and scholars to get a visa rejection from the U.S. Embassy in China for various reasons. It was a traumatic experience. Without a green card, even as a professor in the United States, when I returned to China, I had to go to one of the U.S. embassies in China to apply for visa approval to re-enter the United States.

I started my green card immigration application as soon as I started my employment at Georgia State University in 2004. The U.S. Immigration Office offered me an H-1 visa with a 6-year temporary work permit. However, with the delay in my green card application process, I experienced the trauma all over again in 2010. I was scared that my H-1 temporary work status would expire in a few months, which, at this time, could negatively affect my application for tenure and promotion. I pleaded for help from many departments, including my university president and state congressman. Without a green card, my daughter could only apply to universities as an international student and pay full tuition and expenses required for international students even though my husband and I were both American university professors for many years. She was not eligible for any scholarship or financial aid even though she attended public schools in Georgia for 8 years and was a distinguished student in high school and college. The process damaged my daughter's self-esteem and made her feel depressed and less worthy than her fellow students. When we finally received the green card in 2010, she had almost completed college. Regardless, we were excited and grateful as the green card gave us a real sense of belonging, security, mental relief, and freedom for the first time since we came to the United States. The struggle and painful experience taught me to be patient, resilient, and hopeful. It helped me become more understanding and empathetic with immigrants, refugees, and any ethnic and cultural groups in less privileged positions.

Building bridges and promoting global and cross-cultural education has been my passion for the past 2 decades. I have taken advantage of my dual language, cross-cultural knowledge, immigration experience, and professional assets to serve my students and community. I am proud to have created many opportunities for my students to collaborate on projects and communicate with international peers, especially Chinese college students, about important educational and cultural issues in their respective countries. I have led my students to China and hosted Chinese visiting scholars and exchange students. I have lectured about Chinese culture and education at American K–12 schools and universities and presented about American culture and education at Chinese schools and universities. My college and university highly praise and recognize my efforts in improving students' global competency.

Home Visit and Loss of My Father

I left my hometown Xinjiang for college in 1983 and went back a few times to visit my parents while I was at college and working in Beijing. After I moved to the United States, I didn't go to my hometown for the first 10 years due to my immigration status. My parents, however, did come to the United States and stayed with us for 6 months from late 2005 to early 2006. In the last 10 years, I have returned to China quite a few times because of our China Study Abroad program. I went back to my hometown more frequently before the pandemic to see my parents who were getting old and had health issues. I was eager to leave and see the outside world when I was young. In my 50s, I yearn to get close to my hometown to refresh my bitter and sweet memories and to take care of my aged parents. My father passed away right after my birthday in 2021. I was devastatingly shocked, heartbroken, and regretful. I could not fly back to pay my last visit to him because of China's rigid zero-COVID policy, month-long quarantine requirement, and flight cancellation between the United States and China. I lamented deeply over being away from my parents for the last 20 years. I felt guilty of my absence when my father was sick and needed intensive care. The pain of losing my father and the guilt kept gnawing at me for a long time. I could only comfort myself that I did go back to see my parents twice in 2019, the

Figure 5.3 With China study aboard students and Chinese teachers.

last time right before the outbreak of COVID-19. I resemble my father a lot, both in looks and character. He had such a strong influence on me when growing up that often today, I still feel my dad around me, watching me and taking pride in me as his favorite child. I'm relieved my sister and brother are with my mom in Xinjiang.

MY CONCERNS ABOUT U.S.–CHINA RELATIONS

Twenty-two years ago, I came to this new land with hopes and great expectations. Since then, I have lived a peaceful and fruitful life with hard work and good luck. As an immigrant, I was and will be forever grateful to this land and its people that generously embraced me and allowed me to settle down and pursue new dreams and careers. Indeed, I have had some unpleasant experiences, and as most Asian Americans, we feel ignored, invisible, and are often treated and judged based on our looks and perceived foreign nationality. Still, in general, I have not felt overly discriminated against. I have heard and know of cases of anti-Asian sentiment, and I have joined the efforts to fight for equity and social justice for all immigrants and different racial and ethnic groups in all these years.

The U.S.–China relationship has experienced many ups and downs. The past 40 years have been the best time between the two countries in terms of economic trade and cultural communication. This relationship started to change due to a series of events in the past 4 years and is worsening, profoundly affecting all Chinese Americans. The first cause was the U.S.–China trade war under the administration of President Trump in 2018. Then it was COVID-19 that started in China in early 2020, accompanied by other complicated issues around Xinjiang and Taiwan. U.S. Speaker Nancy Pelosi's early August visit in 2022 to Taiwan greatly enraged China and deepened the U.S.–China rupture. With recent years of anti-American sentiment due to the Trade War, COVID-19, and rising nationalism, Pelosi's visit to Taiwan was considered a severe interference by the U.S. government in Chinese national affairs and split Taiwan's relationship with mainland China (Chen, 2022; Lee & Wu, 2022; Xu, 2022). This anger led to Chinese economic sanctions against Taiwan and military exercises around Taiwan, and the end of dialogue and cooperation with the United States on a range of issues. All these tensions and conflicts have caused incredible frustration, anxiety, and a sense of insecurity among Chinese Americans, including among professors and scholars in higher education.

Discrimination Against Asians and Asian Americans

Historically, in the United States, there has been systematic discrimination against Asians and Asian Americans such as the Chinese Exclusion Act, implemented between 1882 and 1943, and the Japanese Internment Camps during World War II. However, due to COVID-19 and blaming the Chinese for the global pandemic, there has been a new surge of anti-Chinese and anti-Asian discrimination, violence, and hate crimes in a time of public health crisis and economic anxieties. Thousands of physical and verbal attacks against Asian Americans have been reported and made national headlines (Chan, 2022; Ruiz et al., 2021; The Associated Press, 2021). The Stop Asian American and Pacific Islander (AAPI) Hate Coalition (2022) launched in March 2020 in response to the alarming escalation against the Asian population, has documented 11,500 hate incidents between March 19 and March 31, 2022. The attacks against Asian Americans escalated dramatically when a gunman in Atlanta killed eight people at spas, six of whom were women of Asian descent (Hansen, 2021). This brutality shocked, traumatized, and angered all AAPI communities. People across the country took to the street to grieve the victims, protest racism, and march against hate crimes against Asians. On March 20, 2021, I joined thousands of people in the anti-Asian Hate March in downtown Atlanta. I accepted a Fox News media interview about anti-Asian discrimination and hate crimes and their impact on our lives since the pandemic. With the global pandemic still going on, anti-Asian discrimination and violence continue in the United States, severely affecting our lives. Since 2020, many of us Asians, my own family included, have been physically or at least verbally attacked and often live in fear, distress, uncertainty, and isolation. On a positive note, this harsh

Figure 5.4 (a) Anti-Asian Hate March in Atlanta; (b) On FOX News

reality has motivated me to do more teaching and research about the history and contributions of Asian Americans in the United States.

ETHNIC CONFLICT IN XINJIANG AND REKINDLED INTEREST

During the early 1990s, when I was living in Beijing, there were sporadic ethnic incidents in Xinjiang, mainly between the Han and Uyghur, but in general, the Han and the ethnic minorities got along in peace. However, the bloody conflict that erupted on July 5, 2009 between the Uyghur and Han people in the capital city Urumqi of Xinjiang was a total shock to everyone. Almost 200 people (mainly Han people) were killed and over 1,000 were wounded in the deadliest ethnic violence in contemporary Chinese history. The riots started with a gathering and protests on July 5 by the Uyghurs to contest Guangdong province authorities' response to a conflict in June between Han workers and Uyghur migrant workers in a toy factory and the arrests of three Uyghurs afterwards. The protests in Urumqi soon deteriorated into widespread violence and damage (Ryono & Galway, 2015). Although Chinese government attributed the primary cause of the bloodshed to foreign influences and terrorism (The Global Post, 2021; Xinhua News Agency, 2009), many other factors also played a role in the tense relationship and riots: economic inequality, linguistic and cultural differences, preferential policies for minorities, lack of religious freedom, the incompetence of local governments as well as implementation of bilingual education in Uyghur schools (Dwyer, 2005; Han, 2010; Wei, 2010). This riot forced the government to make drastic efforts to promote ethnic unity, strengthen security measures, and alleviate poverty for ethnic minorities in Xinjiang.

The July 2009 violence in Xinjiang deeply shocked my family and me. I felt panicked and heartbroken that my beloved hometown was split ethnically and even fought against each other. I felt obliged to do something for my hometown and, hopefully, I could work with Chinese colleagues to better the relationship, at least in the field of education. Before 2009, I collaborated with Chinese scholars on multiple research projects but, regretfully, I never conducted any research in Xinjiang. With my love for Xinjiang and many years of teaching and research experience in multicultural and global education, I decided to focus more on multicultural education in Xinjiang. Starting in 2011, I went to Xinjiang every time I returned to China. I have visited Han-dominated schools and Uyghur-dominated schools. The Han-dominated schools are in the Han communities and offer all subjects in Mandarin Chinese. The Uyghur-dominated schools are in the ethnic minority area attended mainly by Uyghur students, and courses are taught partly in Mandarin and partly in Uyghur. I have observed in bilingual classrooms where the ethnic minority students learn Mandarin and Uyghur (or another local minority language) in different subjects. I have met and talked with many Han and Uyghur students, teachers, and administrators about their experiences and thoughts about bilingual and ethnic education in the region. I also have shared with them about American multicultural education and how to promote cross-cultural understanding and respect. I have learned the benefits and challenges of bilingual and ethnic education and collaborated with local professors on research. However, in recent years, such dialogues have become more challenging due to my identity as a Chinese American, the worsening and intense U.S.–China relationship, and the Western world's accusation of China for human rights issues in Xinjiang and other places. Regardless, I will continue my efforts with Chinese colleagues in building cross-cultural bridges and promote the common good between the Han and the Uyghurs in my hometown. I hope our collaborative efforts will improve the ethnic education policies and instructional practices in Xinjiang schools and the interethnic relations in Xinjiang.

REFLECTIONS

In retrospect, I feel like I am always living in multiple worlds. I was born into a socio-politically discriminated family in China where I grew up as a poor Han Chinese girl in a remote, isolated ethnic minority area in Xinjiang during the Chinese Cultural Revolution. My only dream then was to become an elementary teacher in my local school and become a teacher just like the teachers I admired. I never expected that one day I would become a professor, not only in Chinese universities but also in an American university. In my 57 years of life, I have lived through the best and worst moments in China's and U.S. history. I feel genuinely lucky to have witnessed tremendous changes in all aspects of life in both countries. I'm forever grateful for all these life experiences that have enlightened me, strengthened me, and shaped me into who I am today. My 2 decades of immigrant life as an Asian American and my academic work in cross-cultural and global education have made me a better person, personally and professionally.

REFERENCES

Bureau of Statistics of Xinjiang Uyghur Autonomous Region. (2020, June 14). *Key data of the Seventh National Population Census of Xinjiang Uyghur Autonomous Region*. https://www.chinanews.com.cn/gn/2021/06-14/9499339.shtml

Chan, M. (2022, March 16). A year after the Atlanta Spa shootings, Asians in America are facing a different kind of abuse. *Time Magazine*. https://time.com/6157468/asian-americans-abuse-atlanta-spa-shootings-anniversary

Chen, W. (2022, August 5). Pelosi's trip reckless, dangerous and irresponsible. *China Daily*. http://www.chinadaily.com.cn/a/202208/05/WS62ec502ea310fd2b29e70610.html

Dwyer, A. (2005). *The Xinjiang conflict: Uyghur identity, language policy, and political discourse*. East-West Center Washington.

Han, E. (2010). Boundaries, discrimination, and interethnic conflict in Xinjiang, China. *International Journal of Conflict and Violence, 4*(2), 244–256. https://doi.org/10.4119/ijcv-2829

Hansen, C. (2021, March 19). *The Atlanta spa shootings and the year of hatred against Asian Americans.* https://www.usnews.com/news/national-news/articles/2021-03-19/the-atlanta-spa-shootings-and-the-year-of-hatred-against-asian-americans

Jiang, W. (2022). *Xinjiang Production and Construction Corps statistical bulletin on national economic and social development in 2021.* http://tjj.xjbt.gov.cn/c/2022-03-25/8204754.shtml

Lee, Y., & Wu, S. (2022, August 2). *Pelosi arrives in Taiwan vowing U.S. commitment; China enraged.* https://www.reuters.com/world/asia-pacific/pelosi-expected-arrive-taiwan-tuesday-sources-say-2022-08-02/

Ryono, A., & Galway, M. (2015). Xinjiang under China: Reflections on the multiple dimensions of the 2009 Urumqi uprising. *Asian Ethnicity, 16*(2), 235–255. https://doi.org/10.1080/14631369.2014.906062

Ruiz, N., Edward, K., & Lopez, M. (2021). *One-third of Asian Americans fear threats, physical attacks and most say violence against them is rising.* Pew Research Center. https://www.pewresearch.org/fact-tank/2021/04/21/one-third-of-asian-americans-fear-threats-physical-attacks-and-most-say-violence-against-them-is-rising

STOP AAPI Hate. (2022). *Two years and thousands of voices: What community-generated data tell us about anti-AAPI hate.* https://stopaapihate.org/year-2-report/

The Associated Press. (2021, August 12). *More than 9,000 Anti-Asian incidents have been reported since the Pandemic began.* NPR. https://www.npr.org/2021/08/12/1027236499/anti-asian-hate-crimes-assaults-pandemic-incidents-aapi

The Global Post. (2021, July 7). *Never allow hostile forces to reverse the "7.5" incident.* http://www.china.com.cn/opinion2020/2021-07-07/content_77611822.shtml

Wei, S. (2010). Explaining ethnic protests and ethnic policy changes in China. *International Journal of China Studies, 1*(2), 509–529. http://scholarbank.nus.edu.sg/handle/10635/128476

Xinhua News Agency. (2003). *Role of Xinjiang Production, Construction Corps important* [white paper]. http://news.xinhuanet.com/english/2003-05/26/content_887338.htm

Xinhua News Agency. (2009, July 6). *China hopes that other countries can recognize the true nature of "East Turkistan" terrorist and separatist forces.* Retrieved on July 20, 2022 from http://politics.people.com.cn/GB/1026/9610205.html

Xu, Y. (2022, August 8). US' one-China policy eroded by Pelosi visit. *China Daily.* http://global.chinadaily.com.cn/a/202208/08/WS62f04ad8a310fd2b29e70c66.html

Zhao, Y. (2013). Straddling multiple culture worlds and promoting cross-cultural understanding as a social science educator. In Y. Wang & Y. Zhao (Eds.), *Seeking the common dreams between the worlds: Stories of Chinese immigrant faculty in North American higher education* (pp. 113–140). Information Age Publishing.

CHAPTER 7

PEOPLE'S REPUBLIC OF CHINA

TEACHING FOR A SUSTAINABLE FUTURE

Crafting a Pedagogy for Sustainability Education

Guichun Zong

I came to the United States in July of 1995 to pursue my PhD in curriculum and instruction with a concentration in secondary social studies education from Florida International University. Since then, I have taught at three American universities in the capacity of assistant professor, associate professor, and full professor. During that time, I have had the privilege of teaching 19 different courses, mentoring hundreds of graduate research projects, and publishing in national and international peer-reviewed journals. As an immigrant woman faculty from China, I ask myself what impact did I have on students and colleagues at American universities? What

The Power of Oral History Narratives, pages 135–154
Copyright © 2023 by Information Age Publishing
www.infoagepub.com
All rights of reproduction in any form reserved.

experiences have helped me with the knowledge, skills, and dispositions required to navigate the higher education landscape and its shifting policies and practices in the United States? These questions guide my inquiry into the impact of personal experiences, particularly the cultural resilience on the professional journey of an immigrant faculty practicing global pedagogy in the American South. I have discussed different aspects of my work, such as increasing intercultural experiential learning through community-based inquiry and computer-mediated communication technology in other publications. In this chapter, I trace my experiences from my upbringing during the Mao Zedong era of China to my professional journey as a senior faculty member who has served with three major universities in the United States. Reflecting on my own trajectory and the totality of my experiences, I hope to shed light on much broader questions through a descriptive and interpretive analysis. Questions such as, "What curriculum and instructional strategies can help prospective and practicing teachers better prepare students for global sustainable development?" or "How can international and immigrant professors contribute to making colleges and universities institutions of diversity, inclusion, and global learning?"

The focus of my analysis centers around my own observations and reflections on the Mao era's gender equality policies and the profound changes in Chinese society since Deng Xiaoping's Open-Door policy and Four Modernization initiatives. I explain how these transformations have shaped my consciousness about global diversity and commitment to making global and multicultural awareness and action a centerpiece of contemporary teacher education. I also discuss how these lived experiences have helped me build the cultural resilience which is crucial to my success in navigating the U.S. higher education landscape, decoding, and adapting to its unique power dynamic, and managing challenges and opportunities during this unique professional journey. I describe and analyze how my lived experiences, specifically my informal and formal education have shaped my curriculum decisions, pedagogical choices, and commitment to global learning. I share some strategies I have developed and refined for a graduate course in intercultural communication and global sustainability education. This chapter ends with a discussion about the ways I have adopted narrative as an instructional strategy to engage and empower teacher leaders with pedagogy for sustainability education.

Writing about my own trajectory and the adjustments, successes, challenges, and struggles in this chapter allows me to explore the following questions:

- How have my lived experiences shaped my teaching pedagogy today?
- How have I reconciled my duality and marginality and used them as assets to build intercultural communication and collaboration to advance teaching about the world?

- How have I developed a curriculum and pedagogy to engage and empower teacher leaders in implementing an education for a sustainable future?

In so doing, I describe, analyze, and discuss the intersecting issues of intercultural communication, navigating higher education power dynamics, and building collaboration and alliances, and practicing pedagogy for sustainability.

My goal is to shed light on questions of a much wider scope, such as how can our entry as immigrant professors contribute to making colleges and universities institutions of global learning? How can we use narrative to engage teacher leaders in learning and teaching about global sustainability? And how can we make social studies curriculum world-centered and focused on people, places, perspectives, not only for profits but for peace and prosperity and a sustainable future for the planet (Kirkwood-Tucker, 2004; Kissling & Bell, 2020; Seitz, 2020; Shuttleworth, 2020)?

SITUATING MYSELF PROFESSIONALLY

I joined Kennesaw State University (KSU) as an associate professor in the Department of Secondary and Middle Grades Education in August 2006. I was promoted to full professor in August of 2012. Prior to KSU, I was a tenure-track faculty member at the University of Kentucky (1999–2003) and Georgia State University (2003–2006). Over the years, I have worked collaboratively to advance KSU's mission of advancing educational excellence through innovative teaching in an ever-changing global environment through teaching, research, and professional service. I have centered all of my work around the theme of preparing preservice and practicing teachers with the knowledge, skills, and commitment to teach for human diversity, cross-cultural understanding, and global interconnectedness that increasingly characterizes contemporary education.

With the recent intense public debates on the quality and effectiveness of teacher education, the content of curriculum in both K–12 and higher education, it is critical to ground programs, curriculum, and teaching in current research and evidence-based innovations. I have successfully taught courses across several degree programs, such as educational specialist in curriculum and instruction, educational doctorate in secondary and middle grades education, and Bachelor of Science in middle grades education. I have also collaborated with teachers from counties across Georgia to prepare preservice teachers to effectively plan middle school curriculum and assess and analyze the impact of their teaching on all middle school learners. My teaching of 19 courses at my current university in a range of initial and advanced teacher education programs demonstrate my multilevel professional expertise and continuous commitment to preparing effective teachers and leaders to improve learning for all K–12 students.

My philosophy of teaching and learning draws upon the theoretical principles of social constructivism, which view knowledge as primarily a cultural product, shaped by micro and macro cultural influences and evolves through increasing participation within different communities of practice. In contrast to the traditional acquisition-oriented learning model which emphasizes transmitting knowledge and skills, social constructivism conceptualizes learning as a collective participatory process of active knowledge construction emphasizing context, interaction, and situatedness. It believes that effective teachers at any level should encourage students to form a participatory community in the classroom, a community where students actively generate and discuss problems, feel challenged to explore some of these problems deeply, work out their own well-informed answers, and then submit their ideas to the critical appraisal of their peers (Brookfield, 2017). I have used this theoretical perspective to guide prospective and practicing teachers in exploring, examining, and critically analyzing various educational theories, research, policies, and practices.

Over the years, I have created a range of teaching-learning experiences for my students in pursuit of global learning goals. These include writing an intercultural learning autobiography to reflect personal experiences with other cultures; conducting community inquiries to explore historical and contemporary connections between local communities and people and places around the world; developing intercultural competence through experiential learning; participating in computer-mediated multinational discussion forums to practice cross-cultural communication; integrating literature and other narratives with research-based learning about people, places, and perspectives; writing women into the formal school curriculum; and engaging in critical analysis of discourses on globalization to deepen understanding of global connections and interdependence (Zong, 2015).

Course evaluation results, students' comments, and administrative reviews consistently identify the strengths of my teaching as: up-to-date content, connections between university courses with educational policies and practices in K–12 settings, engaging pedagogy, passion for the subject, community building, emphasis on technology, diversity, multiple resources and perspectives, intercultural competencies, and global learning. The following quote from our university's anonymous teaching evaluation system exemplifies the comments of many students in their course evaluation:

> I really enjoyed this course. Reading about student perceptions, teacher perceptions, social justice, and sustainability were very interesting. I learned a lot about

culturally relevant pedagogy and teaching for sustainability. I thought that the readings were both relevant to the course content and interesting to read.

Theoretical Orientation and Relevant Research

I draw upon theory and research on the impact of lived experiences on the development of multicultural and global educators (Freire, 2021; Gay, 2003; Merryfield, 2002; Merryfield & Wilson, 2005), the power of teachers' stories and narratives (Connelly & Clandinin, 1999), and autobiographical research of other faculty of minority or international background (Espino, 2018; Li & Beckett; 2005; Stanley, 2006) to write this chapter. Guided by the tenets of interpretive autobiography and reflective inquiry to investigate social interaction and lived experiences (Ellis & Bochner, 2003), the account is based on my own recollections of and reflections on classroom events, program, department, and college meetings, and a close reading of documents and archival materials such as student evaluations, syllabi, discussion notes, and samples of students' work.

This chapter is also informed by the growing field of scholarship on narrative inquiry in teacher education (Carter, Andrews, & Castillo, 2019; Connelly & Clandinin, 1999; Espino, 2018; Milner, 2007). As research methodology, content, and pedagogy, narrative inquiry has been increasingly used as a valid and viable way to shed light on the complex nature of teaching and learning. McEwan and Egan (1995) argue that narrative is "essential to the purpose of communicating who we are, what we do, how we feel, and why we ought to follow some course of action rather than another" (p. xiii). Similarly, Gay (2003) suggested that by "engaging in dialogue with ourselves and sharing our stories with other travelers, we can find confirmation, companionship, and community" (p. 5) of becoming and being innovative educators. She further argued that personal narratives serve the dual function of helping us to look inward and outward since "narratives allow us to visualize these ideas in storied behaviors, as well as reveal and examine the thoughts, feelings, beliefs, and intentions of the agents of the action" (p. 7).

I am particularly inspired by Carter Andrews and Castillo's (2019) work on practicing humanizing pedagogy in teacher education programs to focus on narratives of excellence, resistance, and hope that is enacted by members of marginalized communities. They suggest that a crucial element of implementing a humanizing pedagogy for teacher educators is to engage in sustained critical self-reflection as they argue that

> we must first come to terms with our own identity, values, assumptions, beliefs, and stereotypes, a process often not encouraged or facilitated by our own pathways into the profession. Incidentally, we must practice critical internal

> reflection and question our role in the classroom and engage in truth-telling, valuing narrative and personal experience, and acting. (p. 15)

In searching the literature on understanding lived experiences, I find Van Manen's (1990) comments on the temporal nature of lived experiences particularly relevant to my own inquiry:

> Various thinkers have noted that lived experience first of all has a temporal structure: it can never be grasped in its immediate manifestation but only reflectively as past presence...Lived experience is the breathing of meaning...Thus, a lived experience has a certain essence, a "quality" that we gain in retrospect. (p. 36)

Van Manen (1990) also points out how reflective writing interacts with experience to teach us what we know. Britzman's (1994) and McCarthy's (1998) perspective on the dynamic influence of one's identity and the contexts of power on how experiences are seen and interpreted over time also inform my writing. They argue that power undergirds the construction of identities and interpretations of experiences. The interaction across identity, power, and experience is central to understanding how lived experiences create meaning in people's lives. Through oral and written forms, who a person is and what the person has experienced become important and meaningful. I recognize that learning from lived experiences may differ among those who differ in race, class, gender, language, and national origin.

In recounting my journey from a girl growing up during the Cultural Revolution in China to becoming an immigrant senior faculty in the United States, I try to understand my past experiences in relation to where I am today, and how these experiences have shaped my work in and commitment to intercultural communication and education about global sustainability. In documenting and analyzing my own pathway to the professoriate and beyond, I focus on navigating higher education institutional structures and using narrative curriculum in my teaching about global sustainability.

FAMILY AND CHILDHOOD EXPERIENCES IN THE 1960s IN CHINA

Merryfield (2002) pointed out that many of the multicultural and global educators begin with memories of family or their childhood community, who they know affected their work today. This is also the case with me. My family's tradition in storytelling, Mao's gender equity policies, limited water resources, and deep roots of sustainability living, and experiential learning during the Cultural Revolution had a significant impact on my initial understanding of the world and on my professional trajectory in becoming a scholar committed to peace, resilience, and global learning.

I was born in a small township, Yebaishou, in the Jianping County of the Liaoning province located in the northeastern region of China in the mid-1960s. The city is situated between two sets of railroad tracks that connect two major cities of China: Shanyang and Beijing. The province where I grew up is part of the region historically known as Manchuria, an area which was invaded and occupied by Japan in the 1930s. The eastern part of Liaoning County borders North Korea on the Yalu River. The northern part of the county borders the inner Mongolia. My childhood education and initial understanding of the world were significantly influenced by both the rhetoric of the historical era and the unique geographic place. Yebaishou was typical of many other cities in its time and location. Early social studies learning experiences included listening to stories from my parents, particularly my father, watching revolutionary movies, and reciting the poems written by Chairman Mao.

I grew up listening to my father's stories about how he and his friends were badly treated in their own homeland by the Japanese imperialists. He shared accounts of how they were stripped of their cultural symbols, forced to learn and speak only Japanese in school, and to convert their names from Chinese to Japanese. He also told how he and his classmates battled to resist Japanese colonialism and maintain their identity and dignity during one of China's most difficult and turbulent times, an experience very similar to the one encountered by many Koreans and chronicled in the young adult literature titled, *When my Name was Keoko*, by Linda Sue Park (2010).

Another significant influence of my childhood is the message of gender equity. My father was a strong advocate for women and girls' education. In his early career as an educator, my father traveled to remote and rural parts of the county to persuade peasants to send their daughters to school. At school, I was deeply influenced by mantras such as: "Women were holding up half of the sky"; "Equal pay for equal work"; and "Girls can do everything boys can do" (Rong, 2002, p. 132). I always enjoyed participating in sports and studying math and science. During 3 years of high school, my academic achievement was always in the top 1% among 200 students in the science track. My childhood dream was to become a scientist to build a strong and prosperous China. In our home, gender equity was learned and practiced by observing my mother, my older sisters, and my brothers' wives. My mother, undereducated but experienced in life after having 10 children, encountered many hardships and obstacles with stoic tenacity. She challenged unfairness and injustices openly, so much so that I considered her a hero. During the Cultural Revolution, our family was sent to the countryside for about 10 years. It was my mother who rebelled in silence, yet used her hard work, wit, and diplomacy to gain power in the community, supporting my father's career in education, first as a teacher, then as an administrator, seeking various employments for my brothers and sisters, and constantly finding ways to feed the family on a shoestring budget. Her tenacity, resourcefulness, and problem-solving skills have a profound impact on me, both personally and professionally. Later in a similar vein, I witnessed the resilience, hopefulness, and perseverance from my three sisters as they navigated the economic challenges and opportunities transformed by Deng Xiaoping's economic policy and the impact of globalization on their jobs, families, and communities. Thus, the feminism that I understood from them was not about becoming "like a male" but about being an equal and shouldering family financial and economic responsibilities.

Growing up in Liaoning province in the 1960s has also deeply influenced my initial understanding of key concepts of poverty, sustainability, reduce and reuse of resources, conservation, as well as my later commitment to preparing sustainability-literate teachers (Nolet, 2009). A key geographic feature of my hometown is being surrounded by many big mountains with very few rivers or lakes. The water supply in the region has always been scarce and limited to evening use when the use of water by agriculture and industry is suspended. My parents implemented many creative ways to conserve water to make sure we had enough for cooking and cleaning. Reducing and reusing water consumption was and is part of daily practices both at home and at school. During my 2019 visit to schools in Yebaishou, I saw many innovative signs encouraging water conservation.

By today's American standards of living, I grew up in a highly impoverished environment. However, at the time I was oblivious to the fact that China was seen as a poverty-stricken developing country. While my family did not have much, my parents tried their best to ensure that my siblings and I had enough food to eat and learned about other places outside of the town we lived in. Education and literacy were always important at home. During the Cultural Revolution, when books were rare and most schools were closed, my father copied pages and pages of ancient Chinese poems on large pieces of paper and posted them on the wall for us to read and recite. Those home literacy education activities have had a long-lasting impact on me and my siblings. Contrary to today's highly structured and tightly scheduled childhood activities, both in urban China and in the United States, memories of my childhood include exploring open spaces in the countryside and endless outdoor play during all four seasons. I did not grow up with a television. Life was neither defined by engagement in virtual spaces nor by online experiences. Community-based experiential learning was very common in the school curriculum. My experiences growing up poor not only have made me more aware of the culture of poverty that some of my students are facing in the American South but have also my commitment to teaching about the United Nations Education for Sustainable Development

(ESD) sustainability goals and emphasizing community-based experiential learning pedagogy (Zong, 2015).

COLLEGE AND WORK EXPERIENCES IN CHINA

At the age of 18, I passed the rigorous national college entrance exam and was admitted to Beijing Normal University (BNU). As one of the leading national universities in China, BNU's prestige lies not only in its academic excellence, but also in its long history of active student participation in the nation's social and political movements, including the famous student-led anti-imperialist cultural and patriotic May Fourth movement in the 1920s that grew out of dissatisfaction with the Treaty of Versailles settlement, termed the "Shandong Problem" (BNU, 2008) and leading the 1989 student protest on Tiananmen Square. The students at BNU were selected from each province, autonomous region, and municipality in China, and represented many of the 56 official ethnic groups or nationalities across the country. As a result, I studied together with students from many ethnic groups and regions such as Mongolians, Tibetans, Uighurs from the Northwest; Koreans from the Northeast; and Miao, Yi, and Zhaung people from Southwest China. This provided me with my first richly constructed cross-cultural learning experiences.

During the same time that I was studying at the BNU for my bachelor's and master's degrees between 1984 to 1991, China went through many profound changes, economically, ideologically, socially, as well as politically. The country gradually opened to the international community after decades of isolation. Responding to this open culture among the society, there were many student organizations on campus that promoted various ideas, such as the History Society (Chun Qiu Xue She) and the May Fourth Literature Society (Wu Si Wen Xue She). These organizations often brought guest speakers to campus with competing views to discuss and debate the dynamic changes happening in China, which always drew huge crowds of young and enthusiastic students. In retrospect, the fact that several key student leaders of 1989 Tiananmen Square protest came from BNU directly resulted from a campus culture that fostered free exchanges of ideas and student activism. Major changes of the world during this time also had a profound impact on campus culture, such as the end of the Cold War, the fall of the Berlin Wall, and the political transformation of the East European countries.

After graduating from BNU with my master's degree, I was employed by China's National Research Institute for Curriculum and Instructional Resources, both as an editor and as a research associate. I participated in several national projects in the areas of K–12 curriculum development and school-based reform research. This experience provided me a unique opportunity to work with educators in many different parts of China as well as with educational leaders from Great Britain, Japan, North Korea, Russia, South Korea, and the United States. It also helped me realize that while there was much discussion about improving the quality of math, science, and technology education in China, the discussion about social education in general, and how to teach about the changing world in particular, was extremely limited.

IMMIGRATING TO THE UNITED STATES AND BECOMING AN AMERICAN

In November of 1992, Dr. Jan L. Tucker, an internationally known social studies educator and one of the earliest advocates for global education, delivered a keynote address on global education during an academic conference at BNU in which he called for teacher educators in universities to be at the vanguard of the change process in global education. His speech was received with great enthusiasm. Afterward Dr. Tucker and I had a long conversation with a Chinese journalist and Dr. Zhang Min Xuan, who later became the president of Shang Hai Normal University, about the role of social studies education, the importance of people to people exchanges, and collaboration between educators from China and the United States. Upon Dr. Tucker's return to the United States, he sent me manuscripts to review for two professional journals in the United States: *Social Education* and *Theory and Research in Social Studies Education*. Ultimately, Dr. Jan Tucker sponsored me to be able to attend Florida International University (FIU) to further my education and obtain a scholarship for inclusive education. Most of my coursework at FIU was centered on understanding various global issues and their implications for education. I was actively engaged in inquiries about historical and contemporary connections among nations.

I studied with classmates and professors from many countries such as the Bahamas, Canada, Columbia, Cuba, Greece, Cyprus, India, Jamaica, Japan, Nigeria, Sierra Leone, Spain, Sudan, Trinidad and Tobago, and Venezuela, as well as with American students from various cultural and ethnic backgrounds. Together we discussed and debated issues such as race and racism, population policy, environmental pollution, power, the Cold War, globalization, and the implications of all these issues for education policies and practice. World history and politics meant engaging in competing stories rather than monolithic textbook stories. Together with course readings, I was able to hear many other views about the world besides the "Americentric" or China-centric perspective. Looking back and reflecting upon my experiences at FIU, I was able to learn about intercultural competence through experiential learning and knowledge, and skills on sustainable development through a program of study that contained a balance of courses from the fields of geography, social science education, and educational foundations. Collectively, these courses examined core issues related to human and environmental interaction. The professors in my graduate programs employed a range of resources and opportunities to engage students in learning and teaching about the world. Readings such as *Clash of Civilizations* (Huntington, 1996), *Preparing for the 21st Century* (Kennedy, 1994), and *Lexus and Olive Tree* (Friedman, 2012) uniquely prepared me with knowledge, skills, multiple perspectives, and theoretical lenses to analyze the dynamics of global connections in the new century.

Navigating American Higher Education Landscape

I graduated from FIU with an EdD degree in social studies education with emphasis on global education in 1999. Since then, I have worked as a faculty member in three universities, University of Kentucky, Georgia State University, and now Kennesaw State University. I have overcome many barriers, developed intercultural competencies, and built many collaborative teams across disciplines. Researchers who study the learning journey of East Asian students in Western universities point out that East Asian students embark on their graduate courses with their own particular set of cultural norms, values, and beliefs about the nature of knowledge, how best to teach and learn, and what makes a good student. This line of research indicates that East Asian students (from China, Vietnam, Japan, Korea, Singapore, Taiwan, Hong Kong, and Malaysia) are products of the Confucian Heritage Culture (CHC) and are learners who place great emphasis on avoiding disagreement and conflicts to save their own and the others' "face" at any price. These beliefs manifest themselves in classroom behavior, in written assignments, as well as in their perceptions of what roles teachers and learners should play. Many East Asian students avoid expressing their personal opinions in class to avoid embarrassment by either appearing silly or by humiliating others. They also question the college classroom environment, where the teachers act more as a guide and facilitator, of near equal status with students, in contrast to the view of the teacher's guru-like role of absolute authority and knowledge in the CHC.

I argue that the learning journey of East Asian students can be equally applied to the career trajectory of women faculty of East Asian background teaching in American universities. Both face significant challenges in adjusting CHC thinking and to being in a Western academic environment and adjusting to Western norms. Many Asian women faculty members serving in

American universities have to go the extra mile to make up for their cultural and linguistic differences to construct their professional niche and win support from colleagues and students (Lin, 2005). Many feel isolated, lonely, and unsupported. Some experience rejection, exclusion, and stereotypes. Personally, I have traveled the same path as most women immigrant faculty from East Asia. I have struggled long and hard to find my footing and to carve out a place for myself in the profession. I have adjusted my thinking style, writing style, and teaching style. Over the years, while I developed critical perspectives to analyze social problems as a scholar, I have also formed a constructive outlook on how we should work together to facilitate positive change through communication and collaboration.

As a Chinese American living in the United States, the last 2 years have been emotionally exhausting because of the global pandemic, Donald Trump's China virus rhetoric, and the spike in hate crimes against Asian Americans and Pacific Islanders in several cities of the United States. My university office is less than 10 miles away from the first crime scene of March 16, 2021 mass shooting of women of Asian heritage in Atlanta-area spas. The trauma and hurt are still palpable in the Atlanta Asian-American community. Due to all of these events, I often recently have had doubts about my decision to immigrate to the United States.

In preparation for this chapter, I examined the numerous positive feedbacks I received from my students over the years. The following two messages stood out:

> Dr. Zong, I just wanted to thank you for a wonderfully engaging semester! I thoroughly enjoyed the readings, videos, and websites that you provided to us and the very interesting topics that you required us to write about!

> Dr. Zong, I just want to send you a quick note to thank you for such a great course! It was such a breath of fresh air, and I truly enjoyed all the assignments, and especially appreciated your feedback! I feel like this course has given me tangible, attainable things to consider in my practice and pedagogy, and I'm so grateful to you for that.

These two comments were from one semester in 2020 that I was so afraid to teach because of the former U.S. president's insistence on the China virus claim and the larger anti-globalization sentiment within U.S. society. The two doctoral students who wrote the above messages to me are from the same county where crimes were committed against Asian women. These messages provided much needed assurance and validation that intercultural communication and global learning are important. It also prompts me to reflect deeply on my curriculum decisions and pedagogy for global education.

GROWTH, DEVELOPMENT, AND COMMITMENT TO GLOBAL EDUCATION

My commitment to global education has grown out of the interplay between my personal background and professional responsibility at the university working with preservice and practicing social studies teachers who are mostly from states in the Southeastern United States. My philosophy of teaching has been informed by the tenets of global pedagogy, which posits that teaching from a global perspective differs from traditional approaches to studying peoples and places such as communities, cultures, geography, and history. My earlier work was influenced by Hanvey's (1976) five dimensions of global perspectives: perspective consciousness, state-of-the-planet awareness, cross-cultural awareness, knowledge of global dynamics, and awareness of human choices. More recently, I increasingly draw on theory and research on sustainability education and global citizenship education (Merryfield & Wilson, 2005; Noddings, 2005). Noddings (2005) argues that global education should prepare students to become citizens who are concerned about social and economic injustice, protection of the Earth, preservation of cultural diversity, and cultivating peace. Merryfield and Wilson (2005) suggest 10 essential elements for global citizenship education: global/local connections, perspective consciousness and multiple perspectives, the world as a system, global issues, power in a global context, nonstate actors, attention to prejudice reduction, cross-cultural competence, research and thinking skills, participation in local and global communities, and use of electronic technologies. Kirkwood-Tucker (2004) proposes that global education embraces a pedagogy of peacebuilding and citizenship education that promotes knowledge, attitude, and skills grounded in debate, deliberation, and discussion.

Learning About Global Sustainable Issues

In its report *Global Campaign for Education* (GCE), the United Nations Educational, Scientific, and Cultural Organization (UNESCO) advocates for "empowering learners of all ages to assume active roles, both locally and globally, in building more peaceful, tolerant, inclusive, and secure societies" (UNESCO, 2020, p. 3). The report's education sector of UNESCO (2020) argues that sustainable development involves more than taking care of the environment and conserving resources for humanity to survive (UNESCO, 2020). The United Nations strives to create a more prosperous, equitable, and peaceful world. Its 17 Sustainable Development Goals (SDGs) address concerns with social needs of inequality, wellness, poverty, and economic growth that go hand in hand with the other more environmentally focused goals (UNESCO, 2020). There are many moving pieces, so it takes everyone worldwide to work together to create a more sustainable life for our present well-being and for future generations. All 17 goals work together to impact humanity and the sustainability of all life on Earth.

In keeping with the United Nations' vision, I work to build a curriculum that is world oriented, and I craft a pedagogy that employs a range of teaching and learning experiences that engage my students to pursue these goals. These include writing autobiographies to reflect on personal experiences, conducting community inquiries to explore real-life connections between globalization and local communities and people and places around the world; integrating literature and other narratives in learning about people, places, and perspectives; and engaging in critical analysis of discourses on globalization and teaching for sustainability (Zong, 2015, 2022). Over the years, I have developed a narrative approach to engage teacher education students in learning about global sustainable issues. First, I have selected and integrated young adult literature into the teacher education curriculum. The books I have frequently used are: *A Long Walk to Water* (Park, 2010); *The Boy Who Harnessed the Wind*, written and illustrated by Kamkwamba and Mealer (2009), and *Unbowed: A Memoir*, written by Nobel Prize winner Wangari Maathai (2007). These books not only address global sustainable development issues but also highlight the theme of individual activism in shaping policies and practices that promote ecological citizenship. Most recently, I have built a collection of current event articles from major news organizations to engage candidates in understanding the urgency and relevance of sustainability issues.

I have found that the following articles on air pollution, consumption and production of fast fashion, and water scarcity and uneven distribution are particularly compelling and powerful in empowering the conscience of teacher leaders toward a concern for the global issues of the planet: "The Modern Gold Rush That's Destroying the Amazon" (Weir, 2017); "The Dirty Industry of Fast Fashion is Causing an Environmental Emergency" (Bain, 2018); "Delhi, Blanketed in Toxic Haze, 'Has Become a Gas Chamber'" (Kumar & Schultz, 2017); "Losing Earth: The Decade We Almost Stopped Climate Change" (Rich, 2018); "No Drips, No Drops: A City of 10 Million Is Running Out of Water" (Pathak, 2019); "How Marginalized Communities in the South Are Paying the Price for 'Green Energy' in Europe" (de Puy Kamp, 2021); and "'Dying of Thirst': The Cucapá in Mexico Fight Against Climate Change and Oblivion" (Linares, 2021).

Through effective storytelling, rich narratives, and grounded analysis, these articles powerfully document the toll of human consumerism on the global environment, specifically the destruction caused by a modern gold rush and the scarcity of water, a result of both climate change and mismanagement. Weir (2017) reports that the modern gold rush is destroying the

Amazon because tens of thousands of men from the poorest parts of Peru are mining for treasure in Madre de Dios. However, the use of mercury methods can be very toxic to every form of life in the Amazon. This illegal mining has transformed hundreds of square miles of pristine rainforest in Madre de Dios into toxic wasteland. Health problems can occur for all since the fish swim in the same waters that are polluted by the miners. In fact, the illegal gold pop-up mining camps are the reason for the increase of mercury poisoning since they release as much mercury as a coal-fired power plant. Unfortunately, there is no proof of this slowing down. "As global markets roil and the price of gold stays high, the healthy Amazon disappears" (p. 2). Linares' (2021) story reveals that Mexico is having the worst drought in 3 decades due to climate change. The rainfall is concentrated in fewer days, which creates floods that destroy farmers' crops. There is also an increase in temperature, which heightens the risk for forest fires and heat-related deaths. This drought has affected the relationship of the Cucapá people, "people from the river, with the river," who live in the northern part of Mexico. They are fighting for the water supply of the Colorado so that the fish can gather, and they can earn a livelihood. The Hoover Dam, which lowered the flow for Mexico, also affects the Cucapá people. It has caused a shortage of fruits and grains, as well as trees and shrubs to build houses and boats and make clothing. As a result, the Cucapá people are dying from the declining river flow.

In Garysburg, North Carolina in the United States, Enviva, the world's largest biomass producer of industrial wood pellets, is cutting down hardwood trees to generate energy. The European Union market has increased the demand for wood pellets to the point that the American South has become Europe's primary source of biomass imports. It also created a loophole by not preventing the leveling of rooted trees for wood pellet production. Enviva has impacted the environment and marginalized communities located in Northampton County, such as Garysburg, by emitting pollution. The population of Northampton County is predominantly African American and has been in a constant battle against environmental racism for decades. In fact, its population has been in decline because of pollution. Enviva's plants have led to an increase in asthma, insomnia, cardiovascular disease, and death (de Puy Kamp, 2021). One of the largest users of water globally is the fashion industry, noting that one cotton shirt requires 2,700 liters of water. Also, some worldwide fashion workers are put in unsafe conditions, mostly girls and women. The United Nations Economic Commission for Europe (UNECE) cannot ignore the fashion industry as it aims to promote economic integration and cooperation among its member countries. The commission is focused on meeting such goals as reducing poverty, providing people everywhere with clean water and sanitation, promoting gender equality, and offering decent work for all. The fashion industry's increased production of cheap and disposable clothing is an "environmental and social emergency" that needs to change. The energy used to grow materials and produce fabrics causes heavy pollution. These effects should motivate us all to urgently create an action plan to reduce the damage the fashion industry is causing (Bain, 2018).

Education for Sustainable Development (ESD) is a lifelong process for educating and preparing poverty, zero hunger, good health/well-being, quality education, and gender equality for everyone. The next seven goals represent ambitions needed for economic policies that ensure clean water with sanitation, affordable/clean energy, work that is decent with economic growth, infrastructure with industry/innovation, inequality reduction, sustainable cities/learners to make informed decisions about the environment UNESCO (2020). ESD, a major attribute of education for sustainability, advocates for the globalization and unification of all countries to focus on meeting all 17 SDGs by 2030. The first five goals can be characterized as much-needed social goals that include no communities and responsible consumption/production. The remaining five goals focus on environmental concerns along the lines of taking action with climate changes, protecting underwater life, protecting land life/ecosystems, establishing peace/justice/strong institutions, and establishing global partnerships for achieving the goals. ESD (UNESCO, 2020) states that another major feature of sustainability is to provide everyone with facts in order to conduct the best course of action and embrace accountability for an equitable society, the endurance of an effective economy, and the probity of the environment. Seitz (2020) reviewed literature pertaining to incorporating ecological citizenship into social studies curricula. Ecological citizenship recognizes the connection between all living things, both human and nonhuman, and stresses the responsibilities humans have to be good citizens of the planet to ensure a sustainable future for all. Seitz (2020) identified six areas that ecological citizenship can be incorporated into social studies lessons: water issues, pollution, climate change, climate activism, sustainability and economic growth, and ecological citizenship/ethics.

In my own teaching, I try to stress to my students the interconnection that exists between people around the world. I try to explain to them and give them learning activities that allow them to see that what happens in one area of the world can ripple across the globe to affect them too. Teaching environmental issues creates a fantastic opportunity for this concept. I attempt to provide what Shuttleworth (2020) describes as Global Citizenship Education (GCE): "Rethinking classrooms through a global citizenship education lens that prepares teachers and students to see world issues as challenges and responsibilities arising from membership in a world community—not as curricular tangents" (p. 70). Muchmore (2004) has argued that teaching is an autobiographical endeavor:

It is autobiographical in the sense that the values and beliefs that guide teachers' actions are inevitably shaped by their personal histories. All their past experiences—as children, as students, as preservice teachers and, as adults, play a significant role in determining the kinds of teachers that they become. (p. 6)

REFLECTIONS

As an immigrant woman faculty member of Chinese origin, my experiences and understandings about people, places, and perspectives have deeply shaped my curriculum and instructional decisions with my students in the teacher education programs at universities in the United States. I found Espino's (2018) work particularly resonates with my own professional pursuits in teaching about sustainability. In reflecting upon the impact of her lived experiences in transforming educational structures, policies, and practices to ensure educational equity and opportunity for Latina/o/x students and faculty, she wrote:

> My formal training beckons me to see the world through a distant lens and to keep at an arm's length so that I can approach a problem with objectivity. My spirit calls me to engage, to immerse myself as a whole person so that my understanding of the world is enhanced with compassion and care. (Espino, 2018, p. 2)

After spending a quarter of a century in the United States, I have adapted to life in America, culturally as well as linguistically. Both of my parents have passed away, but their resilience, optimism, and sustainable ways of living have planted deep roots in my thinking and being. I decided to become an American citizen in 2013. I hope my work in improving global understanding through teaching, research and scholarship, and service honors my parents in a small way.

As I finish writing this chapter, Russia's war in the Ukraine is still waging; extreme heat has been recorded in many places in Europe, in Asia, as well as in the United States; historic flooding in eastern Kentucky has claimed at least 37 lives; and a record number of gun violence deaths have been recorded since 1999 in the United States (Ebrahimji, 2022). The new and enduring challenges and mounting tide of public concern about where the world is heading have brought global perspectives to the forefront of the education discourse (Jules & Arnold, 2021; Kenyon & Christoff, 2020).

We are living in a critical time in which we must declare our moral responsibility to confront the ways in which we are complicit in the hatred and violence embedded in today's societies, both local and global, through our own silence, our own hedging, and our own unwillingness to dialogue. Rather than remain silent and silenced, scholars and practitioners in global education must respond to the pressing need to produce a citizenry that is culturally literate and globally competent. The field of global education has taken on a new urgency, importance, and needs to focus on teaching about hope, joy, resilience, communication, conflict management, and building peace.

REFERENCES

Bain, M. (2018, March 6). *The dirty industry of fast fashion is causing an environmental "emergency."* Quartz. https://qz.com/1222569/fast-fashion-is-causing-an-environmental-emergency/

Beijing Normal University. (2008). *Brief history of Beijing Normal University*. Retrieved June 10, 2008 from http://www.bnu.edu.cn/focus/survey/history.htm

Britzman, D. P. (1994). Is there a problem with knowing thyself? Towards a poststructuralist view of teacher identity. In T. Shanahan (Ed.), *Teachers thinking, teachers knowing: Reflections on literacy and language education* (pp. 53–75). National Council of Teachers of English.

Brookfield, S. (2027). *Becoming a critically reflective teacher* (2nd ed.). Jossey-Bass.

Carter Andrews, D. J., & Castillo, B. M. (2019). Beyond the damage-centered teacher education: Humanizing pedagogy for teacher educators and preservice teachers. *Teachers College Record: The Voice of Scholarship in Education, 121*(6). https://doi.org/10.1177/016146811912100605

Connelly, F. M., & Clandinin, D. J. (1999). *Shaping professional identity: Stories of educational practice*. Teachers College Press.

De Puy Kamp, M. P. (2021, July 9). *How marginalized communities in the south are paying the price for 'green energy' in Europe*. CNN. https://www.cnn.com/interactive/2021/07/us/american-south-biomass-energy-invs/

Ebrahimji, A. (2022, August 7). *He was shot and killed playing the sport he loved. Now this Ohio 15-year-old is one of the country's latest victims of gun violence*. CNN. https://www.cnn.com/2022/08/07/us/gun-violence-ohio-shooting-issa-jeylani/index.html

Espino, M. M. (2018). Positionality as prologue: Encountering the self on the journey to transforming Latina/o/x educational inequities. *Teachers College Record: the Voice of Scholarship in Education, 120*(14). https://doi.org/10.1177/016146811812001413

Freire, J. A. (2021). Conscientization calls: A white dual language educator's development of sociopolitical consciousness and commitment to social justice. *Education and Urban Society, 53*(2), 231–248. https://doi.org/10.1177/0013124520928608

Friedman, T. (2012). *The Lexus and the olive tree: Understanding globalization* (2nd ed.). Picador.

Gay, G. (Ed.). (2003). *Becoming multicultural educators: Personal journey toward professional agency*. Jossey-Bass.

Hanvey, R. G. (1976). *An attainable global perspective*. Center for Global Perspectives in Education.

Huntington, S. (1996). *Clash of civilizations*. Simon & Schuster.

Jules, T. D., & Arnold, R. (2021). Constructing global citizenship education at the regional level: Regionalism and Caribbean citizen education. *Globalisation, Societies, and Education, 19*(4), 393–404. https://eric.ed.gov/?id=EJ1302309

Kamkwamba, W., & Mealer, B. (2009). *The boy who harnessed the wind: Creating currents of electricity and hope.* Harper Collins.

Kennedy, P. (1994). *Preparing for the 21st Century.* Vintage.

Kenyon, E., & Christoff, A. (2020). Global citizenship education through global children's literature: An analysis of the NCSS Notable Trade Books. *Journal of Social Studies Research, 44*(4), 397–408. https://doi.org/10.1016/j.jssr.2020.05.001

Kirkwood-Tucker, T. F. (2004). Empowering teachers to create a more peaceful world through global education: Simulating the United Nations. *Theory and Research in Social Education, 32*(1), 56–74. https://doi.org/10.1080/00933104.2004.10473243

Kissling, M. T., & Bell, J. T. (2020). Teaching social studies amid ecological crisis. *Theory & Research in Social Education, 48*(1), 1–31. https://eric.ed.gov/?id=EJ1245664

Kumar, H., & Schultz, K. (2017, November 7). Delhi, blanketed in toxic haze, 'has become a gas chamber.' *The New York Times.* http://www.nytimes.com/2017/11/07/world/asia/delhi/-pollution-gas-chamber.html

Li, G., & Beckett, G. (2005). *"Strangers" of the academy: Asian women scholars in higher education.* Stylus Publishing.

Lin, J. (2005). Building bridges, working for a better world. In G. Li & G. H. Beckett (Eds.), *"Strangers" of the academy: Asian women scholars in higher education* (pp. 289–305). Stylus Publishing.

Linares, A. (2021, June 15). '*Dying of thirst': The Cucapá in Mexico fight against climate change and oblivion.* NBC News. https://www.nbcnews.com/news/latino/dying-thirst-cucap-mexico-fight-against-climate-change-oblivion-n1270806

Maathai, W. (2007). *Unbowed: A memoir.* Anchor.

McCarthy, C. (1998). *The use of culture.* Routledge.

McEwan, H., & Egan, K. (1995). *Narrative in teaching, learning, and research.* Teacher College Press.

Merryfield, M. (2002). Why aren't teachers being prepared to teach for diversity, equity, and global interconnectedness? A study of lived experiences in the making of multicultural and global educators. *Teaching and Teaching Education, 16*(4), 429–443. https://doi.org/10.1016/S0742-051X(00)00004-4

Merryfield, M., & Wilson, A. (2005). *Social studies and the world: Teaching global perspectives.* NCSS.

Milner, H. R. (2007). Race, narrative inquiry, and self-study in curriculum and teacher education. *Education and Urban Society, 39*(4), 584–609. https://doi.org/10.1177/0013124507301577

Muchmore, J. (2004). *A teacher's life: Stories of literacy, teacher thinking, and professional development.* Backlong Books.

Noddings, N. (Ed.). (2005). *Educating citizens for global awareness.* Teachers College Press.

Nolet, V. (2009). Preparing sustainability-literate teachers. *Teachers College Record: The Voice of Scholarship in Education, 111*(2), 409–442. https://doi.org/10.1177/016146810911100207

Park, L. S. (2010). *A long walk to water*. Houghton Mifflin Harcourt.

Park, L. S. (2012). *When my name was Keoko*. Clarion Books.

Pathak, S. (2019, June 25). *No drips, no drops: A city of 10 million is running out of water*. NPR. https://www.npr.org/sections/goatsandsoda/2019/06/25/734534821/no-drips-no-drops-a-city-of-10-million-is-running-out-of-water

Rich, M. (2018, August 1). Losing earth: The decade we almost stopped climate change. *The New York Times*. https://www.nytimes.com/interactive/2018/08/01/magazine/climate-change-losing-earth.html

Rong, X. L. (2002). Teaching with differences and for differences: Reflections of a Chinese American teacher educator. In L. Vargas (Ed.), *Women faculty of color in the white classroom* (pp. 125–144). Peter Lang.

Seitz, R. Z. (2020). Rubber ducks to ecological citizenship: A review of practitioner-oriented research on ecological issues in the social studies. *Social Studies Research and Practice, 15*(3), 261–275.

Shuttleworth, J. M. (2020). Framing the pandemic within global citizenship education. *Journal of International Social Studies, 10*, 67–75. https://eric.ed.gov/?id=EJ1266471

Stanley, C. (2006). Coloring the academic landscape: Faculty of color breaking the silence in predominantly White colleges and universities. *American Educational Research Journal, 43*(4), 701–736.

UNESCO. (2020). *Education for sustainable development: A roadmap*. https://unesdoc.unesco.org/ark:/48223/pf0000374802.locale=en

Van Manen, M. (1990). *Researching lived experiences: Human science for an action sensitive pedagogy*. State University of New York Press.

Weir, B. (2017, November 13). *The modern gold rush that's destroying the Amazon*. CNN. https://www.cnn.com/2017/11/10/world/wonder-list-bill-weir-peru-amazon-illegal-gold-mining/index.html

Zong, G. (2015). Teaching about globalization through community-based inquiry. In B. Maguth & J. Hilburn (Eds.), *The state of global education: Learning with the world and its people* (pp. 92–110). Routledge.

Zong, G. (2022). Integrating global sustainability into social studies teachers' education: A collaborative self-study. *Social Studies Research and Practice, 17*(1), 94–113.

SECTION III

CARIBBEAN

CHAPTER 8

CUBA

FLIGHT TO FREEDOM

A Cuban Immigrant's Journey Through Education

Bárbara C. Cruz

It was my first day of kindergarten in the Fall of 1966 in Playa de Santa Fé, a small town near Havana, Cuba. Fidel Castro and his bearded army of revolutionaries had ousted the dictatorship of Fulgencio Batista on New Year's Day in 1959. Of humble peasant origins, Batista rose quickly through the military ranks. He ruled Cuba twice: 1933–1944 and 1952–1959. It was in his second rule that he emerged as a brutal dictator, incarcerating political opponents, and enriching himself on the backs of the citizenry. As popular unrest grew on the island—and after the United States' withdrawal of support in 1958—the guerrilla army of Castro and his rebels were able to wrestle power from Batista and establish a new revolutionary government.

By the time I entered school, the revolution was still in its heady days, flush with promises of bringing access to medical care and education, eradicating poverty, and hunger, and achieving equality for all citizens regardless of race, creed, or gender. Schooling and literacy were hallmarks of the new government and the country's massive literacy campaign was being touted the world over.

Having spent the previous 5 years in the warmth of family, I cried bitterly of having to go to school. My mother dropped me off at the start of the school day, anxiously standing outside the classroom, the door shut tight, but with a gap between the bottom of the door and the floor. She could hear the teacher trying to shush my wailing, trying to explain that someone would pick me up at the end of the school day. My mother watched helplessly as my breakfast of *café con leche* and buttered Cuban bread rolled out from underneath the door in the form of vomit. To this day, she marvels at how I went on to love school and to become an educator despite this inauspicious beginning. Little did we know what this journey would entail.

JOURNEY TO THE UNITED STATES

The exodus from Cuba to the United States and other countries is still poorly understood by non-Cubans. While it is true that many wealthy and well-educated Cubans left their homeland in the immediate years preceding and following Castro's revolution in 1959, there were also other subsequent waves of immigration by Cubans of decidedly more modest means. My family was in this last category. My family was of the socioeconomic class the revolution spoke to directly. My mother Elsa, as best we can tell, received schooling until about fourth grade, at which point she stopped going to school so she could beg for alms in the town square to supplement her family's meager income. My father, Ignacio, attended school until about second grade, cutting sugarcane and tobacco on a plantation whose owners took him in after he was orphaned as an infant.

By the time I was born, my father had already left the island, convinced the new socialist government would be autocratic, with plans to send for his family once settled in the United States. In 1965, my mother saw the opportunity to emigrate via a new program, the *Vuelos de la Libertad* (Freedom Flights), which eventually transported nearly 300,000 Cuban exiles to the United States between 1965 and 1973. The night before we left Cuba, we were anxious, not knowing what was on the other end of our plane ride. Some of our Cuban neighbors and family shunned us, repeating the epithet of *gusano* (worm) Castro used to describe those leaving the island and, by extension, turning their backs on the revolution. We were allowed one suitcase of clothing and belongings. As we waited to board the one-way

PanAm flight to the United States, my mother Elsa still did not believe we would actually be leaving and began to worry. What if we could not find my father? How would we manage without knowing English? How could we live without any money? But at 22 years of age, my mother was still young and full of hope that a new, better life would be waiting for us in America.

Arrival in America

We arrived in Miami in September 1966, an event my mother commemorates every year, gently reminding me of our roots. After a medical check at repurposed barracks on the airport outskirts, we were processed at *La Torre de la Libertad* (Freedom Tower; Figure 7.1), now a national historic landmark and a beloved monument for Cuban exiles. There we got our first taste of American peanut butter, homogenized milk, and spongy white bread—none of which I liked and refused to eat. I also deeply missed my grandparents who had helped raise me. My mother does not remember how she answered my question when we would be able to see *abuelita* (grandmother) and *abuelito* (grandfather) again. She could not have known at the time, but it would be another 14 years until we would be reunited with those we left behind—grandparents, aunts and uncles, cousins, and neighbors. Soon we were on our way to Southern California, part of the Cuban

Figure 7.1 *La Torre de la Libertad* (Freedom Tower) in Miami, Florida. *Source:* Photographs in the Carol M. Highsmith Archive, Library of Congress, Prints and Photographs Division. https://www.loc.gov/item/2011630393/

Resettlement Program that aimed to find places to live for the thousands of Cuban exiles arriving in the country. My father was already there, having found work as a cemetery gravedigger.

Starting kindergarten anew, in a language I did not understand, with a culture and environment vastly different to that I was used to, posed daily challenges. I was enrolled in a school with no Latino children or staff. Those early days are a blur, just faint memories of confusion and frustration. Most of my teachers were kind and patient, trying to teach me during a time when English for speakers of other languages (ESOL) programs did not yet exist. (The U.S. Bilingual Education Act, Title VII of the Elementary and Secondary Education Act of 1968, was the first piece of federal legislation that recognized the needs of English language learners.) Others, like my second grade teacher who repeatedly admonished me for including the accent mark over the "a" in "Bárbara" ("We are in America now!"), challenged my very identity.

With time, I learned English and like so many immigrant children, served as the liaison between home and the outside world. The ability to "live on the hyphen" (see Pérez Firmat, 1994) would prove to be important later once I became an educator and strived to assist teachers in being inclusive linguistic and cultural facilitators in their classrooms. As many immigrants will attest, living with one foot firmly planted in one's home culture, while the other navigates life in America, can result in a "never fully here nor there" identity. On the one hand, one must acculturate and adopt the language and customs of the new home in order to not just survive, but ultimately be successful. But at home and with family, linguistic and cultural practices endure, often directly at odds with the new home country. Life in between these two spaces—life on the hyphen—was a never-ending source of dissonance and conflict.

By the time I entered junior high (we had moved back to Miami by then), I was confident in the English language and excelled in school. I often helped neighbors and friends in our Little Havana neighborhood fill out government forms and accompanied them to government offices. I tutored younger children in the neighborhood, including my younger siblings. I loved helping others learn and make sense of their world. In high school, I continued to achieve academically while working 20–30 hours per week at a fast-food restaurant. Money was tight in our working-class home, but my sights were set on attending college. I made an appointment with my high school's college advisor, as I saw my peers doing. Suffice it to say that the meeting did not go as I envisioned, walking out of the counselor's office with a stack of secretarial school brochures the advisor suggested I should explore.

But with the encouragement and financial help of my 11th grade history teacher, I took the SAT exam, a college admissions test, scoring high enough to qualify for a Presidential Scholarship at the University of Miami (UM). I told my parents a fib—that first-year students were required to live on campus—since their traditional values made them uncomfortable with my leaving home. Since UM was just a few miles away from our house, they relented. I requested to live on the international floor in my dormitory. I decided that if I could not go out into the world, the world would come to me. I majored in secondary social studies education while continuing to work 20–30 hours a week. I took advantage of living on campus to attend gallery openings, poetry readings, film showings, and concerts. Every day brought new learning both inside and outside the classroom.

TEACHER PREPARATION AND FINDING A MENTOR

After earning my bachelor's degree in 3 years at the University of Miami, I began teaching full time at the same high school in which I had completed my final internship. When the Miami Public Schools district offered tuition support for teachers to continue with their graduate education, I enrolled in my first graduate course at Florida International University (FIU) located in Miami. My life as an educator would be forever changed. I met Dr. Jan L. Tucker in late summer of 1983 by accident. I was looking for FIU's Office of Educational Research convinced that I wanted to pursue educational research as my graduate major but no one from that program was available. Always perceptive, Dr. Tucker must have noted my expression of disappointment as he saw me in the hallway and kindly asked if he could be of assistance. Once he realized I was a social studies teacher in pursuit of a master's degree, he invited me to his office and persuaded me to consider the program he directed.

In Dr. Tucker's classes, I learned new ways to think about the mission of social studies education. He had recently published a paper (Tucker, 1982) wherein he urged educators to consider the implications of our global realities on social studies education. In the classroom, he pushed his students to consider counternarratives and for me in particular, he encouraged me to share my perspectives as an immigrant and as a Latina. I thrived under his tutelage and mentorship, chagrined to realize with each class and with each assigned reading, how much I still had to learn. When I completed my master's program, he brought me to his office once more, asking: "Have you thought about a doctorate?" As a first-generation high school and college graduate, a doctoral program had never figured into my plans. But here was someone whom I deeply respected and admired telling me that I was suited for the academic rigor of doctoral work (see Cruz & Bermúdez, 2009a, for an extended recounting of Dr. Tucker's mentorship). And before I let self-doubt thwart my excitement, I applied for the program, was admitted, and in my second year, was awarded sufficient scholarship funding to pursue the degree full time. Ever the intentional mentor, Dr. Tucker provided opportunities for me to teach courses, attend professional conferences, and serve as a facilitator and curriculum developer in the Global Awareness Program.

The Global Awareness Program

As I have written elsewhere (Cruz & Bermúdez, 2009b), the Global Awareness Program (GAP) in the Department of Teacher Education at FIU was directed by the late Jan L. Tucker (see Figure 7.2). Identified by Merryfield (1991) as one of six model global teacher education programs in the nation at the time, the program created and published curricula, hosted professional development seminars, and offered study abroad opportunities for educators. Founded in 1979 in response to a Florida State Board of Education resolution urging the development of school programs with a global perspective, the GAP was entering its seventh year as I began my doctoral studies.

It is not hyperbole to assert that participation in this program changed my worldview so profoundly that both my professional and personal lives were forever altered. Since that formative introduction to global education,

Figure 7.2 Author, Jan L. Tucker, and Toni Fuss Kirkwood-Tucker (ca. 1987) on a local television program.

its tenets, and pedagogy, my academic journey has had at every step the indelible stamp of GAP's lessons. In addition to the mark it left on my teaching and scholarship (to be discussed later in this chapter), I noted that Dr. Tucker treated teachers with deep respect which they richly deserved. Dr. Tucker (almost 40 years later and I still can't call him by his first name!) ensured that during the global education professional development seminars he conducted, his grant proposal budgets included teacher substitute release days so the participating teachers would not have to attend workshops on their own time. He also included funding requests for teachers' meals (so they would have one less thing to worry about) and tuition waivers (so they could continue their professional education). The GAP program also embraced the "teachers teaching teachers" model, where teachers who participated in the workshops and seminars would then conduct their own professional development sessions at their home schools, sharing their newfound knowledge and skills with their colleagues. I continue to incorporate these features into the project proposals I write today, certain that they result in higher quality programming and participation.

As graduation time neared, Dr. Tucker called me into his office to discuss next steps. He coached me in applying for postsecondary positions, encouraged me to consider leadership opportunities in professional organizations, and asked me to ponder how I would continue to make contributions to our field through scholarship. As the conversation came to a close, he slid an envelope across the desk. He explained that he was gifting me some of his frequent flyer miles for a trip to a place I had not visited. The graduation gift, he said, was a reminder of the importance of travel as an educational means and the opportunity to learn experientially. That gift would be the beginning of a lifetime of travel, both domestically and abroad, a gift that I have passed on to my own children.

One other important life lesson by Dr. Tucker was imparted to me as I was completing my doctoral education at FIU. After defending my dissertation, Dr. Tucker asked me if I had filled out the application to participate in commencement. I replied that I had not planned on attending the ceremony, since I had not done so for either my bachelor or master's degrees. He became very serious and replied: "Commencement is not for you, Bárbara, it's for those who supported you along the way and helped to make this happen, starting with your parents who sacrificed so much for you to be here." Needless to say, I scurried to submit the application. I will always be grateful to him for that admonition. At the graduation ceremony, my parents proudly watched as Dr. Tucker hooded me on stage (see Figure 7.3).

Figure 7.3 Jan L. Tucker hooding author at FIU Spring 1991 commencement.

ENTERING THE PROFESSORIATE

Soon after graduation, I was hired as a new assistant professor at the University of South Florida (USF) in Tampa, Florida. About 5 hours by car from Miami, I figured it would be a great institution to gain experience, apply my knowledge of Florida curricula, and be able to visit family and friends on long weekends. I imagined I would stay for a few years and then move elsewhere.

Paying the Cultural/"Minority Tax"

Although I had shadowed Dr. Tucker for the previous 5 years, I entered the professoriate not truly understanding the myriad demands of the profession (not to mention the responsibilities of simultaneously being a young mother). I tried to continue my scholarship when I could, but most weeks I could barely find an hour or two to write for publication, a critical requirement for tenure-earning faculty. Teaching, with its continual demands of curriculum development, class preparation, grading, and meeting with students, took up much of my time. But equally time-consuming were the constant requests to serve on committees, task forces, and community projects. There was hardly a week that would go by without being asked (or appointed) to serve on a new university initiative.

Soon after arriving at USF, I found out I was the first Hispanic faculty member ever hired in the university's College of Education; this proved to be both an opportunity and an overwhelming responsibility at times. As several scholars of color have written (e.g., June, 2015; Padilla, 1994; Trejo, 2020), the steep cultural/color "tax" minority faculty pay in academia can result in a number of negative outcomes, including stressors on personal and family life, not achieving tenure and promotion, and professional burnout. It took a few years to figure out how to set boundaries, but at least I never felt, as others have described, "the burden that faculty of color have to bear in order to fit into and survive within the unique political and cultural paradigm of American higher education" (Canton, 2012, p. 9). With the exception of a handful of times I experienced blatant discrimination (such as a check-out clerk at the university library demanding I prove my faculty status for reserved material), my colleagues and institution embraced me and what I had to contribute. Since those early days in academia, I have learned to be selective in my professional service, having at the center of my decision-making a clear focus on those core values that continue to serve as a guiding compass in my teaching and scholarship: the imperative of a global perspective, the importance of cross-cultural understanding, and a commitment to educational equity and access for all.

Global Professional Teacher Development

Following in the footsteps of Jan Tucker, I was able to secure funding for establishment of the Global Schools Project (GSP), a teacher professional development program that operated from 2004–2010 under the auspices of the university's Global Research Center. Following my mentor's lead, I ensured that the program's budget included substitute teacher release days, graduate tuition support, and meals for participants. The seminars with experts in the field—both in terms of global content as well as pedagogy—incorporated the teachers-teaching-teachers model, with participants leading their own workshops in their schools.

The GSP teachers were critical to the success of two additional projects. I was able to bring to campus teachers from all over the world to study with us in 6-week programs funded by the U.S. Department of State. These experiences led to work in disparate places such as Haiti, Mexico, the Dominican Republic, Latvia, and Spain; they also made their way into my teacher education classroom, with prospective and practicing teachers benefitting from these global connections. First in 2009 and then in 2010, teachers spent 6 weeks on campus learning about American democracy, considering cutting-edge pedagogy, and developing dissemination plans for sharing their skills with colleagues upon their return to their home countries. The GSP teachers in turn were able to learn from their international colleagues, bringing them in as guest speakers to their classrooms and engaging in cross-cultural teacher exchange.

My Teaching

My teaching assignment the first few years at USF centered on social studies teaching methods, preservice courses such as Teaching Elementary Social Studies, Secondary Teaching Methods of Social Studies, and Practicum in Social Studies Instruction. I was also tasked with supervising interns in the field and facilitating the program's capstone course, Senior Seminar. Graduate courses, such as Current Trends in Social Science Education, were added to my teaching load a few years later. Once I got my bearings, I was able to introduce a new course to our curriculum, Global and Multicultural Perspectives in Education, reflecting my experiences at FIU. Then, when our program began offering a doctoral degree, I started to teach the advanced graduate course, Issues in Social Studies Curriculum and Instruction (I would go on to hood 21 doctoral students of my own, with 27 more in various stages of their doctoral programs as of this writing).

At every opportunity, in every course, I incorporated issues of immigration and modeled teaching strategies using content from my native culture and history. Although Tampa Bay has a long and rich immigrant history, many of the Italians, Spanish, Cuban, and Greek immigrants in the region trace their backgrounds to the turn of the 20th century. For many of my students, meeting a first-generation immigrant, especially one who was their college professor, was a first. Discussion of immigration, diverse histories and cultures, and global issues have always been at the center of my teaching. As a social studies teacher educator, I use these topics to illustrate and model best teaching practices. If I would like preservice teachers to experience the power of effective cooperative learning, I might use an example from Latin American history to model the jigsaw technique. A political cartoon on global migration might be selected for its ability to foment a critical thinking discussion in class. Or the paintings of Mexican artist Frida Kahlo might be used to illustrate how to incorporate art, biography, geography, and politics into a historical timeline activity. My interest in Latin American studies also resulted in young adult books on the life and work of notable individuals such as Rubén Blades (Cruz, 1997), José Clemente Orozco (Cruz, 1998a), Raúl Juliá (Cruz, 1998b), Simón Bolívar (Cruz, 2017), César Chávez (2005, 2016), and Frida Kahlo (Cruz, 1996). These, too, were incorporated into my teacher education classroom as ways to show how inspirational Latino/as and Latin Americans can enrich social studies instruction.

Graduate students in my classes also receive a global education through in-class discussions, readings, and assignments. Some graduate courses I teach (e.g., "Global and Multicultural Perspectives in Education" and "Teaching Social Studies to English Language Learners") lend themselves naturally to the infusion of global issues and topics. Other courses (e.g., "Teaching About the African Diaspora in Latin America and the Caribbean") discretely and directly reflect a global perspective. But ultimately, every course I teach is infused with who I am, where I come from, and who I've become as a scholar, Cuban American, and human being. I impress on my students that they, too, have a duty to share with *their* students their own journeys.

However, not all courses and classroom experiences were met with universal appreciation by students. Teaching in a diverse metropolitan city in the U.S. South invariably results in varied and divergent life experiences and points of view. One semester, when I taught the "Multicultural and Global Perspectives in Education" course, resulted in such consternation that I doubted my own self-efficacy as an instructor. A student in the class challenged me at every opportunity, on every issue and every topic discussed in class. On the first night of class, we introduced ourselves, with instructions to include aspects of our cultures and life experiences as we felt comfortable. I began by sharing a little about myself, including that I had immigrated to the United States as a child. After a short break, we reassembled to begin the course content. To provide historical background, we began by reviewing landmark legal cases in education; one of them was *Plyler v. Doe* (1982), in which the Supreme Court ruled that children of undocumented immigrants could not be denied enrollment in public schools. The student, visibly angered, blurted that since "illegals" and their children don't pay taxes, they should not be entitled to a free, public school education. I have written (Cruz, 2014) about this incident and how I used the technique of distancing the speaker from the comment and thus diffusing the situation, so I will not elaborate on that strategy here. However, what was apparent by his enraged claim is that he was questioning my very identity, my very education, and perhaps even my right to be at the front of that classroom. I would like to report that by the end of the semester the student had made a miraculous turnaround or, at the very least, had moved a little closer to understanding and appreciating the myriad contributions made by immigrants to our community and society, but he finished the course as embittered and adamant as he began. He was one of a handful of students during my professional life that I was not able to persuade to be more inclusive and accepting.

Fortunately, that experience was an anomaly. Much more common were the many students who embraced a global worldview, and who have contacted me years after our time together on campus with stories and photographs of their classroom adventures. I receive messages about successful cross-cultural simulations, geopolitical role-playing exercises, and high-level discussion on the global economy and human rights. It is satisfying to see how they incorporate and modify lessons learned in my classroom into their own.

RESEARCH AND SCHOLARSHIP

When I entered the professoriate, I intended to exclusively focus on global education in my research and scholarship. It was my goal to further the aims of those who came before me so that global perspectives would be palpable at all levels of education, emphasizing the preparation of social studies educators. For the most part, I have kept true to that original intention, publishing and presenting at the Florida Council for the Social Studies (FCSS), the National Council for the Social Studies (NCSS), and the International Assembly of NCSS. I was grateful when the latter invited me to give the annual Jan L. Tucker Memorial Lecture in 2017, the 20th anniversary of his death.

Although the core of my scholarship continues to center on social studies teacher education, with an emphasis on multicultural and global perspectives, three lines of inquiry have emerged in the past decade that have decidedly branched off from my original intent: socially conscious contemporary art, LGBTQ+ history and issues, and meeting the needs of English language learners (ELLs). I have found a (mostly) receptive audience for each of these in the field of social studies education and a clear need to infuse global perspectives in each.

Socially Conscious Contemporary Art

As the Global Schools Project was ending in 2010, by serendipity I began exploring the use of socially conscious contemporary art in the social studies classroom after a chance encounter with a colleague at our university's art museum. This work led to the creation of a new teacher professional development program, *InsideART* (http://www.usfcam.usf.edu/InsideART; see Figure 7.4). The interdisciplinary initiative brings together social

Figure 7.4 InsideART participants touring the art exhibition, Climate Change, at USF Contemporary Art Museum in Spring 2018.

studies and visual arts teachers to explore critical social issues through contemporary art. Many of the teachers who had participated in the GSP joined the new initiative, applying the global education skills and knowledge they had acquired.

Using art exhibitions from the university's contemporary art museum that change every semester, a team of faculty, graduate students, and staff collaborate to develop curricula, offer workshops, and host special events. Nearly every exhibition has a global connection. Past art shows have reflected global issues such as environmental concerns, human rights, immigration, and political repression. In many ways, this program reflects many of the lessons learned from FIU's GAP (e.g., curricular infusion, treating teachers as professionals, and teachers-teaching-teachers). Working closely with colleagues in art education, and with artists themselves, affords an opportunity to continue to grow, evolve, and explore new approaches to the teaching of global concerns. Our self-study (Cruz et al., 2020) revealed that *InsideART* was not only effective in helping both teachers and their students develop global awareness, but it also contributes to teachers' self-efficacy as educators.

This same line of inquiry resulted in a Fulbright Scholar Award in Alicante, Spain, where I had the good fortune to not only realize cross-national research in social studies education, but also develop relationships with international scholars that have been enormously fruitful and soul satisfying. We have been able to write bilingual (Spanish/English) curricula centering on global women's issues, contribute to a tome on the international preparation of teachers of young adolescents, and present in both the United States and abroad on teaching about gender equality through contemporary art. In the works is a study abroad experience for graduate students I will lead in Spain in the future that will enable educators to experience the curricular infusion of contemporary art into social studies education.

LGBTQ+-Inclusive Social Studies

Although I had always believed in the imperative of a social studies education that reflected the complexity and diversity of the human experience, it was in 2012 when my concern regarding the inclusion of LGBTQ+ history and issues into social studies reached the point that I was spurred to action. That year, the Democratic Party publicly called for support of same-sex marriage, the first major party to do so in the United States. In the November elections, Tammy Baldwin became the first openly gay politician to be elected to the U.S. Senate. As the movement picked up momentum and support, the U.S. Supreme court ruled in *United States v. Windsor* (2013) that legally married same-sex couples are entitled to federal benefits. By 2015, the Court ruled in *Obergefell v. Hodges* that states cannot ban same-sex marriage, opening the door for marriage equality for all.

Prospective and practicing teachers in my courses asked about best practices for teaching about these issues and managing (sometimes hostile) inquiries from parents and members of their communities. I usually steered them to organizations such as GLSEN (Gay, Lesbian, and Straight Education Network) that published helpful educational resources and offered professional development opportunities for educators. But sometimes students pressed me, asking me for materials specific to social studies. So, in collaboration with practicing teachers, I used their secondary social studies classrooms as laboratories to try new approaches to the infusion of LGBTQ+ content. We wrote about some of these efforts (see, e.g., Bailey & Cruz, 2017), eager to share what we had learned with others. The best part is that these same colleagues, many of them former doctoral students, have gone on to carve their own niche in the field (some continue their work in school districts, others have gone on to postsecondary careers, yet others are museum educators), resulting in a growing body of research and curricular contributions.

English Language Learners

It is remarkable that despite having attended universities in South Florida with large immigrant populations from around the world, I never completed a course in meeting the needs of English learners. Although some courses claimed to infuse ESOL methods, I cannot recall a single class that discretely presented a case study, illustrated a theory or approach, or demonstrated a teaching strategy. This lack of knowledge and skill was reflected early in my career. Teaching at a high school near Little Havana in Miami, a number of my students were English learners, with Spanish as their home language. Some had been born in the United States (as most ELLs are), while others were recent immigrants, contending with not just a new language at school, but managing a whole host of difficult situations resulting from being political refugees, or being separated from close family members, or struggling with economic uncertainty. I was able to (mostly) meet the academic needs of this student population because I relied on my native Spanish to help fill in the gaps of my pedagogical training. It was when Thanh, a recent arrival from Vietnam, was transferred into my 10th grade World History that those gaps became glaringly apparent. Together, Thanh and I worked to meet his academic needs (at times he was teaching me much more than I was able to teach him). But this early experience stuck with me and a few years after I entered the professoriate, I embarked on a course of self-study that eventually resulted in a number of publications I never intended to write. Often collaborating with my trusted colleague Stephen Thornton, these works include scholarly tracts, practitioner-oriented pieces, and materials intended for student use (see, e.g., Cruz & Thornton, 2013).

Like my work in LGBTQ+ curriculum, my students often expressed frustration at the general nature of the ESOL materials they encountered. Although my home state of Florida now requires that a general ESOL methods course be completed for teaching certification, many students complain that what they really needed were illustrative teaching materials that would help them teach social studies content to students who might have arrived in the United States last week, last month, or last year. How does a teacher reach and teach this vulnerable population vital social studies content when, in many instances, their English language skills consisted of only rudimentary vocabulary? Or how does a teacher teach students who had left war-torn countries and were worried about family members and friends back home? Or how does a teacher teach students who were not literate in their home language in the first place (including their parents)?

Although I think I had a better understanding on how to teach linguistically diverse students than most teachers given my background, I was still unprepared for the pointed questions posed by my students. Again, working with practicing colleagues who graciously welcomed me into their K–12 classrooms, I began to make sense of the theories, approaches, and strategies advocated by linguistics scholars. I attended national and state conferences of organizations such as Teaching English to Speakers of Other Languages (TESOL), participating in as many sessions as I could, eager to soak up the information and then apply it to our social studies education field. Armed with new understandings and techniques, I revised my teacher education courses and created a new one with my colleague Steve Thornton called "Teaching Social Studies to ELLs," which we co-taught in the Fall of 2013 for the first time in the state of Florida. At times, this work has felt as if my academic journey has come full circle, from kindergartner to ELL to Latina academic.

Food Studies and Foodways

As the years have transpired, I have learned to keep my mind and my heart open to new scholarly experiences and initiatives. A recent example is how my appreciation for international migrations, cultural diffusion, and interconnected histories took yet another unexpected academic turn. In 2020, I began my collaboration with two colleagues with a keen interest in food studies. Like me, they are aficionados of culinary memoirs and the study of foodways. Our co-authored book, *The Cuban Sandwich: A History in Layers* (Huse et al., 2022), was as much fun to research as it has been to discuss at Hispanic Heritage Month events and other venues. Curriculum integration of foodways and food studies into a globalized social studies education will be another project to start soon. The book, an exploration of a culinary tradition that has become global, was published in the fall of 2022. A few months later, we were honored with a Florida Book Award Gold Medal.

REFLECTIONS

It has been nearly 6 decades since I left Cuba. We returned as a family only once to visit, in Spring 1980, soon after U.S. President Jimmy Carter removed travel restrictions to travel to the island. Just a couple of months after our return to Miami, on May 1, 1980, Fidel Castro, facing civil dissent and popular discontent, announced that any Cuban who wanted to leave the island would be permitted to do so, provided they could secure transportation from the port of Mariel. Calling the *Marielitos* (people from Mariel) "undesirables," Castro claimed that Cuba was better off without them. President Carter responded by promising to welcome the Cuban refugees and support them under the Refugee Act of 1980.

Over the course of the next 6 months, about 1,700 boats financed by Cuban exiles arrived at the port of Mariel to pick up relatives. But when the Cuban exiles arrived to retrieve their family members, the Cuban government demanded that they also take back with them other people. Castro took the opportunity to deport what he considered "escoria" (waste or trash): those with a criminal past, mental health issues, members of the LGBTQ+ community, and others deemed on the fringe of Cuban society. Eventually, about 125,000 Cubans left the island in what would come to be known as the Mariel Boatlift. Sometimes treated with suspicion and receiving prejudicial treatment from fellow Cubans in the United States, the vast majority of the *Marielitos* went on to become productive citizens in their new homeland, achieving stability and becoming American citizens (Triay, 2019).

Since our family trip, I have never visited the island again, although my parents have several other times by themselves. Like many Cuban American families, we want to see and help family members still on the island but are conflicted about materially contributing to the authoritarian government that emerged from Castro's revolution. Still, we maintain contact with family in Cuba and continue to embrace and practice many Cuban values and practices in our home. The more than one million Cuban immigrants in the United States have changed the fabric of American society—from politics, to commerce, to entertainment, to sports, and more.

As I bring closure to this book chapter, our nation and world are in the throes of political upheaval and polarization, recovering from a pandemic with global impact, and an economic crisis imperiling families the world over. Now more than ever our schools need to embrace a global perspective, one that reflects cross-cultural understanding and at least a modest comprehension of global dynamics. Although I believe that curricular materials with a global perspective have improved overall in the last few decades, the last few years have also brought about a renewed resistance to progressive education. I am working with colleagues (and fellow immigrants) Jing Williams and Anatoli Rapoport, to update Merryfield and Wilson's (2005) important annual bulletin for the NCSS. Intended as a resource for secondary school social studies teachers, the bulletin will provide practical teaching strategies supported by theories, frameworks, and practical experiences in global social studies education.

Global education must be a priority throughout the K–12 curriculum, as well as at the postsecondary level (such as the Global Citizens Project at USF). My husband, Kevin A. Yelvington, a professor of cultural anthropology, also endeavors to infuse global perspectives into his teaching and scholarship. As an extension of our work, we formed a family that cherishes inclusivity, loves global travel, and shares our curiosity about our world. We are proud of our two daughters (second generation immigrants themselves), Cristina and Amanda, who are also educators in their own right, continuing the global vision.

We can hope that our country will continue to welcome immigrants to our shores, incorporating their stories and experiences into the narrative of American society, and furthering the mission of global education as a unifying force in our schools.

REFERENCES

Bailey, R. W., & Cruz, B. C. (2017). An LGBT-inclusive social studies: Curricular and instructional considerations. *Social Education 81*(5), 296–302. https://eric.ed.gov/?id=EJ1231676

Canton, C. (2012). The "cultural taxation" of faculty of color in the academy. *California Faculty,* 9–10. https://www.calfac.org/wp-content/uploads/2021/07/cultural_taxation_cfmagfall2013.pdf

Cruz, B.C. (1996). *Frida Kahlo: Portrait of a Mexican artist.* Enslow Publishers.

Cruz, B. C. (1997). *Rubén Blades: Salsa singer and social activist.* Enslow Publishers.

Cruz, B. C. (1998a). *José Clemente Orozco: Mexican painter.* Enslow Publishers.

Cruz, B. C. (1998b). *Raúl Juliá: Actor and humanitarian.* Enslow Publishers.

Cruz, B. C. (2005). *César Chávez: A voice for farmworkers.* Enslow Publishers.

Cruz, B. C. (2014). Social studies teacher education: Promoting and developing inclusive perspectives. In B. Cruz, C. R. Ellerbrock, A. Vasquez, & E. Howes (Eds.), *Talking diversity with teachers and teacher educators: Exercises and critical conversations across the curriculum* (pp. 99–114). Teachers College Press.

Cruz, B. C. (2016). *César Chávez: Civil rights activist.* Enslow Publishers.

Cruz, B. C. (2017). *Simón Bolívar: Fighting for Latin American liberation.* Enslow Publishers.

Cruz, B. C., & Bermúdez, P. R. (2009a). The power of one: Continuing the dream. In T. F. Kirkwood-Tucker (Ed), *Visions in global education: The globalization of curriculum and pedagogy in teacher education and schools* (pp. 256–269). Peter Lang.

Cruz, B. C., & Bermúdez, P.R. (2009b). A retrospective on the global awareness program, 1986–2006: Challenges and future directions. In T. F. Kirkwood-Tucker (Ed), *Visions in global education: The globalization of curriculum and pedagogy in teacher education and schools* (pp. 90–115). Peter Lang.

Cruz, B. C., Ellerbrock, C. R., Denney, S. M., & Viera, C. M. (2020). The art of global education: Using contemporary art to develop global perspectives. In J. Myers (Ed.), *Research on Teaching Global Issues* (pp. 93–113). Information Age Publishing.

Cruz, B. C., & Thornton, S. J. (2013). Teaching social studies to English language learners (2nd ed.). Routledge.

Huse, A., Cruz, B. C., & Houck, J. (2022). *The Cuban sandwich: A history in layers.* University Press of Florida.

June, A. W. (2015, November 8). The invisible labor of minority professors. *Chronicle of Higher Education.* https://www.chronicle.com/article/the-invisible-labor-of-minority-professors

Merryfield, M. M. (1991). Preparing American secondary social studies teachers to teach with a global perspective: A status report. *Journal of Teacher Education, 42*(1), 11–20. https://doi.org/10.1177/002248719104200103

Merryfield, M. M., & Wilson, A. (2005). *Social studies and the world: Teaching global perspectives.* National Council for the Social Studies.

Padilla, A. M. (1994). Ethnic minority scholars, research, and mentoring: Current and future issues. *Educational Researcher, 23*(4), 24–27. https://doi.org/10.2307/1176259

Pérez Firmat, G. (1994). *Life on the hyphen: The Cuban American way.* University of Texas Press.

Trejo, J. (2020). The burden of service for faculty of color to achieve diversity and inclusion: The minority tax. *Molecular Biology of the Cell, 31*(25). https://doi.org/10.1091/mbc.E20-08-0567

Triay, V. A. (2019). *The Mariel boatlift: A Cuban American journey.* University of Florida Press.

Tucker, J. L. (1982, June 2–5). *Our global future: Implications for social studies education in the United States* [Paper presentation]. Annual Meeting of the Social Science Education Consortium, East Lansing, MI. https://eric.ed.gov/?id=ED216991

Williams, J., Cruz, B. C., & Rapoport, A. (submitted for publication, 2023). *Teaching with a global perspective: Approaches and strategies for secondary social studies teachers.* National Council for the Social Studies.

SECTION IV

EURASIA

CHAPTER 9

UKRAINE/RUSSIA

TEARING HUMAN MINDS TO PIECES

The Power of Hypocrisy and the Hypocrisy of Power

Anatoli Rapoport

For many years, I have been teaching my social studies methods class at 7:30 in the morning. Readers can only imagine how "excited" my students are about hauling to class, particularly on dark freezing Indiana mornings in January. I, however, discovered a trick that helps me wake them up in the first minutes of our introductory class. When my students hear my accent and ask where I originally come from, my answer is "Indiana"—with a grin, I tell them I came from the country that no longer exists. I immediately see the change: Students' eyes, dreamy and half-closed a second ago, brighten up; they take the challenge. After initial suggestions of Ancient

Rome, Yugoslavia, or Syria comes the correct answer—the Soviet Union. This game is fun but at the very moment when I tell them about the country of my origin, I subconsciously make myself an object of additional scrutiny. I play in my head an imaginary dialogue that my students *might* have with themselves: "Oh, he is an immigrant. What can we learn from an immigrant? Come on, he is a professor, after all, and looks like a cool guy. So what? What does he know about the United States or American education?"

For almost 20 years, I have been teaching in the United States. There were very few days when I didn't question my value as an instructor of future American teachers. Education, as a field of human activity, is deeply rooted in ideological, social, and cultural contexts of the society. As a person who was born, raised, and educated in another country, I ask myself, am I truly valuable to my students who will be teaching their students in *their* environment? My students are future social studies teachers who will be teaching others how to be a good citizen. My socialization and understanding of good citizenship were originally shaped by many ideas and policies that are not only different but are completely opposite to the ideas and policies that my colleagues and I expect future social studies teachers must adhere to.

My Birthplace

> *Odessa is both celebration and lament and equally impressive as both.*
> —Harold Bloom

Every country has a place that is the embodiment of joy, humor, and free spirit: New Orleans in the United States, Rio de Janeiro in Brazil, Gabrovo in Bulgaria. Everyone in the Soviet Union, when they heard the word "Odessa," would grin from ear to ear, imagining warm weather, smooth seas, a lot of funny jokes, and a very specific accent that many unsuccessfully tried to imitate. That was the place where I was born in the time later called the Khrushchev Thaw, exactly 2 weeks and 2 days after the Soviets launched Sputnik. The world panic caused by Sputnik did not bother my family; a much bigger problem worried them, namely, if they could find a *mohel*, an observant Jew who performed...well...an action (ouch!) that would prove to the world that I was a Jewish boy. They found one, trust me. Little did I know how that symbolic and painful act of prescribed Jewishness would affect my life. Even if I had known, I couldn't have done much, as I was only 8 days old.

Odessa in the 1960s resembled one of Jackson Pollock's paintings: a seemingly random mosaic of ethnic, social language, and cultural groups which, if observed from afar, looked like a beautifully arranged chaos. I was born in one of the most notorious suburbs, *Moldavanka*, glorified by many writers as the birthplace of famous bloodthirsty criminals and a cradle of the most heinous crimes. This myth about Moldavanka criminals was gladly supported by all residents, who in real life were very loud, poorly educated, but extremely nice and kind people in the very specific Odessite meaning of nice and kind. Not only was Moldavanka famous or infamous, depending on who you ask for its barely existent mythological criminals, but it was also the world's largest center of what became known as *Odessa dvorik*. (Obviously, one would think, where else can the world center of Odessa dvorik be if not in Odessa? I heard that Tbilisi, Georgia, has something like that, but whether it is true or not, I cannot know, as I've never been to Tbilisi). The Russian dvorik is a small courtyard, but the Odessa dvorik is a separate concept, a phenomenon that could only be found in Odessa: a relatively small space surrounded by two-storied dilapidated houses with terraces filled with anything that did not fit into tiny apartments. And the Odessa dvorik won't be a dvorik if it does not have four most important distinctive features: a hand water pump, countless clothes lines with drying linen, a strong smell of frying fish, and a slovenly dressed woman who scolds and yells at everyone she sees.

TESTING MY SELF-IDENTIFICATION

Although Kazakhstan a glorious country, it have a problem, too: economic, social, and Jew.
—Sacha Baron Cohen

It was in one of these dvoriks where my growing self-identification was first tested. I was 8 years old, when one day I went to a neighboring dvorik to play with my schoolmate. There were six or seven children playing there. I don't remember why one of the children, a boy approximately my age, was upset, but he decided to take his anger out on me: "You kike!" Words have meanings. I heard this word so many times, in the talk of random people, in school, or in jokes among kids, but it was always about someone else, never about me. I don't remember why that happened, but I remember how I felt: scared, disgusted, and humiliated. I knew I was Jewish, but before that day I had not known I was also a kike. Many years and antisemitic abuses later, I tried to explain to myself whether I was really Jewish.

In the Soviet Union, Jewishness was very loosely tied to religion. It was more like ethnicity, something that very few of my American friends and colleagues understand. Secular Jews were more similar to the rule rather than the exception. Unlike my paternal grandparents, my father, mother, and later stepmother belonged to the generation born in the Soviet antireligious time. They were not religious, nor was I. My grandmother and her many siblings spoke Yiddish; my father did, too—in the 1930s. He and his sister attended *die Schule*, a Jewish public school. These schools were all closed in 1939. My dad kept a textbook from the Schule, a thin primer with texts in Yiddish and Hebrew characters and a large portrait of Stalin on the front page. It was annoying to hear my dad, granny, and other relatives talk to each other in a language I didn't understand. Once, when I was 6 years old, I asked my father to teach me Yiddish. His reply was short: "You'll never need it." After the 1953 "Doctors' Plot," the 1967 Six-Day War, and particularly after the 1973 Yom Kippur War between Arab states and Israel, the Jewish/Yiddish culture was almost nonexistent in the Soviet Union. So, was I really a Jew without culture or language? When I turned 16 this question was resolved by the Soviet government which handed me my national ID card (internal passport) that clearly stated in thick black ink: JEW.

Petty, social-trivial antisemitism became particularly unbearable in the early 1970s after the exodus, a mass emigration of Jews to Israel. It was fairly customary to hear people yelling at children or the elderly calling them names and telling them "to go to Israel" which implied, "Know your place, we don't want you here." I and other Jewish children were often bullied in school. Jews who wanted to emigrate were called traitors. Those who wanted to leave had to receive special permission from the authorities, an exit visa. Those people immediately lost their jobs and sometimes had to wait for a long time without any means to support their families before they received official permission. Students were expelled from colleges. The grade of vulgar antisemitism grew higher and higher. All this was happening in my beloved Odessa where Jews, in the late 1960s before the exodus, made up almost 20% of the population. By 2010, this number dropped to less than 1%.

The "Jewish Question" in the Soviet Union

Reality exists in the human mind, and nowhere else.
—George Orwell

But one would never know what was really going on in the country if they read the official newspapers since there were no other newspapers; or watched official television since there was only one official network that broadcast on one channel. According to the media, the multinational population of the Soviet Union successfully continued to build a communist society expressing boundless love to each member of the society and adulation to the leaders of the Communist Party and the government. Soviet Jewry, as asserted by the official propaganda, was an integral part of the Soviet people consisting of a new political and social community whose only goal was to build a brand-new Communist society. There is no antisemitism, there are no persecutions, and there are no violations, preached a famous and very popular Soviet TV analyst who was allowed to travel to the United States and later told Soviet viewers how unjustly the American government treated workers and Black Americans. Another famous and very popular TV analyst pontificated that there is only a small group of irresponsible derelicts who smeared our country and lied about Jewry in the Union of Soviet Socialist Republics (USSR). These statements, of course, were an official lie, easily disproved by hundreds of people who encountered antisemitism and humiliation daily.

Even now, I wonder why the Soviet Government had to sugarcoat the problems that Jews faced at that time. The most reasonable explanation is a desperate desire to demonstrate to the world that everything was well in the USSR and that people were happy to live in a country building a classless homogeneous society. The hypocrisy of official propaganda couldn't help but result in growing duplicity and doublethink among people. Although these were no longer the bloodthirsty years of Stalin terror, many people who had recently lived through the horrors of purges and repressions were very sensitive to the signals from the official propaganda.

The Jews in the Soviet Union who wanted to emigrate had to go through several circles of hell: Not only were they fired from their jobs and positions, ostracized, and called traitors, but they also had to sell almost all their possessions in order to buy tickets to Israel or the United States. One of my many uncles had to sell his apartment in a very prestigious district of Odessa to pay for four plane tickets. The tricky thing was that people could not sell their apartments legally. By law, Soviet citizens rented apartments from the state or municipalities and had to "return them to their legal owner" if they decided to vacate them. People were only allowed to exchange their apartments. The legal loophole was an "exchange" with a surcharge, when a person could receive money for "exchanging" a high-quality apartment for an apartment of a lesser quality or smaller size. For that, one had to get a fake document asserting that their apartment was in much better shape than it really was. Everyone knew about these tricks, including the government, but the government and law enforcement pretended that they knew nothing. I remember how happy my uncle was when he managed to "sell" his apartment and buy one-way tickets to the United States.

Obviously, not all Jews could afford to leave. Some had a fear of the unknown, lacked language skills, had old and sick relatives who had to be taken care of, and had lost hope that something would change. The inability to conform to the growing antisemitism and oppression, on the one hand, and the fear of leaving, on the other, forced many of the remaining Jews to do some sort of mental gymnastics to reconcile reality with television. You can lie to others, but it is difficult to lie to yourself or to the people you love.

I was a witness to many quarrels in my extended family. For example, my dad, who knew perfectly well about the toxic antisemitic environment, was against emigration because he was respected at work.

The number of Jewish families in Odessa decreased significantly. When I was in eighth grade, half of my class of 35–36 students were Jews. By the time I graduated from high school, there were only seven Jews left in my class, and two of whom were waiting for their exit visas. We rarely heard from our friends who had left. People were afraid to admit they had friends or relatives abroad to avoid being treated as "traitors" or lose their job. Still, to maintain contact with those who had left was particularly important for those who planned to leave in the future.

The first Jewish émigrés were trailblazers, pioneers who were supposed to tell those who stayed behind the truth about life in Israel or the United States. There were rumors that the mail was being censored by the Komitet Gosudarstvennoy Bezopasnosti (KGB) and that letters with any positive information about life abroad were destroyed. But it was not easy to outsmart Jews from Odessa. Lyonya Levinson, one of my classmates whose family wanted to leave, told us that his father's brother who had already emigrated promised to send them a coded message about the life of the *olims* (new immigrants) in Israel. If a picture of the family sent to them was with the family sitting down that meant life is bad, don't go. But if the family members were standing it meant everything was alright, and come. Lyonya told us he received a picture in which his uncle's family was standing with hands up in the air. Was Lyonya's story true? I don't know, however, urban legends like this made us feel like conspirators who knew something of which others were unaware.

My schooling was almost over and the time came to decide what I wanted to do after graduation. In the Soviet Union, young people rarely went to college away from where they lived. I wanted to apply to a foreign language program at Odessa State University (OSU). College education in the Soviet Union was free, but placements were limited, creating strong competition for prestigious programs. OSU was a reputable school with good traditions. With my grade point average (GPA) of 4.75 out of 5.0, awards in several academic Olympiads (local and regional competitions in various school disciplines), and 3 years of a specialized advanced program in English, I believed I did have a chance. Or so I thought. I still had a flaw: I was Jewish. For some time, we had heard rumors that colleges and universities intentionally failed Jewish applicants during entrance exams (usually four exams that applicants had to pass to be admitted). One of my aunts, who worked in the admission's office of one of the colleges, saw a directive that set a quota of newly admitted Jewish students at 1% (in a city with a 20% Jewish population). One of my best friends, Peter Gelman, who had a 5.0 GPA and had won numerous Math Olympiads, suspiciously "failed" his entrance exam in mathematics. My concern was that if I am not being admitted to college, I would be drafted to serve in the army for 2 years, an alternative that every reasonable person, regardless of their ethnic origin or social background, tried to avoid. I had to go to college at any cost! The decision was made: My family and I decided that I should apply to the Pedagogical University in Tula, located in a large industrial city in Central Russia, more than a 1,000 kilometers north of Odessa. Why was remote Tula, where I had never been, a more suitable place to apply than my beloved Odessa? First, because Jews made up less than 1% of the half-million residents of Tula and there was less antisemitism. Second, I had relatives in Tula to keep an eye on me.

My Encounter With the KGB

> *Doublethink means the power of holding two contradictory beliefs in one's mind simultaneously and accepting both of them.*
> —George Orwell

Life at the University of Tula was fun. It was a new place with new friends and no parental control. But even here some random people and the government kept reminding me from time to time that I was special. During my freshman year, I rented a room from an old lady in a small wooden house. The house had no natural gas or doors other than the main entrance door. The landlady cooked on a stove with wood and coal and used fabric curtains to separate rooms. She was small and kind and always asked me to lower the volume when I watched television because she believed it saved electricity. All her children lived elsewhere. One day, she brought me happy news: Her son from Vladivostok was coming to visit! Also, he was a KGB officer and he didn't like Jews. Several days later, the following dialogue happened between her son who was visiting and me:

> So, you are renting this room?
> The son who entered my room without knocking (for the lack of the thing to knock on) was in his mid-30s, skinny as a beanpole, and shorter than me (I am 5'9"—or at least I was then).
> Yes.
> I was a normal kid and, as all normal people, scared of the KGB.
> Student?
> His colorless eyes stared at something to the left of me. He was drunk.
> Yes.
> Jew?
> Yes.
> I don't like "kikes."

That was the end of my first KGB interrogation. Yes, the first. What were the odds for an average Soviet citizen like me to meet with KGB officers in their lifetime? Probably 1:1,000. I was "lucky" enough to meet them only twice that year. And the second time, it was not a skinny drunk antisemite but someone more sinister.

It was a warm Tuesday in March in 1975. Our dean's secretary was looking at me with curiosity, stating: "Rapoport, they want to see you in Human Resources." Me? In HR? Why? In my 17 years, I had never been to HR.

When I slowly entered the HR office and gave my name, a woman shouted to another room, "He is here!" Two stocky wrestler-type characters showed up. One of them quietly but very convincingly told me, "Come with us." They took me to a large room across the hallway. When we entered the room, one of them said, "We are from the state security service." (This is exactly what he said: not KGB, but state security service.) "Take a seat." He shut the door with the leg of a chair. I will never forget the next few seconds as I was desperately looking for a chair in a room full of chairs frantically thinking, "Why? Did something happen in Odessa? Did someone snitch that I was telling political jokes? What do they want from me?"

These men were professionals. They immediately proved that they knew everything about me, about my family, my friends, how I spent my days and nights. They knew that my uncle secretly (or so he thought) taught Hebrew to those who planned to emigrate to Israel, what role I was rehearsing for our college theatrical production, and even how much I paid for a pair of jeans (Levi Strauss, three sizes too big, which I bought on the black market for an amount equal to the monthly salary of a highly qualified professional, an object of pride and the envy of my peers). That was their strategy, as if to say: "We know all about you so don't play games with us." And then the agents started asking me questions.

Do you tell political jokes?
Of course not.
Does anybody among your friends mock the government?
No, God forbid.
Who comes to your uncle to learn Hebrew?
I have no idea (which was true).
What did Professor XYZ tell students 2 weeks ago?
I don't remember.

I denied everything or demonstrated a rare-for-my-age case of complete amnesia. They wrapped up our conversation with the following: "We will meet with you next week and you will tell us what your professors talk about. And do not tell anybody about this meeting." They needed a snitch among the students, and I was their choice.

After this meeting I needed to talk to someone badly. Somehow, I never took their warning about disclosing the conversation seriously. The only person I could think of to talk to was my uncle. After my detailed description of the conversation and a panicked question: "What do I do?" he looked at me and said, "You are a big boy now. It's up to you to decide." I was scared and angry. Scared because I had no idea of the consequences, and angry because I was by myself. I had to make a decision that could potentially affect my whole life, and I had to make this decision by myself. I also felt humiliated. Those two stocky guys knew very well how miserable I would feel, how disgusted I would be with myself for agreeing to meet "next week." Suddenly I realized that those middle-aged KGB agents did to me exactly what that young bully had done to me 10 years before in my Odessa dvorik. They treated me like a dirty kike and left chuckling quietly with a sense of superiority.

I have had many tough weeks and months in my life. That week in March of 1975 was one of the most memorable and toughest. I could hardly sleep or study. I tried to avoid my friends to make sure I wouldn't hear or see anything that could compromise them. I rehearsed my imaginary dialogue with the KGB guys hundreds of times, trying to make my voice, looks, and gestures as truthful and convincing as possible. Novelists write about nightmares that people experience before making vital decisions. I didn't have nightmares because I could not sleep. I knew I would deny everything and make up stories about innocent conversations, but I also knew that the upcoming rendezvous wouldn't be the last one. And that was the scariest part as I was thinking: "Okay, I will lie to them, lie, lie, lie, lie. They will eventually understand that I am useless and let me go. They won't arrest or kill me, for God's sake, it's not Stalin time. And what if they do? What if it is Stalin time and I simply didn't pay attention?" The next Tuesday came. Nobody called me. I have never heard from them again.

HYPOCRISY AS MODUS OPERANDI

I don't remember when I realized that life around me was a lie. That is, there were two lives, one at home with family and friends in the dvorik, and the other everywhere else: in school with "free" education when parents had to collect money to fix a leaking ceiling or bribe teachers for a better grade, in hospitals with "free" medical care that could be provided for bribes, in stores with empty shelves although the state media cheerfully reported the unimaginable success of the economy, and in everyday life where you were afraid to utter your Jewish last name for fear of being bullied although you heard and read about friendship of all people in the USSR from television and newspapers.

Everybody knew that outside the sweet and warm world of home and friends, there were lies, a lot of lies. And almost everyone was alright with it. We knew that the government on every level, from the country leadership to the school principal, lied. And the government on every level knew that we knew it. And we knew that the government at every level knew that we knew. And the government knew that we knew that the government knew that we knew that the government at every level lied to us. And almost everybody pretended that this was okay. Perception is reality. Lies became reality. We grew up with this reality. As a child, you simply don't know that there is a lie beyond your small world. Later, you take it as a norm—everyone does it. Then you become a part of it. The power in the USSR in the 1970s and early 1980s was not in the omnipotent and omnipresent KGB or Communist Party bureaucracy, but rather in this perverse social contract of a vicious circle of lies and hypocrisy, a mean-spirited esprit de corps.

The aim of totalitarian education has never been to instill convictions but to destroy the capacity to form convictions.
—Hannah Arendt

I began working in education immediately after a year and a half of mandatory military service. Many technical colleges and universities in the Soviet Union had so-called "military departments." All male students at those colleges had to take mandatory military preparation classes for the duration of their 5-year study. These classes were counted as military service and male graduates of the colleges with military departments were not drafted for 2-year mandatory service in the Soviet Army or 3-year service in the Soviet Navy. Unlike future Soviet engineers, future Soviet teachers were not as fortunate: Pedagogical and liberal arts colleges did not have military departments (although some military preparation classes were mandatory there too, but only for freshmen and sophomores) and their male graduates had to serve in the military for a year and a half.

My career in education was preceded by a remarkable event. My future wife Inna and I met when we were freshmen in college. We married after 4 years of dating and, by the end of my military service, we had been married for almost 3 years. Following tradition, Inna, who is ethnically Russian, changed her very Russian-sounding maiden name to mine and became Inna Rapoport. If only we knew at that time what would follow. While I was in the army, Inna moved to Leningrad (now St. Petersburg) and started looking for a job. She, as well as I, graduated with a degree in foreign language education and she tried to find a position related to translation or education. Wherever she applied, she heard the same response: "Sorry, your husband is Jewish, you have a Jewish last name, we cannot hire you." Her ordeal lasted for almost a year. She lived with her sick grandfather and barely had money for food. I would send her ruble bills in my letters from my monthly allowances of 10 rubles, which was approximately 8–10% of a regular monthly salary. We didn't know what to do. Someone suggested that she change her name back to her maiden name. She did and was able to find a teaching position in a high school. When our daughter and son were born, we decided that they should have Inna's Russian last name. That is why I am the only Rapoport in my family.

After Inna's ordeal, I decided not to tempt fate and went to work in the same Leningrad school where she worked. Luckily, they needed a foreign language teacher. Leningrad, which returned to its original name St. Petersburg in 1991, was the absolute opposite of Odessa. The vast former capital of the Russian Empire was cold, reserved, arrogant, and smug. Have you ever seen snow in summer? I have. It snowed on June 2, 1981, a week after I returned from military service. On the other hand, the city breathed culture. It possessed the best museums, the best theater companies, concerts, and exhibitions, and was truly the cultural capital of the country. We lived in one of the most fascinating parts of the city, Petrogradsky Island, where almost every building looked like an architectural masterpiece and related to a historical event or personality. We technically lived in a museum! But only technically. We actually lived in a 300-square-foot room in a communal apartment. The concept of the communal apartment is usually misinterpreted by non-Russian speakers. A communal apartment was a multiroom apartment shared by several families. Our six-room apartment was shared by six families with one shared kitchen, a shared bathroom, and a shared toilet. Imagine here that there also was an alcoholic neighbor in one of the rooms and, in another, a schizophrenic antisemite who reminded me daily that Jews are evil, and you will have an incomplete but fairly accurate picture of our first abode. In the 1980s, Inna and I were two of 800,000 Leningraders who lived in communal apartments, many of which were in even worse shape than ours. Still, the television kept telling us that all Soviet people, including us, lived happily in the best possible conditions.

Teaching in Leningrad

The beginning of my teaching career at a Leningrad school was full of hope and enthusiasm. Like all young teachers, I envisioned my role in showing my students the importance of knowledge, the wonders of new cultures, and the value of critical thinking. I had reason to think so, for I was now in Leningrad, the city mythologized in history and literature, adored by everyone, particularly those who had never been there. Unofficially, it was called the second capital. I hoped to see highly intelligent and refined students as well as colleagues. Unfortunately, reality proved me wrong. The school was a regular Soviet school with the traditional strengths and vices of regular Soviet education: rigorous academic curriculum, students of different calibers, underpaid and overworked teachers, and a feared empress-like principal. During my almost 20 years in the Soviet Union and later, in Russian schools, I met hundreds of teachers, mostly nice people and hardworking professionals but, as in every society, my school was a Soviet society in miniature, which meant that lies and hypocrisy were a part of school life. Inflated grades, false reports, and insincere declarations of full support of government and Communist Party policies were a daily reality. The English-language reader knows the expression "Potemkin village," which means window-dressing or a fake façade. During Catherine the Great's reign Prince Potemkin set up painted house façades on the banks of the Dnieper River during the empress's voyage to the Crimea to hide the poverty and squalor of local villages. There is evidence that the empress believed what she saw. I am not sure if this expression is fully applicable to the Soviet school system since, unlike Catherine the Great, all levels of the Soviet education hierarchy knew that what they saw was a fake painted Potemkin village façade.

Pokazukha

Since I started teaching you a little Russian (remember dvorik?), another word worth learning is *pokazukha*. This concept refers to window-dressing where both parties know that what they see is not true. Schools had to demonstrate high academic performance no matter how this performance might be achieved. In a 5-point system of assessment (in which 5 is the highest grade and 1 is the lowest) teachers technically could only use grades 2–5 to assess their students. I witnessed several times how teachers under pressure from administration had to draw a hook to turn "1" into "4" in class grade registers. Even giving a student a "2" was a teacher's nightmare. The directive to teachers repeatedly stated at weekly teacher meetings was the following: "If you cannot teach (and that's why your student has a "2"), stay with this student after classes and present to administration a written journal detailing how you worked with your students to improve their grade." Although the latter threat was mostly hypothetical, most teachers did not want to take chances and gave students a "3" instead of "2." Did school districts or provincial education authorities know about this pokazukha? Not only did they know, but they quietly encouraged such skewed performance reports from schools in order not to jeopardize their cushy jobs.

In 2000, I was admitted to a doctoral program at Purdue University in the United States and participated in several international exchange programs since then. In 2005, two education professors from the United States and I visited a school in Northern Russia as part of an exchange project. We were invited to a 10th grade history lesson. My American colleagues were afraid that they wouldn't understand much because of the language barrier. The principal told us not to worry because the lesson would be in English. "Does the history teacher speak English?" "No," the principal said, but explained that the students will be speaking English. And there it was: The teacher read questions from a cheat sheet in very poor English (I suspect that the questions were written in Cyrillic letters) and the students answered with brief, memorized, and clearly rehearsed responses in English. After every response, the teacher, who didn't understand a word in English, nodded, said "Good," and gave each student a "5," which means "excellent" in Russian schools. My American colleagues were shocked by this dog-and-pony show. I was not, for I had seen and participated in many such lessons when I lived in the Soviet Union. These lessons were called "open lessons." Originally, these lessons, to which a teacher invited colleagues and school administrators, were organized for the mere purpose of demonstrating new activities or best practices. Unfortunately, they became pokazukha: Instead of motivating teachers to share their best practices with peers, school administrators simply mandated such open lessons and made them a measure of a teacher's efficacy. As a result, teachers who had been told to conduct open lessons simply rehearsed these lessons with students several times before the required demonstration to the authorities.

The social science textbooks in schools told students about the grand achievements of the Soviet Union and compared them to the misery of the "decaying West." School wall posters depicted glorious accomplishments of local Communist Party leaders while students, who lived in communal apartments with three-four-five families in each, saw daily the long lines in stores for food or imported clothing and heard their parents' complaints about low salaries. If you were asked to make a presentation at a teachers' meeting, or conference, or to write a paper, you had to first thank the head of the Communist Party in the first paragraph and only then proceed to write about the topic of the presentation. The entire education system as well as the whole country lived in Wonderland where all wonders had vanished leaving teachers and students very little choice: either pretend or else... I don't think many people knew what "or else..." meant. Anyway, pretending was easier. Students knew that teachers lied to them, and teachers knew that students knew, and students knew that teachers knew. The same perverse social contract, the same vicious circle of lies and hypocrisy, the same mean-spirited esprit de corps.

MOVING TO THE UNITED STATES

I was admitted to the doctoral program in social studies education at Purdue University in 2000. My interest in citizenship education, particularly its global and comparative aspects, was triggered by an international 6-week professional development program in which I participated in 1999. At that time, despite practical efforts of several liberal scholars and classroom educators, the concept of civic and citizenship education was barely known to many teachers in Russia. My move to the United States was fairly smooth; I did not experience any problems with the U.S. visa or Russian authorities. I received an assistantship (I worked as a research and later teaching assistant) that provided my family and me with minimal financial support. The inevitable culture shock was mitigated by the fact that I had visited the United States twice before starting the graduate program and teaching about the United States in school. Although my transition was probably easier than my colleagues from other countries, there still were several issues that made me go, "Hmmm...." One of such issues was my rationalization of authority in academia. It took me a long time, probably years, to overcome "the fear of authority," a sensation that administrators and other authorities are here to punish you and you should avoid them at any cost. The idea that the purpose of my superiors, the leadership of the department and college, is not to micromanage and punish me for every misstep, but to help me succeed was foreign to me. I remember very well what a colleague of mine once told me: "Anatoli, you are not in the Soviet Union. They [college and department administration] do not tell you what to do. You tell them what you accomplished." In essence, my colleague's phrase summarized my struggle with the remnants of a Soviet mentality. Another issue was...surprise, surprise...my identity. When I was asked who I was and I answered: "I am Jewish," the usual reaction was: "Oh, we do not care about your religion. Who are you ethnically?" My attempts to explain that I am not religious and I consider myself Jewish ethnically were not helpful. When my interlocutor found out that I came from Russia, I was immediately labeled Russian. It took me a couple of years to realize that my efforts to convince people who I think I was, were futile. I eventually gave up. So, I am "Russian" now.

Does My Experience Count?

The above narratives of my chapter are comprised from my acute memories and experiences of my 30+ year life in the former Soviet Union. How useful are they for young Midwestern girls and boys for many of whom the USSR is as ancient as Babylon or William the Conqueror? These inner thoughts and doubts continued to torment me ever since until one day—It was a regular class of my secondary methods course where we talked about multicultural education and whether citizenship education benefits from cultural diversity. "With all due respect, Dr. Rapoport, but don't you find it disingenuous that you, a White male, are teaching us about the importance of diversity and ability to hear the voices of the others?" That was a legitimate question, and my first knee-jerk reaction was to say something about acknowledgement of biases and instructor's neutrality... but I suddenly realized that I am a White middle-aged male, seen by many as a regular American (until I open my mouth and they hear my accent) only here, in the United States. Back in the USSR, I was a living part of a minority, and I know what it means to be bullied and deprived of my voice.

We often talk to students about power. We ask them to read Hannah Arendt, George Orwell, Francis Fukuyama, and Timothy Snyder. We want them to know the origins of power in the hope that they will teach future democratic citizens to resist possible abuses of power. We show movies and talk about dictators and dictatorships. But we rarely hear personal accounts of how power, in Orwell's words, tears the human mind in pieces by forcing people to live simultaneously in two worlds, the world of reality and the made-up world of hypocrisy and lies, flouncing about between these two worlds in the attempt to find some resemblance of balance. Having lived in those two worlds, I feel I can explain to my students and colleagues what it means to live surrounded by official hypocrisy and even participate in it. American society and even more democratic societies are far from perfect. Democratic development is vulnerable as we witnessed in the United States in 2017–2020 and in other European countries. We can only hope that young people can recognize hypocrisy, particularly the hypocrisy from the power and the powerful, and resist it.

At a conference in 2012, I had lunch with a group of colleagues, one of whom was my former compatriot who now works in the United Kingdom. In the middle of a fairly amicable conversation, she turned to me and so that everybody at our table could hear, said: "Anatoli, why do you hate Russian teachers?" Hmmm. To say that I was stunned would be an understatement. Apparently, she read a couple of my articles with the analysis of the patriotic education policies in Russia. My critical analysis had nothing to do with teachers.

Most teachers I had met in schools during my 20-year experience in Soviet and later Russian schools were hardworking professionals who had to do their noble work in a mostly toxic environment of hierarchical bureaucracy and omnipresent pretense. I wrote about the threat of indoctrination masqueraded as a noble cause and draped in patriotic sentiments that now was mandated in all Russian schools. I argued that the then new Russia's official patriotic education campaign aimed at militarization of conciseness, uncritical glorification of questionable historical events, and mobilization of masses against mostly imaginary enemies resembled in style, forms, and content indoctrination campaigns used in the Soviet Union. Teachers, I believe, were mostly victims of that campaign but were unable to voice their concerns. I recalled this strange 2012 lunch when I was writing this text in March 2022 when Putin's army invaded Ukraine, destroying cities and villages, killing civilians, and threatening my beloved Odessa where my terrified family, an elderly sick aunt, her daughter, and my 21-year-old nephew had to hide in a nearby shelter when they heard air raid sirens. At this very time, on the Internet and Twitter, I saw pictures from Russia of the elderly, children, kindergarteners, and their teachers lining up in the form of a Z holding pictures of this new symbol of death and destruction. Why was I not surprised?

REFERENCES

Orwell, G. (1977). *1984*. Signet Classics. (Original work published 1950)

SECTION V

EUROPE

CHAPTER 10

FRANCE

MY DREAM OF BECOMING A CONTEMPORARY CLASSICAL COMPOSER ADVOCATING FOR THE ARMENIAN GENOCIDE

Hayg Boyadjian

I am a contemporary classical composer. I am presently working on my third symphony, *Black Lives Matter* in four movements and will, therefore, compose my personal and professional history in four movement narratives. The first movement narrative addresses my family members who were victims of the Armenian Genocide of 1915, forced on a death march through the desert. My second movement narrative takes place in Paris surviving the German occupation and bombing attacks of World War II with horrifying memories. My third movement narrative speaks to my immigration to Argentina in 1948 where, as a little boy, I sold stockings, sewing needles, and threads at the street market. There, I learned about classical music which was the critical time in my life when I knew that music was my calling. My fourth movement narrative begins with my immigration to the United States and my life-long dream of becoming a composer. My compositions incorporate the global mindedness of music reflected in the inner desires and longings of diverse groups as well as global issues that are permeating the world. My proudest work is *Time of Silence* (Boyadjian, 1986), a 1-hour oratorio on the Armenian Genocide referred to as "Esse Aeternam," accompanied by my poem. My story can only be understood in the context of the Armenian Genocide.

THE ARMENIAN GENOCIDE

The Armenian Genocide was the systematic killing and deportation of Armenians by the Ottoman Empire that began as early as 1894 and reached its peak in 1915. Approximately one and a half million Armenians, half of the Armenian population, were killed in the most barbaric way that the human being can concoct. The dream of the Turkish government had always been to create a geographic and demographic territory that united all Muslim populations of the Caucasus region of Eurasia as represented in the crescent moon of the Turkish flag.

Who Are the Armenians?

To fully understand the magnitude and scale of the Armenian Genocide the reader must know about the history and culture of the Armenian people. Armenians lived in the Caucasus region of Eurasia for some 3,000 years. Their country stretched from the Caspian Sea to the Mediterranean Sea. I possess an original map dated in 1715 drawn by Isaac van der Putte showing the original land of the Armenian people in Asia Minor. At the beginning of the fourth century AD, it became the first nation in the world to make Christianity its official religion. Armenians were a thorn in Turkey's plan for a homogenous country. The Turks destroyed the world-famous centuries-old churches often located in the mountains, almost inaccessible except by long hikes. I have seen some of the ruins when I traveled by train from Yerevan, Armenia to Moscow, Russia. On the border between Armenia and Turkey on the Turkish side, I could see the centuries-old famous city called Ani, the city of a thousand churches. During the 10th century, it was the capital of Armenia. With the genocide, Armenians became foreigners in their own country.

The Roots of Genocide

For a time there existed a Kingdom of Armenia as an independent political entity. During the 15th century, Armenia was absorbed into the Ottoman Empire. The Ottoman rulers, like most of their subjects, were Muslim. They permitted religious minorities some autonomy, but subjected Armenians, who they viewed as "infidels," to unequal and unjust treatment. The Armenian community thrived under Ottoman rule despite possessing few political and legal rights. They tended to be better educated and wealthier than their Turkish neighbors who resented their success. This resentment was compounded by suspicions that the Christian Armenians would be more loyal to Christian governments (Russia) than to the Ottoman caliphate. These suspicions grew more intense as the Ottoman Empire crumbled. At the end of the 19th century, the despotic Turkish Sultan Abdul Hamid II decided to solve the "Armenian question" by means of state-sanctioned pogroms. Between 1894 and 1896, Armenian villages and cities were destroyed and 80,000 Armenians massacred in cold blood. Following international condemnation of Abdul Hamid, the systemic killing began to taper off in 1897.

Young Turks

In 1908, a group of reformers, the *Young Turks*, came to power with what history refers to as a Triumvirate of three brothers: Kemal Pasha, Enver Pasha, and Talaat Pasha. Their objective was to "Turkify" the empire, blaming the non-Muslim population of Turkey for undermining the unification of their Muslim state. Their names are infamously engraved into every Armenian's consciousness for planning and carrying out the Armenian Genocide.

Talaat Pasha was the master mind of the genocide. In Istanbul, on April 24, 1915, he ordered the arrest of all Armenian intellectuals, leaders of the Armenian population, and leaders of the church. They were either crucified or hanged. Armenian men of age were conscripted to work for the state as slaves and, once the work was finished, they had to dig their own graves while being shot or thrown in and buried alive. Once all able-bodied men were exterminated, women and children, and the elderly were driven out of their homes and forced to march in caravans through the Mesopotamian desert without food or water into exile. Frequently, the marchers were stripped naked and forced to walk under the scorching sun until they dropped dead. People who stopped to rest were shot. "Killing squads," or "butcher battalions," carried out "the liquidation of Christian elements." These killing squads were often made up of ex-convicts. They drowned people in rivers, threw them off cliffs, crucified them, or burned them alive. The countryside was littered with Armenian corpses. In the "Turkification" campaign, government squads also kidnapped children, forced them to convert to Islam, and gave them to Turkish families for adoption. They raped women and forced them to join Turkish "harems" or serve as slaves. Muslim families moved into the homes of deported Armenians and seized their property. The Young Turks' goal was to eradicate the Armenian presence in the region and populate it instead with Turkish families.

During World War I (1914–1918) the Turkish government allied with Germany and the Austro-Hungarian Empire while, simultaneously, the Ottoman religious authorities declared a holy war against all Christian Armenians declaring them to be traitors. As the war intensified, Armenians organized volunteer battalions to help the Russian army fight against the Turks in the Caucasus region. This event combined with the Turkish suspicion of the Armenian people and their religion, led the Turkish government to push for the "removal" of the Armenians living on the eastern front. With the collapse of the Ottoman Empire in 1918, Turkey expanded its territory by adding Western Armenia to its country. I recommend two books written about this historic era: the first book, by Armenian American Pulitzer Prize Winner poet Peter Balakian (2009) titled *Black Dog of Faith*, addresses in great detail the history of the Armenian Genocide. The second book, *Ravished Armenia*, by Aurora Mardiganian (2015), describes a young Armenian woman's experiences during the genocide. One needs a strong stomach to read this heart-wrenching book.

Side note: After the defeat of Turkey (and Germany) in World War I, Woodrow Wilson, president of the United States in the Lausanne Treaty of 1920, decided to honor the Armenians for fighting with the Allies and presented them with a map that showed their original country (Figure 10.1). Unfortunately, to pacify the Turkish government, the treaty was rescinded with a new treaty in Sèvres in 1923 canceling the Lausanne Treaty. The "Wilsonian borders," the dream of the Armenian people, became a myth. The Armenians' dream remained a dream.

After the Ottomans surrendered in 1918, the leaders of the Young Turks fled to Germany for safety. Talaat Pasha was assassinated in Berlin in 1921 by the Armenian Soghomon Tehlirian. The German court found him innocent of the crime. Armenian American playwright and actor, Eric Bogosian, wrote *Operation Nemesis* (Bogosian, 2015) about the assassination

Figure 10.1 Map of the original size of Armenia.

and trial. There were about 2 million Armenians living in the Ottoman Empire at the time of the massacre. By the early 1920s, when the massacres and deportations ended, historians estimated that approximately 1.5 million Armenians were killed, with many others forcibly removed from the country—388,000 Armenians remained in Turkey. April 24 is a special day for Armenians around the world commemorating the onslaught of the Armenian Genocide.

Turkey Denies Armenian Genocide

At this point I would like the reader to know about a conversation between Talaat Pasha—the Young Turk who spearheaded the Armenian Genocide—and Henry Morgenthau Sr., the American ambassador to Turkey. Talaat Pasha requested that Morgenthau arrange for American banks to transfer the life insurance money of Armenians to the Turkish government since there were no more Armenians living in Turkey who would be able to claim the insurances (Lang, 1978, p. 289). I ask, is this not sufficient proof alone that the Armenian Genocide took place?

The Turkish government, to this day, has denied that a genocide took place. The Armenians were an enemy force, they argue, and their slaughter was a necessary war measure. On October 29, 2019, the U.S. House of Representatives passed a resolution that recognized the Armenian Genocide. The Senate did the same by unanimous consent on December 12, 2019, which made recognition of the Armenian Genocide part of official U.S. policy. On April 24, 2021, President Biden issued a statement, saying, "The American people honor all those Armenians who perished in the genocide that began 106 years ago today" (Biden, 2021). To date, a total of 33 nations have acknowledged the Armenian Genocide.

MY FATHER ARSEN BOYADJIAN

My father Arsen Boyadjian was born and lived in the village of Gürün surrounded by mountains with altitudes of over 4,000 feet above sea level. His village is in Western Armenia (now central Turkey) between the city of Adana on the Mediterranean Sea and the city of Trabzon on the Black Sea. Some of the mountains have deep caves where people lived for centuries. Near Gürün is the closest city of Kahramannmaras (Marash for Armenians)—85 miles away. My father lived with his mother Mariam, his father Katchadour (Katcho for short), and his grandfather Parsegh. Two of my mother's cousins had emigrated to Paris, France, before the genocide. My father's cousin on his mother's side, Garabed (Charly) Kasparian, had moved to Arlington, Massachusetts, in the United States also before the genocide. He was the person who later sponsored my immigration to the United States.

A curious fact about my father and many Armenians, especially those living in the villages, is that they do not know their exact birthdate as the official municipal birth records were destroyed during the genocide. In those times particularly, village people had no knowledge about birth control which resulted in large families. Individuals like my father had to guess when they were born and adopt a birthdate they could easily remember. My father adopted May 28 as his birthdate since it is the date in 1918 when Armenia became independent for a short time until 1920 when it became part of the Soviet Union. My best guess is that my father was born around 1900 since he was a teenager when the genocide took place. My father spoke of having siblings who had died due to illness. When a child would die, the next child born would be given the same name as the dead child. He mentioned several names of siblings, but I have not been able to find out how many were alive when they were taken on the death marches. Whatever the number, two of his brothers were killed before the rounding-up of women, children, and the elderly.

The Genocide Begins

First, the Turkish soldiers killed all able-bodied men of a village or town. Then they evicted women and children from their homes and forced them through the wilderness to climb mountains and cross rivers, and march through the desert of Deir-ez Zor in today's Syria. The soldiers raped women and girls of all ages, took women hostage for harems, removed children from their mothers to be raised as their own, cut open the bellies of pregnant women, and tore out the unborn bashing their heads on the ground. They cut off women's breasts. To save their children from brutality, mothers threw themselves with their children into the Euphrates River(Morgenthau, 1918/2003). When the caravans moved along the Euphrates in Mesopotamia (Syria) it is said that the river ran red with Armenian blood for years. Tens of thousands of women and children died of hunger or disease during these marches.

The city of Aleppo, Syria, became a central stopping point for the caravans. A map of the region of western Armenia (now central Turkey) clearly shows the many villages that existed in that region—just like my father's Gürün. There were almost no Turkish people living there at the time. The hundreds of villages were like branches of a giant tree with the trunk representing Aleppo, the main stopping point. The final destination of these caravans was Beirut, Lebanon. The distance to Beirut from my father's village is about 450 miles. From Aleppo the Turks did not take a direct route to Beirut but took the caravans on a detour through the Syrian desert Del-El-Zor. To this day there are caves in this desert with human bones of Armenians who have died there.

My Father's Family Evicted

My father clearly remembered how, after his family was evicted from its home, his mother Mariam and two sisters, Nazeli and Serpouhi, were forced to join the caravan. My father's father Parsegh (my grandfather), who was of age, decided to hide in the village. One can only guess his fate. The caravan consisted of 100 to 200 villagers escorted by two gendarmes (police). Often, during the night, a band of armed Kurdish convicts (released from prison by the Turkish government to assist in the roundup and forced marches) would come to steal the food that they had brought along. At gunpoint they demanded money, or you were killed. One time, after robbing the Armenians in my grandmother's group, these released convicts returned the next morning and took their shoes. The two police escorts did nothing to protect them.

The Armenians in my father's caravan had a mule. As he and four of his friends were taking the mule to pasture, they were able to sneak away and go back home to Gürün. They found that everybody had left the village and that Turkish families had moved into their homes and businesses. Starving, my father climbed up a fig tree to reach for some fruit when the branch broke, and he fell onto a concrete wall that surrounded the flat roof of the house. He does not remember how long he was unconscious. A passerby found him and told him that his forehead was badly cut as they could see his skull. They took him to an old medicine woman who applied concoctions, and he slowly healed. Since staying in Gürün did not make sense, he decided he would rejoin his mother and his two sisters on the caravan. On his way a childless Turkish family gave him refuge and treated him like their son. He became a delivery boy and helped them with their chores. He stayed with them for approximately 2 years. My father told me that those 2 years were the best of his life.

Searching for Mother and Sisters

Missing his mother and sisters more and more, my teenage father decided he must find them. One fateful night and without saying good-bye, my father left this kind Turkish family who were like parents to him. Barefoot, hungry, and alone he wandered about in the countryside following the route of the caravans, always being careful as not to be apprehended since this could mean his death. Following the littered tracks, with dead bodies piled up in heaps, somehow he found his way to Beirut. I am certain of the fact that he must have seen some of the atrocities that happened during these death marches. Fortunately, he managed to not be detected by the watchful eyes of gendarmes. I estimate that it took my father about 2 years to reach Beirut.

Finding Mother and Sister Serpouhi

Beirut was the city where all the death march caravans ended their journey. He eventually found his mother and one sister. The Lebanese government had set up refugee camps. In one of the refugee camps, a miracle happened: He saw his mother leaning against a fence. He remembers his mother bending over in agony when she told him that his second sister Nazeli had died along the march in Aintab, Aleppo. Now only his other sister Serpouhi and his mother were alive. But Serpouhi became blind during the excruciating march through the desert and was placed in an institution for blind and deaf refugees in Beirut. My grandmother Mariam never spoke a word about their march through the desert. What the Turks and Kurdish convicts did to her and to her two daughters during the death march from Gürün to Beirut we will never know. But one can only imagine what experiences they might have had, including likely being raped multiple times. Their breasts were still intact. My grandmother's answers were silence.

In their despair, with my grandmother being incapable of making decisions, my teenage father decided, with the help of a nongovernmental organization, to contact his cousin on his grandfather's side of the family in Arlington, Massachusetts, for help. But there were complications regarding immigration to the United States. Although technically they were citizens of Turkey, they did not have a Turkish passport since the Turkish government did not recognize their citizenship.

Invitation to Come to France

Two brothers, second cousins on my grandmother Marian's side of the family, who lived in Paris, France, invited her and my teenager father to come to Paris. They desperately needed a passport. Fortunately, the League of Nations had endorsed the "Nansen" passports, created especially for Armenian refugees, issued by Fridtjof Nansen, a Norwegian humanitarian. These passports were being sold in Beirut but often with names already listed inside. My teenage father, nevertheless, managed to secure a passport which was issued to a person named Alexanian who, according to the passport, was married, had a mother, and a child. I have no idea why the passport was not picked up by the actual family or whether it was stolen. Now my teenage father's main problem was that according to the number of individuals listed in the passport he had to have a wife.

Finding a Wife

Needing a wife, my father went to visit an orphanage. The director paraded a group of young women in front of him from whom he could choose. My father chose a very beautiful girl who did not look like an Armenian woman. Armenian women are known for their beautiful dark eyes, but her eyes were very blue, her skin was of light complexion, and her facial bone structure was typically European. She had no idea where she came from, who her parents were, or how she ended up in Beirut, but she knew her name: Margrite. Members of my family guess that she must have been a few years younger than my father, a very young teenager.

LEAVING FOR FRANCE

Leaving behind my teenage father's blind sister Serpouhi (my aunt) in Beirut, my father, his mother Mariam (my grandmother), and his new wife Margrite (my mother) boarded a ship to Marseille, France, with other Armenian families (Figure 10.2). Upon arrival, the customs officer asked my father about the child that was listed in his passport. Thinking on his feet, he told the customs officer that the child had died during the passage and was buried at sea. I have no idea when they arrived in Paris or how long it took them to get there. But eventually the three of them were able to join my mother's two cousins, Miran and Hratch.

Four Sons are Born in Paris

In Paris my three brothers and I were born to teenage parents: My oldest brother Mourad in 1932, my second oldest brother Katchadour (K) in 1933, I, Hayg, in 1938, and my younger brother Armen in 1944 (see Figure 10.3). We lived in a small house on the outskirts of Paris called Issy-les-Molyneaux on the Isle St. Germain on the Seine River. At first my father worked at the Renault car factory.

Figure 10.2 Survivors of the Armenian Genocide leave Beirut, Lebanon, for France with Grandmother Miriam (front row, first from right) and Wife Margrite (front row, second from right).

Figure 10.3 Me [right] and my second oldest brother Katchadour [left] in Paris in the mid-40s.

My parents were relatively comfortable in their new country despite linguistic issues. But then World War II began, and everything changed. After Hitler invaded Poland in 1939, he occupied parts of France. To save civilian lives, Paris was declared an open city. One of the hardest times of our lives had arrived. It was an especially terrible time for my parents and other Armenians who had survived a genocide and had moved from Lebanon to France. Food became scarce or nonexistent. The French government issued ration cards for small amounts of food, just enough to survive. There was hunger everywhere. Having become resourceful after having survived a genocide, the Armenians managed to somehow do better during the war than the French.

The Renault factory near our house was now under Nazi control producing armaments. I remember my father bringing waxed papers from there, recovering the wax by heating it and making candles. I would go around the neighborhood and sell the candles which were badly needed because the electricity was often shut off. My father had a Moroccan friend who occasionally brought us coffee, tea, sugar, butter, and cigarettes which we would barter. Somehow, we managed to survive during these war years, but the worst was yet to come.

The Allies Landing in Normandy

With the Allies landing on the coast of Normandy and heading towards Paris, the bombing was relentless. When the sirens sounded, we would immediately run to the shelter which consisted of a big hole in the nearby soccer field. Our misfortune was that the Allies decided to bomb the Renault factory and a military base under Nazi control. Some errant bombs fell on residential housing. When we came out from the shelter after the raid, we saw the four-story building across the street had turned into a crater. Residents, who instead of going to the shelter hid in the basement, were buried under the rubble. A second horrifically loud bomb that fell on the biggest building on our island in the Seine River left no survivors. I am sure my hearing loss and tinnitus (ringing in the ears) were a result of this bombing. One day my father and I were standing in front of our porch when suddenly a big piece of a bomb fell right behind us. If we had stood just a little bit closer toward the street, we both would have been killed. We kept that bomb piece as a souvenir.

My father decided to move us to our summer cottage which had a forest in the back of the house only an hour by train away from Paris. He

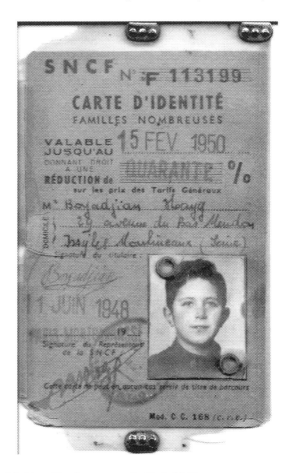

Figure 10.4 My identification papers in Paris 1948.

thought that the bombing would not reach the countryside. Unfortunately, a small airport nearby spoiled his plan. One Sunday, I still remember, when we were eating pea soup for lunch, the siren blasted, and we ran for shelter which was a hole in the ground in the forest behind our cottage. The bombs were falling. As my father and my two older brothers were running toward the hole, with my mother and me closely behind, a tree shattered from the explosions crashed what seemed like inches behind us, almost killing the two of us. My mother was in shock. When we returned from the shelter our neighbor's house had been flattened with nothing left but a crater. Our neighbors and visiting friends were buried in their basement, their remains were never found. With this terrible experience we returned to our little house on Isle St. Germain on the Seine River.

During the war, my mother had been pregnant with my youngest brother Armen. When she was in the hospital, a bombing attack rattled and shook the windows of the hospital just when he was about to be born. We think that the tantrums he developed were a direct result from this experience. To calm him, we would pour cold water on his head whenever he had one of his tantrums. Fortunately, Armen slowly recovered from his ailment when we lived in Argentina.

One of my best memories from the war is that of an American soldier giving me a whole loaf of bread; it was heaven. I will never forget that. I could have devoured it all on my own, but I went home and shared it with my brothers. Very gradually life in Paris returned to normal. During the German occupation, the schools were used by the Nazi army. After liberation the schools reopened, and I attended half a year of elementary school. Finally, the war ended. Having survived these hard times, my father told us that France and Western Europe are places where there would always be wars. Having four sons would mean four soldiers to fight in a war. Argentina became a choice for him, since nobody "makes wars way down in South America."

LEAVING FOR ARGENTINA

My grandmother Mariam had a sister, Alsina, who lived in a suburb of Buenos Aires. She had left Armenia before the genocide. The name Alsina is famous in Argentina because of a tango called *Puente Alsina* (Alsina Bridge) which separates the suburb of Alsina from Buenos Aires, the capital of Argentina. Mariam's sister had two sons and two daughters. One daughter was married to Guiragos who was the main person to arrange for our immigration to Argentina. He had a custom tailor shop.

From Le Havre, France, in November of 1948, with other refugees, our family boarded a ship that took 1 month to reach Buenos Aires (Figure 10.5). Upon their arrival, the customs agent decided that my mother had

Figure 10.5 Back row from left to right: My father with Armen, grandmother Miriam, and mother Margrite; Front row from left to right: Katchadour, me, and Mourad leaving for Argentina, 1948

trachoma and had to remain on the ship. After bribing the officials—a common practice among authorities of all ranks in Argentina—she was released. To begin with, my mother did not have trachoma in the first place.

Our relative Guiragos—who was the son-in-law of my father's cousin's daughter from his mother's side and lived in Alsina, Buenos Aires, Argentina—had written to my father that he would do everything possible to help us. He had rented a very small place for us consisting of one room and a small kitchen with just enough space for the seven of us to sleep on the floor, like sardines. We jokingly called it our "sardine house." Our lives were difficult. Guiragos proposed to my father that he should work for him. Custom tailor stores were common in Buenos Aires because Latin people like to be well dressed. My father's job was to assemble pieces of men's jackets and sew them together. He already had experience in this kind of work working in Paris after he had left working in the Renault factory. My job was to travel by bus and take the finished jackets to Guiragos' shop.

Buying Our First House in Argentina

Our sardine house became too small with the seven of us sleeping on the floor. Working too many hours to make ends meet, we ventured out to buy our first little house. With bad advice from Guiragos, the house became a thorn in our difficult lives in Argentina. It was too small for us. Guiragos told us that we could evict the tenants that lived in the other part of the house and, thus, gain more space for the seven of us. But he did not know the law in Argentina. Once you rent in Argentina, it is very difficult to evict the tenants. Tenants can literally stay forever. We did not have much choice. To improve our living conditions, we built two rooms above the main floor for us four brothers. This decision became a big financial burden which forced all of us to work. A positive outcome of the situation was that our house was on a street corner, and the streetlight gave me sufficient light to read and study during the night since I never needed much sleep. My studying during nights became very useful for my future. Instead of attending the university, I had to work. I worked at a stand in the street market where I sold small household items such as sewing thread, needles, stockings, shoe polish, and other items. My youngest brother Armen, then 6 years of age, had to help me.

Working Different Jobs

In addition to my father working in Guiragos' custom tailor shop, my oldest brother Mourad worked in Krikor's tailor shop. Krikor had lived across the street from us in Paris and had traveled with us from France on the same ship. My second oldest brother Katchadour (we called him K) was working as what in Spanish is called an *aparador*—a person who takes the top part of the shoe, shaves the edges of the parts, and glues and sews them together. The half-finished shoe is then taken to a shop where the soles are attached to the shoe. When K had had enough of Buenos Aires, he left for France. Due to his French citizenship, he was drafted into the French army and sent to Africa where he became a cook for the army. After K left, I took over his job. K's two bosses, who were brothers, were now my bosses.

During the carnival season, like the famous one in Brazil, people dressed in beautiful imaginary costumes and many people wore boots. The boots had to be inexpensive since they only had to last for 2 days and, very importantly, the boots had to be ready on time. For many years I had to work nights without sleeping. One year, I will never forget, I did not sleep for 5 nights. In my young life, I generally worked an average of 16 hours a day, 6 days a week, all this at the age of 11.

In the meantime, my older brother Mourad worked in the custom tailor shop of Krikor who loved to listen to classical music on the radio. Exposed to classical music, my brother decided to buy the best radio there was to get, a German Grundig. When he would turn on the radio, out came this fascinating music. I wish I could remember the piece I heard, but I know that I realized immediately that it was my calling to compose classical music, become a composer, and make it happen despite any difficulties.

Unfortunately, years later, Mourad developed tuberculosis and was sent to a sanatorium in the province of Entre Rios. I do not remember how many years he stayed there. His doctor told him that the climate of Buenos Aires was very bad for his condition. As a result, Mourad moved to the south of Argentina to Tierra del Fuego, literally across from the Falkland Islands (Las Malvinas). He stayed there all his life until his death 2 years ago from COVID-19 in 2021. My younger brother Armen's tantrums gradually became less and less as time went on. He eventually moved to Caracas, Venezuela, where he became a well-known theater director.

My Education

In France, I had half a year of elementary school since schools did not operate during the war. Now in Argentina, I was required to attend elementary school. The school did not know in which class to place me because according to the teacher, I was "overeducated" for the Argentinian school system. Thus, I was placed in the highest grade of elementary school which was still too easy for me. Throughout my life I have always educated myself. But in Argentina, where I wanted to continue my education to higher levels, my family's financial situation did not allow it. I had to work. Mostly, I wanted to study music. There was a small inexpensive Conservatory of Music in Alsina in the suburbs of Buenos Aires where I was able to take piano lessons and study music theory and counterpoint with the well-known pianist Beatriz Balzi. She was a concert pianist specializing in contemporary music. She mostly performed works by Latin American composers. Later, when I left for the United States, she moved to Sao Paulo, Brazil, where she had a successful career. Ms. Balzi often performed my works, including my second piano sonata, which I dedicated to her.

Debating to Leave Argentina

Having experienced my two older brothers leaving Buenos Aires, I was thinking about leaving, too. Two things preoccupied me for a long time while living there. First, the weather. The humidity in Buenos Aires was literally 100% all year long, with very hot summers and winters not cold enough. The second aspect I disliked about Buenos Aires were these colorful bugs flying all around you that you could not escape. Moreover, my parents never knew that, in 1955, I was on the Plaza de Mayo in Buenos Aires where military planes carried out their attacks during the uprising against Peron. I almost lost my life when running for cover.

Figure 10.6 Back row from left to right: my father, my mother, my father's cousin Hratch; Seated: my father's cousin Miran and my grandmother in Argentina.

I did not want to go to France because of my French citizenship, like my brother K, I would be conscripted. I was thinking about going to Canada instead. For quite some time, I had been considering telling my parents about wanting to leave. Maybe my father read my mind because he had already written to my uncle Charley who lived in Arlington, Massachusetts, about my intention. Charley gladly invited me and sent money for my airfare. Unfortunately, I had to wait for 2 more years due to quota restrictions for immigrants.

My Father's Unsuccessful Investment

Having to wait for 2 years to immigrate to the United States, my father and I decided to invest the airfare money. It was a bad idea. We were too innocent about scams. We went to an office in Buenos Aires that had advertised an opportunity to invest in a restaurant. The problem was that the restaurant had perhaps 12 different owners/partners of which we were not aware. Four of us kept the restaurant running by showing up daily from morning until night because in Argentina anyone could enter a restaurant, take it over, and claim it to be his. Again, a strange Argentinian law. I kept a gun on my lap for protection.

Unfortunately, one of our partners in the restaurant who came from the Canary Islands of Spain tricked us by selling the restaurant behind our backs. I never found out how he did it. I became so very angry at him that he had betrayed us—especially because we were close friends and once when he was very sick with a bad flu, I nursed him and even gave him injections. Because of his betrayal, I decided to kill him. We found out that he was planning to go back to the Canary Islands. I decided to observe his house from a close distance in which he, his wife, and two children were living. Someone must have noticed my presence and called the police. I had no identification on me and ended up being arrested and put in jail: a tiny room, a container for body relief, and a concrete floor to sleep on. I don't remember how long I was kept in jail. I can only remember that the wife of one of the inmates brought a cake which he shared with me because it was Christmas. Eventually, I was released. When my business partners rumored that he was about to leave for the Canary Islands, I went to the dock with the gun in my pocket, still ready to kill him. Fortunately for him and me, he did not show up when his wife and kids were boarding the ship. Maybe he suspected something. He saved me from being a murderer.

IMMIGRATING TO THE UNITED STATES

While waiting for my immigration visa I worked hard and saved. Finally, after exactly 10 years in Buenos Aires, from my arrival in November 1948 until my departure in November 1958, I took a plane to the United States. Leaving my parents was one of the most difficult moments of my life. The plane first stopped in Lima, Peru, and then in Havana, Cuba, where a revolution, led by Fidel Castro, was about to overthrow the Batista government. I was immediately put on a plane to Miami, being its only passenger.

In Miami I had my first American experience. I saw the word "sandwich" and, not being able to communicate in English, I pointed to the "sandwich deluxe." And there arrived on my table a sandwich that seemed two stories high. I sat there trying to figure out how to eat a sandwich of that size. I then continued my trip to Boston, Massachusetts, where Uncle Charley was waiting for me on a cold, snowy November day. After 10 years of heat in Buenos Aires, I welcomed the cold air that embraced me. I gratefully settled down in my uncle's beautiful house on Mystic Avenue in Arlington. It was very difficult for me to leave my parents alone in Buenos Aires. My departure was especially heart-wrenching for my mother as I was her favorite son, although she had hoped that I had been a girl.

Learning English and Meeting Brigitte

Speaking three languages fluently did not help me to learn English. I enrolled in a class for English for foreigners at the local Arlington High School. At an evening gathering of non-English speaking students, I met my future wife, Brigitte Kuelzer. We had problems communicating with each other because she spoke German and I spoke Armenian, French, and Spanish. We discovered that both of us knew sufficient Italian and so Italian became our language of communication.

In Arlington, I first worked in a shoe factory during the day doing the same work as I did in Argentina, and in the evenings, I worked in restaurants, first as a busboy and later as a waiter. While Brigitte took a trip to California to visit her aunt, I applied for a high school equivalency diploma. I also bought a grand piano. After the High School Equivalency Test, the teacher told me that she was impressed with my proficiency in English, but I needed to have more knowledge in algebra and American history. As a result, I took some extension courses at the Massachusetts Institute of Technology (MIT) in Cambridge, passed my High School Equivalency Test, and earned my high school diploma in 1960. Having obtained my high school diploma, I applied at Northeastern University where I earned a bachelor's degree in economics. For a time, I was also a special student of music at the New England Conservatory in Boston. One of my teachers suggested that I should become a piano tuner instead of working in restaurants. Following this advice, I attended a technical trade school in New York for over a year to accomplish this goal. Piano tuning came very naturally to me as I loved the instrument.

My Wife Brigitte

After Brigitte returned from a trip to California, she was delighted to hear that I had bought a grand piano and asked if she could practice on my piano. We realized that we had a common interest in music, and music became our common language. Her father was a concert pianist, and I was very impressed by his performances. Brigitte had arrived in Arlington the same month as I did. She was hired as an au pair for the son of a well-known art restorer, Christa Gaehde, who specialized in the restoration of works of art on paper. Interested in art, Brigitte became her first apprentice. The family did not live far from my uncle's house, and Brigitte and I saw each other often and played the piano. We fell in love and decided to marry in 1961. Christa Gaehde's husband Joachim Gaehde, a renowned professor of art history at Brandeis University in Waltham, Massachusetts, had an excellent school of music specializing in music composition for aspiring composers. Thanks to Professor Gaehde, I was accepted into the school of music.

My goal in life was to become a contemporary classical composer. Before this dream could be realized, I had to work as a piano tuner and waiter. At this time the Vietnam War had broken out. In Boston, people, especially young students, organized peaceful demonstrations against the war. I joined the anti-war movement. When we found out that the authorities were bringing buses into the city to pick up draftees, we decided to block the doors of the buses. Once, when I blocked a door, two men grabbed me and pulled me forcefully back. They wore black raincoats, sunglasses, black hats, and had gloomy dispositions, perfectly fitting the profile of FBI or CIA agents. Being a French citizen, I expected the worst: being jailed or deported. Fortunately, Brigitte, in an advanced state of pregnancy, pushed herself through the crowds and talked to them—and they let me go. Our daughter Iskuhi was born on July 13, 1964.

BECOMING A CONTEMPORARY CLASSICAL COMPOSER

I had the great fortune of having excellent teachers from whom I learned the critical tools for composing music. My career started in the 1970s after I left Brandeis University and after Brigitte encouraged me to start composing. Her work in art restoration was lucrative and we could now afford to realize my dream. I first concentrated on composing chamber works, designed to be performed by 1 to 10 musicians. Concertos, sonatas, oratorios, choral music, and symphonies followed in quick order. I have gradually developed my own musical language and style. My work is unlike that of any other composer. I use aspects of my diverse heritage to guide my musical forms and compositions. My compositional style is unique. Over time, my 150 plus compositions have been performed in renowned music halls in Armenia, Argentina, Germany, Poland, Ukraine, United States, South Korea, and the Soviet Union. I am particularly proud that the world-renowned Boston Symphony Orchestra has taken an interest in my work. One of the biggest moments in my life as a composer arrived in 1980 when I was invited to Yerevan, the capital of Armenia, by renowned Armenian musicologist Cicilia Proudian where several of my compositions were performed in a solo concert. Since that first concert, I have returned to Yerevan every 2 years or so for solo or joint concerts. All my symphonic works, including my piano concerto and, more recently, my violoncello concerto, have been performed in Armenia.

So far, I have composed three symphonies. My first symphony for orchestra, *Of Life and Death: Genocide* (Boyadjian, 1990), was premiered in Lviv, Ukraine, in 1996, and again performed in Yerevan, Armenia. My heart goes out to the Ukrainian people who were invaded by the Russian Federation on February 24, 2022. It is strange, as if I had envisioned it, that they now experience the horror of genocide in real life. I specifically composed my second symphony, *Oratorio "Time of Silence"* (see Figure 10.7), to present genocide as a human tragedy that has occurred around the world. It is written for orchestra, choir, solo soprano, and speaker, and was premiered on April 21, 1986, in the prestigious Sanders Theatre at Harvard University,

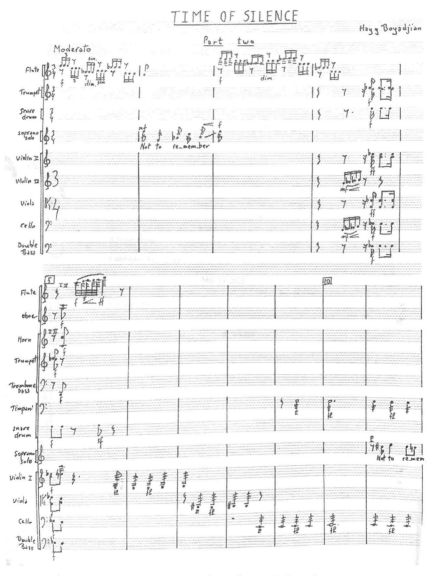

Figure 10.7 Score sheet of "Time of Silence." *Note:* Before the computer was developed, all scores were written by hand. Now I use the software Sibelius, one of most important software applications for composing music.

Cambridge, Massachusetts. The main text of the oratorio comes from my poem *Genocide* (unpublished), whose last line, "Time of Silence," is its title. The oratorio reflects my deep feelings about genocides, but particularly about the Armenian Genocide of which I am a survivor thanks to my teenage father. The poem is placed at the end of my chapter. My third symphony, *Black Lives Matter* (unpublished), is in four movements. Each movement reflects the suffering of Black people and includes a funeral march and a last movement of apotheosis.

The following seven compositions have been recorded on CDs:

- *Vientos*—a solo recording of my chamber works consisting of "Cassiopeia," "Mi Tango," "Perseus," "De Profundis," "Menschheit" (humankind), "Der Tod des Dichters" (death of a poet), and "Pleiades"; recorded by Albany Records.
- *Places Not Remote*—"Odessa," "Clown Bearlee," and "Vignettes"; recorded by Living Artists Recordings.
- *Visions, Dreams, and Memories*—"Sevan" (Native flute, American flute, string orchestra, and timpani); recorded by Opus One.
- *Hayg Boyadjian et al.*—"Scorpius Rising" (orchestral piece); recorded by Opus One.
- *Hayg Boyadjian et al.*—"Armenian Suite" (orchestral piece); recorded by Opus One.
- *Final Bell*—"Sonata No. 3" (performed by pianist Max Lifchitz); recorded by North-South Consonance Records. My Sonata No. 3 was nominated for a Grammy Award in 1960.
- *Variations on a Theme by Bach* for piano performed by Armenian virtuoso pianist Armen-Levon Manaseryan (September, 2022). This concert was performed at the famous Steinway Hall in Frankfurt, Germany, sponsored by the Harvard Club of Germany in April 2022; recorded by Naxos Recordings (2022). Musicologists are agreed in general that the variation form is the most difficult form of musical composition.

Themes Flowing Through My Music

My narrative essentially reveals my extensive struggles in life starting with my family, genocide, war, and my own brushes with death. I suppose I was destined to write music, paint, and write poetry, and death had to wait. However, what has touched me the most in my life and has left in me an empty space is my mother Margrite's suffering. I think she never really discovered who she was and why she had to suffer so much. My father had to guess her age when he met her in the orphanage since she neither knew her age nor her parents' names or whereabouts. As if being an orphan, having no idea about her background, being selected by a teenage boy as his wife, emigrating to France and then to Argentina was not enough. On top of that, her mother-in-law Mariam (my grandmother) disliked her because, in essence, she took her only son away from her when she became my father's wife. She suffered through those long years in silence. Fortunately, one of our neighbors in Argentina, who lived next door to our sardine house and who was like a second mother to us four brothers, became her confidante. Her name was *Lousaper* which, appropriately, means "bring me light" in the Armenian language.

During my mother's long silence, she once did break down and told of an experience during the genocide that I can never forget for its brutality. I heard her describe a scene that other survivors of the genocide have corroborated. During her march through the desert without shoes, the Turks forced the Armenians to dig rows of holes in the ground the size of a person up to their shoulders, so their head would stick above the ground. Then the Turkish soldiers mounted their horses and galloped up and down the rows over the people's heads while still alive. Fortunately, my dear mother, in her late years, also experienced a happy time when she was able to visit Paris again, the city she loved. She admitted that she did not want to leave France in the first place, secretly wishing that the ship taking her and our family from France to Argentina would turn around. Her hope was realized 30 years later. Returning from France, my parents came to visit us in Arlington, Massachusetts (Figure 10.8).

Figure 10.8 Parents return from Paris, visiting me in Lexington, Massachusetts.

I Honor My Wife

My wife Brigitte deserves deep acknowledgement from me. First, I honor her for reviewing my oral history narrative and making suggestions. Second, I honor her for her contributions to the success of my career as a composer; and third I honor her for her critical comments throughout the years from a listener's point of view. She has been my mentor and my supporter, and she believes in me as a composer. Without her, I would not have been as successful as I am today. Her own achievements also deserve acknowledgment. In the 50 years of her professional work in the field of art restoration she has specialized in the restoration of works of art on paper. She has developed a reputation for excellent work. She also deserves acknowledgement for her talents in playing the piano. She has performed publicly in student recitals and given solo performances of classic composers such as Bach, Beethoven, Brahms, and others as well as of modern composers such as Bela Bartok, Schoenberg, and of the compositions I dedicated to her. She performs by memory as her outstanding teacher Daryll Rosenberg demands of all his students. I thank Brigitte for being my wife and my partner.

THE GLOBALITY OF MY WORK

Several of my symphonic compositions speak to the horrors of genocides perpetrated against innocent people of different nationalities, as we witness today in Ukraine where the Russians, under Putin's order, are mercilessly killing innocent civilians. I want to reiterate here that it is crucial to understand the uniqueness of the Armenian genocide, the first genocide of the 20th century, when Talaat Pasha admitted to the American ambassador, Henry Morgenthau, that all Armenian men were dead. The surviving Armenian women, children, and elderly were sent on death marches to Beirut from where they were dispersed to countries around the globe. Thus, the Armenian diaspora consisted almost only of women and children, accompanied by a few men, miraculously including my teenage father, who managed to survive the genocide. This clearly is conclusive proof of the Armenian Genocide which Turkey cannot deny and still does to this day.

REFLECTIONS

I have learned much about my family's suffering in the Armenian Genocide later in my life. Throughout my entire life, neither my father, my mother, nor grandmother broke the silence—except once. My mother broke her silence once in Argentina with her neighbor which I overheard when she described how her people were forced to stand in dugout holes up to their shoulders with their heads sticking out of the hole, with Turks on horses galloping over their heads. My father broke the silence—slowly and painfully on his last visit to us in Lexington after he and my mother joyfully returned from Paris.

Recounting his vivid memories, he slowly and painfully began to tell his story: his mother and sisters being evicted from their house, all able men shot on the spot before their eyes, women and children forced through the desert, being separated from his mother and sister, one sister who died, the other blinded from the death march, finding a wife required in his passport, emigrating to France, and later, Argentina. Suddenly, in the middle of a sentence, my father stopped and said, "I can't talk about this..." These hours were some of the most earth-shattering and heart-breaking times in my life. Thanks to my own research, an occasional visit from a survivor, and the golden opportunity of my father's interview when he and his wife Margrite visited us in Lexington, I have gathered sufficient knowledge and courage to have composed this agonizing chapter.

My father, Arsen, passed away in 1986, 6 years after my mother's death. My father's mother, Mariam (my grandmother), died after I left Argentina; and so did my three brothers: Mourad in 2021, Katchadour (K) I am not sure of the date; and my youngest brother Armen in 2012. At the ripe age of 84, I am the only survivor of the Boyadjian family from ancestral Armenia. Music saved me.

Figure 10.9 My brothers and me in Buenos Aires.

Time of Silence (Boyadjian, 1986)
Salvame—Save me

Genocide
Empty Cribs
Mothers raped
Fathers butchered
Tears empty
No recognition
No yesterday

Genocide
Seeds blown by wind
Demands unretributed
Questions unanswered
Faces dying
Remembrances marred

Genocide
A generation asking
Waiting despairing
Murder crime
Accuser accusing
Innocents dying
Lies upon lies
Breathing lies
Only lies

Genocide
Undreamed dreams
Forgotten paths
Dust covered
Unborn infants
Hidden from light
In silence buried
Forever lost

Genocide
Distant land
Memories past
Minds of ruins
Stones demolished
Masquerade of history
Footnotes erased
Stories untold

Genocide
Not to remember
Corpes upon corpes
Rotten flesh
The dying undead
Smiles of murderers
Neighbors and friends
Love and hate
Knife and blood
Spurring rivers
Red of sunset
Carnage unseen

Genocide
Tears of lovers
Of lost mothers
Desert sands
On severed hands
Fearful sight
Enemies might

Genocide
Strewn dismembered bodies
Unstaining stench
Swords slashing
Scorpions biting
Daggers unleashed
Raven's final feast

Genocide
Walk stumble
Bleeding shapes
Trailing blood
Soaking earth
Essential life

Genocide
Snow cover
All remnants
Unseen unheard
Fragile memory
Time of silence.

ADDITIONAL RESOURCES

Boyadjian, H. (n.d.). *Hayg Boyadjian: Composer.* https://www.haygboyadjian.com/
History.com.editors. (2021, April 26). *Armenian Genocide.* https://www.history.com/topics/world-war-i/armenian-genocide
National Alliance on Mental Illness. (n.d.). *Mental health conditions.* https://www.nami.org/Learn-More/Mental-Health-Conditions
YouTube. (n.d). *Hayg Boyadjian.* https://www.youtube.com

REFERENCES

Balakian, P. (2009). *Black dog of fate: A memoir.* Basic Books.
Biden, J. (2021, April 24). *Statement by President Joe Biden on Armenian Remembrance Day.* https://www.whitehouse.gov/briefing-room/statements-releases/2021/04/24/statement-by-president-joe-biden-on-armenian-remembrance-day/
Bogosian, E. (2015). *Operation nemesis: The assassination plot that avenged the Armenian genocide.* Little Brown & Co.
Boyadjian, H. (1986). *Time of silence.*
Boyadjian, H. (1990). Symphony 1. Of life and death: Genocide. https://www.youtube.com/watch?v=x3Gs8HMaK5o
Lang, D. M. (1978). *Armenia: Cradle of civilization.* Allen & Unwin.
Mardiganian, A. (2015). *Ravished Armenia: The story of Aurora Mardiganian, the Christian girl who survived the great massacres.* Ararat.
Morgenthau, H. (1918/2003). *Ambassador Morgenthau's story.* Doubleday, Page & Co.

CHAPTER 11

GERMANY

NAZISM. BORDERCROSSING. RACISM. ALL LIVES ARE OF EQUAL WORTH

Toni Fuss Kirkwood-Tucker

This oral history narrative tells of my life as a young German girl growing up during the Nazi regime and the end of World War II. It recounts my childhood experiences and the stories my father shared with me, his oldest daughter, about the horrors of the Nazi regime and Nazi genocide of tens of millions. I describe the suffering of ordinary people in my village, the death of soldiers at an early age, and the sabotage activities of my dissident father. I recall how we, children-of-war, stood watching the liberation of our village by American forces, fascinated by U.S. tanks rolling down our village streets and the Black and White soldiers throwing us food we had never seen before—like Hershey bars, oranges, and bananas. I describe my immigration to the Deep South of the United States at age 22, and my introduction to the suffering of African Americans and systemic racism in a country to which most of the world's refugees want to migrate. I explain how I began to develop my philosophy of global pedagogy in teaching about the integration of global awareness in the secondary social studies curricula in public schools and in teacher education programs. I share the power of my extensive storied historical narrative with you which comprises one of the richest pedagogical strategies for classroom use (Connelly & Clandinin, 2006).

My Birthplace

I was born in the beautiful farming village of Unterammergau located in the foothills of the Bavarian Alps in Bavaria, the most southern state of Germany only 10 kilometers from the Austrian border (Figure 11.1). The name of our village derives from its location on the Ammer River which flows along the edge of our *Dorf* (village). The name Unterammergau derives from *unter* (below), Ammer (the name of the river), and *gau* (place). With only 1,500 inhabitants the mayor, priest, and teachers were the prominent individuals in the village and were deeply respected by the populace the majority of whom were farmers. Like many inhabitants in the State of Bavaria, the villagers were devout Catholics and very religious.

Growing up during World War II, I was cruelly exposed to notices from the *Wehrmacht* (German Armed Forces) that arrived in our village, telling

Figure 11.1 Author's birthplace of Unterammergau.

of husbands, sons, brothers, uncles, and cousins being wounded, killed, missing in action, or taken as prisoners of war. Forty-one soldiers from Unterammergau were killed, 21 went missing in action, and many more were wounded. Today, a marble memorial in front of our St. Nikolaus Catholic Church is engraved with the name, birth date, and location of death of each fallen soldier. Most died in Russia, others in Poland and France. None of the missing soldiers returned after the war, bringing the death toll of the fallen from our village to 62 soldiers during World War II.

GROWING UP DURING THE NAZI REGIME

My Parents

I have many profound recollections of my mother and father during the Nazi era and the end of World War II (see Figure 11.2). One stark memory I clearly recall was the birth of my younger brother Hartl. In January 1944, as he was soon to be born, I asked my moaning mother why she had not called for Dr. Kohlmeier to come to our home to deliver the baby as he did for my sister and me. My father heard my question and yelled at Mama in the vernacular, "Tell your daughter the truth about why Dr. Kohlmeier is not here to deliver the baby! Dr. Kohlmeier," he yelled, "is a Jew who was arrested, and who is likely

Figure 11.2 Wedding of author's parents, 1936.

in Dachau with his family and other Jews…where they are being murdered in cold blood." Dachau was located near Munich, only 90 kilometers north from our village, and it was among the first concentration camps constructed by the Nazi regime. As my Mama moaned, I begged my father to tell me more about Dachau. He ranted on for what seemed like hours, telling his 7-year-old, first-born daughter about the horrors taking place in concentration camps in Germany and Poland. At that age I could not fully comprehend the concept of concentration camps, but my Papa would never lie to me, I was sure of that.

Intellectually curious, I had a thousand questions to ask him when he came home from Munich. He would take me aside, away from my mother and sister, and describe the Nazi's brutalities against forced laborers, prisoners-of-war, resistance fighters, Jews, Romas and Sintis, homosexuals, Jehovah's Witnesses, and the physically and mentally handicapped. As I reflect on it today, I wonder in horror if my mentally challenged daughter Andrée would have been forcefully euthanized under Nazi rule?

Besides Dr. Kohlmeier and his family, only one other Jewish person lived in our surrounding communities, Herr Foster. With his cart drawn by two tired old horses, he came regularly to our village, ringing his bell and announcing fresh vegetables for sale. After allegiance to Hitler became absolute throughout all of Germany, Herr Foster did not return to our village. So, when Mama complained about the shortage of fresh vegetables, Papa yelled at her, "Don't you know by now where he is? Tell me! Herr Foster was dragged to Dachau just like Dr. Kohlmeier."

Papa

Why had my father been stationed in Munich and not sent to fight on the Eastern or Western front? Papa was injured in the war and consequently assigned the the *Messerschmittwerke* in Munich. He was expected to apply his engineering skills to the smooth operation of large machinery that assembled airplane parts into fighter planes. While working in Munich towards the end of the war when non-relenting bombing destroyed the city to rubble, Papa had to endure mind boggling nightmares—events that he repeatedly dreamed about. One event was the day he and other factory workers were ordered to gather in wheelbarrows the body parts of children that had been thrown into the shattered Munich streets after a nearby orphanage was bombed during an Allied attack. I believe that the cruelty of this bombing may have been a deliberate attempt by the Allies to demoralize German civilians, actions analogous to the Russian bombing of Ukrainian civilians happening right now since Russia's invasion on February 24, 2022.

The second event my Papa had nightmares about was the suicide of his Munich landlord and wife in whose home he had rented a room. The landlord worked as the overseer of the notorious Stadelheim Prison in Munich, a facility where the Nazis confined and tortured German dissidents working against the Reich who had been uncovered by the *Sicherheitsdienst* (secret police). One nightmarish day, Papa's host was ordered to supervise the decapitation of the Scholl siblings, a young brother and sister studying at the University of Munich who led a student resistance group against the Nazis called *Die Weisse Rose* (The White Rose). When Papa came home that night to his rented room, he found the overseer and his wife dead from suicide.

Die *Weisse Rose* Intellectual Resistance Group

Die *Weisse Rose* was an intellectual resistance group founded by three medical students at the University of Munich, Hans Scholl, Willi Graf, and Alexander Schmorel. Under the leadership of Kurt Huber, professor of psychology and musicology, the three students, with others took action to resist the Third Reich. While serving as medics on the Eastern front, the three medical students had witnessed mass killings of Eastern European Jews by Hitler's security, surveillance, and terror organization, the *Schutzstaffel* (SS). Upon their return to the university, under the leadership of their professor, the three joined with other students, including Hans's sister Sophie, to compose and distribute an entire series of leaflets they had started to produce as early as 1942. The pamphlets, later called "Leaflets of the Resistance," blended youthful idealism with an impressive knowledge of German literature and Christian religious teachings. In addition to their widespread distribution throughout Munich, the students traveled by train to various German cities to surreptitiously distribute them. Four days after distributing the sixth edition of their fliers, on February 22nd, 1943, siblings Sophie and Hans Scholl and Christoph Probst were executed by the Nazi regime. (This is the very event when Papa's landlord, who had to supervise the beheading, committed suicide with his wife.) Other group members followed. According to historians, at least 14 of the 30 to 35 group members were executed by guillotine. The resistance and decapitation of Hans and Sophie Scholl is documented in the 1982 West German film, *Die Weisse Rose*.

Mama

Mama was the fourth child in a farmer's family of nine children. At birth, the toes of her feet were webbed, a disability that required many trips to a specialist in Munich, 90 kilometers away from her home, putting an enormous burden on her family. Mama's parents placed her with her much older paternal grandparents, who had the time and means to raise the child and afford the necessary operations. After many surgeries, Mama could walk, but she had to wear specially designed orthopedic shoes all her life. In addition, the neurological damage from the surgeries left her legs strangely underdeveloped from the knees down, so much so that, even as a child, I wondered why she did not wear long dresses to hide them. Mama's smiles were rare, and only later in life did I understand why. Growing up with her grandparents and having to assist them with their daily needs precluded her from playing with her siblings and neighborhood children. Her grandparents made clear, however, that life in her parents' home, with eight siblings and little food, would be much worse. There was little joy in her young life. Her grandparents held quite interesting roles in the community. Her grandmother, the only midwife in the Ammer River Valley, was often picked up in the middle of the night by a farmer's horse and buggy to assist in the birth of a child. Mama's grandfather was the royal mailman to King Ludwig II (1845–1886), the last King of Bavaria. Their frequent absences from home made her life even harder and very lonely.

I vividly remember Mama's grandfather, my great-grandfather Vetter, as I called him. He was one of my favorite people in my young life. Vetter was obsessed with education. When my teacher recommended after the fifth grade of elementary school that I attend the *Oberschule* (preparatory school for the university) in Murnau, some 13 kilometers from my village and requiring a roundtrip train ride each day, he paid for my tuition until he died. Each day, returning from school, I had to report to him what I had learned from each of my teachers. He made me proud of excelling in school.

Collusion of Church and State

With Hitler's invasion of Poland in 1939, Germany became embroiled in World War II. By 1943, it had been 5 years since *Kristallnacht* and Jewish children had been banned from attending school. I was 6 years old at that time and attended first grade in our public elementary school. As in many Catholic villages in Bavaria, religious studies were taught every day, and in Unterammergau this role fell to our local priest, Herr Pfarrer. When he entered the classroom, we were trained to automatically stand and wait for his gesture indicating it was time to pray. Every morning, we said the same prayer to the crucifix hanging on the wall behind the teacher's desk before we were permitted to sit down.

One morning at the beginning of the school year, when Herr Pfarrer arrived in our classroom, he walked behind the teacher's desk, moved the chair against the wall, climbed up, and took down our hand-carved crucifix. The crucifix was especially beautiful. It had been handmade by a well-known woodcarver living in nearby Oberammergau, a town world-renowned for its wood carving school and its centuries-old passion play. We students participated in fundraising activities for the purchase of this cross, so I was surprised to see Herr Pfarrer remove it. I must confess that I was secretly relieved that

Jesus was able to come down from the wall. As a first grader, I had felt sorry for him having to hang there all day with almost no clothes on.

From under his black frock, Herr Pfarrer pulled out a framed picture of Adolf Hitler, hung it on the same nail where the crucifix used to hang, turned to us, and said in an astoundingly severe tone:

> From now on you will not pray at the beginning of class. Instead, when I enter the classroom you will stand up, raise your right arm three times, and each time pronounce *Heil Hitler*! loud and clear. And when you greet the people in the village, which of course you are expected to do, you will no longer say (in Bavarian), *Grüß Gott* ("Greetings to God"), or *Frau* so-and-so. Instead, you will raise your right arm and shout, *Heil Hitler, Frau*-so-and-so! Do you understand?

On that day, I could not wait to run home from school to tell my father about our exciting new *Heil Hitler* greeting. I will never forget how he grabbed me by my arms in no uncertain terms and shouted that I was never to salute Hitler in the classroom nor in the street. He yelled, "Don't let me catch you not listening to me!" I loved my Papa, I would never disobey him. The next day in our classroom, I did not raise my right arm three times to say *Heil Hitler*. My old teacher, Fräulein Grainer (she and Herr Pfarrer were our only teachers during the war) asked to see me after class and tried to persuade me to use the Hitler greeting. When I informed her that my father forbade me to do so, she shook her head, raised her eyebrows, stared into my eyes, and commanded that I must stay 1 hour after school every day to clean blackboards, floors, and windows as punishment for not saluting Hitler's portrait. Fräulein Grainer lived in the basement of our schoolhouse; it was easy for her to check up on me. Once, she threatened that I would have to stay longer if I was not more thorough in my work. After this, my peers ignored me, Herr Pfarrer took a dislike to my family, and the villagers shunned us. When my peers planned activities, they failed to invite me, instead looking over their shoulder at me with disapproving eyes. Along with my family, I was ostracized and my life became difficult. As a 6-year-old, I wondered why my father believed that the *Hitler Gruß* was such a terrible thing? After all, everybody else used it in school and in the village. Yet, I sensed he knew something more about the world and had a good reason for his directive.

Imminent Bombing Attacks

To this day, I can hear the screeching sounds of the rusty hand siren used by the old city clerk. Beginning in 1943, he used the siren to warn the villagers of imminent bombing attacks as he was cycling through the village on his bicycle. Anyone who could manage to get to the church tower first would also ring the small church bell. Our beautifully resonant big church bell could no longer spread its glorious sound as the Nazi government had mandated that all large church bells across Germany be taken down and melted for war material.

The cruel sound of the siren would alert us children to run home from school to take cover in cellars reserved for potatoes, apples, and jars of marmalade. If we could not reach our house in time to escape the low flying bombers soaring over us, we would throw ourselves into a ditch and hold our ears. The shrieking fighter planes would fly so low that I sometimes could see the pilots' faces. They were Allied bombers on their way to bomb the underground Messerschmittwerke (factory) inside the base of the Laber Mountain in the next village of Oberammergau, a bombing goal that was often repeated but ultimately unsuccessful. The main Messerschmittwerk was located in Munich, the capital of Bavaria, but the Nazis had moved essential manufacturing to the countryside to avoid bombing attacks. The Oberammergau villagers were enraged but had no choice to house hundreds of skilled engineers who had been relocated from Munich to work in the new location of the factory (Waddy, 2010). Because we lived only four kilometers from Oberammergau, we feared we would be bombed to death. A blanket of despair hung over our village.

Boy Soldiers. Soldiers. Deaths.

Another profound memory surrounds my mother's decision to hide three boy soldiers who fled to our house seeking refuge during the final days of the war. They were members of the retreating Wehrmacht, many of whom were trying to escape into our surrounding mountains. My mother agreed to hide them in the cellar located under the small rectangular door which was in the corner of the kitchen floor, covered with a carpet. My father shouted at my mother for letting them in since she would be shot if the SS were to discover the boys. At that time, the SS regularly searched the houses in our village for deserters and resistance fighters. Mama refused to change her mind and, as she later said, "Thank God," the SS did not discover the boys. After several days in the cellar, they thanked Mama, stuffed her food provisions into their backpacks, snuck out the back door, and ran to the mountains. We never learned what happened to them.

By 1940, 8.8 million *Hitlerjugend* (Hitler Youth) existed in Nazi Germany, and over 1 million of these boys were positioned on the frontlines of the Eastern and Western fronts where they would face combat against the invading Allies. To this day, I find it difficult to comprehend the magnitude of brainwashing these boy soldiers, still in their formative years of 10- to 18-years-old, had to endure. By early 1944, with the Wehrmacht suffering extensive casualties on both fronts, the boys were mandated to serve in the Hitlerjugend brigades, where they were exposed to extreme physical training and irreconcilable indoctrination into the Nazi ideology. Boy soldiers as young as 14 were sent to the Normandy coast of France to combat the Allied invasion on D-Day. In one Panzer Tank Division, over 65% of the boy soldiers were between the ages of 16 to 18 (Butler, 2019). Brutally disciplined in training camps, these young boys had acquired a formidable reputation for their violence in battle as reported by American soldiers.

The boys from my village were not spared from this reign of terror. I can still see them walking down our street, their uniforms too big and scared to death. And I can still hear the wailing of mothers, siblings, and grandparents at the train station as they said goodbye to their boys on their way to war. One of these boy soldiers who was drafted into the Wehrmacht was my 15-year-old uncle Gustl, my father's youngest brother. My grandfather had forbidden him from joining the Hitlerjugend, just as my father had forbidden me to join the *Bund der Deutschen Mädchen* (League of German Girls). At the time he was drafted, Gustl was a talented woodcarver and had just acquired admission to the famous, highly competitive woodcarving school in Oberammergau. In November 1944, my grandmother received his death notice that Gustl had been killed in Hochsavoyen, near Iacques, France, at the age of 18 (Figure 11.3). My stoic grandfather withdrew into his workshop, but my grandmother's primeval screams gave me nightmares for years. I can still hear her shrieking words of total despair:

Figure 11.3 Author's Uncle Gustl Fuss, age 18, killed in France.

You Nazi killers murder innocent boys to win a useless war! Is it not enough that my oldest son (my father) was injured in the war, that my second son Luisl is fighting in Russia, and now you have killed my youngest son?

We later learned that Gustl was buried in a French cemetery for German soldiers at Andilly, France. My grandparents were never able to make the trip to visit his grave.

Luisl (see Figure 11.4), the second brother of my father, survived the war. He was my favorite uncle who often took me skiing and mountain climbing when I was a little girl. After fighting in the 5-month-long Battle of Stalingrad in 1943, in which almost 2 million Axis and Allied soldiers died, he finally returned home in 1945. Emaciated and wild-looking, he knocked on the front door of his parents' house, but his own mother (my grandmother) did not recognize him and refused until much later as he would not stop knocking on the door. On my many visits home from the United States, I repeatedly tried to interview him about his wartime experiences, he always sadly declined.

As the war raged on, Mama continued knitting socks for the soldiers at the Eastern and Western fronts, as many women did. Mandated by the Nazi regime, the activity seemed to help her to maintain her sanity. Mama was not given to easy emotion; her much older grandparents had taught her not to cry. But despite her deeply stoic approach to life, I watched how she

Figure 11.4 Author's favorite Uncle Luisl Fuss, age 24, returning from Stalingrad, Russia.

Nazism. Bordercrossing. Racism. All Lives Are of Equal Worth ▪ 235

Figure 11.5 Author's maternal Uncle Nikolaus Lindele, prisoner of war killed in Staßdopol, Russia.

broke down sobbing when she learned of the death of her oldest brother Nikolaus, a scout in the Wehrmacht who died in a prisoner-of-war camp in Staßdopol, Siberia, Russia (Figure 11.5).

At the war's end, her second oldest brother Toni (Anton) who also had fought in Russia, came home from a Russian prisoner-of-war camp and later died of his wounds (Figure 11.6).

Figure 11.6 Author's maternal Uncle Anton Lindele died of his wounds after returning home from Russia.

VILLAGE LIFE

Nightly Footsteps

I still remember how, as a 7-year-old lying in bed listening to the nightly clacking of a young woman's passing footsteps as she hurried to the 10:45 night train. Marie went every evening to await the arrival of her fiancé Leonhard on furlough from the war. Night after night, the clattering footsteps passed our bedroom window. It must have been a year before the clacking stopped. Leonhard never arrived; Marie finally learned that he was killed at age 24 in Stalingrad, the site of one of history's bloodiest battles. Before the end of the war, Leonhard's mother and father would suffer the loss of two more sons, both killed at the Russian front. Marie would never marry.

My childhood memories are filled with stark images of a village population scarred by war, desperately yearning for peace. The many death notices from the Eastern and Western fronts had reduced the male population and in our village where, by the end of the war, 41 husbands, sons, uncles, cousins, and neighbors were dead, 21 were missing-in-action, and many more were wounded. On June 29, 1941, Lieutenant Hubert Menninger was the first soldier from the village to lose his life. The villagers remembered him proudly waving goodbye in his brand-new *Luftwaffe* (Air Force) uniform. He fell in Russia at the age of 25. Death at an early age.

Bread and Milk for Forced Laborers

To this day, I will never forget how every evening Mama sent me on a mission to bring milk and bread to the labor camp near a sawmill on the other side of the Ammer River. Encased with a barbed wire fence, the huge camp housed Poles and Russians, forced laborers who had to live in the open without a roof over their head or indoor plumbing. During the day they worked in the sawmill cutting trees into boards and loading them onto railroad cars at the nearby train station. They replaced the local farmers who had worked at the sawmill to subsidize their income before they were sent to war.

I clearly remember carrying a two-liter, white metal milk can with a lid and my mother's warnings not to spill a drop, as "every drop of milk will make a prisoner happy." I remember walking down the street that crossed the Ammer River bridge, and standing at the gate of the workers' enclave holding up the milk can and the bread. A prisoner would take a sip or two from the milk can and pass it on to the next prisoner and so on until the milk can was empty. Then each would tear a piece from the loaf of bread and pass it on to the next prisoner until the loaf was devoured. As a little girl I was amazed how the prisoners did not fight over my mother's big treats. When I left the camp, some feverishly asked, "*Morgen*"? (tomorrow) and said good-bye to me in a language I did not understand. And, yes, Morgen would come, and my mother would again send me on this journey to the forced laborers who anxiously awaited a little German girl with pigtails. This daily "Mama mission" would repeat itself until the end of the war, when the forced laborers were liberated by a contingent of General Patton's Third Army 10th Armored Division. How did my Mama manage to get milk and bread when we were short of food ourselves? She traded pieces of her precious jewelry.

Refugees

I remember hundreds of weary refugees seeking shelter in our village after the war ended in 1945. They came from as far away as the Sudetenland (now reconstituted as the Czech Republic) and from as close as Munich, the capital of Bavaria, 90 kilometers away. The first group was expelled from Czechoslovakia after being conquered by the Nazis. This group had lived in the Sudetenland regions of Bőhmen (Bohemia), Schlesien (Schleswig), and Mähren (Moravia) for centuries. The latter group contained city dwellers, many of whom had vacationed in our village in peacetime. They were homeless and hungry, trying to escape the Allied bombings that had destroyed their city. They begged for a place to stay.

Of the 3.4 million Sudeten Germans forced to flee their homeland at the end of the war, 1.02 million were sent to the state of Bavaria. Of these, 600 arrived in our village. Every homeowner was required to provide housing for one refugee family. Mama took in a family with four children. At school, our classroom suddenly became overcrowded with refugee children speaking a strange dialect. They seemed to feel afraid, as did we. When they excelled in sports and beat our soccer team, we realized that they were kids just like us and overcame our fear. As I recall those tragic days, I can't help but think of the more than 1 million Ukrainian refugee children who, with their mothers, have fled to neighboring countries to escape Russian bombing attacks since the Russian invasion of Ukraine in February of 2022. Months into the war with Russia, our own village of Unterammergau has received its first Ukrainian refugee families.

The Role of the Village Church

How well I remember the frequent church services held in our village, a reflection of the deeply entrenched Catholicism in southern Bavaria. On Sundays, the high mass was held at 10 a.m. and the *Vesper* (a prayer meeting) at 2:00 p.m. My mother required me and my siblings to attend both.

In addition, throughout the war, a *Kriegerandacht* (service for soldiers) was held every evening of the week to pray for the safe return of the local soldiers fighting on the Eastern and Western fronts. We had to say an entire rosary during these services. I disliked this boring ritual.

The most traumatic church services were those held after a fallen soldier's death notice arrived in the village. At that time, the city clerk, with his rusty bell, would bicycle through the village announcing a special service at a certain day and time. The villagers knew that this special service was for another of our village boys or men who had been killed. Between 1941 and 1945 of World War II, 41 soldiers had been killed in battle. I remember the pitiful assembly of old men, distraught women, and children like me at these special church services. Hymns would be sung by a small female choir, alternating with parishioners' prayers in the local vernacular and the priest's prayers in Latin. Then the priest, standing before us, would announce the name of the fallen soldier and the place where he died, as women screamed in anguish. In front of the altar would stand a cross made of birch trunks with a photograph of the uniformed soldier attached on the front of the birch trunk and a helmet on top of the cross surrounded by flowers.

THE NAZIS IN OUR VILLAGE

Some members of our village served as Nazi appointees. They wore perfect-looking uniforms with Nazi insignias on their jackets and shouted commanding "Heil Hitler" greetings as they marched around the village. They carried themselves with great authority and evoked deep *angst* (anxiety) among the villagers who wondered with fearful anticipation what they might do.

By 1943 or so, the Nazis had grown increasingly suspicious of my father. Every time he was home from Munich, there was a big sigh of relief in my house when they did not knock at our door. The local Nazis had the authority to order those suspected of disloyalty to the Nazi regime to be forcefully removed from their home, even in the middle of the night. Our apprehension was multiplied by my father's constant warning, "Trust no one, including your own mother, the *Spitzel* (spies) are everywhere." I think my father feared that my mother might inadvertently mention his frequent outbursts to her sister who lived down the street from us, outbursts about the murdering Nazis who even trampled *über Leichen* (dead bodies) in their brutality. During the mandated evening blackouts, Papa would frequently jump up from our peaceful dinner table and pull back the window curtains to see if a Spitzel was eavesdropping.

Of all the fears I experienced as a young girl during the Nazi era, the greatest fear was that my father would be shot. Often in the night, I would awaken to the sounds of gunshots fired in the distance, and I would run to wake my mother who would assure me that Papa was alright working at the

Messerschmittwerke in Munich. I knew, however, that Mama was not privy to all his activities. In the nearby coal-mining town of Penzberg, the SS had recently hanged 17 men and women from lamp posts. They had attempted to remove the appointed Nazi leader of the village who had commanded them to destroy nearby bridges and industrial sites to prevent the approaching Allies from reaching southern Bavaria.

During the months before the war ended on May 8, 1945, the German army and the *Waffen* (weaponized) SS retreated to southern Bavaria to regroup. They feverishly prepared for the last stand at the alleged *Alpenfestung* (Alpine Fortress). They wanted to be ready to fight against the approaching Allies who had landed on the French coast and were sweeping with lightning speed through Germany, overrunning the Wehrmacht. By this time, millions of German soldiers had surrendered en masse, but there were true believers among the Waffen SS forces who were refusing the Allied demand for unconditional surrender. These fanatical SS officers gave a hellish choice to the retreating German soldiers who anxiously awaited the end of the war: Continue to fight against all odds or be shot on the spot.

The Schutzstaffel (SS) of the Nazi Regime

The *Schutzstaffel* (SS; security agency), was a major paramilitary organization under Hitler. The Schutzstaffel had begun as a small group of party volunteers to provide security at meetings. By the outbreak of World War II in 1939, the SS consolidated and took its final form with three branches: (a) The *Allgemeine* (general) SS responsible for enforcing the racial policy of Nazi Germany; (b) the Waffen SS consisting of combat units in the military, and (c) the SS–*Totenkopfverbände* (death squads wearing uniforms labeled with skulls) which were in charge of concentration camps and extermination camps. Specialized groups of the SS included the *Gestapo* (Geheime Staatspolizei, Secret Police) and the *Sicherheitsdienst* (SD; Security Police) which together were tasked with detecting and interrogating potential enemies of the state, neutralizing the opposition, policing the German peoples' commitment to Nazi ideology, and providing domestic and foreign intelligence.

The SS carried out systematic genocide of approximately 17 million individuals during World War II of whom six million were Jews and approximately 11 million consisted of other groups that included the Roma and Sinti, the mentally and physically handicapped, forced laborers, homosexuals, Jehovah Witnesses, prisoners of war, and political dissidents. It is not surprising that the SS and its branches were the foremost, deeply feared agency of security, surveillance, and terror within Nazi Germany and Nazi-occupied Europe.

Figure 11.7 Feared Waffen SS of the Nazi regime.

The *Auerhahn* Resistance Group

Nazi Germany's looming defeat meant that more and more retreating soldiers and Waffen SS officers were arriving in our village. At the same time, Bavarian underground resistance groups, who were aware of the imminent arrival of General Patton's Third Army 10th Armored Division in Bavaria, grew bolder in their acts of sabotage. Among those engaged in underground activities was the *Auerhahn* resistance group of Upper Bavaria which managed to burn down the *Hundigungshütte*, the largest wooden cabin on a nearby mountain in the *Graswangtal* valley, a cabin around the corner from our village that was designed for hikers to spend the night. The Auerhahn group was informed that the Waffen SS intended to store food and ammunition in case they needed to escape to Austria, approximately 10 kilometers away. The group also planned to eliminate the district leader, Kreisleiter Schiede, a ruthless Nazi official who, along with his staff, had brutally governed our entire *Gau* (county) of *Garmisch-Partenkirchen*. Due to the unexpected speed with which the advancing U.S. Army arrived in the nearby Bavarian villages, the plan failed. It is fitting that the Auerhahn resistance group was named after one of our most beautiful Alpine birds soaring in our mountains.

MY FEAR FOR MY FATHER

By the time I was about 8 years old, I was convinced that my father would be shot by the Nazis for many reasons. One reason for my fear was his refusal, from the start of Hitler's takeover, to wear the Nazi pin. I witnessed him tearing the Nazi insignia off my mother's blouse and telling her to never wear it again. Moreover, despite his compulsory military service, Papa was highly critical of the "murderous Nazi regime," as he called it. He spoke openly about it to educate other villagers to recognize its dangers, but to no avail. In fact, the villagers began to look at him and our family with suspicion. The frequency and suddenness of his unexplained appearances, disappearances, and reappearances, allegedly to and from Munich, suggested he might be involved in anti-Nazi activities. Papa did not tell me about his sabotage endeavors at that time but, instead, ranted on for hours about the horrors of the concentration camps and their victims. I think he felt that I, his young daughter, was the only person he could trust to share his deep rage boiling inside of him. Besides, his earlier admonitions forbidding me to say "Heil Hitler" in school and in the street, or to join the Bund der Deutschen Mädchen, exacerbated the local Nazis' suspicions about our family.

THE PEACEFUL SURRENDER OF MY VILLAGE

When the villagers attended the evening *Kriegerandacht* (devotion to the warriors) for a fallen soldier on April 28, 1945, they did not know that the liberating American troops would arrive in Unterammergau the next day. While in church, deafening artillery fire came from behind the Schergen mountain and echoed in the church. I thought the noise must be Hitler fanatics and SS officers shooting at the approaching American tanks and the American soldiers returning their fire. Filled with terror, we ran out of the church to our cellars. What we heard in the church that night, however, was the prelude to the most momentous next day in the history of our mountain village. On April 29, 1945, around 10:00 a.m., our liberation from a regime of immeasurable destruction, unspeakable horrors, and human suffering became a reality. A contingent of U.S. General George S. Patton's Third U.S. Army 10th Armored Division was assembled at the entrance to our village, awaiting the villagers' peaceful surrender.

I can still hear my Marxist grandfather, equipped with a white flag hanging from a pole, tearing open our front door and yelling, "Are you ready?" to my father, who instantly appeared at the door with a pole to which he had nailed a white bed sheet. I remember watching them both shakily balance the poles on their shoulders as they wobbled down the street on their bicycles, crossing the Ammer River bridge, and continuing to the edge of the village, yelling along the way, "The Americans are coming... hang white sheets from your windows!" The American commander would not accept my father and grandfather's peaceful surrender of the village to the "enemy," however, until he met with the *Bürgermeister* (mayor) of the village and obtained its official surrender. Papa turned around and raced on his bicycle to the home of the mayor, who was hiding in the cellar, and persuaded him to appear before the U.S. commander. So, here were my grandfather and father, white flags fluttering in the wind, next to the mayor of Unterammergau, peacefully delivering our village to the American forces. My two role models, predicting that the Nazi mayor would not emerge from his cellar when the victorious "enemy" arrived, had long planned this act of bravery. Their action defied SS commander Heinrich Himmler's emergency order to shoot all males who were caught with white flags. To this day I am deeply proud of my father and grandfather who defied Himmler's directive.

Unfortunately, on this glorious day of liberation by the American troops, the inevitability of death reared its ugly head. Frau Reindl, whose house and gas station were located at the very village entrance where the American tanks halted, ran panic-stricken to the surrounding fields and was shot by a reconnaissance plane circling over the village; she died 2 days later. Moreover, four 18-year-old German boy soldiers who were hiding behind Frau Reindl's gas station were also killed as they attempted to flee. They were buried in our village cemetery and years later, exhumed and returned to the cemetery in their hometowns. Given the might of the U.S. Army at the edge of our village, the large number of retreating German soldiers hiding in the mountains, and the feverish resistance of Nazi fanatics, it is surprising that not more unnecessary deaths occurred. Finally, a week later, on May 8, 1945, 11:05 p.m., commanders of the Wehrmacht officially signed the documents of unconditional surrender of the Nazi regime.

My Paternal Grandfather

Who was my grandfather, the father of my father, who welcomed the Allies at the entrance to our village? He was born in the small farming village of Alteglofsheim, near Regensburg on the Donau (Danube) River in lower Bavaria, where vast fields of wheat danced in the sun of rich farmlands beautifying the countryside. The son of a struggling farmer and one of nine children, he decided to become a metalworker. His education and certification required him to become an apprentice for 3 years and travel from place to place to make a living with his craft. When he arrived in Unterammergau to find metal work, he met my paternal grandmother, fell in love, and became the father of an illegitimate son, my father. He decided to remain in the village, marry my grandmother, build his own house, and open a metal shop. My teenage father had to work for years at the big farm of a landowner to "work off" the debt his father had incurred when borrowing a hay wagon and horses for transportation to move building materials. My father never forgot the landowner's oldest son mocking him: "You are a poor boy, eh?" These words carved a deep pain in my father's psyche.

Despite settling in the village, my paternal grandfather remained an outsider. Bavarian villagers did not look positively upon newcomers in their village and did not accept him as an equal. Moreover, my grandfather's ideas about the world were controversial and out of step with those of the conservative Catholic farmer. He believed in the philosophy of Karl Marx and proudly challenged the status quo. He held regular meetings of likeminded individuals at his home until the local Nazis forbade him to do so threatening his arrest. My father never discussed Karl Marx with me, but I knew that early in his life he had recognized the grave dangers of authoritarianism and fanaticism evident in the policies of the Hitler regime.

American Soldiers on Tanks Rolling Down Our Village Street

After the peaceful surrender at the village entrance, it seemed like hundreds of American tanks with soaring flags bearing the stars and stripes rolled down our street. On the day American forces entered our village, we children-of-war enthusiastically waved to the Black and White soldiers sitting on top of their tanks (Figure 11.8). We were overwhelmed to find the soldiers throwing us bananas, oranges, and Hershey bars—items we had never seen before. One contingent of the Third U.S. Army 10th Armored Division settled in our village, and the remaining division moved on to Oberammergau and other villages close to the border of Austria, only 10 kilometers away, to liberate the German (and ultimately Austrian) people from the Nazi regime. They encountered spontaneous skirmishes with retreating Waffen SS officers who ultimately, at the cost of their lives, succumbed to the overpowering forces of the Americans. The American contingent in my village was part of the larger Allied occupation of defeated Nazi Germany,

Figure 11.8 U.S. Black and White soldiers on tanks rolling down our village street.

in which British, French, Russian, and American victors divided the country into four occupation zones. Our Bavaria was occupied by the Americans.

As the Americans settled in the village, they evicted several residents of two-story houses in order to set up U.S. headquarters and sleeping quarters. When we were so ordered, and given just 1 hour to leave our house, my mother quickly borrowed an ox and hay wagon from our neighbor so we could throw our featherbeds down from our second-floor balcony. By the time Mama had found a neighbor to take us in the Americans no longer needed our house, as they had found bigger ones for their purposes. Used to a hard life, Mama showed no anger towards the Americans. She was just relieved that we could stay in our pretty 18th century house, even without its blooming geraniums on the balcony which had been her pride and joy before the war.

One afternoon, when we children apprehensively gathered near some of the soldiers who had kicked us a soccer ball (another surprise we had never seen before), we slowly lost our apprehension as we sensed their genuine kindness. After that, we often gathered around them, communicating with our hands and facial expressions and the little English we had learned in school. One momentous day, I mustered all my courage and asked an African American soldier in my halting school English if I could touch his arm as I had never seen anyone with black skin before. When he laughingly consented, I licked my right forefinger and swiped it along his forearm, certain that the black paint would rub off. I remember him smiling at me with perfect white teeth, patting me on the back, and shaking his head. The special kindness and generosity of the African American soldiers towards us war-scarred German children remains deeply carved in my memory. It is the same kindness I later re-experienced with African American colleagues after I moved to the United States.

Emerging German American Friendship

After the American troops settled in our village, it did not take long before Mama was washing, starching, and ironing officers' uniforms in her makeshift *Waschküche* (wash house). In return, she received generous supplies of her sought-after cigarettes and coffee beans which she ground with an almost religious fervor. During the war, Mama had laboriously grown tobacco plants on the roof of a low shed behind our house, rolling her harvest within whatever paper she could find. One afternoon, the American officers asked Mama to cook the trout they had caught in our Ammer River. This was the first time our family ever ate fresh trout as fishing in Germany, even today, requires an expensive license. Another memorable highlight of Mama's emerging friendship with the Americans was their surprise gift of a turkey on Thanksgiving. The whole neighborhood feasted on this unknown bird that has no habitat in the Bavarian mountains.

WAS PAPA A MEMBER OF THE *AUERHAHN* RESISTANCE?

Papa was undoubtedly a fearless dissident defying the Nazi regime, but was he a member of the organized Auerhahn resistance? During my many visits home from America he had always taken off work to share time and talk with me—sometimes we took a cable car to a mountaintop restaurant or went to sit in the log cabin he had built nearby during the war for possible shelter. He would speak of the profound evil of the Nazi regime, and I would fill the pages of my now-treasured diaries to overflowing with these inexplicable human tragedies. But it was not until my visits to Unterammergau late in my father's life that he shared with me, for the very first time, his part in sabotage activities at the Messerschmittwerke in Munich and the *Echelsbacher Brücke* (Bridge). At the Messerschmittwerke, while assembling airplane parts for fighter planes, he and two confidants from a nearby village deliberately left out key components to impair the reliability and effectiveness of the aircrafts. They did this under the threat of grave danger as monitors constantly walked through the huge halls of the factory, looking over the workers' shoulders. Papa knew that if he had been discovered he would have been shot on the spot. If caught, Papa would not have been the first saboteur to be shot in front of the workers. His most daring deed, however, was in helping to safeguard the *Echelsbacher Brücke*, a huge bridge spanning the steep cliff beds of the Ammer River about 10 kilometers north of our village (Utschneider, 2012). The Nazis had targeted it to be blown up to delay or prevent General Patton's advancing Third U.S. Army 10th Armored Division tank columns from crossing the Ammer River. At great risk, in the middle of the night, Papa worked with others to remove the explosives that the Nazis had positioned there. Even though SS officers with deadly force could have appeared from anywhere and at any moment, Papa and his group miraculously avoided detection. Papa's keen mind kept his memories fully intact until his death in his late 1980s. His nightmares worsened with age and his hope for a better world essentially ceased.

One aspect of his resistance activities still remains a mystery to me. Was Papa also a member of the organized Auerhahn resistance group of Upper Bavaria? Based on the frequency and suddenness of his unexplained appearances, disappearances, and re-appearances, and his frequent alleged trips to and from Munich, I believe that he was an active member of the Auerhahn resistance of Upper Bavaria.

IMMIGRATING TO THE UNITED STATES

Once the war had ended, the German population desperately tried to make sense of the Nazi nightmare. I continued my college prepatory education, graduated, and registered for my first semester at the University of Munich since my father wanted me to become a teacher. On the weekends, despite my mother's worries that I might fall off a mountain, I frequently went hiking and climbing some of the highest mountains of the Bavarian and Austrian Alps. (Perhaps my mother's concern was well-placed as I often faced extreme danger due to changing weather conditions and lack of proper equipment.) My hiking companion was usually my friend Gittl who had moved with her family to my village during the war and who loved the mountains like I did. One of our hiking trips at the young age of 17 remained happily in my heart for all these years of my life. Gittl and I were scaling the Zugspitze summit (the highest mountain in Germany at 2,964 meters or almost 10,000 feet) when we encountered a handsome young hiker from another village who had reached the top of the summit first. As was customary among German hikers, the first young woman reaching the summit would have to kiss him. I did, and Helmut became my first love.

In 1957, when I was 20, I took a summer job working at the American Express office in the village next to mine, with the goal of improving my English. There, I met an American military officer who happened to wear civilian clothes. We fell in love and decided to marry. My father had prohibited me from ever marrying "a man in uniform" but my future husband was a lieutenant in the counterintelligence corps (CIC) responsible for the security of the North Atlantic Treaty Organization (NATO) and Special Weapons School in Oberammergau. He was fluent in German and he did not wear a uniform. My parents hesitantly allowed us to marry. After I became pregnant with our daughter Andrée in 1959, my new husband and I left for the United States and settled in his hometown of New Orleans, Louisiana. I can never forget the faces of my crying parents as they said goodbye to me, their oldest child, at the Munich airport. Two years later, in 1961, our son David was born in New Orleans, completing our family.

The American Deep South

My arrival in the United States heralded a profound epoch in my young life during which time I greatly broadened my Western-centric perspective on the world. Over the next 50-plus years I gained what the global educator Robert Hanvey (1976) referred to as a higher level of "perspective consciousness" about the world and its people (p. 163). In his seminal article, "An Attainable Global Perspective," Hanvey advanced the idea that it is critical for individuals to recognize that their view of the world is not universally shared, and that it has been and continues to be shaped by often unconscious influences. As human beings, Hanvey argued, we must accept that others hold views of the world that are profoundly different from our own.

This perspective consciousness concept could not have been reinforced more strongly than by my border crossing in the early 1960s as a transplant from Southern Germany to the American Deep South. The change proved overwhelming when I found myself confronted with the customary Southern way of life. In my choice to marry an American I had chosen shotgun houses, rocking chairs on front porches, cooling fans, debilitating humidity in 110-degree heat, and systemic racism. I was shocked by the blatant and ubiquitous segregation of African Americans in daily life as reflected in "Colored" water fountains, confinement to the back of city busses, access to doctor's offices in the rear of buildings, and the hateful spitting by Whites on Black children being bussed to newly integrated schools. I observed the South's deliberately slow desegregation efforts and their terrible impacts in the hesitation of my mother-in-law's maid Yvonne to eat with me at the same table, and in my naïve insistence to drop her off at her housing project when she finally consented to let me drive her home.

In my newly adopted country, I discovered different forms of discrimination and victimization, similar to what I saw happen to Jews in Hitler's Germany. In the United States, it was African Americans who had been the target of injustice and systemic racism for centuries. My German education had not prepared me for this traumatic experience. For a young girl from the Bavarian countryside, it was difficult to understand the environment in which I now lived. Only with time and education was I able to put together the pieces and grasp the underlying circumstances that had produced this other slow deliberate genocide over time—a reality made more shocking because it was occurring in a country where most of the world's migrants want to emigrate. In reflecting on the numerous injustices occurring in the world today, another genocide is presently being committed at this very moment in Ukraine since the Russian invasion on February 24, 2022.

I arrived from Germany to the State of Louisiana at the dawn of the civil rights movement. Within the next decade, I experienced the assassinations of civil rights leaders Medgar Evers, Malcolm X, and Martin Luther King Jr., as well as President John F. Kennedy and U.S. Attorney General Robert Kennedy. What a profound learning experience for a country girl from the Bavarian Alps. I experienced cities burning, demonstrators beaten and killed by police, racial profiling, and unnerving race riots. We lived near the 9th Ward in New Orleans, an African American neighborhood that later was the very place where, in 2005, Hurricane Katrina drowned more of its victims than in any other part of the Crescent City. Were these victims of systemic racism not the same kind and generous African Americans I had encountered as a child-of-war, the ones who had liberated my village from the Nazi regime? How could they be treated this way in the land of the free? My introduction to the Deep South of the United States was a painful one.

Navigating Cultural Differences

Like all immigrants in coming to America, I had to overcome cultural differences. What I missed most from my native Bavaria was celebrating Christmas Eve with an emphasis on the birth of Jesus and attending midnight mass in the cold of winter. Mama always kept the Christmas tree hidden until we left for church when she would ring the bell and call us children into the living room to find a beautifully decorated tree lit with real wax candles. Before we were allowed to open our presents, we sang in harmony, *Stille Nacht, heilige Nacht (Silent Night, Holy Night)* with Papa singing in his golden tenor voice that gave one chills, and I harmonizing in my alto voice. When Papa sang the *Ave Maria* in church, the parishioners cried as his tenor voice soared to heaven. I maintained the Christmas Eve celebration in my adopted country and taught my children to sing *Silent Night* in German. To this day, I have trouble accepting the American tradition of telling children on Christmas Day that St. Nick left presents the night before. In Bavaria, Saint Nikolaus, the patron saint of little children, sailors, merchants, and students, arrives on the sixth of December, when he goes from house to house to fuss at or praise children on their school performance and distributes small presents.

After coming to *Amerika* (as Germans refer to the United States), I also missed celebrating my "name day." In Bavaria, Catholic children are named after Catholic saints. When a child shares the same name as a saint, the child celebrates her/his name day on the saint's name day. In fact, my mother once told me that in Bavaria, name days are more important than birthdays. I was given the name "Antonie," after St. Anthony, as my parents expected me to be a boy. Since that first year in my adopted country, no one congratulated me on St. Anthony's name day—except my sister phoning me from Germany. Since living in the United States, I have also missed the Bavarian cultural tradition of wearing a *Dirndl* (Bavarian dress), especially after being told by an American that I forgot to take off my apron. The *Dirndl* consists of a sleeveless dress with mother-of-pearl or silver buttons down the front, a white blouse, and a half apron tied around the waist with long ribbons. Another effect of living in the United States was that, like many immigrants, I feel compelled to perform with 200% competency. On the other hand, despite my continuous efforts to fit in and gain acceptance, I remain vigilant for some unanticipated consequence of my actions. Although I think I will always feel marginalized to some degree in this country, there is no doubt that in the years following my arrival, I fell in love with the United States.

My Life as an Immigrant and Teacher

My emigration from Germany to the United States also gave me insight into the complex experiences of life as an immigrant. African American scholar W. E. B. Du Bois (1903) best articulated this experience in his notion of double consciousness and the ever-present invisible veil that minorities choose to wear for survival. Although his ideas refer to the African American experience in a predominantly White racist society, I found that they also capture the dilemma that kept me separate from my newly adopted country. What caused this separation if not race? It was, at least in part, inescapably linguistic. My accent clearly points to a non-native American cultural and linguistic background and although I speak both Goethe's high German and the Bavarian vernacular in my home country, it continues to separate me in my adopted country. Even today I still struggle with the pronunciation of the "th"—a nonexistent sound in the German language as well as with the ubiquitous American "w."

Working in the Miami School System

When my husband, who was now a United States Customs agent, was transferred from New Orleans, Louisiana, to Miami, Florida, and our two children, Andrée and David, were settled in school, I began to study at Miami Dade Community College and Florida Atlantic University to obtain my bachelor's degree in secondary social studies education. Upon graduation in 1982, I taught at Ida Fisher Junior High School in Miami Beach. Little did I know that my first teaching position would lead to experiences I could never have anticipated. One early morning, while trying to decipher the Yiddish of the elderly women walking too slowly in front of me as I rushed to get to school on time, I saw the school buses roll up to the entrance of the school with Black children emerging with fear on their faces as protesters spit on them, yelling "Go back to your ghetto," and extremist parents obstructing their path into the school. After I discovered in my overcrowded integrated classroom of over 50 students that the bussed-in children from poverty-stricken inner-city Miami had never seen the Atlantic Ocean nor learned how to swim, our first field trip was to the beach. I still remember my principal's warning about the risks I was taking as I nonetheless pleaded with him to allow us to see and feel the ocean. My students were thrilled and overwhelmed by the glistening waves of the sea touching their toes.

When we studied the interconnectedness of global issues with local issues my students and I, along with others, marched in the Miami streets to demand economic, political, and social rights for migrant farmworkers who worked under inhumane conditions in the fields of South Florida, as elsewhere in our country. We visited one of South Miami's huge factory farms so my students could experience first-hand what it means to have to stoop all day to pick tomatoes and potatoes with aching backs. We also picketed Miami's Winn-Dixie grocery stores to support a national boycott of Gallo wine called for by the United Farm Workers of America (UFW). Based on these experiences, I composed my first publication, "Migrant Farmworkers: The Invisible Minority" (Kirkwood, 1977).

I also taught at Turner Technical Arts High School, a brand new inner-city high school located in the poorest section of town where 95% of my students were African American. Being German in South Florida where many Jewish refugees had settled after World War II I, once more, was painfully reminded of the Nazi genocide and its horrors inflicted on the Jewish people. One of my very painful memories from that time was my experience with a Jewish teacher who taught English next door to my classroom. When we first met, she was friendly and welcoming, and when I proposed that she might require students to read *The Diary of a Young Girl* by Anne Frank (2003) at the same time I taught the Nazi genocide in my social studies class, she happily agreed. On my way out of the door, she stated, "I love your soft French accent." When I responded that the soft accent is a German one, she shrieked. She never spoke to me again.

BECOMING A GLOBAL EDUCATOR

Empowering learners of all ages to assume active roles, both locally and globally, in building more peaceful, tolerant, inclusive, and secure societies
—UNESCO, 2018

My proclivity for and commitment to the pedagogy of global education dates back to my enrollment in the master's degree program and, ultimately, the doctoral program, at Florida International University (FIU). Under the leadership of Professor Jan L. Tucker, my mentor and later husband, I was exposed to the philosophy, literature, moral dimensions, and pedagogy of global education, concepts that made my head spin. I was fascinated by these new ideas for teaching social studies and the possibility of integrating a global perspective in curriculum and instruction in my teaching. Then, as if by magic, a momentous moment arrived. When the superintendent of the Miami Public Schools mandated the interdisciplinary infusion of global education in curriculum and instruction across all age levels, I was appointed principal trainer of in-service teachers, media specialists, and administrators in the district to demonstrate how global education is most effectively integrated into the mandated curricula across all disciplines and age groups. This position ultimately led to my appointment as coordinator of the newly established International Global Education Program of the Miami Public Schools. In my edited book, *Visions in Global Education: The Globalization of Curriculum and Pedagogy in Teacher Education and Schools* (Kirkwood-Tucker, 2009), I devote two chapters to describing the 10-year integration of global programs in Miami's schools. My chapters, along with the other chapters in this book, describe the power of global education when visionary, knowledgeable, and caring leaders in education are convinced of its promise.

As the coordinator of the International Global Education Program of the Miami Public Schools, one of my proudest achievements was the creation and implementation of the Model United Nations, known as the Model UN program, in Miami's 43 high schools in 1984. Within a short time, student teams from surrounding counties (including Okeechobee County, northwest of Miami, with its large farmworker student population) asked to join our UN simulation program. In collaboration with the Political Science department at Florida International University, members of the United Nations Association of the United States of America (UNA-USA), and the Miami Quaker community, I accomplished this feat for 10 years. Although challenging, implementing a Model UN program in Miami's schools was a long-held dream of mine (see "Empowering Teachers to Create a More Peaceful World Through Global Education: Simulating the United Nations" [Kirkwood-Tucker, 2004a]). Not only did I want Miami's students to learn about the seminal documents of the Universal Declaration of Human Rights (United Nations, n.d.-b) and the Convention on the Rights of the Child (n.d.-a), both which I consider to be commensurate with the global education philosophy, I also wanted Miami's students to know that it was former First Lady Eleanor Roosevelt, my heroine, who had chaired the original United Nations Human Rights Commission from which these unique documents originated. I also wanted Miami's students to know that it was her husband, President Franklin Delano Roosevelt, who coined the name United Nations. Deeply convinced that human rights are basic to all humankind, I later penned two publications about my conviction. In "Eleanor Roosevelt and Civil Rights" (Kirkwood-Tucker, 2011), I analyzed the first lady's fearless advocacy for African Americans in their struggle for equality. I see Eleanor Roosevelt as an inspirational figure who viewed racial discrimination as a blatant form of injustice that had been tolerated for too long in the United States.

In my second article, "Preparing Global Citizens Through the Study of Human Rights" (Kirkwood-Tucker, 2012), I spoke to the multiplicity of global issues confronting humanity (premature death of children, refugees, forced labor exploitation, child laborers, poverty, human trafficking, etc.). Most importantly, I addressed the moral responsibility teachers must possess in order to cultivate global awareness in their students and ensure that future generations have the knowledge, attitudes, and skills essential for competent citizenship in a global age. I should note that the Model UN Program in the Miami Public Schools is still in operation today.

Assistant Professor at Florida Atlantic University

Upon attaining my long-sought-after doctorate in education in curriculum and instruction, with an emphasis on global education, from Florida International University (FIU) in 1995, I accepted a position as assistant professor of social studies education in the School of Teacher Education at Florida Atlantic University (FAU) in 1996. My golden opportunity to globalize curriculum and instruction had arrived and, this time, it was at the university level. I introduced five new global education courses into the teacher education program: Global Perspectives in Education, Global Perspectives of Curricular Trends and Issues Across Nations, Methods for Teaching Global Perspectives Across Curriculum, Simulating the United Nations, and I co-authored Methods and Materials for Teaching the Holocaust and Other Genocides. My world was beautiful. My new role as an assistant professor offered new possibilities to engage in travel-study trips abroad to such places as England, China, Japan, Nepal, and Vietnam. These trips were some of my most enjoyable and highly educational endeavors, exposing me to multiple perspectives and cultural similarities and differences. Meeting teachers in each of these countries also demonstrated how much we had in common in our efforts to educate the youth of our respective nations. I am fortunate to have experienced the kindness, warmth, and intelligence of educators, colleagues, teachers, and students in many spaces around the world.

Banned From Tibet

During my study-trip to Nepal in 2005, I embraced the breathtaking views of the Himalayan Mountains, exquisite temples, and caring people, but found I was banned from visiting Tibet. To my surprise, the Chinese consulate in Germany (I traveled with a German academic group) refused my visa application. I tried again, and regretfully gave up after a second rejection without a requested explanation. "Why?" I asked myself. I hypothesized that the visa rejection might have been related to a research project I supervised which required my graduate students to investigate human rights violations in a given country in lieu of the final semester exam. One of the exchange students from China asked if she could investigate her home country to which I agreed. When permitted to leave the class before the end of the semester in order to visit her family in China, she asked me if she could send her final paper from home, and I consented. Although she had the distinction of ranking among the top students in the School of Teacher Education, her research paper never arrived. Upon her return from China, she assured me that she had emailed her work via attachment and, indeed, the hard copy she provided was the best paper of all those submitted by my 23 graduate students. I had to wonder if the security apparatus of the Chinese government intercepted her research and made note of her German American professor at Florida State University? Or, was the daughter of a Nazi dissident a possible danger to an unjust Chinese regime governing Tibet?

My worldview was expanded even more as I began to deliver research presentations at international conferences around the world in Canada, Germany, Jamaica, Korea, Mexico, Russia, and South Africa. I especially benefited from the authentic and principled scholarship of international teacher educators and their creative and ingenious efforts to improve education in a wide variety of ways. Each conference offered me the chance to hear unique perspectives about the meaning and purpose of global education from scholars from the Eastern, Western, and Southern hemispheres. Their research challenged my deeply embedded Western perspective. Equally important as the intellectual exchange with academics from around the world were my encounters with the local people in the street. I watched as they sold goods in the market, I ate in remote places, and I conversed with engaging young men and women about their dreams.

GLOBAL EDUCATION: CATALYST IN THE NEW RUSSIA

In 1991, I reached the climax of my professional career with an invitation to participate in the radical education reform movement in the former Soviet Union with a group of global educators from Indiana University and FIU (see "Global Education in Russia: Catalyst in the Russian Education Reform

Movement" [Kirkwood-Tucker & Tucker, 2001]). It was the golden educational opportunity of a lifetime. On the historic day of December 31, 1991, the Union of Soviet Socialist Republics (USSR) superpower ceased to exist, and the Commonwealth of Independent States (CIS) was born. Stalingrad reverted to Volgograd, Leningrad to St. Petersburg, and 15 nations that had comprised the former Soviet Union gained independence. After working more than 70 years within a closed society, Soviet leadership, now Russian leadership, faced the enormous challenge of joining the community of nations. The country lurched forward to begin the process of democratizing its major institutions. One of its greatest challenges was to restructure education, the seedbed of new ideas in a free society. The goal was to replace an educational curriculum based on Marxist/Leninist thought with a global education curriculum.

While we implemented global education programs in Russian schools and universities, we were unaware of the extent to which hunger had become an enduring condition in Russian communities since the fall of the Soviet Union in 1991, especially among children and elderly in rural areas. When Dr. Edvard Dneprov, Minister of Education (whom I knew from the 1991 Key Biscayne conference when he and his delegation visited the United States) appeared on U.S. national television to ask for assistance in addressing Russia's hunger catastrophe, his request traveled like wildfire through the Miami-Dade public schools. Hundreds of globally-trained teachers responded by placing empty milk cartons on school cafeteria dining tables encouraging students to drink water and place their milk money (a quarter) into the container labeled "For Russia's Hungry Children." To this day, my deep gratitude goes to Delta Airlines which transported, at no cost, tons of vitamins, medicines, and dried food to Moscow for distribution.

Another highlight of my teaching career was the 1994 U.S.–Russian Student Exchange Program sponsored by the American Forum for Global Education funded by the United States Information Agency (USIA). The program paired 10 global high schools in Connecticut, Florida, Illinois, and New Jersey with 10 global schools in Russia (see "Building Bridges: Miami 'Ambassadors' visit Russia" [Kirkwood-Tucker & Tucker, 2001]). A colleague and I took minority students from our high school to the cities of Ryazan and Cheboksary to homestay for 3 weeks with Russian families. The following year, the children of our Russian hosts home-stayed with American families in Miami. The U.S.–Russian Student Exchange Program resulted in most meaningful educational and social benefits for Russian and American students and parents alike, in particular for the Miami inner-city students of color (Figure 11.9).

Fulbright Senior Specialist

Missing my Russian colleagues, students, and their parents, I returned to Russia for a seventh time in 2003 as a Fulbright senior specialist. At Ryazan

Figure 11.9 Miami's student ambassadors visiting Russia.

State Pedagogical University where I had previously attended international conferences between 1992 and 1994, I presented lectures on global education research and taught student teachers and in-service teachers the pedagogy of integrating global content into curricula and instruction across disciplines and grade levels. This 3-month return to Russia re-introduced me to the extraordinary scholarship and deep commitment to global education of Russian teacher educators, administrators, and teachers. Of all my foreign travels my repeated trips to Russia most penetrated my psyche, because I was able to immerse myself in the Russian way of life and develop deep and lasting friendships. The country's superb literature, music, dance, and folktales, the serenity of its countryside of pines and birches, and the warmth, superior intelligence, and generosity of the Russians I realized are experiences I will forever treasure. I remain amazed at how, despite centuries of suffering throughout their turbulent history, the Russian people have survived and successfully navigate their complex lives.

Professional Organizations

An integral part of my professional life derived from an awareness of the criticality of membership in professional organizations and active engagement in leadership positions. After completing a master's in social studies education degree at FIU, and teaching in the Miami Public School District, the fourth largest in our country at that time, I founded the Miami Social Studies Council (MSSC) with the intention of offering Miami's secondary social studies teachers the opportunity to engage in professional development, state and national conferences, and express their concerns about the teaching conditions in their schools. As the MSSC president, I spoke before the Dade County School Board to register our complaints about the consistently oversized social studies classrooms and other concerns. I eventually served on the executive board of the Florida Council for Social Studies (FCSS) before joining the National Council for the Social Studies (NCSS), the largest national professional organization for social studies educators, and its affiliate, the International Assembly (IA), where I served as vice-president and program chair and, eventually, as president from 2004 to 2006. These professional engagements greatly contributed to my intellectual growth and development as an academician.

WRITING ABOUT WAR

Since early childhood, I have been obsessed with the question of how to stop the madness of war. My deeply embedded hatred of war, which I credit in part to my dissident father, eventually resulted in two publications, "Germany's Opposition to the Iraq War and Its Effect on U.S.–German Relations" (Kirkwood-Tucker, 2004b) and "From the Classroom to the Battlefield: A National Guardsman Talks About His Experience in Iraq" (Kirkwood-Tucker, 2006). In the first article, I discussed the major reasons why Germany refused to join the 2003 U.S. invasion of Iraq. I wanted the American public, and in particular American high school teachers, to understand modern Germany's revulsion to war due to the horrors of the Nazi genocide. For most of my life I felt ashamed to be German-born, wondering how so much darkness could emanate from a cultured people with a strong work ethic as I have sought to make sense of this inexplicable nightmare.

In my second published article influenced by my early experiences with war, I recounted the story of my former Haitian American high school student, Bikransky Athouriste. During his senior year in high school, Bikransky and five of his friends signed up for the military. At our high school the recruiters for the Army, Navy, Marine, and National Guard had a table outside the main office which students had to pass to go to class. He joined the Florida National Guard, reasoning that he could attend the required monthly training in his area and simultaneously attend college. It is public knowledge that many American high school students from lower socioeconomic backgrounds see military service as a vehicle for advancement. For poor youth seeking a career, the various branches of the U.S. Armed Forces provide one of few such concrete opportunities. Enlistment holds out the promise of generous benefits, adequate pay, college tuition, and specialized training that would otherwise be unattainable for them. Yet, I strongly believe that these very young people, who choose the military in their quest for a better life and risk emotional and physical debilitation and death, could choose a different path to their future if our society prioritized high-quality education for *all children* regardless of socioeconomic status/ethnicity/race. Bikransky's classmate Candice went into the Air Force while others, like Yoruba and Jonathon, joined the Marine Corps. St. Todd enlisted in the Army and Bikransky and his friend Reggie signed up for the Florida National Guard. That year, a total of 160 high school graduates were recruited from Miami's public high schools, and the majority were students of color (Florida Department of Education, as cited in Kirkwood-Tucker, 2006). The memory of these students grappling with social and educational inequalities (as do so many others in the United States) along with my deeply felt opposition to war, led me to become a Quaker. The Quakers belong to the Religious Society of Friends and are conscientious objectors. My father would be pleased with my anti-war academic work and my personal life decisions..

MY LOVE OF TEACHING

Muchmore (2020) argues that teaching is an autobiographical endeavor:

> It is autobiographic in the sense that the values and beliefs that guide teachers' actions are inevitably shaped by their personal histories... their past experiences play a significant role in determining the kinds of teachers they become. (p. 109)

My storied narrative supports this assertion. After retiring from Florida Atlantic University as associate professor emeritá in 2004, I moved to Tallahassee, Florida, with my special needs daughter Andrée to live in closer proximity to my son David. He had moved to Tallahassee years before to earn a bachelor's degree in criminology and a master's degree in social science education from Florida State University, and decided to stay. For 30 enjoyable years, he taught Advanced Placement (AP) World History and Advanced Placement (AP) Psychology at Wakulla Senior High School, just south of Tallahassee. The rolling hills, pine forests, and a Southern way of life in the capital of Florida have provided a welcome change for Andrée and me after years in the overcrowded, fast-moving, and unmercifully hot climate of South Florida.

Soon after my retirement, however, I began to miss teaching and the beautiful young people who aspire to become social studies teachers. I returned to academia and taught two semesters at Florida Agricultural and Mechanical University (FAMU), an historic Black college in Tallahassee founded in 1859. Shortly after, Florida State University (FSU) offered me a position as a visiting professor and social studies program coordinator in the School of Teacher Education. With the approval of Assistant Dean Sissi Carroll and the curriculum committee I was able to integrate a global perspective into the existing social studies program. To learn about the significance and criticality of the United Nations students engaged in my newly developed Model UN course which required them to simulate the United Nations which became one of their favorite activities in the Department of Teacher Education. I was gratified to find that my proclivity for and commitment to global education teaching had reached unexpected heights of educational and personal satisfaction, since I strongly believe that teachers are among the most powerful forces to lift their beloved students to their full potential. After my second retirement from teaching at FAMU and FSU, I again found myself unable to relinquish my love for teaching. I am now teaching classes for the FSU Osher Lifelong Learning Institute (OLLI) that include: Experiences of a German Girl During the Nazi Era, End of World War II, and Mandatory Teaching of the Nazi Genocide in German Schools; The Rise and Fall of the Berlin Wall; Eleanor Roosevelt: A Woman of the World; and The United Nations: An International Forum Working for Peace Among Nations.

As part of my service as an immigrant to my new homeland I raise funds for the mentally impaired clients at the Hilltop Residential Program in Madison, Florida, a group home 55 miles east of Tallahassee where my daughter Andrée resides. Except for two of the 16 residents, no family member or friend has paid them a visit over the last 10 years. I also serve as a Florida Guardian ad Litem volunteer, a position in which I act as the "voice" for Florida's abused, neglected, and abandoned children. Seven years ago, I met two teenage brothers of color at our local Boys Town (a group home for boys and now also for girls originally founded by Father Flanagan in Nebraska in 1917) whom I mentor and represent in court. This volunteer work has exposed me to the stark reality of what it means to be poor. Here in Tallahassee, I have developed a new understanding of the inextricable intersections between the neglect of the mentally ill, the abuse suffered by children, and the impacts of poverty.

REFLECTIONS

My childhood years in Germany during the Nazi era, my dissident father, immigration to the United States, work in the Miami Public Schools, participation in the Russian education reform movement, travel and study trips abroad, tenure at two public Florida universities, and love for teaching—all have shaped who I am today. At each crossroad and with each relationship, lessons emerged that shaped my philosophy of education and of life itself, deepening my global perspective. My philosophy of life commensurates with the mission of the Universal Declaration of Human Rights (United Nations, n.d.-b) and the Convention of the Rights of the Child (n.d.-a).

My childhood experiences of war and genocide molded my worldview and determination to prevent the horrors of war through global education as reflected in my high school and college teaching, curriculum development, and academic publications. My worldview also has its roots in the deep affection I felt for the African American soldiers who threw oranges and bananas and Hershey bars to us children-of-war when their tanks rolled into our village at the end of World War II. Coming to "Amerika" at age 22 into unfamiliar territories and cultures, further affected my perspective. I did not anticipate the discriminatory practices against African Americans that I witnessed, and which I perceive to be another form of genocide in slow motion over time in my new homeland. In experiencing the interrelationships between social and racial injustice, identity, and power, I have come to recognize the multiple realities surrounding us. This recognition has led to my international sensitivity, intercultural competence, and world mindedness. My interactions have laid the foundation for my deep friendships with individuals of racial and cultural backgrounds, and for the love I share with two abused teenagers-of-color whom I have nurtured in the Guardian ad Litem Program in my community.

Why do I possess a proclivity for and commitment to a pedagogy of global education that teaches about the equality of all members of humankind, an understanding of the perspective consciousness held by individuals and groups, respect for cultural similarities and differences, the interconnectedness of the world, and the moral decisions and actions we must engage in to improve the human condition (Kirkwood-Tucker, 2018)? My experiences, lived in the context of certain historical times and geographic spaces, have sensitized my cross-cultural awareness, and challenged my thinking. I have witnessed poverty and despair that has scarred me forever, but I also gained deep professional and personal fulfillment from work with the Russian education reform movement and its brilliant and committed education leaders. Above all, however, it is my father whose influence shaped me into the individual that I am today. His abhorrence of fascism and distrust of government and authority ignited, kindled, and cultivated in me a critical mind, deep respect for the due process of law, and awareness of the criticality of separation of church and state.

My first teaching experience began at a junior high school in Miami Beach, Florida, at the height of school integration in the 1960s. My career continued at an inner-city high school in the trenches of poverty and crime in the 1990s, and ended in the 2000s at two public Florida universities, where I trained future secondary social studies teachers to teach from a global perspective. As I reflect on my life, I cannot imagine a more rewarding professional and personal journey.

REFERENCES

Butler, R. (2019). *SS-Hitlerjugend: The history of the twelfth SS division, 1943–45*. Trade books. E-Bay: Quality Books.
Connelly, F. M., & Clandinin, D. J. (2006). Narrative inquiry. In J. Green, G. Camilli, & P. Elmore (Eds.), *Handbook of complementary methods in education research* (pp. 375–385). Lawrence Erlbaum.

Du Bois, W. E. B. (1903). *The souls of Black folks*. A. C. McClurg.
Die Weisse Rose (The White Rose). (1982). *Documentary on the Geschwister Scholl: Resistance and decapitation*. Wikipedia. Retrieved May 15, 2022 from https://en.wikipedia.org/wiki/Die_Wei%C3%9Fe_Rose_(film)
Frank, A. (2003). *The diary of Anne Frank: The revised critical edition*. Doubleday.
Hanvey, R. (1976). *An attainable global perspective*. American Forum for Global Education.
Kirkwood, T. F. (1977). Migrant farm workers:The invisible minority. *Trends in Social Education, 23*(2), 13–23.
Kirkwood-Tucker, T. F. (2001). Building bridges: Miami "ambassadors" visit Russia. *Social Education, 65*(4), 236–239.
Kirkwood-Tucker, T. F. (2004a, Winter). Empowering teachers to create a more peaceful world through global education: Simulating the United Nations. *Theory and Research in Social Education, 32*(1), 56–74. https://doi.org/10.1080/00933104.2004.10473243
Kirkwood-Tucker, T. F. (2004b). Germany's opposition to the Iraq war and its effect on U.S.- German relations. *Social Education, 68*(4), 285–288.
Kirkwood-Tucker, T. F. (2006). From the classroom to the battlefield: A national guardsman talks about his experience in Iraq. *Social Education, 70*(2), 99–103.
Kirkwood-Tucker, T. (Ed.). (2009). *Visions in global education: The globalization of curriculum and pedagogy in teacher education and schools*. Peter Lang.
Kirkwood-Tucker, T. F. (2011). Eleanor Roosevelt and civil rights. *Social Education, 75*(5), 245–249. https://www.socialstudies.org/social-education/75/5/eleanor-roosevelt-and-civil-rights
Kirkwood-Tucker, T. F. (2012). Preparing global citizens through the study of human rights. *Social Education, 76*(5), 244–246. https://www.socialstudies.org/social-education/76/5/preparing-global-citizens-through-study-human-rights
Kirkwood-Tucker, T. F. (2018). (Ed.). *The global education movement: Narratives of distinguished global scholars*. Information Age Publishing.
Kirkwood-Tucker, T. F., & Tucker, J. L. (2001). Global education in Russia: Catalyst in the Russian education reform movement. *The International Social Studies Forum, 1*(1), 63–75.
Muchmore, J. (2020). The legacy of a murder. In C. Edge, A. Cameron-Standerford, & B. Bergh (Eds.), *Textiles, and tapestries: Self-study for envisioning new ways of knowing*. EdTech Books. https://edtechbooks.org/textiles_tapestries_self_study/chapter_109
United Nations. (n.d.-a). *The convention of the rights of the child*. https://www.ohchr.org/en/instruments-mechanisms/instruments/convention-rights-child
United Nations. (n.d.-b). *Universal declaration of human rights*. https://www.google.com/search?client=firefox-b-1-d&q=United+Nations+%281948%29+Universal+Declaration+of+Human+Rights+
United Nations Educational, Scientific and Cultural Organization. (2018). *Global campaign for Education* (GCE). https://sdgs.un.org/statements/global-campaign-education-gce-13514
Utschneider, L. (2012). *Oberammergau im Dritten Reich 1933–1945*. Historischen Vereins Oberammergau 1999.
Waddy, H. (2010). *Oberammergau in the Nazi era: The fate of a catholic village in Hitler's Germany*. Oxford University Press.

CHAPTER 12

THE NETHERLANDS

ON CROSSING THE BIG POND

Frans H. Doppen

Before I immigrated to the United States, I knew that New Amsterdam, founded in 1625 by the Dutch, had become New York in 1664. However, I was clueless when it came to *Hans Brinker and The Silver Skates* by Mary Mapes Dodge published in 1865, the very same year the American Civil War came to an end. My mother-in-law recommended that I read this classic. So, I did. Having grown up in The Netherlands, little did I know that Hans Brinker actually saved my country by sticking his finger in a leak in one of the many dikes that protect our country from the sea. As a recent immigrant, I soon realized that stereotypical images of The Netherlands as a country of wooden shoes, windmills, and tulips remained alive and well. As a teacher and teacher educator, it became my never-ending mission to instill a sense of global awareness in my students.

GROWING UP IN THE NETHERLANDS

Marienvelde

In 1930, Pastoor Deperink, then a chaplain in the nearby parish of Beltrum, was appointed by the Vatican to build a church in a to be established new parish in Achter-Zieuwent in The Netherlands. When construction of the church was completed in 1932, it was christened *Onze Lieve Vrouw van Lourdes* (Our Dear Lady of Lourdes). That same year, referring to the Virgin Mary, Pastoor Deperink also decided to name the new parish *Marienvelde*, meaning "Mary in the Field." Marienvelde is part of a Catholic enclave, the result of having remained under Spanish control during the Twelve Years' Truce (1609–1621). It is located in the eastern Dutch province of Gelderland (Guelders), about 10 miles from the German border. And it was in Marienvelde where in 1956 my parents decided to build a house and my father operated his barbershop (Figure 12.1) directly across the street from the church, and where I was born 1 year later. I was 15 years of age before

Figure 12.1 The house my parents built in 1956.

I first crossed the border into Germany to proudly purchase a transistor radio with my own money earned in our neighbor's grocery store. Reminiscent of the religious divisions that have marked the history of Ireland, but without its history of violence, Zieuwent at the time was part of the Catholic municipality of Lichtenvoorde whereas Achter-Zieuwent was incorporated in the largely protestant municipality of Ruurlo. As a result, my father's customers included virtually no Protestant customers even though they lived less than a mile north of the village.

My Parents

My father, Antoon Doppen, was born in Zieuwent, the second child in a large family of eight children, five boys and three girls (Figure 12.2). Three of the five boys, including my father, followed in my grandfather's footsteps by becoming barbers. My father set his eyes on Marienvelde and built his clientele base by starting off cutting customers' hair in the cow stable of one of our neighbors. During the final days of his life, my father revealed to me for the first time that during the Nazi occupation of our country in World War II he had been forced into the *Arbeitsdienst* (labor service) at Mook, a small village on the Maas (Meuse) River south of Nijmegen. Each morning the camp commander would sit down stark naked on a stool to be shaved and remind my father that if he would ever cut him, he would be facing the firing squad.

Like my father, my mother was also born into a large Catholic family in nearby Lichtenvoorde (Figure 12.3). She was born into a family as the

Figure 12.2 My father, 3rd from right.

264 • F. H. DOPPEN

Figure 12.3 My mother, 3rd from right.

youngest of eight children, three boys and five girls. The youngest child in the family, her father was a farmer. As a young woman my mother helped with the harvest and later worked as a house maid for a family in town until she married my father in 1956. She served in the traditional role of a housewife and daily prepared fresh meals. I distinctly remember, in the days before the arrival of washing machines, that Monday was laundry day, all day long.

Memorable Events

As I reflect back on my youth in Marienvelde, several events stand out distinctly in my memory. In 1963, when I was in second grade, we got our first television. I remember how excited I was when a local carpenter installed a special shelf in the corner of the kitchen, and a local electrician mounted an antenna on top of the roof of our house. This event began to open my eyes to the larger world. My father and I religiously watched the evening news and also daily read *De Gelderlander*—the regional newspaper. At that time there were only two Dutch television channels, but we also had access to three German television channels, which we occasionally watched even though I did not fully understand German. I also remember the birth of the current Dutch King Willem-Alexander, in 1967, which we celebrated at my elementary school with all students eating a "beschuitje" (rusk) with orange *hagelslag* (sprinkles), the color of the royal House of Orange. Most notably, due to Queen Wilhelmina's radio messages to the nation from her exile in London during World War II, the monarchy continues to symbolize what it means to be Dutch. In 1969, my father and I sat up late on the night of July 20–21 to watch Neil Armstrong become the first human being to set foot on the moon and famously proclaim, "That's one small step for man, one giant leap for mankind." Another vivid memory is the hostage crisis at the Munich Olympics in 1972, which resulted in the death of five of the eight Palestinian hostage takers, 11 members of Israel's Olympic team, and a German policeman. The Oil Embargo of 1973 is another highly memorable event of global importance that stands out. In retaliation for supporting Israel during the Yom Kippur War, the Organization of Petroleum Exporting Countries (OPEC) cut off the oil supply to the United States and, among other countries, The Netherlands. A fond memory, during our car-free Sundays even Joop den Uyl, our prime minister, as well as many other ordinary citizens, were able to bicycle on our empty highways.

Village Life

Although today the village only has a car repair shop, when I grew up in Marienvelde it had three bakery shops, three grocery stores, three bars—two of which were directly across the street from the church, a butcher shop, a bicycle repair shop, a feed mill, as well as a blacksmith and a paint business. We even had a milkman who daily delivered fresh milk, fresh yogurt and *vla*, a delicious kind of Dutch custard. Our neighbors operated a grocery store, a café, a restaurant, and a snack bar. I mostly worked in their grocery store where I became well acquainted with many villagers. I most clearly remember a customer who each time he came into the store was offered a cup of coffee and, in keeping with an old tradition, he always turned the cup upside down on its saucer after finishing the drink. The grocery store also accepted weekly orders from its customers which—when they were delivered to their homes—always included a small gift bag of candy, apparently an international tradition as I found out after moving to Ohio some 30 years later when I found out that the immigrant father of a new friend had brought that same tradition with him from nearby Oberhausen, Germany, located about 40 miles across a border.

Special annual events in Marienvelde included the annual *kermis*, a fair that involved no animals and featured dancing floors with live bands in the two cafés across the street from the church, the local "harmony" marching band, *vogel shieten* (shooting down a wooden bird from the top of a high pole) whose winner became the ceremonial king for the duration of the fair, *vogel gooien* (throwing clubs at a wooden bird on a high pole) whose winner then became his queen. And, of course, there were also exciting attractions such as a carousel, bumper cars, and a fairground mill. Carnaval was also a special annually recurring event. My siblings and I would dress up in special outfits and go door to door singing the "*foekepotterij*" song. Instead of the *foekepot*, which is an old folk music drum, we rattled our piggy banks. Each time after singing the song, the tenant of the house would drop a coin in each of our piggy banks. Also, on the 11th of the 11th month (November 11), the village elected a Prince Carnaval, an honor once bestowed upon my father. Another memorable annual event was the Easter bonfire during which time our pastor, accompanied by the marching band, blessed and lit an enormous pyre aflame to symbolize the resurrection of Christ and mark the end of winter darkness.

The elementary school I attended, St. Theresia, was less than a block from my parents' house, and each day I simply walked to school in less than 5 minutes. I came home for dinner at noon and returned to school for the afternoon. Dinner typically included potatoes, vegetables, and fruit that my parents grew in the garden behind our house. Having become an altar boy, being a favorite of the pastor, I often had to leave school for church service. For some unknown reason, it seemed like no one ever could get married or buried without me having to be there. Another important memory of my elementary school happened when I was in sixth grade. Unacceptable as our response may seem today, I distinctly remember running to the front of the school when I heard students shouting, "There he is!" A reflection of how culturally homogeneous my childhood experience was, here was the first person of color I ever saw in my life: a native of Suriname, which at that time was still a Dutch colony. He was the first person of color I ever saw in real life. Needless to say, our geography school curriculum included learning where our colonies in Asia and the Caribbean were located.

World War II Stories

Although I was a schoolboy in the 1960s, I recognize some of my own experiences in Ian Buruma's (1994) introduction to his study on how Germany and Japan have responded differently to the question of their guilt for World War II. In general, Buruma argues that, soon after the war, contemporary Germany atoned for its guilt whereas Japan did not. As I grew up, Nazi Germany's guilt for invading The Netherlands was always beyond question: The Nazis were the aggressors by brutally attacking a peaceful neighbor. On the question of Nazi Germany's guilt for invading The Netherlands, Buruma—being a schoolboy in the 1950s growing up in The Hague—wrote:

> There was never any doubt...who our enemies were. There was the Soviet Union, of course, but that...was rather remote. No, the enemies were the

Germans. They were the comic-book villains of my childhood in The Hague. When I say Germans, I mean just that—not Nazis, but Germans. The occupation between 1940 and 1945 and the animosity that followed were seen in national, not political terms. The Germans had conquered our country. They had forced my father to work in their factories. And they had left behind the bunkers on our coast, like great stone toads, squat relics of a recent occupation, dark and damp and smelling of urine. (p. 3)

On the timeless question of whether the Dutch should have joined the resistance, Buruma wrote:

The question that obsessed us was not how we would have acquitted ourselves in uniform, going over the top, running into machine-gun fire or mustard gas, but whether we would have joined the resistance, whether we would have cracked under torture, whether we would have hidden Jews and risked deportation ourselves. Our particular shadow was not war, but occupation. (p. 6)

Like Buruma, I also grew up with stories about events that happened locally during World War II, which in my case were stories from Marienvelde. Between September 1944 and May 1945 during the war, the western part of The Netherlands experienced a food crisis, known as the Hunger Winter. Our neighbors, *Ome* (Uncle; "Ome" in the local dialect rather than "Oom") and *Tante* (Aunt) Heutinck, in whose grocery store I worked, as part of a national effort to evacuate children (De Swarte, 2016), accepted a young girl by the name of Marietje Siderius from Amsterdam, into their home so she would no longer be starving. After the war, when I was a teenager, Marietje returned each year for a visit to thank Ome and Tante for what they had done for her.

In September 1944, after liberating the south of The Netherlands, the Allies launched Operation Market Garden in their attempt to cross the Rhine River at Arnhem to reach Germany. The operation failed as Arnhem became "a bridge too far." The *Wehrmacht* (German army) ordered that Arnhem be evacuated. Our neighbors then decided once again to offer shelter, this time to a refugee couple by the name of Putman from Haalderen, a village near Arnhem. One day, a group of German soldiers came into their restaurant for some food and drinks after just having executed a local farmer by the name of Ten Dam who had been forced to dig trenches. Apparently, Ten Dam had either refused to dig more trenches or said something that displeased the Germans. He, with the commanded assistance of another villager, was then forced to dig his own grave and was executed. Mrs. Putman suggested they should put rat poisoning in the soup they were preparing for the German soldiers in their restaurant. This terrified Ome and Tante who had to persuade her not to do so. On another occasion Ome had hidden half a pig under the billiards table on which the German soldiers, who were regulars in the restaurant, played their competitive games. Ome was terrified, but fortunately the Germans never noticed the pig.

Even our Pastoor Deperink helped hide two local villagers who were wanted by the German occupier between the church's vaulted ceiling and its roof. His housekeeper, Maria Rolfes, whom I regularly visited across the street, tended to a beautiful garden with dahlias that she used not only to decorate the altar in the church each week for Sunday Mass but also the war graves in our cemetery of five Royal Air Force (RAF) members. On the night of September 18–19, 1940, an RAF plane crashed near our village, killing its four crew members, all between the ages of 22–27. While I do not know the cause of his death, a fifth RAF flying officer, age 39, who died on July 26, 1942, was buried in our cemetery as well. Each time I visited their graves with Maria, I was reminded of how war especially claims the lives of young men.

Church

Although The Netherlands is today a rather secularized society, as I was growing up the church still played a central role in most people's lives, including mine. Each time I crossed the street to visit Maria, she inevitably led me to the *pastoor kamer* (pastor's room) to shake hands with Pastoor Deperink who always struck me as a kind, old person. An important event that happened during Pastoor Deperink's term in Marienvelde was the Second Vatican Council, which decided to dramatically turn around the altars in our churches so that the priest now faced the congregation and the parishioners no longer had to observe mass watching the pastor's back. Also, for the first time, mass was now delivered in Dutch rather than in Latin. To top things off, my mother no longer had to wear a head scarf or hat during church service. After Pastoor Deperink retired, our new pastor, Pastoor De Graaf was quite different from our former pastor. Rather than keeping to himself in the pastor's room as Pastoor Deperink did, he was rumored to spend too much time in the housekeeper's part of the church building, which led to his ouster by the church council. The central role of church in my life was further emphasized by the ever presence of a picture of Cardinal Alfrink, archbishop of Utrecht from 1955–1975, on our kitchen wall.

MY EDUCATION

High School

After passing the admissions test in 1969, I was accepted at the *Marianum Scholengemeenshap* (School Community) a secondary, Grades 7–12, school in Groenlo. For 6 years I biked the daily eight miles to and from school, rain or shine. After the first *propaedeutic* (preliminary) year, I qualified for the college preparatory track. Excited to be learning another language and curious about the "outside" world, during my second year at the school, I convinced my parents to host a visiting student from the United Kingdom, which was my first major personal intercultural experience and my family's first direct experience with a foreigner, having to communicate in a foreign language.

The Marianum was—and is to this day—a publicly funded Catholic school. Since 1917, at the end of the *Schoolstrijd* (School Struggle), a long political battle over how to publicly finance education, all schools in The Netherlands have received equal government support and are held to the same national standards. Although the Marianum was a Catholic school founded by Marist priests, it did not have a strong focus on religion. I only had one class period each week dedicated to religion which included the study of world religions. I don't recall ever attending any church service in the school's chapel, but I do remember that we once did have a transcendental meditation session in the building. I also distinctly remember that we watched the musical *Jesus Christ Superstar* in religion class. Since I was a better student in the humanities than in the exact sciences, I opted for the "*Atheneum A*" college track that included the study of Dutch, English, French, and German language as well as history, economics, and business administration as national examination subjects for graduation. Particularly the language classes, which all required a literary reading list to be read over several years and to be orally examined in front of a panel of several teachers, opened my eyes to different cultures.

At the Marianum, my history classes were very teacher centered. Studying history basically meant that you read the textbook, took notes, and answered some questions at the end of the chapter. I do not recall any classroom discussions about any historical events. Nonetheless, I was very much interested in history. Then a powerful event occurred in 1973 when, during my sophomore year, Alexander Solzhenitsyn's *Gulag Archipelago* trilogy was published in the West. Reading all three volumes, I was stunned by what I learned about Stalin's forced labor camps, show trials, and the terror he unleashed on every Soviet citizen as even parents were too afraid to discuss any political issues in front of their own children, family members, or friends in fear they might be reported to the secret police. It was during my junior year on February 12, 1974, that Heinrich Böll, a famous German author, welcomed Solzhenitsyn at the Frankfurt airport in West Germany after he was stripped of his citizenship and expelled from the Soviet Union. With all the attention that my history teachers bestowed upon Hitler and World War II, I wondered why Stalin's Great Terror was not part of the curriculum? This personal questioning further unleashed in me a desire to learn more about what had happened in the history of other countries that we did not learn about, such as, for example, Mao Zedong's communist rule in China.

My history classes also did not include any critical examination of Dutch colonization and involvement in the slave trade. The emergence of the Black Lives Matter movement that originated in the United States and spread to other countries, including The Netherlands, has led to a welcome and highly needed surge in research on the role of the Dutch in the enslavement of Asians and Africans. After the publication of a report on Amsterdam's deep involvement in enslaving people in Asia and Central and South America (Brandon et al., 2020), the city of Utrecht has published its own report on its notables' commercial interests in enslaving innocent people (Jouwe et al., 2021). The lack of any deep critical perspective on Dutch involvement in the slave trade continued even during my undergraduate studies at Utrecht University where I completed a minor in overseas history that focused, among other topics, on "17th century Dutch traders' opinions on Natives of the colonies."

Utrecht University

Upon graduating from high school in 1975, the lottery system, a consequence of national admission quotas, resulted in my admission to the University of Utrecht (now Utrecht University) to study history. It was a big change to move from my small hometown to a big city with more than 200,000 inhabitants. However, I felt liberated having left Marienvelde and its social constraints behind. As the son of the local barber, my parents always emphasized the importance of never doing anything which might cause my father's customers to go elsewhere for their hair cuts. Freedom was calling!

After I completed my *Kandidaat's* (bachelor's) degree in 1979, a friend challenged me to be more adventurous. This prompted me to visit the *Bureau Buitenland*, the foreign programs office at the university, to inquire about the possibility of joining an exchange program at the Sorbonne in Paris to hone my French language skills. The office's director told me there would be little chance that I would be accepted at the Sorbonne as I would be competing for a spot with French language majors. Instead, she recommended the exchange program at the University of Florida (UF) in Gainesville, Florida, where acceptance was virtually guaranteed. I told her I had no desire whatsoever to spend a year in a capitalist and militarily aggressive world power country that was in the process of developing the morally despicable neutron bomb, a thermonuclear weapon designed to maximize lethal neutron radiation in the immediate vicinity of the blast while minimizing the physical destruction of the blast itself. My perspective on the United States was reflective of a nascent peace movement that was emerging in The

Figure 12.4 My departure for Florida, August 18, 1980.

Netherlands at that time. Despite my reservation about spending a year in the United States, I decided to add my name to the list of applicants for the exchange program at UF. Although I had traveled in Germany, France, England, Belgium, and Luxembourg, this would be my first major foreign overseas experience. Thus, it came to be that in August 1980, together with four other exchange students, I boarded a Sabena airplane in Brussels to fly across the big pond (Figure 12.4).

Because of my participation in the foreign exchange program, the Department of History at Utrecht University allowed me to complete my teacher education early. It was a one-semester-long full-time program, alternating between weeklong classes at the university and student teaching in Schiedam. This community near Rotterdam proved to be an important diversity experience for me as most students appeared to lack any significant knowledge of the history of Christianity and religious practices. Furthermore, many students' parents worked in the Rotterdam harbor, a culture I was totally unfamiliar with. Upon completing the program, I became certified to teach history at any secondary track level but as fate would have it, I never became a teacher in The Netherlands. During my time at Utrecht University, I also learned important lessons about life by working jobs through temporary employment agencies. These experiences taught me to appreciate factory workers' lives. I walked country roads in the midst of winter snow to read gas meters. I worked on a bottle washing machine in a soda drinks factory. I worked in the cooling cellar of a margarine factory with Turkish immigrants who observed Ramadan and thus exposed me to an unfamiliar culture. These were experiences that have stayed with me all my life.

University of Florida

During my exchange program at the UF, I intended to complete my master's thesis on American perspectives on the European revolutions of 1848. However, since the Department of History did not offer any course on this specific topic, I was advised to take a course on immigration history with Dr. George Pozzetta. It was in this class that I met my future spouse, Loraine McCosker, whom I would marry 3 years later. The course with Dr. Pozetta—an inspiring expert on immigration to the United States, especially on Italian immigration—led to my master's thesis titled, "Dutch Catholic Immigration in Little Chute, Wisconsin." After completing my doctorandus degree, the equivalent of a master's "plus" degree, I subsequently published my thesis in *U.S. Catholic Historian*, a history journal in the United States (Doppen, 1984). To my dismay the editor, without consulting me, removed any references I had made to how the native Menominee nation was negatively impacted by the arrival of White settlers such as the Dutch immigrants who Van den Broek, a Dutch Catholic missionary among the Menominee, recruited to come live in Little Chute.

While I was an exchange student in the United States, global events once again caught my attention. On November 4, 1980, Ronald Reagan was elected president. The next month, on December 2, three American nuns and a lay worker were savagely murdered in El Salvador. And yet another month later, surprisingly, the Iran hostages returned home on January 20, 1981, shortly after Reagan's inauguration.

Conscientious Objector

After returning home to The Netherlands at the end of the exchange program, I filed for conscientious objector status. The history I had learned about World War II, my questioning—like Buruma—whether I would have had the courage to join the resistance, my interest in global affairs, the civil war in El Salvador, and the Iran hostage crisis deeply motivated me to successfully file for conscientious objector status. Consequently, I completed 18 months of civil service at the Directorate of Emigration in The Hague instead of the regular 12 months required for military service. The directorate was a direct outcome of World War II as the Dutch government decided that economic recovery would be a slow process. It subsequently promoted

Figure 12.5 My parents' 25th wedding anniversary, September 27, 1981. From left to right: Anja, Mia, vader, moeder, Frans, Gonnie, Nico.

and subsidized large-scale emigration to Australia, New Zealand, Canada, the United States, and South Africa. A distinct memory of my time at the directorate is that I was told by one of its long-time employees that in order to be granted a higher immigration quota for the United States they deliberately flew the American ambassador far out over the North Sea to exaggerate the Dutch flood of 1953. My experience at the directorate further opened my eyes to an awareness of the interconnections among nations. Interestingly, after I immigrated to the United States, in 1997 the Dutch fully ended the military draft and converted the army into an all-volunteer force.

University of Utrecht: Reverse Exchange

Loraine, my future spouse, and I decided that she should come to The Netherlands on the same exchange program in which I had participated and attend the University of Utrecht during the 1981–1982 academic year. After she arrived in Utrecht it became my "job" to show her around The Netherlands. We traveled all over the country to places big and small. That experience opened my eyes to how important it is to know the history of one's own country. Subsequently, I have included local history topics and field trips in my courses after I became a social studies teacher educator. I strongly believe that future teachers need to become familiar with the history and culture of communities in which they teach, regardless of location. Who would have thought that the son of a barber from a small village in The Netherlands would one day end up as a teacher in the United States?

Soon after Loraine's arrival, on November 21, 1981, together with 400,000 other demonstrators, she and I participated in the largest peace demonstration held in Amsterdam against the decision by the North Atlantic Treaty Organization (NATO) to install 48 nuclear cruise missiles in The Netherlands in response to the Soviet Union's SS-20 cruise missiles. The big organizer behind the protest in Amsterdam, and of a second protest in The Hague in 1983 that drew 550,000 protesters, was Dutch peace activist Mient Jan Faber. Although he has been largely forgotten, as I write this chapter, the Dutch news reported his passing on May 15, 2022, at the age of 81. Despite the fact that the peace movement put enormous pressure on the Dutch government, it nonetheless agreed to install the cruise missiles in 1985. Fortunately, in the Intermediate-Range Nuclear Forces (INF) treaty, signed on December 8, 1987, Reagan and Gorbachev agreed to destroy their cruise missiles.

MY IMMIGRATION TO THE UNITED STATES

My immigration process to the United States began with my decision to join Loraine in the United States and to live there. As part of the process, I had to submit one of her letters to the American consulate in Amsterdam to prove that we were in fact in a committed relationship and that the *Partij van de Arbeid* (Labor Party), of which I was a member, was not a communist organization. Imagine, I was able to immigrate on a K-1 fiancé visa that gave us 30 days to get married or else I would face deportation. Furthermore, my future sister-in-law had to sign documents that in case I would become a burden to the government she would provide for my sustenance. Within a week after having returned to the United States, Loraine and I married on June 30, 1984. We decided to settle in Gainesville, Florida, where I hoped to begin my teaching career.

Teaching in Florida

My first teaching experience in Florida involved commuting to North Marion High School, a rural school near Ocala where I encountered my first instance of racism. The teachers at the school informed me that they used to meet on Fridays at a nearby bar but no longer patronized the establishment after they had been refused service when an African American colleague had joined their get together. Residing in Gainesville, to my amazement, and contrary to what I had thought I had learned in my education about the success of the civil rights movement in the United States, I learned the meaning of living on "the other side of track" which still is very much evident in the segregated residential patterns in Gainesville. I also was astounded when a friendly elderly neighbor referred to her yard maintenance person with the n-word. Having grown up in a society known for its history of tolerance, I experienced a frightful protest by opponents of a planned anti-gay ordinance, which city council had planned and ultimately did pass. After my first year of teaching in Ocala, I was offered a teaching position at a basically all-White school in rural Branford, a small community in Suwannee County near Live Oak. While I had an overall positive experience teaching in Branford, some locals still referred to the part of town where the family of one of my African American students lived, as the "quarters." In fact, one year Klansmen even burned a cross in one of my male African American students' yard to warn him to stop dating one of my female White students.

Upon receiving my green card—which turned me into a "permanent resident alien"—I was able to apply for annual temporary Florida teaching certificates. Despite having more than the equivalent of a master's degree, the Florida Department of Education required that I take a series of additional courses, including six credit hours of English, after which I would then be able to receive a regular 5-year teaching certificate. When the Bureau of Teacher Certification continued not to respond to my application for a regular 5-year teaching certificate, during my third year of teaching, my principal told me to take the day off and drive to Tallahassee. Simply walking into the department apparently was reason enough for one of the attending civil servants, to on the spot waive the 6 hours in English, finally ending the ordeal to get my foreign credentials accepted and becoming eligible for a regular 5-year certificate.

Interestingly, the first time I returned to Europe for a visit "back home," after a mere 2 years, I came across a Dutchman on a camping site who also came from the *Achterhoek* (literally: back corner), a region in the eastern part of the province of Gelderland (Guelders) near the German border where I grew up, told me that, even in my dialect, I now had an American accent. This experience distinctly planted Du Bois' (1903/2014) idea of double consciousness in my mind, making me wonder: "Am I then no longer a Dutchman?"; "Have I already become a hyphenated Dutch-American?"

In 1993, after 8 years of teaching in Branford, I obtained a teaching position at the racially diverse P. K. Yonge Developmental Research School at UF in Gainesville. At this school, I was inspired by W. D. Myers, a wonderful African American author of children's books for adolescents who presented his book *Now Is Your Time* (Myers, 1991) to our students and staff, to develop a middle school curriculum that explicitly integrated African American history into my teaching (Yeager et al., 1997). Moreover, when one of my 15-year-old students, to my dismay, pointed to India on the world map when I asked him to show us where the continent of Africa was located, I felt compelled from then on to always include basic physical and cultural geographical concepts into my teaching to expand their knowledge about the larger world.

At P. K. Yonge, I became convinced of the importance of the concept of *glocalization*—a term later made popular by Thomas Friedman (2007), which is to teach local history while making global connections. Consequently, each year I organized a major daylong field trip to a significant historical site. For example, I took my students to: nearby Micanopy, Florida's second oldest town, established in 1821, after St. Augustine which was founded on September 8, 1565 by Spanish admiral Pedro Menéndez de Avilés; nearby Paynes Prairie, once the home of the Seminoles to teach them about William Bartram's exotic descriptions of Florida's fauna and flora; nearby Rochelle to show them the grave marker of Madison S. Perry, governor of Florida when the state seceded from the Union; historic Cedar Key on the Gulf coast, while stopping at the site of the Rosewood Massacre that led to the total destruction of this African American community in 1923, left eight people dead, and forced its survivors to flee in order to escape with their lives; and the Kingsley Plantation near Jacksonville. Making global connections, at Zephaniah Kingley's plantation, for example, my students learned that his wife, Anna Madgigine Jai, came from Senegal, West Africa, and was actually purchased by him as a slave.

In the aftermath of 9/11, realizing my students' lack of knowledge of the larger world, I spoke with the director of my school about the importance of offering a new elective course on global issues, something she wholeheartedly agreed with. However, by the time the next school year rolled around, 9/11 had begun to take a backseat in people's collective memory and, unfortunately, the course did not materialize.

As a faculty member at P. K. Yonge, I had the privilege of being able to take tuition free courses at UF. As a result, in 1995, I decided to pursue a specialist in education (EdS) degree, which I completed in 1998. By then, I was the parent of our son Juliaan who was born in 1990 and our daughter Elsbeth who was born in 1994. Attaining a PhD in educational leadership required a major time commitment that I decided would interfere too much with my parental responsibilities. As a result, I decided instead to pursue a PhD in curriculum and instruction with a concentration in social studies. As part of my dissertation research, I conducted classroom observations at four different schools to assess how novice teachers who had recently graduated from the teacher education program at UF, used technology in their classrooms. After completing my PhD in 2002, I published my findings in *Theory and Research in Social Education* (Doppen, 2004).

MY POSITION AT OHIO UNIVERSITY

Teaching in Ohio

After earning my doctorate at UF, I accepted a position at Ohio University in Athens, located in southeast Ohio about 70 miles from Columbus, the state capital. As I drove from the Columbus airport to Athens for the interview, coming from essentially a flat, mostly below sea level, country, I instantly fell in love with the hills of Southeast Ohio. I had no idea of the history of Southeast Ohio. Little did I know that this part of Appalachia would open a whole new world to me that greatly differed from my life in Florida. In many ways, it almost felt like a homecoming as Southeast Ohio's climate and daily weather reminded me of that of The Netherlands.

As an assistant professor in the Department of Teacher Education, I taught courses in middle childhood education and social studies education. While I continued teaching these courses, I received tenure and promotion to the rank of associate professor in 2008. I also served as assistant chair of the department. In 2013, I was promoted to the rank of professor and elected to serve as chair of the department, a position which I continuously held until 2021. As chair of the department, I was able to incentivize several faculty members to globalize the curriculum by offering small stipends for including a global perspective in their courses. Also in 2014, during our annual retreat, I was able to invite Ken Cushner, professor of international and intercultural education at Kent State University, to deliver a full-day professional development workshop on how to infuse global education into the teacher education curriculum. At Ohio University, I have had the opportunity to develop and, unfortunately only twice, teach Dynamics of Change in Educational Institutions, a course on the impact of globalization on institutions of education with a focus on teacher education. The course included texts by Kirkwood-Tucker (2009), Spring (2009), and Zhao (2009). I also served as chair on 14 of 15 dissertation committees. Several of my supervised dissertations are related to glocalization, an increasingly critical issue in the interconnectivity between local and global issues and sustainability of the world.

Topics of dissertations I have supervised include injection wells in rural Ohio, perspectives of overseas student teachers on American national identity, experiences of graduate Muslim students with religious microaggressions, fracking for funding in Appalachian Ohio, understanding elementary teachers' perceptions toward the national examination in central Java, Indonesia, teaching about fracking in the American Government high school course, parental involvement in non-native English speakers' postsecondary enrollment, and American teachers' perspectives on Chinese American students' culture.

Little Cities of Black Diamonds

Southeast Ohio, the location of my university, also has several boom-to-bust coal mining communities such as Shawnee, where there are still buildings with upper story balconies that are reminiscent of New Orleans. One late Sunday afternoon, after arriving in Shawnee, one of the locals came out of the one country store in town and asked whether we were from out of town. "How do you know?" I responded. Pointing at our old Volvo station wagon, he said, "They don't drive those around here." This serendipitous encounter marks the beginning of a long friendship with John Winnenberg, a local historian and civic activist, that would have a significant impact on the curriculum I developed for my social studies methods courses at Ohio University.

Shawnee has a long history as a coal mining town since it was founded in 1872. The town is part of the Little Cities of Black Diamonds (LCBD), a microregion in Southeast Ohio with a shared history of mine labor organizing and ethnic immigration. As a result of conversations with John, and as I educated myself about the history of the Little Cities, I decided to organize field trips into these former mining communities for my students, most of whom had never having left the "bubble" of Athens and were astounded to learn about these communities which they had never visited.

My involvement with the Little Cities also led me to develop a summer course called Southeast Ohio: The Appalachian Experience. I used *Coal: A Human History* by Barbara Freese (2003) as a core text in this course and focused on the role of coal in climate change. Her text examines coal's historical and contemporary impact in Great Britain, the United States, and China. Now, 20 years later, as the world is experiencing significant climate change, it is once again apparent that we seem to have learned little about climate change, especially since the oil crisis of 1973. As a result of my involvement with the Little Cities, I decided to concentrate my efforts on saving what remains of the "little city" of Rendville, a once-thriving coal mining town which, unlike other coal mining towns in Southeast Ohio, has a unique history of racial integration. In 2015, I was part of founding the Rendville Historic Preservation Society which seeks to preserve the town's history, heritage, and two major physical structures: the town hall and a miner's house which we seek to convert into a museum. Through my efforts we were able to install two Ohio Historical Markers in 2010 and 2018. Finally, my research on Rendville has led to the publication of my book *Richard L. Davis: An African American Mine Labor Organizer from Rendville* (Doppen, 2016). Davis broke the color line by serving on the National Executive Board of the United Mine Workers of America (Figure 12.6).

Figure 12.6 Richard L. Davis, United Mine Workers of America, National Executive Board, 1896–1897, 2nd from right.

ACCOMPLISHMENTS IN HIGHER EDUCATION

International Assembly

One of my biggest accomplishments in my professional career is my extensive involvement with the International Assembly (IA). IA is an associated group of National Council for the Social Studies (NCSS) and was formally established in 1994 by key global educators including former NCSS President Jan L. Tucker, professor of social studies and global education at Florida International University. The group provides a home base for global scholars from other nations as well as global international scholars in the United States (Kirkwood-Tucker, 2018, pp. 411–414).

In 2005, while attending the NCSS conference, my interest in global education led me to attend a meeting of IA. At this meeting, I met Dr. Toni Fuss Kirkwood-Tucker, associate professor and chair of the Department of Social Studies, at Florida State University, and president of IA at that time, who encouraged me to seek a position on IA's executive board. My election in

2006 to the executive board of IA, with members from different countries including the United States, marks the beginning of my involvement in IA. In 2010, I was elected vice president and program chair, in charge of organizing the 2012 IA conference held in Washington, DC, and the 2013 conference held in Seattle, Washington. As president of the IA, I was responsible for planning the 2014 conference in St. Louis, Missouri, and the 2015 conference in Boston, Massachusetts.

Sponsored by the generosity of the Eleanor and Elliot Goldstein Family Foundation (EGEG Foundation), I was instrumental in identifying and inviting four keynote speakers for the Annual Jan L. Tucker Memorial Lecture. The intent of the memorial lecture is to honor the legacy of Jan L. Tucker, founder of IA among others, and to provide a forum where prominent international scholars and foreign scholars based at U.S. institutions of higher learning deliver a keynote address that captures their perspective on the prevailing global challenges confronting the word of education in the 21st century (Kirkwood-Tucker, 2018, pp. 419–420). During my 4 years as vice president and then president, our keynote speakers for the General Assembly were: Guomin Zheng, dean of teacher education at Beijing Normal University in China (2011) who addressed teacher education reform in the People's Republic of China; Graham Pike, dean of international education at Vancouver Island University in Canada (2012) who addressed the state of global education in times of discomfort; Francis Godwyll, associate professor at University of North Florida, USA (2013) who addressed globalization and education with a focus on Ghana; and Gustavo E. Fischman, professor at Arizona State University (2014) who addressed civic education in Latin America.

IA each year also honors a Distinguished Global Scholar at its annual luncheon, sponsored by the EGEG Foundation as well. The annual selection and honoring of these scholars were initiated in 2005 by Toni Fuss Kirkwood-Tucker, then president of IA. This competitive program, via a selection committee, identifies leading scholars in global international education who have dedicated their lifelong careers to the field and have an extensive record of scholarship and engagement in global education (Kirkwood-Tucker, 2018, pp. 415–417). To learn about all 13 Distinguished Global Scholars between 2005–2016, see Kirkwood-Tucker (2018).

During my 4 years as vice president and then president, the recipients of the Distinguished Global Scholar Award were: Kenneth Tye, professor emeritus, College of Educational Studies, Chapman University, Orange, California (2011); Josiah Tlou, professor emeritus, College of Human Resources and Education, Blacksburg, Virginia (2012); David L. Grossman, senior adjunct fellow, East-West Center, Honolulu, Hawaii (2013); and Angene Wilson, professor emerita, Secondary Social Studies Department of Curriculum and Instruction, University of Kentucky (2014).

Malawi: Adopt-A-Well Project

IA, over the years, has played a significant role in assisting less industrialized nations in their educational efforts. For example, as a member of the executive board of IA, I initiated the Adopt-a-Well Project in Malawi, Africa. Recommended by Josiah Tlou, in 2007, the initiative first provided backpacks for students at the Mwanje Primary School in Malawi. When I learned that the school lacked access to clean drinking water, I initiated fund raising activities with my university teacher education students to sponsor the Adopt-a-Well Project at their school. Since Mwanje Primary School did not have Internet access, my students were excited to have a "live" teleconference with the school's principal who was very grateful about the prospect of drilling a borehole at her school (Figure 12.7). In 2013, with the additional support of Jennifer Tesar, one of my former doctoral students and then an assistant, and now associate, professor at Davis & Elkins College in West Virginia, we were able to contract with a local company to drill the borehole for the school and its surrounding communities (Doppen & Tesar, 2012).

Figure 12.7 The borehole at the Mwanje school in Malawi, 2021.

The borehole remains functional to this day. The project offered an excellent lesson to my future social studies teachers about the true meaning of global education in its efforts to demonstrate the interconnectedness of the world's people and their schools. The project further promoted the criticality of empathy for those in need.

After serving as vice president and program chair and as president of IA for 4 years, I remained a member of IA's executive board until 2018. I take pride in the work I did for IA and cherish the crystal globe I received when I completed my term as president. To this day it has a special place in my office.

Consortium for Overseas Student Teaching

A golden opportunity in the Department of Teacher Education at Ohio University to promote global mindedness and interconnectivity among nations was the offer to replace a departing faculty member in her role as the university's sending site coordinator for the Consortium for Overseas Student Teaching (COST). Established in 1973, COST is a collaboration of 16 colleges and universities in the United States that provides opportunities for teacher education students to have an overseas student teaching experience.

Since 2008, I have sponsored nearly 150 student teachers to complete their student teaching in Australia, the Bahamas, Belize, Costa Rica, Ecuador, Germany, Greece, India, Ireland, Mexico, The Netherlands, New Zealand, South Africa, and Spain (Figure 12.8). Unfortunately, due to COVID-19, the university required nine students who were placed in Belize, Costa Rica, Germany, Greece, The Netherlands, Spain, and South Africa, Greece, and Germany, to return home to Ohio during the Spring 2019 semester. The pandemic further rescinded 22 projected placements for the Fall 2019–Summer 2021 semesters, and an additional four projected placements for the Fall 2021 semester canceled due to the program's suspension. Fortunately, Ohio University has now once again been able to send three students teachers overseas again to Australia, New Zealand and Italy during the Spring 2023 semester.

In my role as a sending site coordinator, I have been instrumental in adding The Netherlands and Belize to the COST program. In my efforts to add another country from Africa to the program, despite a whole-hearted welcome at several schools in Botswana in 2016, which included a personal meeting with Unity Dow, then minister of the Ministry of Education and Skills Development, I was regretfully unable to add Botswana as a receiving site for the COST Program.

COST has been an avenue for my research on student teachers' experiences while teaching overseas. The research has been focused on how COST contributes to personal and professional growth. Ohio University's student teachers typically have gone overseas for 12 weeks which has provided them with the opportunity to immerse themselves in another global culture. Amongst other assignments, such as completing the edTPA, a state-required educational portfolio, I have required each student teacher to complete five reflective essays on their student teaching experiences abroad. In their final reflection during their last week overseas, I have asked them to respond to what they have learned about themselves as an American and answer Michel Guillaume Jean de Crèvecoeur's (J. Hector St. John, a naturalized French-American writer, 1735–1813), timeless question, "What's an American?"

As a result of the COST program, I have published two single-author and four co-authored articles with my former doctoral students Jing An (Williams), Kristin Diki, and Bahman Shahri. My research has focused on global awareness, intercultural experiences, and national identity. Although the overseas student teachers generally unanimously indicated that the 3-month-long COST experience broadened their global awareness, the extent to which they became immersed in intercultural learning remained limited. I found that my student teachers often knew little about the world (Doppen, 2010b). While most of my COST participants appeared to remain in the *minimization* stage in which people tend to minimize differences among the diversity of people around the world by believing that all humans are essentially the same, some reached the *acceptance* stage in which individuals begin to analyze cultural differences (Bennett, 1993; Cushner, 2018). However, two surveys of former COST students (one for participants between 1995–2013 and one for participants between 2013–2014), found that COST not only increased their ability to consider multiple perspectives and incorporate cross-cultural perspectives into their curriculum, but that the program also increased their opportunity to get hired as a first-year teacher (Doppen & An, 2014; Doppen & Diki, 2017). Finally, the COST experience not only led to significant personal and professional growth but also increased students' awareness of their own national identity (Doppen, 2015; Doppen et al., 2016; Doppen & Shahri, 2019).

As a result of my extensive work with COST, I was also honored, in 2019, to receive IA's Best Paper Award on the Belize Project, a pre-COVID-19 annually recurring 1-week school immersion experience for Ohio University student teachers in Belize's Corozal district, which was subsequently published in the *Journal of International Social Studies* (Doppen & Wentworth, 2020; Figure 12.8). In this article, my co-author and I argue that while the research literature is replete with studies on student perspectives and their development of cross-cultural sensitivity, research on the perspectives of educators who host international preservice teachers is woefully lacking and presents a gap in the research. We found that completing a field experience in the classroom in another country is truly a reciprocal process in which both participating partners, the teacher candidates, and the host school community, reap the benefits of a cultural and educational exchange.

Figure 12.8 School visit in Corozal, Belize, 2018.

Moreover, I have co-presented at an Ohio Council for the Social Studies and published an article with two former doctoral students (Hollstein et al., 2020) to share our research on how to foster media literate global citizens, a new area in global research that needs to be urgently addressed. Matt Hollstein and I were also able to publish a book chapter on fracking which has become a significant global issue in today's world (Hollstein & Doppen, 2021). Throughout the years, I have thoroughly enjoyed working with my doctoral students as I have supervised 15 dissertations. I have especially enjoyed working with my international students from Canada, China, Egypt, Iran, and Indonesia. As a global scholar, I have learned as much from them as I hope they did from me.

COST also rekindled my own interest in Dutch national identity and resulted in the publication of two articles related to the assassinations of Pim Fortuyn (1948–2002), a politician who spoke out against the Islamization of The Netherlands; and Theo van Gogh (1957–2004), a film director, who strongly criticized the treatment of women in Islam (Doppen, 2007; Doppen 2010a). This interest has also led to the recent publication of a book chapter with another former doctoral student, Mohamed Amira, in which we compared national identity in Egypt, The Netherlands, and the United States (Amira & Doppen, 2019).

REFLECTIONS

After having spent 40 years of my life living in the United States, I continue to possess a sense of double-consciousness (Dubois, 1903/2014). On one hand I am an American, on the other, I am a Dutchman. This double consciousness has been part of my identity since I first immigrated to the United States. In many ways technology has made double consciousness easier as I can now daily not only check the news in the United States but also the news in The Netherlands. I can even watch the Dutch daily news right on my phone or laptop. All this is to say that it has become so much easier in many ways to cling to the Dutch part of my identity.

Yet, it has been too long since my last visit to The Netherlands. I can't help myself wanting to spend more time back home. I want to go ride a bike again on Vlieland, one of the Dutch islands in the Wadden Zee, where no cars are allowed. I want to visit my siblings and old friends. I want to walk the streets of Utrecht where I went to college, go *lekker fietsen* (enjoy bicycling), and be part of a society that is more tolerant and more committed to social justice than the United States. As the United States appears to be backsliding on civil liberties and human rights, something that makes me proud of The Netherlands, for example, is that while same-sex marriage did not become legal in the United States until the Supreme Court ruled in *Obergefell v. Hodge* in 2015, it became legal in The Netherlands in 2001, 14 years earlier.

Unfortunately, the grass is not always greener on the other side. Historically, immigrants typically remember the home country as they have left it. It may be tempting to return to The Netherlands, but I am well aware, especially now that it has become so easy to keep up with news from back home and to talk with and visually connect with family and friends through Skype or WhatsApp at no cost, that it is no longer the same country that I left. I realize that The Netherlands has its issues as well. For example, a recent controversial issue has been the Zwarte Pieten (Black Petes), the "clownesque" helpers of Sinterklaas (Santa Claus), who to many Dutch citizens are blatant examples of racial discrimination. As after the assassinations of Pim Fortuyn and Theo van Gogh, the Dutch continue to struggle with what it means to be Dutch as, similar to in the United States, White privilege is being questioned.

When I first immigrated to the United States in 1984, The Netherlands did not allow for dual citizenship, and I was content with my status as a permanent resident alien in the United States. Although the Dutch government has allowed for dual citizenship since 2004 if one is married to a citizen of the country to which one applies for citizenship, I have not felt compelled to seek American citizenship as I've wanted to make absolutely sure to keep the option open of being able to move back home to The Netherlands at any time should I decide to do so. Having a son and a daughter in the United States has made this unlikely to happen. But as I approach my retirement part of me longs to return to my country. When I worked at the Directorate for Emigration between 1982–1984, a mantra, often mistakenly held by emigrants, was that "the grass is always greener on the other side." In the aftermath of World War II when prospects for economic recovery seemed dim, between 1946–1959 more than 350,000 Dutch citizens left the country to seek a better life in another country. However, as part of my responsibilities at the directorate I had the opportunity to travel across The Netherlands to interview emigrants who had decided to return, often disillusioned with their new life in the other country or simply missing the typical Dutch *gezelligheid* (coziness). After all, The Netherlands is a small country you can cross in less than 2 hours from East to West and in less than 4 hours from North to South.

So here I was, after nearly 40 years, that I finally decided to apply and was sworn in as a citizen of the United States on August 18, 2022 (Figure 12.9). Yet, I have serious doubts about my newly acquired citizenship as my confidence in American democracy is faltering due to the ongoing assault on voting rights, as exemplified by the Big Steal, the Supreme Court assault on human rights in overturning of *Roe v. Wade,* and the limitations it imposed on the Clean Air Act. To illustrate the assault on our democracy and controversial presidential election of 2000, which is well documented in *Unprecedented* (Brave New Films, 2020), the Republican Party was able to steal the election with the help of Kathleen Harris, Florida's Secretary of State, and the United States Supreme Court. After the court stopped the Florida recount, Al Gore conceded the presidency to George W. Bush. Then, once again, after we had moved to Ohio, the same thing happened anew in the presidential election in 2004, which is well documented in *How Ohio Pulled It Off* (Barker et al., 2007). By delivering the state to George W. Bush, Ohio's Secretary of State Kenneth Blackwell, made it possible for George W. Bush to steal the election from John Kerry. Now, in a reversal of fate, Donald Trump alleges his reelection in 2020 was stolen by the Democratic Party and that Joe Biden is an illegitimate president.

I feel unease about living in this highly polarized country that is in the process of rolling back the clock for decades on such controversial issues as voting rights, abortion, LGBTQ+, and gun control. The prospect of being able to vote for progressive candidates is not very encouraging. America' democracy is on the edge of a deep abyss. Nevertheless, I hope this alarming phase will pass and that the time will come when we can talk once again respectfully across ideological lines in a less divided country. I have had a rewarding

Figure 12.9 Being sworn in as a United States citizen, October 6, 2022.

personal and professional life in the United States. I have much enjoyed being a middle and high school teacher as well as a college professor and department chair. My son and daughter are now adults and live their own lives. I can only hope that in an increasingly globalized world, among all the many challenges we face, we will meet the challenge to address the reemergence of authoritarianism and global threat against democracy as well as climate change in order to preserve our imperiled planet for future generations.

REFERENCES

Amira, M., & Doppen, F. H. (2019). The struggle for national identity: Islam in Egypt, the Netherlands and the USA. In A. Rapoport (Ed.), *Competing frameworks: Global and national citizenship in education* (pp. 71–91). Information Age Publishing.

Barker, C., Kraus, M., & Quiroga, M. (Directors). (2007). *How Ohio pulled it off*. Ohio Film Makers LLC. https://vimeo.com/192861432

Bennett, M. (1993). Towards ethnorelativism: A developmental model of intercultural sensitivity. In M. Paige (Ed.), *Cross-cultural orientation* (pp. 27–69). University Press of America.

Brandon, P., Jones, G., Jouwe, N., & Van Rossum, M. (Eds.). (2020). *De Slavernij in Oost en West: Het Amsterdam onderzoek* [Slavery in East and West: The Amsterdam study]. Spectrum.

Brave New Films. (2020, August 18). *Unprecedented: The battle for the Presidency in Florida and the undermining of democracy in America* [YouTube video]. https://www.youtube.com/watch?v=mL8ME0SS_Y0

Buruma, I. (1994). *The wages of guilt: Memories of war in Germany and Japan*. Farrar, Straus Giroux.

Cushner, K. (2018). *Teacher as traveler: Enhancing intercultural development of teachers and students*. Rowman & Littlefield.

De Swarte, I. (2016). Coordinating hunger: The evacuation of children during the Dutch food crisis, 1945. *War & Society, 35*(2), 132–149. https://doi.org/10.1080/07292473.2016.1182359

Doppen, F. H. (1984). Theodoor J. van den Broek: Missionary and emigration leader. The history of Dutch catholic settlement at Little Chute, Wisconsin. *U.S. Catholic Historian, 3*, 202–225.

Doppen, F. H. (2004). Beginning social studies teachers' integration of technology in the history classroom. *Theory and Research in Social Education, 32*(2), 248–279. https://doi.org/10.1080/00933104.2004.10473254

Doppen, F. H. (2007). Now what? Rethinking civic education in the Netherlands. *Education, Citizenship, and Social Justice, 2*(2) 103–118. https://eric.ed.gov/?id=EJ845676

Doppen, F. H. (2010a). Citizenship education and the Dutch national identity debate. *Education, Citizenship, and Social Justice, 5*(2), 131–143. https://doi.org/10.1177/1746197910370723

Doppen, F. H. (2010b). Overseas student teaching and national identity: Why go somewhere you feel completely comfortable? *Journal of International Social Studies, 1*(1), 3–19. https://iajiss.org/index.php/iajiss/article/view/10/30

Doppen, F. H. (2015). Student teaching in South Africa: An intercultural experience. *Ohio Social Studies Review, 52*(1), 55–65.

Doppen, F. H. (2016). *Richard L. Davis and the color line in Ohio coal. A Hocking Valley mine labor organizer, 1862–1900*. McFarland.

Doppen, F. H., & An, J. (2014). Student teaching abroad: Enhancing global awareness. *International Education, 43*(2), 59–75. https://www.researchgate.net/publication/304747826_Student_teaching_abroad_Enhancing_global_awareness

Doppen, F. H., An, J., & Diki, K. (2016). Why do student teachers go global? *Journal of Social Studies Research 40*, 85–95. http://dx.doi.org/10.1016/j.jssr.2015.05.002

Doppen, F. H., & Diki, K. (2017). Perceptions of student teaching abroad: Upon completion and two years after. *Journal of International Social Studies, 7*(2), 78–97. https://files.eric.ed.gov/fulltext/EJ1160535.pdf

Doppen, F. H., & Shahri, B. (2019). Overseas student teachers' reflections on American national identity: A longitudinal study. *Journal of International Social Studies, 9*(1), 72–92. https://eric.ed.gov/?id=EJ1215091

Doppen, F. H., & Tesar, J. (2012). The Mwanje project: Engaging preservice teachers in global service learning. *Journal of International Social Studies, 2*(2), 52–65. https://files.eric.ed.gov/fulltext/EJ1149757.pdf

Doppen, F. H., & Wentworth, L. F. (2020). The Belize project: A host school perspective. *Journal of International Social Studies, 10*(1), 138–153. https://www.iajiss.org/index.php/iajiss/article/view/497/361

Du Bois, W. E. B. (2014). *The souls of Black folk.* CreateSpace Independent Publishing Platform. (Original work published 1903)

Freese, B. (2003). *Coal: A human history.* Penguin Books.

Friedman, T. L. (2007). *The world is flat: A brief history of the twenty-first century.* Farrar, Straus and Giroux.

Hollstein, M. S., & Doppen, F. H. (2021). Socio-scientific issues-based instruction: The case of fracking as a controversial environmental issue. In R. W. Evans (Ed.), *Handbook on teaching social issues* (2nd ed.; pp. 163–176). Information Age Publishing.

Hollstein, M. S., Hinkle, J. K., Doppen, F. H., & Guedel, E. A. (2020). Fostering media literate global citizens: Tools for understanding. *Ohio Social Studies Review, 56*(2), 21–33. https://oaks.kent.edu/article/fostering-media-literate-global-citizens-tools-understanding

Jouwe, N., Kuipers, M., & Raben, R. (Eds.). (2021). *Slavernij en de stad Utrecht* [Slavery and the city Utrecht]. Walburg Press.

Kirkwood-Tucker, T. F. (2009). *Visions of globalization: The globalization of curriculum and pedagogy in teacher education and schools: Perspectives from Canada, Russia, and the United States.* Peter Lang.

Kirkwood-Tucker, T. F. (Ed.). (2018). *The global education movement: Narratives of Distinguished Global Scholars.* Information Age Publishing.

Meyers, W. D. (1991). *Now is your time! The African American struggle for freedom.* Harper Collins Publishers.

Spring, J. (2009). *Globalization of education: An introduction.* Routledge.

Yeager, E. A., Doppen, F. H., & Middleton, D. (1997). Now is your time! A middle school history unit. *Social Education, 61,* 207–209.

Zhao, Y. (2009). *Catching up or leading the way: American education in the age of globalization.* ASCD.

SECTION VI

MIDDLE EAST

CHAPTER 13

TURKEY

FRACTURED VISIONS OF REMEMBRANCE

Varteni Mosdichian

Why won't they let me speak my tongue?

My oral history narrative describes my life from the Armenian perspective. I was born in the unsophisticated lively town of Gedik-Pasha in the ancient section of Istanbul on the Sea of Marmara, in Turkey. The protecting warmth of my grandparents, their traumatic experiences in the Armenian genocide, the poets in the family, my father's immense love for the sea, my mother's passion for freedom—all impregnated my soul towards a creative world. Moving to a relatively more cosmopolitan part of the city and my acceptance to the selective Sankt Georg Austrian Gymnasium where lectures were conducted in German, intensified the dialectical process of my early development for becoming a painter of international issues permeating our troubled world. One irreplaceable memory in attending Turkish schools was the absence of Armenian history and culture in Turkish textbooks, omitting the extensive contributions Armenians made to civilization. One of my other strongest memories is my departure in the autumn of 1969 to the United States to join my mother in Lynn, Massachusetts, where I attended high school and, later, obtained a bachelor's degree from the University of Florida. A foreigner in my newly adopted country and feeling alone, my consistent release of thoughts and my feelings of my remote loved ones were expressed through drawing and painting. My art displayed in this chapter reflects the multiple layers of injustices I have witnessed and lived through in the Old World and New World. Whether it is the Armenian genocide and continuous suffering of the Armenian people, the asylum seekers from the former Yugoslavia and later Afghanistan, or the political dissidents from the Middle East, and now the refugees from the Ukraine, the pain of this universal suffering is omnipresent in my artwork. My life experiences and my inner world shaped my work into a global mindedness of artistic expression that reflects the interconnectivity and cross-cultural integrity of the world's people.

THE ARMENIAN GENOCIDE

To begin my story, I first must address the Armenian genocide at the turn of the 20th century and the forced Islamization of the remaining Armenian women and children illustrating the systematic destruction of the Armenian people by the Ottoman Empire during World War I. Spearheaded by the ruling Committee of Union and Progress (CUP), more than 1.5 million men, women, and children were murdered, the majority of which were forced to death marches through the Syrian Desert. To date the Turkish government, contrary to its own notable Turkish intellectuals and academicians, denies the Armenian genocide. The United States Senate unanimously recognized the genocide with Senate Resolution 150 on December 12, 2019. On April 24, 2021, President Joe Biden officially recognized the massacre. As of 2022, 33 countries have acknowledged the Armenian genocide.

I am an Armenian woman who was born in Turkey after my country Armenia was almost obliterated from the world map by the Ottoman Empire and became part of the official country of Turkey. I was born in the unsophisticated lively town of Gedik-Pasha of Istanbul in the ancient section of Istanbul on the Sea of Marmara, a simple, friendly community, poor in wealth, yet so rich in heart. The Armenian church and the elementary school I attended for my primary education; the long curvy, old, and narrow stony streets with steps; the Armenian peasants from Eastern Anatolia and their colorful ceremonious lives; all these places are deeply rooted within me. At the Sea of Marmara with its beautiful islands, I called them princess islands, every day I would journey to them in my mind, but they would distance themselves from me in the horizon. But once I learned to swim towards their shores, my swimming reached the first island, then the second, then the third in the longing Sea of Marmara until, in my imagination, I reached the big waters of the Atlantic Ocean.

Gedik-Pasha was one of the oldest Greek, Armenian, Assyrian, and Jewish populated neighborhoods in Istanbul. *Saray ici sokak* was the Turkish name of the street where my extended family lived during my early years. This name created such fantasies in me. *Saray ici sokak* in Turkish means "inside of a palace," which is the translation of my street name that perhaps exists today and certainly in my dreams. Our house was on top of the hill and possessed the most spectacular view of the Sea of Marmara. I would often run to our long terrace every time a foreign ship paid a visit to our shore, and I would greet them loudly. From our house, cobble stoned old curvy streets led downhill, forming numerous steps, and finally arriving at the coast where the old Armenian fisherman community lived. "You can only run downhill as far as the fountain" my grandmother used to tell me, and I followed my ball as far as the running cold water of the fountain, where the reclining bear was bathing himself and his Romani owner recognized my childish fearlessness playing his violin.

My Extended Family

The protecting warmth of my maternal grandparents, their traumatic experiences as survivors of the Armenian genocide, the poets in the family, my father's immense love for the sea, my mother's passion for freedom all impregnated my soul towards a creative world of an artist. My maternal grandfather originated from the region historically called Gesaria or the Romanized name of Mazaca. Gesaria was the capital of the Roman province of Cilicia where they recruited generals for the Byzantine army. Before the invasion by the Ottomans, it was called Caesaria. My maternal grandparent's family were originally from Angora, today's capital of Turkey called Ankara. My maternal grandfather's side can be traced to the town of Elma Dagh (around Angora). Before the genocide they were harassed by the Catholic missionaries and, to survive, they became Catholics. The Armenians are Christians and are known as the Eastern Apostolic Gregorian Christians named after Gregory the Illuminator.

My maternal grandfather's side eventually migrated to Gesaria (Caesaria). Feeling safe, they founded the village of Erkilet where they built the city's water system. In 1915, when the Turkish army had come to Erkilet to massacre the Armenians, the Turkish inhabitants of the village defended the Armenians impressing on the soldiers that they had intermarried and were a mixed population of Armenians and Turks, and the soldiers miraculously left, and the village remained unharmed. But my grandfather's family knew that would not be the end. They already had had family members murdered through public hangings before the genocide during the Sultan Abdul Hamid II pogroms against Christian Armenians of 1894–1896. My grandfather and his immediate family ended up moving before the Genocide of 1915 to the Black Sea coast in the Greek Pontus region where they thought they would find more freedom of expression under the Ottoman millet system. The millet system was an autonomous self-governing religious community where many national groups existed side by side with less repression than in other areas.

My maternal grandmother's adept voice resonates a turbulent history, the history of my ancestors, and I remember vividly hearing her speak fondly of that area at the Black Sea where they lived. She would tell me how silk was refracted out of cocoons and how she took her horse riding among the lush tobacco lands and the vineyard right at the shore, where they spent their summers near a windmill. How proud my grandmother was when she counted her family names going back to the times of Pontus when the Black Sea area was predominantly reigned by Pontus Kingdom before the Ottoman invasion. There were four brothers and four sisters in her family, all pulsating with the marvels of learning music, art, literature, and science. She would spin around my soul fancy like caterpillars with all the colors of her sea and land starting from mulberry trees to cherry, fig, quince, pomegranate, from primordial times to now except for that lethal, intoxicating fleet of horrible despotic Ottoman Turkish Forces. For some reason, my grandmother cannot forget her havoc-infested ancestral home. How the Black Sea concealed the mutilated, lethargic corps of her kin, relatives who were murdered in the genocide, during that fateful spring. She spoke of her wondrous puberty times, her blossoming times of falling in love and of childbearing times. But the blissful times became times of desolation; the genocide robbed her from her mother and brothers. Sporadic vile forces extinguish innocent lives of nature. "Do gulping sharks prefer to consume ancient vital minorities? What is the impetus of big fish versus small fish in a given society?"

My Armenian Culture

The country I was born into was Turkey and our official language was Turkish, but it was not my native language. The first spoken language I learned from my mother was Armenian. For example, good morning in Armenian is *Pari Louys* and means "kind light"; dignity in Armenian is called *louys*. I believe that a person without dignity is a xerox copy (my way of referring to people without a personality or special appearance) defeated in the homogenization of our gloriously civilized world. The Armenian language predates Christianity and Islam. It is one of the oldest living Indo-European languages. Our forebearers were Zoroastrians and before that, they worshiped the Pantheon. In Ani, the city of 1,001 churches, you can see the ruins of a Zoroastrian fire temple and on the slopes of Mt. Aragatz there is an obelisk dedicated to Astghig, the goddess of beauty.

"Now that I had to live in the country of Turkey, why won't the Turkish government let me speak in my own tongue? What if you did?" A hundred years ago, the government would have cut out your tongue. By the mid-20th century, Turkey did not cut out tongues anymore but penalized you for speaking anything but Turkish because of your identity. In fact, there are penalties for those who speak foreign languages in Turkey (Figure 13.1). Punishments such as imprisonment and monetary fines were very common. And if you were convicted of speaking your own language, you were put on a list which consequently unabled you to enter such career fields as science, medicine, law, teaching, or journalism. Half of the monetary fine was given as a reward to those who reported the foreign language speakers to the government. You were diminished to very low-level labor jobs. The policy was heavily publicized throughout the country.

I am proud to say that for centuries Armenians were the original blacksmiths, silversmiths, jewelers, shoemakers, tailors, bakers, bookmakers, and other professionals in the Ottoman Empire, the very master craftsmen of the Sultans and "padishahs." And who built Istanbul and the most prominent edifices, the most renowned buildings, mosques, fountains, and the infrastructure? The engineers were all Armenians. Prominent architects of the Balyan family practically built the entire Istanbul and Anatolia. These Armenians were very popular with the people, and the Sultan actually executed a few of them fearing that they would win the hearts of the populace

Figure 13.1 Turkish newspaper article (September 1, 1938) prohibiting the speaking of a foreign language in Turkey.

even more. Turkey has repeatedly killed and raped its Armenian people and taken their lands and homes. Today, it is doing this to the Kurdish people in Turkey, Syria, and Iraq's Kurdistan.

Varteni Saying Goodbye to her Mother

One of my unforgettable memories is aunts, uncles, cousins, grandmama, and grandpapa gathered at the Bosporus port on the Marmara Sea to wave good-bye to my mother leaving for Egypt. After her divorce from my father, she visited her uncle and his family in Egypt for several months which felt like an eternity to me. I was only 5 years old. Those huge boats would just kidnap your loved ones to any kind of destination. My family members were waving, appearing to be hugging silhouettes. At my young

Figure 13.2 *Departure.* Dedicated to Leyla Zana, a Turkish parliamentarian of Kurdish origin who was imprisoned upon her return from Sweden where she had dared to utter the word "Hello" in Kurdish.

age I decided not to wave goodbye to my only parent and crouched on the wet concrete, determined to wait for her return, thinking: "I worship you my Marmara Sea, but why am I left here alone salty, shivering wet, without my Mama?" Being an only child made my life harder. With the divorce, my mother received custody of me and, legally, I now belonged to her. She and I were going to live in our maternal grandparent's big house in Istanbul where my uncle with his family also lived. The unconditional love that I began to receive from my grandparents gave birth to an immense faith and optimism in my soul. Their love became my refuge of hearths.

Of all the wonderful birthday celebrations I had, my fifth birthday is unforgettable until this day. The house was decorated in such a festive way: balloons in different shapes, sizes, colors, cordons of glitters stretching from one corner to another in swinging lines of color from the ceiling. The large oval dining table offered lush delicatessen from Armenian, Turkish, and French cuisines. I remember chimes, masks, hats, adults as well as children related or unrelated, and known or unknown faces singing or screaming, dancing, blessing, or cursing. Embarrassed with all the overwhelming décor and audience, I finally blew out my five candles. I realized at that moment how the delicious food from different nationalities served at my birthday celebration connected me to the larger world. Yet, the silence of my early years returned. The absence of my father carved the strength of silence in me. In addition to missing my father, I was always admonished not to call my mother "Mama" in public places so the Turks would not notice that we were Armenians. This demand was very hard for me to survive in Turkey while growing up as an Armenian. These early memories reminded me again of my beloved, extended family spoiling me to no end. The international cuisine also made me realize how interconnected we are as a human family joyously sharing our foods together regardless of our backgrounds.

Finding the World of a Magic Doll

The internationality of my family who often traveled abroad was also evident in a special doll I possessed. "She" came all the way from another continent and one of its largest cities—New York. I loved this doll more than any other. My mother even gave it a name. The other dolls were on a higher shelf and untouchable and unreachable for me. Only on my birthdays, I had the permission to play with all the dolls from all the countries we had visited: France, Italy, Portugal, and New York and Miami in the United States. These dolls had a special significance for me because they represented the larger world outside of Turkey and made me aware of my global awareness at my young age—thanks to my family. This doll sometimes was a baby boy and other times it was a baby girl. Its gender didn't make any difference, but what could have made a thrilling difference was that if it could only talk to me. Every night I prayed to the sky that my doll would talk. It was at the time that both of my parents disappeared from my life at the age of four and five. It was a civilized divorce, and my mother now legally owned me. I was scared my father would take me away someday. I always had a vivid imagination about that. I was shocked about their divorce because they were never fighting.

MY EDUCATION IN TURKEY

As an Armenian child, it was hard to survive in the Turkish school system. After graduating from elementary school, I had to take entrance exams at middle schools that offered foreign language instruction. My mother's dream was for me to get an international education that offered different European languages. I had already begun learning French in the Armenian elementary school in the third grade. I was quite apt in it because when we traveled to France, I could use my French very effectively, and I was only 4 years of age. At that time, we were in search of a safe haven following Turkish pogroms against the native Greek inhabitants of Constantinople (Istanbul in the mid 1950s), when the Turks burned and looted Greek homes and businesses, targeting all Christian minorities by association. These horrors became known as the events of the 5th and 6th September of 1955. After France, we traveled to New York in 1957 to escape the pogroms but, ultimately, returned back home. I eventually immigrated to the United States in 1969 to live with my mother who worked for a wealthy Armenian family.

Indoctrination in Education

The education system in Turkey had great systematic brainwashing mechanisms. We, at the age of six, had to do citations first thing every morning. These recitations were really like prayers before the school day at which time we were required, with fervor, to thank the Turkish government for how great it was to be a Turk, how right and how great Turks are, for being able to speak the Turkish language, and that we will respect our elders and the laws, and so forth. It was a whole cartoonish melodrama reoccurring repeatedly and so superficial that even I, as a child in the third grade, was aware of the farce. These citations in Turkish schools somehow are not really different from American students who, usually during morning announcements, are required to stand up before the U.S. flag and pledge allegiance to their country.

Falling prey to the indoctrination, I authored a poem about the aggrandized military state of the Turkish government. My fantasy patriotic poem won me praise from my Turkish teachers. I was around 8 years old and so ecstatic that I had received the praises of my Turkish language teachers and that I was passing my oral exams just by reading my poem. Instead of asking me any academic questions, the teachers would call me in front of other inspector teachers to read my patriotic poem before them. I was given an excellent passing grade in all my Turkish subjects. This was in my elementary school, and it happened only out of my innocence. They knew how to manipulate this innocence.

Attending the Austrian Gymnasium

Moving to a more cosmopolitan part of the city of Istanbul and my acceptance to the select Sankt Georg Austrian Gymnasium where lectures were conducted in German, intensified the dialectical process of my early development for becoming a painter. I went to the exam center holding my grandfather's hand to check out my scores to find out which school could be my future secondary school. I was accepted to several of them. Istanbul, a historically cosmopolitan city of the world, had prestigious foreign schools with high tuition operating in their city and only accessible to the elite. I passed Die Deutsche Schule of the *Sankt George Austrian Gymnasium* with excellence. In Turkey in the 1950s, the German School was the most prestigious one with the English School and the French School second and third in ranking respectively.

My mother had the option to enroll me in different institutions including the Deutsche Schule (German School) or the Österreichisches Gymnasium (Austrian Gymnasium), a type of high school. Die Deutsche Schule required 1 year of preparatory schooling and was coeducational whereas the Österreichische Gymnasium required 2 years of preparatory schooling and was designed for girls only. This Gymnasium was like a Jesuit Catholic school founded in 1882 by Austrian Lazarists and was originally intended for German speaking Catholic children living in the Ottoman Empire. After the Ottoman (and Austrian) defeat in World War I, the school was ordered closed by the occupying Triple Entente forces in Istanbul, and the school administrators and teachers were sent back to Austria. The Gymnasium did reopen when the Republic of Turkey was founded in 1923. After the annexation of Austria by the Nazi Germany in 1938, the school turned into a "German School," and it was closed once again in 1944 due to the negative political relationship between Turkey and Germany. The school was again reopened in 1947.

After 2 years of preparatory classes where all subjects were taught in German, I was now in my third year at the Österreichische Gymnasium. As a Turkish citizen, I also had to take classes in the Turkish language, in history, geography, and civics. In my Turkish language class, I began to question the absence of the history of Armenians who were born in Turkey and were left out of the textbooks, a phenomenon that is also true in other countries where the history and culture of minorities are ignored. But regarding my own people's absence in Turkish textbooks, none of our well-known Armenian actors, musicians, scientists, novelists, and poets who contributed to the shaping of Turkish culture were discussed in our classes. Neither the Armenian composer Edgar Manas who composed the Turkish national anthem was mentioned nor the world-famous Armenian linguist Hagop Martayan whom Ataturk renamed Dilachar (meaning tongue opener) who converted the Ottoman Arabic orthography into the modern Turkish alphabet. I wrote these famous Armenian names in my composition book so I would never forget their contributions to Armenian culture. I also examined existing textbooks used in other Turkish schools and found that our history and culture were not included on their pages and, in fact, referred to Armenians as "traitors." I have learned from my grandparents that Armenian history dates back over 3,000 years and I ask respectfully, "Why is our history not mentioned anywhere in Turkish textbooks and barely, or not at all, in Western textbooks today?" These censored history books and educational tactics affected me deeply.

Without any reference to Armenian history and culture in Turkish textbooks used in the education of students, I began to question who I was and where I came from. Although I was not struggling in any of my classes except in the Turkish language and the Turkish/Ottoman history classes, the Turkish teachers were clearly antagonistic towards me. In my sixth year, when I had to take the final examinations for graduation—knowing that I would leave the country to join my mother in the United States in 1969—I told my teacher that I refused to take the final tests and that I would accept a zero for my grade. In fact, I had the courage to say to one of my teachers, "There are Armenian ghosts in this country who must be reconciled with; give me a zero, I don't care." After I said that to her, I triumphantly left the classroom. My classmates were stunned.

While studying at the Österreichisches Gymnasium, I developed a special friendship with Nilufer. We became blood sisters around the age of 13. At the time, Ludwig von Beethoven was our God. This adoration for him and his music enabled in us the vision to realize the strength of musical imagination which stretched living colors and shapes into all moments of my life until today. We would spend all day together until the sun went down at the old silver beach leaving behind burning traces of waves. I was refreshed by internalizing the external serenity of the shivering water. We asked each other why, at such a youthful age, do we have to get married and then become pregnant. Sometimes I wanted these waves to grab and drown me forever. No more questions, no more pondering, no more waiting for a loved one.

Decades later, around 2011, while living in the United States, I was comforted by telling the above story of the biased history test in the Österreichische Gymnasium to Hasan Cemal, professor at Harvard University in Cambridge, Massachusetts, who had given a talk about the 1915 Armenian genocide. Hasan is the grandson of Djemal Pasha, one of the three architects of the Armenian genocide. Known as the triumvirate, Talaat Pasha, Enver Pasha, and Djemal Pasha planned and orchestrated the Armenian genocide of 1915 in the Ottoman Empire under the rule of the Committee of Union and Progress during the years the empire was collapsing. The Ottoman Empire had been shrinking and collapsing since the late 19th century. Many of its territories in the west became independent countries (i.e., Bulgaria, the Balkans, and Greece). The Committee of Union and Progress emerged after the Young Turk Movement of 1908. One of the reasons that they targeted Armenians for genocide was their fear that the Armenians would rebel and form their own independent nation.

Figure 13.3 *Grief.* Dedicated to the grieving women of the world.

FEAR AS AN ARMENIAN

I can trace the momentum of all my paintings to my emotions and the inner workings of my psyche. Among my own personal trauma and joyful moments, I also breathe memories of my ancestors. They are memories overshadowed by pain and suffering. The genocide of the Armenians in 1915 by the Ottoman Empire that took the lives of many of my family members and exiled most of the survivors, is the epicenter of these memories. The fear of losing your very life, fear of losing the lives of your loved ones, fear of deportation, fear of losing your livelihood by losing your job, fear of having your properties confiscated, fear of having your wife abducted or your daughter... fear, fear, fear. This fear has passed on to multiple generations echoed through the Armenian genocide and traveled and spread out with the diaspora of Armenians all over our earth.

IMMIGRATION TO THE UNITED STATES

In 1969, I joined my mother in the United States. My mother had come to the United States to work as a private nurse for a wealthy Armenian family to take care of their mother who had had a stroke and only remembered her mother tongue. Upon my arrival, I remember the plane hovering over Boston, and I noticed all the buildings looked like in the movies I'd seen before in Istanbul. I liked seeing those buildings; they were not Byzantine or Romanesque, yet I favored their authenticity. The American sky was immense. I had never seen such a majestic sky! I ended up at the seacoast where my mother rented an apartment. The ocean near our apartment became such a paradox to my feelings and so were the people with smiley faces and their rehearsed stylized greetings. The endless ocean marked the separation between me and my loved ones back home in Turkey, and I looked with tearful eyes into the sea in search of them. Now every time I gaze at the sea, I vividly remember what my beloved father would tell me, "You were a mermaid once." He repeated these words every time we took a boat ride. I do not remember my history as a mermaid, but I know I was a fish-maid because my mother and I would cook giant red fish in our kitchen.

Attending Lynn High School

After my arrival in the United States at the age of 16, I attended Lynn High School in Lynn, Massachusetts. It was full of noise and strangers walking by. I lost myself in incipient reveries while memories were coiling in the cradle of my existence. Being a foreigner in the United States and feeling alone, my consistent release of thoughts and my feelings of my remote loved ones were expressed through drawing and painting. I met Polish, Irish, Italian, and Greek immigrants and heard Yiddish for the first time. I felt like I was part of *West Side Story*. I felt left out many times at that school. I was this odd stranger although welcomed by the teachers. I remember meeting an Irish girl who lived with many siblings and a half-blind Mama in the projects. She became special to me as she stood out among many xerox copies. My Irish friend and I participated in Vietnam anti-war demonstrations in Boston. The police had huge dogs facing us ready to attack us.

I had a marvelous guidance counselor and a Polish art teacher at Lynn High School. The Irish literature teacher told me that he was glad my English was not perfect, otherwise I would detect his mistakes in the English language! He was always interested in my books which I used to read in Turkish by Dostoyevsky and Gogol, and in German by Kafka. I had pass privileges to go to the art room any time I wished during my homeroom. My favorite composer, Ludwig van Beethoven's bicentennial birthday was in 1970 and I was so ecstatic to be able to attend a concert with my mother. The conductor was Michael Tilson Thomas. I even went backstage to meet him out of my joy. Once, I was sent by the school to a student congress to give a talk at Brandeis University, what an honor. While I was at Lynn High School, I developed an awareness of the environment and cosmopolitics. I had entered the world of adulthood.

As a grandchild of Armenian genocide survivors arriving in the United States during the Vietnam War, I started to pose thousands of questions in my young mind. Wars to me mean nothing but destruction; there is no liberation for any nation, only elimination. Colonial anti-revolutionary war structures, Nazi fascist mongers thrive, and the weapon industry benefits. I defend identity but not nationalism. I like to inspire but not control. I do not understand nationalism to sustain our identities, or why we depend on forceful religion or any dogma. The idea of saying no to war started for me right then. Adulthood came crashing in. After my graduation from the University of Central Florida (UCF), I found a job as a costume designer in a children's theater in Boston. My costumes were screened on the local news television. Having been appreciated in public is a supportive feeling for an artist. My admission to the prestigious Studios at the Cité International des Arts at Les Marais in Paris, France, is one of my greatest joys.

I received my Bachelor of Arts degree at the University of Florida where I met my most stimulating and philosophical mentor, Dr. Walter Gaudnek, who himself came from Europe where his father had experienced the cruelty of the Nazis regime. He influenced me as a future painter, encouraging unlimited freedom of spontaneous creativity. My early works reflect the multiple layers of injustice I had witnessed/lived through in the Old World and, again in the New World. My paintings from the 1970s speak of the

Figure 13.4 *Moment.* Dedicated to the refugees of the world.

socioeconomic injustices of my fragile environment in the United States. The Armenian genocide and continuous suffering of the Armenian people as well as others who I have befriended over the years—those coming to the United States on asylum from the former Yugoslavia or political dissidents from the Middle East, and others, are deeply carved in the pain of universal suffering and are vividly omnipresent in my artwork. My global awareness increasingly deepened with my explorations about the world. With pain, however, also comes resistance and resilience, and my work also celebrates the overcoming of tyranny and oppression, and survivors of genocides. Amazingly, their offspring are all resilient. With integrating intuitive and intellectual processes involved with the exploration, the expression, the celebration of life, my art screams in silence, slashing the apathy of emotions in the worlds of advertisement and entertainment.

While living these long years in the United States, our friend Vuk came into our lives who somehow resembled my father and had the same name. He was truly a gift to my family. He injected in my vein gallons of dreams, dreams that forged in me an unbounded essence swooping into my paints, onto my canvases. It is my magic spell that embraces all my unspoken dialogs. It is love which manifested itself only within nature and, especially now, images from far away are gnawing at my memories of him. Every year at Xmas time, my father would send red lustrous shoes for my Zepure, my first-born. In 1978, we waited for this package, but it did not arrive. It was a very weary Xmas with chilly thoughts engulfed in my throat. I was wondering, "Why could I never express my love in words to him? Why did I never visit his home?" I looked at his photos secretly to the degree of scrutiny. And, for a prolonged period of time, I defied my apparent resemblance with him. I suddenly could not endure the pain of not being with him. I believed that my anguish about you would vanish by telling my friends that you were dead since you were too alive in my soul. I loathed myself in mirrors. I would condole myself by sharing the sufferings and losses of their fathers. You were so humble yet so regal, and I was your insolent, unspoken daughter. Now I am his age when he passed. In fact, I am older than him now.

Eastern- and Western-Born Armenians

One day my daughter Zepure was placed in an Armenian Elementary school in Watertown, Massachusetts, where she recognized and acknowledged her roots. However, her Armenian classmates were disputing her roots. The reason was that Armenian-born immigrants from different countries living in the United States today disagree about their roots as they identify themselves as either western or eastern Armenians and speak either the Western or Eastern standard form of the Armenian language. Eastern and Western Armenia developed during the 19th century as a result of the division between the Russian and Ottoman Empires along the dividing line of the border between Turkey and today's Republic of Armenia.

Eastern Armenia went through troubled times during World War I and eventually became one of the Soviet Republics. It flourished for 70 years and when the Soviet Union dissolved, Armenia became an independent nation. The Armenian community of Iran, itself a very old and transitional entity, has always been considered part of eastern Armenia. Eastern Armenian is spoken in Armenia, Nagorno-Karabakh, Georgia, and Iran. Western Armenians lived in the Armenian highlands which is today's Eastern Turkey, bordering Eastern Armenia. They were subjects of the Ottoman Empire until 1915. During the genocide many Armenians were deported to the Der-el-Zor desert in Syria. Those who survived either remained in Syria or fled even further south to Lebanon and other Arabic countries who give survivors refuge and shelter. Some genocide survivors made it to European countries, especially Greece, Bulgaria, Romania, and France. Some also made it to the United States and the Americas as well as to Australia. Western Armenian was spoken by Armenians in Anatolia, Turkey, and today is spoken in places such as Lebanon, Syria, Iraq, Egypt, Ethiopia, Turkey, Australia, Europe, North America, and South America. Of great importance to today's generation is the Armenian language. Linguistic scholars consider the western and eastern Armenian languages as two standardized versions of the modern Armenian language. While scholars and lay individuals debate about how they relate to each other, both versions enrich their unique culture. The above differentiation is not necessarily taught to children whose parents/grandparents immigrated to the United States as they often learn about their history from books and selected storytelling. Zepure, had learned from her mother (me) that her family are western Armenians and speak the western Armenian language.

Visiting Turkey

After 31 years since my arrival in the United States, I visited my birthplace in Turkey with my daughter and my mother. But my memory takes me back to one of my first visits to Turkey after immigrating to the United States when I met Nubar Hadjian. I will not forget his name as long as I live. I saw him in the backyard of the old church Surp Hovhannes. He was already an old man resembling my grandfather Garabed when I migrated to America. I followed him like a ghost. I went to his dilapidated home and climbed the shabby stairs up to his home. He was one of the survivors of the Armenian genocide in my childhood neighborhood. He was the only one still alive. I spoke to him in my imagination,

> You continue life so adamantly, the very life dreams which I have in my mind. I salute you Nubar Hadjian. I can only make paintings with your name on each one of them, dear Nubar Hadjian. You are my existing hero. I bow in front of you. You are not Van Gogh, not a famous mathematician, no, just Nubar Hadjian. You will be remembered as long as I am able to paint colors and lines onto the canvas.

He asked me not to forget his name, stating, "Do not forget who I am!" I sound sentimental, yet you do not know what it means to be erased from the pages of history and to be erased from the neighborhood where you once lived 30 years ago which changed into oblivion.

MY LIFE AS AN ARTIST

In the early 1970s, I began exhibiting my work in such diverse locations as California; Louisville, Kentucky; Boston, Massachusetts; Maine; New York City; Rhode Island; Washington, DC; and Florida as well as in Europe and Armenia. I had become a global artist coming from a disturbed world filled with intolerance and discrimination. I strongly believe that art converges

Figure 13.5 *Threnody to Yezidi Women.* Elegy to the women of ethnic Yezidis of eastern Turkey massacred by ISIS.

people, and I also am convinced that my art gives spiritual satisfaction! An artist, if unselfish and passionate, is a living protest to protest against conformism, against what is official, what is public, or what is national. What everyone else feels comfortable with, an artist is engaged in protest which is always scandalous. I am an artist who feels the pain of injustice from all directions and among all peoples around the world. My works carry the burden of millions who are being dehumanized today and are reflected in the philosophy of global education. My deep feeling for humanity and its interconnectivity between all members of the world are reflective in some of my paintings: *Grief* (Figure 13.3), which honors suffering women of the world; *Moment* (Figure 13.4), dedicated to the refugees of the world; *Threnody to*

Yezidi Women (Figure 13.5), the painting celebrating the Yezidi women massacred by the Islamic State of Iraq and Syria (ISIS); and, foremost in my feeling for humanity, my most recent painting of *An Armenian Woman* (me) *Longing for Peace in the Ukraine* (this volume, p. vi), which addresses the Ukrainian crisis and the burden of families who are being dehumanized seeking refuge in neighboring countries while husbands, sons, and brothers, and cousins are dying in the war against invading Russia. In particular, my paintings challenge the leaders of the world who possess the power to do so, to bring justice to their suffering societies.

I have confronted discrimination firsthand both in America and abroad many times. For example, I once applied to be a tour guide at Disney World while attending the University of Florida. The last few words of the interviewer have been etched on my brain cells permanently. He told me I was not eligible for the position because I did not fit the perfect image of the candidate they were looking for since I was darker than average, had an accent, and my nose and teeth were uneven. Some Armenians have looked down on me because I am from Turkey as being somehow Turkified which can be true for some who were forced to Turkify. What they did not understand was that it was not a choice. In the United States, I also have experienced superficial discrimination regarding my accent and my difficult name. I also have been told by directors of art galleries that the problem is not my artwork but that I do not fit their mold. I have always been different, but not the right kind of different. The silence of my early years slowly evolved into creating numerous paintings of global dimensions and perspectives over the many years in my newly adopted country of the United States. To love, to paint, to dream, to make money, to eat healthy, to dance, to sing, to think, to say everything, to say nothing, to understand is foremost on my mind. With love, all the other senses can stream into its unique expression. I have learned that Americans or, for that matter, Armenians with their spoon-fed conceptions of how eccentric creative people should act, are more interested in the persona than in the true woman/man of her/his expressive abstract art.

Palimpsest: History in a Drawer

A palimpsest is a manuscript that has been reused by writing over the original writing, and sometimes more than once. Frequently it is impossible to say which layer was first inscribed. *History in a Drawer* is an art installation that expresses moments of memories of separations and distances representing letters from loved ones tucked away in a drawer and years later found and read with longing. It is a precious moment for now while we still write letters to each other before all correspondence is captivated in electronic file cabinets.

Fractured Visions of Remembrance • **311**

Starting with my remembrances of my early childhood in Istanbul and my grandparents' old house on the ancient seacoast with a view ranging from minarets and churches to the Sea of Marmara, one piece of furniture precipitates my reflection to date: an armoire with mirrors and four or five drawers. My grandparents and I each had a drawer; my grandmother kept her jewelry in one drawer and all her notebooks and writings written with beautiful calligraphy in another. One drawer was for me where I kept my childhood drawings and secret diary. The bottom drawer belonged to my grandfather; and it was locked. The metal key was at his disposition only. Every time he unlocked his drawer, I would go sit with him as at an altar of a sanctuary and watch a stack of large envelopes carefully piled together. These envelopes had large colorful images printed on them with stamps and Russian writings from Soviet Armenia from his brother, sister,

Figure 13.6 *Palimpsest of my Artsakh.* Dedicated to my memories of the past long ago and faraway.

and father who had left Istanbul in the 1920s. These manuscripts were resonances of separation, nostalgia's only thread of communication. No telephone, no photographs, just these envelopes with big writings on them carefully placed in this drawer.

My experiences of the very act of my grandfather keeping and holding on to these envelopes, reading the contents repeatedly, exist vividly in my mind today and are strongly connected internally to my art. I deliberate this intense human form into an imaginative consciousness to mediate an interaction with the visitors to my studio who become part of my lived experience, that of the moment. I connect the internal and external worlds of day-to-day life, scrape away the solitude and alienation of the human condition, especially via art, and give the observer/participant a totally lived life. The very notion of bringing new beauty into *existence* implies that an old ugliness has been swept away. Beauty defines itself by restoring the ill, the ugliness which is not itself. And tomorrow probably I shall clear this and write anew.

Painting Massive Spaces

The most spectacular thing I have experienced in America is space: space in the thought process, space for creativity. Space is the essence for all the wonderments of art and life. Completely mesmerized with space, I started to paint on the large, stretched canvases or on the walls. No wonder the great American abstract expressionism started the use of space, although the idea came from artists who became aware of the difference between the Old World and the New World just like Antonin Dvorak's (1893) *New World Symphony*. Once experienced, both differences can be valued.

Certain painters are truly expansionists, although it all depends on whether they have the financial means to get the space they need. As for me I got stuck in Watertown, Massachusetts, surrounded with heavy duty obscurantists in terms of evaluating paintings. Because of my art, I have been living a very lonely life; only my immediate offsprings, partners, a few precious friends, and my cousins are appreciative of my art. Still, I am luckier than Vincent van Gogh, and I am grateful for that. In fact, I am totally hijacked as a nonrefundable refugee in my house with a paintings-stuffed studio. I am in the wrong places at the wrong times; the Boston area galleries either have trendy kitsch work or secondhand works of prints of famous artists. Yet, for the sake of my family, I continue to endure all kinds of humiliations and degrading attitudes living here where I am now writing these words. I was ridiculed by even so-called close relatives with their conventional minds who regard artists as subhuman. People ask, "Oh, are you still sleeping all morning?" or "Oh, you still paint?" or "Why do you paint if you cannot sell?" in condescending tones as if I am asking them for money. I leave the presumptuous ones to taste their own life lessons. I was raised with passion and utmost love for my children and grandchildren. I also conduct art workshops for adults as well as students in public schools here in Watertown, Massachusetts.

CONCLUSION

My beloved maternal grandfather died in 1973 and my maternal grandmother in 1977. They had visited me in the United States in 1972 before my eldest daughter was born. My beloved mother, a vibrant, lively, vivacious woman, a mega feminist without even trying to prove anything to anyone, a single mother, a minority Armenian in Turkey, working at a prestigious university as the dean's executive assistant. She was widely traveled and decided to move to America in the 1960s because she felt there existed the freedom she needed. First, she worked in a factory, then as a nurse, and finally ended up at the Harvard University Herbarium. Without exaggeration, she was loved by everyone; she was magnanimous; she always told exciting stories and had an incredible contagious belly laugh. She gave her final breath in 2009 surrounded by her loved ones.

As for me, after immigrating to the United States, I married my musician friend at the age of 18 with whom I had my firstborn in California. Being such a young mother gave me liberation and being closer to nature and my inner core. I was accepted to CalArts. We traveled throughout the country in my early 20s and ended up in Florida. We divorced. I stayed to continue my higher education in art at the University of Florida where I met my influential professor and mentor, Walter Gaudnek. In my late 20s, I moved back North with my daughter to be closer to my mother. I live among Armenian refugees in our community which never fails to remind me of the horror my people experienced during the Armenian genocide. I met my second husband, and we had two more children in the early 1980s. My first daughter is a poet, my second daughter is a lawyer, and my son is a utilitarian artist of sorts, building passive housing. I have five wonderful grandchildren ranging from the ages of 3 months to 11 years old. We all live together in one big house where I often must withdraw from the children's noise to the quietude of my studio, my world.

REFLECTIONS

As a painter of modern art, what matters most to me is the expression of one's soul because that is true art. How this art is perceived in society is another story. All societies need art as art is the lifework of education—genuine art that is. It is neither business nor commercial. The magic of art shapes humanity. It creates culture. It creates philosophy. Why do the Germanic people have such strong art versus Italian craftwork, French seduction, and the Asian world of craft?

What are my dreams now? To continue creating paintings that bring about strong emotions and hope in order to counterbalance the violence and injustice in the world. Naturally, I am enthused to show my works to the public. I am driven to paint and create. Another dream of mine is to visit Armenia again after the devastating war of aggression by Azerbaijan in 2020 backed by Turkey. I dream of bringing my canvasses and vivid colors and develop with the children of Armenia a colorful and strong future together. Another dream of mine is to continue to work with students here in the United States and expose them to the history of art and the genres of art. I enjoy encouraging them to bring out their talent that reaches deeply into their souls, their spirit. I am a global artist who feels the pain of injustice from all directions and among all peoples around the world. In my work, I want to continue to show the global interconnectedness of human suffering and the burden of millions of people around the world who are being dehumanized.

SECTION VII

SOUTH AMERICA

CHAPTER 14

ARGENTINA

FROM BUENOS AIRES TO BUFFALO TO BOOKS

The Politics of Populism

Aixa Pérez-Prado

I was born in Buenos Aires, Argentina, in 1964. Buenos Aires is a bustling metropolis known for a vibrant arts scene and political turmoil. The city is built in the European style and reminiscent of both Paris and Madrid. The 1960s in Argentina were a particularly turbulent time in the country's history. The Perón administration of the 1950s had promoted a social safety net, labor rights, expanding infrastructure, public services, and educational opportunities. During this time wages were increased and healthcare improved. However, not everything was positive. There was disagreement about how Perón went about the business of social reform and wealth distribution. While the administration was popular with the many in the lower

Figure 14.1 Aixa in the city.

socioeconomic classes, many in the middle classes struggled to maintain their family businesses.

Eventually a coup d'état overthrew Perón. The new military government established in 1955, well before I was born, favored a free-market economy and lessened state regulations. In the following years, social inequalities increased, and a housing problem developed. Many properties were taken over by squatters who failed to pay rent but were almost impossible to evict. This happened to my family and is still happening today. Sixty years later, there remain squatters on my grandfather's properties.

SOCIAL CHANGE AND WOMEN'S ROLES

Just as in other parts of the world, the 1960s in Argentina were a time of cultural and political change that reimagined gender roles and challenged the status quo. Young people started to explore and debate new ideas about love, sex, and family. A strong sense of modernism and defiance pervaded the country (Pujol, 2003).

Increasingly, women were working outside of the home and studying a variety of traditionally male professions. My own mother became a medical doctor in the late 1950s despite the misgivings of some of her male family members. Argentine women began to demand equality with men, even in the face of increasingly conservative regimes. The coup d'état of 1966, shortly after I was born, was one of many examples of the political turmoil that would plague the country for years to come. The status quo was being challenged in Argentina much as it was in the rest of the world, yet in Latin America this was happening in the face of repressive regimes.

My memories begin in the late 1960s, right before I left the country, and they have nothing to do with politics. What I remember is the love of my grandmothers, the delicious foods they served me, empanadas, milanesas, tortillas, and my first forays into primary education. I also remember one of my role models, a small girl in a comic strip that bore her name *Mafalda*. This little girl was constantly worried about the status quo and seemed to carry the weight of the world on her shoulders. Although my father strongly objected to some of the stereotypes contained in this long running series, he bought me all of the books and encouraged me to read them throughout the 1970s. Mafalda (Cosse, 2014) was questioning the world and how it worked in Argentina, and I also would be questioning the world and trying for the rest of my life to figure out how it worked.

FAMILY DYNAMICS

My paternal grandfather owned a series of small grocery stores that he bought, made profitable, and resold. With his profits, he invested in properties to use as rental income. During the Perón administration, my grandfather was detained and charged for not selling groceries at the prices the government had established. My grandfather had immigrated from Spain to Argentina on his own as a 14-year-old boy, with nothing. He had built up wealth through hard work and sacrifice. He was not a fan of Perón. Neither was my maternal grandfather, who also happened to be a grocer and who was also detained during this time. The difference was that my maternal grandfather barely got by and ultimately lost his grocery store.

My grandmother, Blanca, the youngest of six sisters, was from the province of San Luis, in Northwest Argentina, a mountainous, arid region known for its natural beauty. Blanca's birth certificate lists only a mother with the same last name she used her entire life. My grandmother was sent to live in a convent because her mother could not take care of her due to a disability. My grandmother often recalled the trauma that she experienced in the convent, something she remembered for her lifetime. She regularly shared the story of how she was forced to kneel on raw corn kernels and pray for hours as punishment for minor offenses. Predictably, she held a low opinion of nuns and priests.

Blanca adored her father and seemed to have little love for her mother, rarely mentioning her. She remembered being taken with several of her sisters, by her father, to her paternal grandmother's house to live as their own mother was unable to care for her daughters. Apparently, her grandmother was well off with plenty of space for the girls. However, after first having agreed to care for her granddaughters, she told her son to take his daughters with him when he was leaving. That may have been when young Blanca ended up in the convent school.

Although my grandmother never stated why her own grandmother rejected her and her sisters, I now believe that she was a White immigrant from Europe and didn't want half indigenous girls as part of her family. All my grandmother would say is, "She didn't want us." I wonder how much my grandmother knew of her own heritage, or how much she understood at that time. Although Blanca was extremely light skinned, several of her sisters were darker skinned with dark hair and eyes. Perhaps because my grandmother was the youngest, she didn't realize the nuances of the rejection at the time. I will never know the true story, but I know that my grandmother lived the rest of her life feeling that she was not quite good enough.

MY COMMUNITY

My home was right in the middle of Buenos Aires, located in one of the oldest and most central neighborhoods of the city, Montserrat. I lived walking distance to every important government building and I spent many afternoons feeding the pigeons in their spacious squares. My neighborhood was also walking distance to the artsy San Telmo district with its hippie street fairs and numerous cafés, and the poorer and more colorful Italian neighborhood known for tango, soccer, and crime—La Boca.

Immigrants and Indigeneity

My neighborhood, like most of the country, was made up of European immigrants and their descendants. The majority of these were from Southern Europe, including my paternal grandparents from Spain, and maternal great grandparents from Italy. The indigenous population of Argentina is small compared to neighboring nations, and I was unaware of indigenous peoples as a small child. In fact, I had no idea that I had any indigenous ancestry until I took a DNA test many years later and was shocked to discover that my maternal grandmother was half indigenous. She described herself as French and Irish and her light skin and blue eyes seemed to cement the fact that she was European. Looking back, I wonder whether she was ignorant of her indigeneity, or hiding it. Racism exists throughout Argentina against indigenous people, and she may have internalized racism for herself.

Los Gallegos y Buenos Aires

My home in Buenos Aires was located in a community composed primarily of immigrants from Spain. My own grandparents had immigrated from Galicia when they were teenagers. In Argentina, "Gallegos," as immigrants from Galicia and all of Spain are called, had a reputation for being stupid. I grew up hearing jokes about Gallegos, similar to Polish jokes in the United States. I also saw these jokes in my beloved comic strip, *Mafalda*, in the form of Manolito, the son of a grocer. His head is square shaped, and he is the least intelligent of all the children. It is a trope, a stereotype that was rampant in the country when I was a child and one that caused a great deal of stress to my father.

My father, Antonio, a medical doctor, writer, and artist, fought against racism directed at Gallegos his entire life. He wrote a book that became quite

Figure 14.2 Aarriba Argentina.

well known in certain circles, called *Los Gallegos y Buenos Aires* (Pérez-Prado, 1973). In his book he explored the history of the diaspora of Galicia to Argentina and the causes and consequences of that immigration. He went on television and wrote articles, even debating the famous creator of the *Mafalda* comic strip, social satirist, Quino. This all happened in the 1970s and was a cause of great embarrassment for me. My mother's family, primarily Italian and of extended Argentine ancestry, made fun of my father for his mission against jokes about Gallegos and ridiculed the awards he was given by the Galician community. Even as a small child, I knew that what he was doing was honorable and good, but in wanting to fit in as an Argentine, I never defended him.

A SERIES OF GOODBYES

My childhood was a childhood of goodbyes. When I was 6 months old my father left for England to do postdoctoral study. I think a great deal of the appeal of England was that it enabled him to temporarily escape being a husband and father. My mother sent him a series of angry letters, demanding his return. She had not been consulted on his decision to go. My father, always the pedantic sort, sent back those same letters after having corrected all of the grammar errors. This action was not well received, and my father did not return to us for over a year. He returned only when his own father was dying of kidney disease.

After my grandfather's death, another goodbye, my parents moved to Holland to do postdoctoral research. Perhaps it was a last-ditch attempt to fix their marriage. They left me behind in Argentina with my grandmothers. I was only 2 at the time and don't remember this period, but I know that my grandmothers became the most important people in my world. Soon after my parents returned, evidently not having fixed their marriage, the next goodbye followed. My mother emigrated to the United States, settling in Buffalo, New York, and leaving me behind. Only my father knew she was emigrating, everyone else thought she had gone to a medical conference. I don't remember missing her, I was only 3. Her own parents thought she had abandoned me.

A Happy Childhood Punctuated by Pain

The final goodbye came a year later when my father took me to "visit" my mother in the United States. I was excited to go. I had recently started school and was eager to show off everything I had learned. I never imagined for a moment that I was emigrating. Had I known, I would have refused to get on the plane. Leaving my grandmothers, my home, and my city, was unfathomable. Yet it is exactly what occurred. Before the cruelest goodbye, I had turned 4 and started pre-Kindergarten in Buenos Aires. The school was close to my home and my grandmother walked me there every day. I remember my crisp white uniform and shiny leather shoes. My grandmother Fé from Galicia fixed my hair exactly the way I liked it, and I proudly held her hand to cross the street. Every morning we stood together on the front steps waiting for the school to open with the other mothers, grandmothers, and their young charges.

I still have the notebook with the cut-out shapes I pasted in those first few months of pre-Kindergarten. I still remember my friend Julieta's curls and watching my grandmother blow me goodbye kisses. I loved school. On the way home, my grandmother and I always stopped by the small grocery store where Don Garcia would give me a bit of cheese or ham to snack on, the bakery where I was always allowed to choose a pastry, and the vegetable and fruit stand where I reached for peaches whenever they were available. It was a good life. Despite being temporarily motherless, I was a happy child.

Years later I saw a comment in one of my father's journals from this time. He had been looking through my school notebook and seeing what I was learning made him question whether he should let me go live in the United States. I wanted to reach back in time and yell, "No! You should not let me go! Especially not the way you are about to!" But it was far too late. My parents' decision changed the course of my life. While there are a multitude of positive outcomes that resulted from my emigration to the United States, there are also a multitude of negative ones. Among these is a lifetime of feeling like I don't really belong anywhere. I left too little to fully belong in Argentia. I left too late, and too abruptly to fully accept the United States as my home. I left my grandmother Fé, the center of my world.

Brought to the United States, the Cruelest Goodbye

A week or so after being brought to the United States by my father, he told me, one morning, that he was going to work. As a doctor, my father worked in Buenos Aires, so I must have thought he'd just pop into a hospital in Buffalo, see some patients and come back—I was wrong. My father never returned. That was the final and cruelest of all goodbyes because there was no goodbye. I remember waiting by the door for him for a long time. My mother explained the situation, but I didn't believe her. I don't remember how long I waited for him, but eventually I determined that he was dead. It seemed the only explanation possible. I was inconsolable, and later, I was furious.

Immigration happened to me. I had no choice in the matter whatsoever. I was not informed of the decision until it was already done. For me, it was a horrible experience. I felt abandoned by my father, the only parent I remembered. Children usually do not get a voice in the decision to emigrate, but they should at least be prepared. At the very least, they should be informed.

Many years later I asked my father why he had agreed to the arrangement and why he hadn't said goodbye. His face told me this was a topic we could not discuss. The only thing he said that I remember, is that leaving me was like cutting off an arm. That is how much it hurt him. I don't think I replied at the time, but I have thought often of that comment. I wish I had responded that I understood how painful that would be, and then continued with his metaphor. If leaving me was like losing an arm to him, then I was just an arm that was lost. An arm is powerless all by itself. An arm does not have a voice to protest, a body to take it where it needs to go, a mind that can understand decisions made for it. If he was left without an arm, then I was just a bloody appendage. That is exactly how I felt, powerless, pained, and incomplete.

CITIZENSHIP AND IDENTITY

When I was 13, my mother became a citizen of the United States and through her, so did I. I remember once again feeling as though I had no choice in the matter, just as I had had no choice in becoming an immigrant. My mother did not ask me if I wanted to become a U.S. citizen. I was not happy with her decision. I felt like I was betraying Argentina. When I protested, my mother dismissed my concerns.

Another aspect that disturbed me about the citizenship process was that my mother told me not to sign the naturalization papers with my full name. My full name includes two middle names, Jimena Beatriz. She said that if I signed that way, then I would always have to use my two middle names every time I signed. I did not want to sign without including my full name. I remember feeling like my names were taken away from me. Becoming a citizen of the United States was not a pleasant experience and the face photo on my naturalization certificate proves it. I look like I am being coerced, and I was. However, I do not regret my citizenship now. I have dual citizenship and that seems appropriate, and I use my two middle names whenever I feel like it.

Beatriz was my mother's name. My father added it to Aixa Jimena because the ladies in the name registration office were concerned. They felt sorry for me for being given such unusual names. Nowadays Jimena is fairly common in Argentina, but at the time it was apparently as strange as Aixa. In order to placate these bureaucrats, my father added my mother's name to mine. I never liked either of my middle names, but I wanted to hold on to them, nonetheless. They were part of my identity, the odd with the familiar, the new with the history. I didn't want to let them go. Despite what any of my documents say, in my heart I am Aixa Ximena Beatriz Pérez-Prado Grisolía Guevara. A name that is way too long and complicated, but that somehow suits me.

Acculturation and Double Consciousness

When I came to the United States at the age of 4, I expected to visit rather than relocate. My idea was to have fun and visit my mother. When I realized that I was not going back, I was furious. Since I was so young, and so powerless, I quickly adapted to my new circumstances. What else could I do? I learned to live in the suburbs instead of a city. I learned to become a different person, at least superficially.

My mother enrolled me in an excellent and very expensive private school with a large outside play area and wonderful teachers. I was fortunate to have the experience of attending that school for several years. Looking back at some of my report cards from the time, I see where the teachers started out concerned that I cried most of the day when I first arrived. I was comforted only when allowed to set the table, or during music time. I can only imagine that setting the table reminded me of being home with my grandmother. Music time also must have reminded me of my grandmother who sang all day as she did the chores at home, often in her native language Gallego.

At my school there was a young French teacher who played guitar and sang French songs with us. I loved French music time. My mother later told me that the teacher was astounded by my excellent pronunciation. Apparently, she did not know that I also spoke Spanish and was surprised at how I could make the sounds of French so effortlessly compared to the other children. I also had a French babysitter for several months who spoke to me only in French. Many years later when I moved to Morocco, I picked up French astonishingly quickly. I believe that my early exposure to the language must have had a strong influence on me and made me more receptive to the language and ready to learn it in later years.

The Color of Childhood

Another aspect that happened once I moved to the United States is that I became aware of skin color. In Argentina, I had never seen a Black person. My own family is composed of pale skinned people of mostly European descent. I have no recollection of seeing any people who were brown skinned before I emigrated. I lived in a very White world.

When I started my new school in the United States my best friend at the school was a black girl named Avian. We spent time together both inside and outside of school. There were quite a few Black children in my neighborhood, and soon I came to believe that all children eventually turned black if they lived in the United States. One day, I was looking at myself in the mirror and touching the skin on my face and arms. My mother asked me what I was doing, and I responded that I was seeing if I had started turning black yet. When she informed me that I would not be turning black, that my friends had been black from birth, I was sorely disappointed. Apparently, I felt that being black was an important part of belonging and understanding how to do things in English and in the United States.

A New Family for a While

When I was 7 years old my mother married a man from Buffalo, New York. My stepfather, Paul, was the best stepfather a strange little kid like me could have asked for. He was kind and loving and had a family who welcomed me into the fold. I told him that he was going to have to take me out for ice cream every weekend because that's what other dads did. By then, I had started to make friends with kids whose parents were divorced, and their weekends were always filled with fun dad outings. My new dad agreed to my terms, and we often went to Dairy Queen on the weekends, blasting "Bye Bye Miss American Pie" on the car stereo on our way to visit family. I felt loved by my stepfamily and felt like I was a part of it.

Later, when my stepfather and mother separated, things changed. The family cut me off along with my mother. I always felt that the fact that we were both from Argentina had something to do with the abrupt break in relationship. I had two younger siblings by then who were not cut off from the family. Even though my mother and stepfather reunited for many more years before separating again, I never again became part of that family. It felt like a big loss to me, another family that had let me go. Families are complicated, and when immigration, alienation, and cultural expectations of family intermingle, even more complicated.

When No Place Is Home

When my mother remarried, she took me along on her honeymoon to Argentina. I was 7 years old. It was the first time I had returned since emigrating. I remember many things about that trip, including the feeling of unease. It was as if I was home but not home, in a place I belonged but would never again belong. My cousins made fun of my accent, my father tried to relate to me as if I was still 4, and the neighbors asked me to speak in English. I had turned into a curiosity, something strange yet familiar, someone who did not quite fit in. Only my grandmothers continued to treat me as if I was still the same old me, and I once again fell happily under their spell. Their stories and their food sustained me throughout that month-long trip. Leaving them again was difficult.

I continued to return to Argentina every few years throughout my childhood. Every time I went it was with the expectation of going home to where I belonged. Every time I arrived, I was faced with the realization that I had changed, and the country had changed without me. No matter what I said or did, it was not quite right. I was always the subject of curiosity, and sometimes teasing. I hated that. Yet, every time I left again it was painful. It felt as if I was on the verge of finding my rightful place in the world just when it was time to leave.

BEING AMERICAN

I am American, by birth and by choice. I do not mean that I am a citizen of the United States and, therefore, "American" as citizens of the United States call themselves. I do not buy into the concept of the American dream or the idea that real Americans are the ones who were born and raised in this country, speak English from birth, and have primarily a northern European heritage. I am not as American as apple pie, as the saying goes. I am as American as empanadas.

Most people from the United States do not realize that everyone from North, South, and Central America is American. We all have the right to that moniker if we choose to use it, and sometimes I choose to use it. Having indigenous ancestry further cements my claim to the label. I have a history on these continents that goes back thousands of years. I have a claim to both the south by birth and the north by lived experience. I speak the three most spoken languages in the Americas: Spanish, English, and Portuguese. I also have started to explore the indigenous languages of Quechua and Guaraní spoken primarily in Bolivia, Paraguay, and Peru. In some ways I am more American, in my opinion, than most people who refer to themselves as American. Yet, I am often excluded from the term. I am often forced to claim it rather than it being a given.

There are several things that peg me as not "American" enough. The first is my name, an odd name for all of the Americas. My name is Arabic, chosen for me by my father from a novel he loved. Sometimes people insist that my name is pronounced with the "x" as is a Puerto Rican name with identical spelling. However, that is not my name. My Arabic name is spelled in Gallego, so the x has an -sh sound. I have spent a lifetime explaining my name and how to pronounce it with two syllables that sound like eye-shaah. Moreover, my last name is hyphenated. It is extremely challenging to convince people that both parts of the name are equally important. I am continuously having to point out that the whole thing is my last name from birth. I did not hyphenate my name after marriage. I cherish my double last name because it represents both of my immigrant grandparents. However, convincing other people that using only one side of the hyphen is not enough has proven almost impossible.

South America is Not Important

What it meant to be American and who qualified as American was made clear to me during my elementary school years in Buffalo, New York. When I started fifth grade, my teacher announced that we were meant to study North and South America in social studies that year. I was excited as it would be the first time that South America would be featured in my education. I was eager to show off my knowledge and learn more about the continent. However, that was not to be. Right after his announcement, my teacher said that we would be skipping everything in the curriculum about South America because it was "not important."

With two words an entire continent was rejected. A continent rich with diverse landscapes, histories, countries, and people. My teacher dismissed my family, my language, and my homeland in one fell swoop. I was stunned into silence. I remember sitting at my seat hoping that none of my classmates would remember that I was born in Argentina. His words had negated the value of my very existence. My mortification was not about the lack of importance of South America. I knew my teacher was mistaken about that. Rather, it was about the other kids believing him and seeing me as "not important," not really "American."

Although in class we did not use the South America section of our textbook, it still existed in the textbook. I remember feeling relieved that we would not be reading about Argentina when I saw that the only image of my country in the book was of a boy who appeared to be a gaucho on a ranch. He was meant to represent life in Argentina. I was mortified. Not because I didn't know gauchos existed, I had heard about them much like children hear about cowboys in the United States. However, because I had never seen a gaucho, it somehow embarrassed me to have anyone think that Argentina was a vast grassland populated by cattle ranchers. The image was so far removed from my experience, and such a narrow slice of Argentina, that I felt it would be better to have no picture at all in the textbook.

My discomfort with the image was compounded by the reaction of a classmate who sat in front of me. He had also looked through the textbook, and knowing I was from Argentina, pointed to the little gaucho and asked me if he was my brother. When I said, "No," he asked me why I was White. The little boy in the image appeared to be indigenous. His questions felt deeply humiliating to me. I tried to explain that most people in Argentina are White and that I really did not know much about Argentina. I wanted to cry in frustration because in some ways he was right. I had not gone to school there beyond pre-Kindergarten. Most disturbingly, I knew in my heart that I didn't belong to Argentina anymore and would never really belong to the United States of America either.

RELATIVES, REVOLUTIONS, AND REJECTION

Before I was taken to the United States at the age of 4, my father and I had a special bond. Although he was not my primary caregiver, as I was raised by my grandmothers. We spent weekends together engaging in our favorite activity attending the theater. Buenos Aires has a wealth of children's theater performances every weekend. Children in the audience were frequently invited to play on stage before and after the show. We were provided with noisemakers and encouraged to interact with the actors during the show. It was participatory and energizing. I have fond memories of that time.

One day at the theater, I noticed a microphone set up on the stage. I took advantage of the opportunity to make a formal announcement that the Argentine revolutionary, Ché Guevara, had been killed, and I added, "We should all be very sad because my uncle, Ché Guevara, was really murdered!" My maternal grandmother, whose last name was Guevara, who came from the same place as Ché Guevara, always told us that he was one of our distant relatives. I heard from somewhere of his death, and I was determined to relay the shocking news to the world.

The next thing I knew was my father scooping me off the stage, holding me tight by the hand and running down the street with me. In later years, my father explained that he feared we would be detained by the military government because of our connection to Che Guevara. I have no idea if my father's fears were justified, I only know that whenever the subject of Ché Guevara came up after that, it was quickly silenced. My mother continued to silence the topic throughout her life. She refused to either confirm or deny the relationship. The connection is still a mystery.

Los Desaparecidos—the Disappeared—the Dirty War

Anything going on politically in Argentina was unknown to me. I now know that the 1970s brought a great deal of political upheaval to my home country including the disappearance of thousands of Argentinians who were considered to be subversives or revolutionaries. Perón had returned to the presidency in the early 1970s but died in 1974. At that time his vice president and second wife, Isabel Perón, assumed the presidency. Not having the political strength to stave off a military coup, a junta led by General Jorge Rafael Videla removed her from office and established a strong grip on power. A grip that proved fatal for thousands of Argentinians.

The junta maintained control by cracking down on anybody they believed might be a challenge to their authority. The regime was responsible for abducting, torturing, and murdering thousands of Argentinians during this time. These included political activists, nonviolent leftists, and creatives, as well as their sympathizers and families. Pregnant women were kidnapped and kept until their babies were born, then murdered. Their babies were adopted out to military families or others and raised without knowledge of their origins. Although much of this was happening in Buenos Aires, most people were either unaware of, or chose to turn a blind eye to the situation. Those who were aware of the atrocities lived in fear.

It was in the midst of this turmoil that I decided to leave the United States where I had lived for 11 years and live in Argentina again. I was 15 at the time and feeling rebellious. I was tired of living under my mother's constantly changing roof. She had moved us so frequently over the years that I had been forced to be the "new kid" at a new school repeatedly. With a name and story like mine, that was difficult. I wanted to go back to a home that did not move. I wanted the stability of my grandmothers and felt the need to reclaim my identity as an Argentinian. My arguments finally wore my mother down and she decided to let me go. However, my father did not want me to return home.

Rejection

After my return to Argentina, I remember how horrible it felt that my father was not eager to have me back. To me it felt like not only being rejected by my father, but somehow also being rejected by my country. The more he resisted, the more my mother insisted that I should go back to Argentina. He kept urging caution and reconsideration. In hindsight, I realize that he was terrified. He was one of those people in Argentina who knew what was going on. He had friends who had fled in exile, and even though I knew nothing about politics nor was I involved in it, he was afraid.

My mother and I got our way, and I boarded a plane "home" in June of 1979. I spent the next 7 months in Buenos Aires, in the midst of the Dirty War. My mother and the rest of the family felt that my father was exaggerating about the unpredictable actions of the government. They treated my father's fear of the government much like his problem with jokes against Gallegos, an unnecessary preoccupation. Many people at that time in Argentina felt they had nothing to fear because they were doing nothing wrong, but others understood the danger.

My father was right to be worried. Although I had no subversive inclinations, I put myself in dangerous situations out of ignorance. At the time, in Argentina, everyone had to walk around with identification at all times. On numerous occasions I would forget to carry around my U.S. passport. My father insisted that I use it as my ID, reasoning that if I was detained for any reason, the military police would not harm a U.S. citizen. I did not have the habit of carrying an ID around, and I eventually lost the passport. This caused a great deal of upheaval since I hid the fact that I had lost it for months. When my mother came to Argentina to retrieve me and found me sans U.S. passport, you could have heard the uproar all the way to Buffalo.

The Streets of Buenos Aires

What I remember most about this period of Argentina's Dirty War is that my father appeared to be paranoid. The rest of the family seemed occupied with Argentina's soccer victories, popular music, and other entertainments. Argentina had recently won the World Cup, and this had caused a major distraction. They were proud to be Argentinians and not eager to speak out against the country that had just handed them this victory. Diego Maradona, perhaps one of the most gifted soccer players of all time, was the darling of the country despite the fact that his darker skin color would have normally caused him to be treated in discriminatory ways. In the face of his talent, his skin color could be excused.

I am younger than Maradona was, but not by much. In some ways we were traveling in similar circles for a while. I remember attending dances in the parts of the city where he sometimes frequented. More than once he was rumored to be around. This would cause kids to try to catch a glimpse of him, or an autograph. I always stayed back, watching from a distance. I wanted to fit in and be one of them, a real Argentinian, but I could not summon the same level of enthusiasm for soccer and soccer players as many of my contemporaries. Not feeling the same way as they did is part of what I knew made me different from other young Argentinians on the inside. No matter how much I wanted to be one of them, I never really was.

I surrounded myself with those who were celebrating the country rather than those who were criticizing it. They were mainly friends of my cousins, my friends only by association. For me, as a kid growing up in the United States, where Argentina was rarely mentioned, it was nice to be surrounded by people I did not have to explain the country to. As always, I wanted to fit in somewhere, anywhere, and not listening to my father was one way to do it. Perhaps if I had grown up in Argentina it would have been a different story, perhaps the friends I would have chosen for myself would have been different people, the kind who disappeared.

Las Madres y Abuelas de la Plaza de Mayo

My home in Buenos Aires is just a few blocks from the government center and I frequently walk in that area. I was not going to school because the schools in Argentina could not accept me due some missing documents that we did not have. Apparently, my parents had not figured that out before I returned. Therefore, I was free from going to school for 7 months. I was perfectly okay with that, much to the chagrin of my parents. For months, I barely studied and mostly roamed the streets of Buenos Aires. On weekends I went out with my older cousins to dances and parties, enjoying the full teenage experience with absolutely no concerns whatsoever for my own safety.

One day while out walking, I saw the women who walked in a circle outside of the Casa Rosada where the Plaza de Mayo is located. These were the mothers and grandmothers of the disappeared, *Las Madres* and *Las Abuelas*. Nobody was paying any attention to them. They were walking around in a circle with white kerchiefs on their heads. To me, they looked like sad old women from fairy tales. I didn't fully understand why they were there. When I asked my grandmother, she explained to me in measured words that these women wanted their children to be released from jail, and that she felt sorry for them. By the way she spoke, it was clear that she did not want to talk about it, quickly changing the subject.

Sometimes I heard my father and grandmother whispering in the kitchen when they thought I was still asleep. I knew they were talking about the political situation in Argentina, but I was not curious enough to listen carefully. I was not afraid of the military government or of disappearing, that was not a reality I understood at the time. I was afraid that the situation would cause my father to force me out of the country once again, replaying my earlier involuntary emigration. I would have done anything to avoid that.

One day while I was walking aimlessly during school hours, I wandered over to where the women walked in a circle. I stood and watched them for a while from a distance. To my surprise I thought I recognized my grandmother walking arm in arm with one of the women. I quickly turned and walked away, not wanting my grandmother to see me. To have made eye contact with her would have confirmed for me a suspicion that I was starting to formulate. Something was terribly wrong with my country. I didn't want to believe that. That day I stayed out much longer than usual. I didn't want to go back home and find that my grandmother was out, and thus possibly confirm that it was her.

Years later my father told me that my grandmother had walked with the Madres in the circle to show her support. He said that he had tried to dissuade her but that she had gone anyway. I learned this long after she was deceased. Apparently, my other family members never knew. When I questioned them, they said they had no idea, but that isn't surprising. They were busy promoting Argentina at the time and either unaware or unwilling to accept the atrocities that were happening.

My aunt and uncle on my father's side were among the most vocal promoters of Argentina. They gave me patriotic bookmarks and stickers to pass out to friends that said: "*Los Argentinos Somos Derechos y Humanos*," which roughly translates to: "We Argentinians Are Right and Human." It was a play on the term human rights. Argentina was being accused of violations by international human rights organizations at this time. My uncle was a kind and loving man, and I am certain, ignorant of what was happening. I never passed any of the stickers or bookmarks out, but I kept them for a long time. Today, I hope it was my grandmother I saw walking alongside those brave women in Plaza de Mayo that day.

MY LANGUAGE. MYSELF

Language has always been, and continues to be, an important aspect of identity for me. I speak, read, and write in both of my strongest languages, Spanish and English, yet there is a big difference between how I feel in both. I am more confident academically in English and write freely without feeling that I need to monitor myself in any way. However, using terms of endearment in English or talking to babies in English feels strange and uncomfortable to me. I don't feel that I can be as loving a person in English as I would like to be.

I am mostly confident when I speak in Spanish, and I read in Spanish as readily as I do in English. However, when I write in Spanish, I often find myself feeling anxious about my grammar and the placement of accents. I am not nearly as confident when writing in Spanish as I am in English, yet using terms of endearment in Spanish, loving in Spanish, comes naturally to me. If English is the language of my keyboard, Spanish is the language of my heart.

Having an Accent

I gave an online workshop not long ago on linguistic and cultural identity and how these come together in teaching and writing for children. As I was preparing the workshop, I reviewed the questions I would ask participants with the event organizer. One of my questions was: "Do you feel that your accent identifies, stereotypes, or labels you in any way?" When the organizer got to this question, she hesitated, and then she said, "I don't have an accent so I guess I can't answer that question." Her response highlights the idea of who is American and who isn't. "Americans" think they do not have an accent. Except they do.

One of the most important things that I have learned, both from my own lived experience as well as from my field of TESOL and applied linguistics is that everyone has an accent. Some are accents of power and prestige, the standard accent that guarantees you fit in. The standard is not the lack of an accent, it is the lack of an accent that would label you as an "Other." Like many, the event organizer I was working with had never considered accent in relation to power. She hadn't considered the fact that her assumptions of people who did not talk like her might in some ways influence how she perceived them or how they perceived her. She had never considered that everyone has an accent, even her.

The idea that an accent is never a bad thing, that it is merely an aspect of our language, is one of the most important concepts that I teach. For many years as a small child, I felt embarrassed by my mother's thick Argentinian accent in English. I am ashamed to say that I asked her not to call for me out loud when I played outside in my neighborhood because I didn't want the other children to hear the way she sounded in English. Her English did not feel good enough to be spoken around my second-grade friends. My parents' accents marked them as Others and thus identified me as an Other as well—even though most people consider that I don't have a foreign "accent" when I speak English. The more accurate description is that I have a mild Buffalo accent that after years living away from Buffalo is now blended with Miami tones. My accent does not place me in any region of this country, or my birth country. Even my accent doesn't belong anywhere.

The idea that all accents, all varieties of a language, and all languages are equally worthy is an important concept in my field. My first language, Spanish, is a language of lower prestige internationally than is English. I have always been sensitive to how it is portrayed in the media, workplace, and classroom. The numerous videos that have emerged in the past few years of people being berated publicly for speaking Spanish among themselves in the United States are hurtful yet not surprising. Even living in a city like Miami, heavily populated by bilinguals and Spanish speakers, it is clear that Spanish is not the language of power.

The Absence of Language Equity

Spanish is spoken widely in Miami but mostly for low-prestige daily tasks such as shopping and ordering at a restaurant. It is not the language that will get you into college. It is not the language that will identify you as "American" even though the first Europeans in Florida were the Spaniards. By the time many of my college students get to my class, they can no longer speak to their parents or their grandparents in ways that go beyond the surface level. They can chat, they can certainly ask for food, they can swear, and they can shop, but they cannot express their abstract thoughts, their hopes, dreams, goals, and fears in the same ways as they can in English. Even if Spanish is the only language they spoke when starting school, their Spanish language has not been supported and nourished by years of reading, writing, critical thinking, and interacting academically in Spanish. If Spanish were as powerful as English in Miami, they would be balanced bilinguals, able to do everything in each of their languages equally well, but the great majority of them cannot. That is a lack of language equity.

MY PROFESSIONAL LIFE: CHOICES AND CHALLENGES

I chose the field of teaching English to speakers of other languages (TESOL) so I could live and work overseas. It was a good choice, I learned a lot and when I returned to the United States with a newborn and a husband, I went on to get my PhD in social science education at Florida State University and now teach TESOL courses at the university level. But as a young assistant professor in 1997 at Florida International University in Miami, Florida, on tenure track, and a divorced mother of two, I had to make a choice. Unlike my own parents who chose to outsource childcare duties, I was determined to be their primary caregiver. This was not easy because I had to teach during hours that my children were not in school or daycare. I had to hire a sitter and hope the sitter would be reliable.

This all came to a head one day when I had an evening class, and my sitter did not show. My 4-year-old son, not the most well-behaved child, had an extra burst of energy that day. About an hour into my class, in addition to knocking over his sister and all the art materials I had provided, he stood on a chair and started shouting out "bathroom words." There was no stopping him. I had to dismiss my class. Lucky for me, mere days after that unforgettable incident, I started a new relationship with the man who has now been my husband for over 2 decades. With four young children between us, we immediately became a six-person unit rather than a couple. On the days that I taught in the evening, my future husband fed the children and got them ready for bed. I then had the privilege of coming home to read books and tell stories to a captive audience of four little ones snuggled under their covers. Very quickly, a family was formed that would soon expand to include two more children of our own. My evening childcare woes were temporarily resolved. However, my parental choices had become an even larger problem.

To Tenure or Not to Tenure

During my tenure earning years I received several concerning/unwelcome comments. These comments highlight how being a mother, and particularly an immigrant mother, affected my professional life. The first was from a colleague at a conference. I was bemoaning the fact that I had to worry about publishing while also teaching a full load of classes and taking care of my children. There didn't seem to be enough time to do all of that well. She, a woman with no children, told me to stop complaining and focus on publishing. She let me know that worrying about childcare was "Hispanic" and would not be getting me tenure. At the time, I felt too powerless to do anything but nod in agreement even though I did not agree at all. Unlike my own mother, I did not have grandmothers available to care for my children and I could not rely on babysitters. I was too Hispanic in my focus on my family.

In another incident, a male colleague advised me to "pause" the raising of my children to work on tenure and after getting tenure, I could refocus on my children. Many of my male colleagues were doing exactly as he advised with their own wives or girlfriends. I imagined putting my children on a shelf like bottles of wine, hoping they would still be there years later just waiting for me. "You have a PhD," he said, "you don't need to be changing diapers." By this time, I was pregnant with what would be our fifth child in a blended marriage. I was in no position to pull my focus away from my children, and there were plenty of diapers in my future.

Faculty View of Gender

Around the same time, I noticed a difference in the perception of faculty according to their gender. My chair pulled me aside one day to caution me against parading around with children into and out of my office. He had no issues with my work, but the children were not appropriate in faculty offices. When I told him that I believed my children were not bothering anybody, he leaned in to tell me that I would be surprised to know what my "friends" on the faculty were saying about all those kids following me around like "ducklings." My chair's words had a chilling effect on me. From that day forward I felt as though I had no real friends at the university and my desire to remain there was significantly reduced. Looking back, I wish I had confided what I had heard to colleagues I considered my friends. I feel that I missed an opportunity to seek clarification and support, and in so doing lost a sense of connection with the university.

I had two male colleagues who would occasionally bring their only child into their offices. I noticed how staff treated male professors whenever they had a child with them. They were widely regaled as exemplary fathers for doing so. I remember hearing the secretaries talk about how adorable it was that they had their child with them. I admit, I almost always had more than one child trailing behind me, and I often kept them in my office for several hours as I worked. I also used my office to nurse my youngest child whenever I needed to do so. Rather than being considered an exemplary mother, I gave a different impression. Seeing me with several kids in tow, was to see someone less professional, less efficient, and less tenure worthy.

During one of our faculty assembly meetings, the dean invited us to his holiday party. He went into detail about how he hoped all of us would attend. His way of inviting us was so notable to me that I remember his exact words. "Everyone is welcome to bring a guest, as long as that person is at least five feet tall." He was looking at me when he said it. I did not attend the event.

The following year, I was called into the office by my new chair to discuss my tenure process. I had been asked to teach online and to deliver classes online at a time when very few professors did, and I had dedicated much time to that endeavor. These time-consuming activities turned out to not be helping my progress towards tenure. I thought the new chair was going to sit me down and help me figure out how I could present my tenure file in the best possible light. I even harbored hopes that she might decrease my teaching load. This did not happen. Instead, my chair let me know that my tenure file with the accumulated documents I had secured thus far over a 5 year period, had somehow been misplaced. I would have to spend the entire summer resecuring the materials that had been accumulated up to that point, including letters of support and file reviews. This was the time before records were electronically created and transmitted. As I was walking out the door, pregnant with my sixth child, pondering how I was going to recollect the materials, she said words to me that remain with me to this day. "Hey, you're not going to come back and teach with a baby hanging off of your tit, are you?"

Dropping out of the Tenure Process

I dropped out of the tenure process shortly before I would need to submit my completed file. It was not only the lack of support at my university, or the middling progress I had made in terms of grants and publications, it was way more than that. My very identity as a Latina, a daughter, and a mother, was pulling me away. In Argentina, my elderly father had begun to need full-time care. As an only child, and daughter, I was expected to step into the role of care provider. The choice was my own and I have lived with the consequences of that choice ever since, most of them negative.

At this point several older female colleagues tried to talk me out of dropping out of the process, but for me it was too late. I had spent the summer trying to maintain my high-risk pregnancy, dealing with my father in Argentina, and taking care of my children. I had not spent the summer working on recovering my lost tenure documents. I had needed support earlier but had never asked and was never offered. I had needed "a village," as the saying goes, to help me raise my children, and I had not had that village. Had I been in my home country, surrounded by family, the situation might have been different, but it was not. Immigration has long-term consequences. For me, one of them was tenure.

I prepared to finish my teaching during the Spring semester of 2006, have my baby, take my maternity time, and then leave the university. I was looking for a way to live and work between countries and responsibilities, I was needed on two continents. Then my father surprised me by suddenly finding himself a full-time girlfriend/caregiver who took over and left no room for me or my children in the house to live in when we were about to leave for Argentina. In a way it was a blessing, but it also upended my plans and I found myself leaving a job without any idea of what to do next. It was then that those same colleagues who had discouraged me from dropping out of the tenure process stepped back into my life.

ESOL Coordinator

I was asked by one of these colleagues to remain at the university in a new position that was mostly administrative in nature and part time. I accepted the offer. I began to work as the ESOL coordinator. For several years I trained faculty in the College of Education in infusing ESOL concepts into their courses and gathering documentation of compliance for the state of Florida. It was work that held little satisfaction for me as I was mainly asking people to do things they did not feel like doing. Some faculty outright refused to comply. It was frustrating, to say the least and my change in status from tenure earning to nontenure earning sometimes felt humiliating.

Remaining at the university, I eventually switched to being a full-time TESOL instructor. I have always preferred teaching to any other part of the job. For the last decade or more I have gone through the nontenure promotion process at my university, and I am now a full teaching professor. I will never have tenure, or the salary and prestige attached to a tenured professor, but I have had a steady full-time teaching job for many years with flexibility that has allowed me to devote time to my family as necessary. Though many women secure tenure while raising children, I am not one of them. My family needed my focus, and I needed to focus on family.

LESSONS LEARNED

There is something lonely about always feeling like an outsider. In my case, as the stepchild in the family, I grew up in Buffalo, New York, where I was the outsider on the inside even in my house. When I returned to my home in Argentina, I was again the outsider on the inside. Life had gone on without me. Everything had changed. When I left my tenure earning position, my program continued without a hitch. Although they asked me to continue as ESOL coordinator, they could have found someone else to do the job. Being the outsider on the inside feels like you are a replaceable part in a functioning system. Worse than replaceable, you find that the system can easily run without you. It might even run more smoothly without you. Though there is a sadness in never truly belonging, there is also a freedom in feeling this way. You are free to go.

Finding My Freedom

It took me a long time to find the freedom in being the outsider. I spent a whole childhood and early adulthood desperately trying to belong. When I left Buffalo in 1985 for graduate school in Monterey, California, I found many wonderful friends there with whom I built a community. But they were the kind of people who quickly moved on and disappeared out of my life. And so, I moved on as well.

I decided to move to San Jose, Costa Rica, where I took a job with the Central American Peace Scholarships (CAPS) program at the Centro Cultural Costarricense Norteamericano. I taught English to high school students who were preparing to study abroad in the United States and, later, for university students who would also study abroad at universities in the United States. I bonded with colleagues and enjoyed my students immensely. But there was a restlessness in me built over a lifetime of moving and though I loved the country, I moved on. I chose to migrate to Morocco where I taught English at the American Language Center in Casablanca, Morocco, for 2 years from 1989–1991. I married a Moroccan, had a child, and immersed myself in the languages and the culture of that beautiful country.

Figure 14.3 Mouse reads in tree.

But there was no way I was ever going to truly belong in Morocco. I was way too different to even come close. Morocco laughed at my attempts to fit in, and allowed me to finally become resigned to, and even enjoy being the Other. I ended up settling into my outsider identity and taking it with me when I left. I decided to return to the United States in 1991 and, ultimately, chose Miami as my home and I have lived there ever since.

Embracing Otherness

Moving back to the United States was challenging after Morocco. The culture had moved on without me and I felt like more of a foreigner than I had in years. Soon I began to adapt once again, only now I was a different person. I was still an immigrant, but I wasn't the same. Every place I had lived had come back with me, all held together with the glue of my languages of Spanish, English, French, and Portuguese.

My languages work together to shape my feelings, thoughts, perspectives, and reactions to the world. All of them make up who I am. I used to think that I had to speak only one language at a time and speak it to the level of a native speaker. Now I know that this is not the case, not for me. My brain is a mixture of languages, and I give myself permission to mix my languages when I speak with bilinguals. I give myself permission to find a word in one language that does not exist in another and to use that word when I need it. All of my languages are necessary to express how I feel at different times, each serving its own unique purpose.

My languages travel with me wherever I go. In some sense, I no longer need to belong anywhere, I have found my home within myself. I am okay now with being the Other. I even enjoy this status. It allows me to step back and observe what is happening without being a part of it. It has allowed me to see things from multiple points of view. It has allowed me to have empathy and understanding for people who differ from me significantly because I know what it feels like to be misunderstood and misinterpreted. I know how it feels to be outside looking in.

DREAMS AND DISCOVERIES

When I think back on my experiences as a migrant, a daughter, a granddaughter, a mother, and a teacher, there is one lesson learned that applies to all the most important roles in my life. The lesson is to listen more, and to listen better. I love language and enjoy the way that words feel in my mouth. I have increasingly started to value the role of listening with empathy and understanding before saying a word.

As a granddaughter, I listened to my grandmother's stories and their stories shaped my understanding of the world and made me a storyteller. As a daughter, I listened to my parents' different versions of reality and began to understand how each of us sees the world differently, and each of us is right in our own way. As a mother, listening is one of the most important things that we can do. I know this intellectually and I try to practice it in my parenting, but I am being constantly challenged by my own children to do better. I believe that being a migrant and a language learner has increased my capacity to listen with empathy and, I hope, to continue to increase this skill throughout my life. As a teacher, the need to listen is obvious. Students will tell you how they are feeling and whether they are learning if you give them a chance to do so. Listening to students, for me, is far more powerful than gaging how they are doing from a traditional paper and pencil test.

HOPES FOR THE FUTURE

Just as most mothers in the history of our species, my dreams center around my children. I dream that they will have all of the experiences that they desire, that their lives will be full of adventures and quiet moments, of books, art and music, good friends, and colleagues, and especially of hope. I dream that the languages that they hold in their heads and in their hearts will serve them well by providing them with the words they need to communicate successfully within and across cultures.

Windows, Mirrors, and Sliding Glass Doors

I have always been a writer and an artist. From my earliest years I wrote poetry and stories and surrounded myself with books and art supplies. My father, an artist and writer himself, encouraged me artistically and was disappointed when I had not produced several books by the time I finished college. He did not understand my choice to teach or my focus on child-rearing. My mother, on the other hand, appreciated my talents but was most concerned with seeing me able to financially provide for myself. In the end, I disappointed both of my parents to some extent. I did not go to medical school as my mother would have liked, nor did I devote myself

Figure 14.4 Don Quixote & Sancho Panza.

to writing and art as my father would have preferred. Instead, I became a mother and teacher because each role allowed me to devote myself fully to the other when I needed to do so.

Now that my children are mostly grown, I find that I have more time to explore the artist within me. During the COVID-19 pandemic my teaching responsibilities became fully online, and my younger children homeschooled. Unlike most teachers, I was already used to online instruction and as a homeschool family, we were used to this form of learning. I found that I had much more flexibility and time than I had before. I used this time to learn everything I could about writing and illustrating for children and started to create books for children and adolescents. My first two children's books include a bilingual biography of an Argentine singer and activist, *Mercedes Sosa: Voice of the People* (Pérez-Prado, in press), and a rhyming celebration of the diversity of city life told from a toddler's perspective, *City Feet* (Pérez-Prado, 2023). In this new creative endeavor, I found a new community of children, writers and illustrators. It is a community where I truly feel at home.

Being published is not what motivates me. My goal has moved from the product to the process. Writing and illustrating bring me joy. I love sharing my work with others. If I can make one child smile with one of my stories or can help one child identify with a character in a book that is an outsider on the inside, an immigrant, a language learner, a stepchild, a special needs child, an Other, then that is enough for me. As children's literature researcher Rudine Sims Bishop (1990) states, books are sometimes windows offering glimpses of new worlds, sometimes sliding doors that readers can walk through in imagination to become part of those worlds, and sometimes mirrors where they can see themselves. If I can offer any of these experiences to a child reader, then that is enough.

Our Stories

Can we really know and understand one another if we do not know one another's stories? I don't think so. I am committed to sharing my personal story of migration, of language learning, and of balancing motherhood and a profession so that others can learn from my experiences. I am even more committed to listening to the experiences of others and reading about their personal stories. I have started to integrate storytelling into my teaching as a way to make content more personal and meaningful. I know that by sharing their stories, my students are able to make connections between their own experiences and the experiences of the immigrants and language learners that they will encounter in future classrooms. I know that by sharing stories of my own experiences with my students, readers, and children,

I will help them to see the world from multiple perspectives and in so doing see themselves. Stories move the world and storytelling has helped me become a better teacher and parent. My dreams have come full circle.

FINAL THOUGHTS

In my professional work as a TESOL professor, I have been able to reach far beyond borders to a global community, the community of language learners. My teaching of language and culture addresses issues of diversity, equity, and intercultural communication. Teaching English and training teachers in Argentina, Brazil, Costa Rica, Morocco, and the United States have helped me to reach an international audience exposing language learners and teachers to the interconnectedness of peoples across languages and cultures. Additionally, my writing and illustrations address themes that introduce children across the world to multiple perspectives and to the value of linguistic and cultural diversity. These stories center on identity and belonging while promoting peace building and empathy. I believe that it is through storytelling that a great deal of learning takes place. My work as a teacher, writer, and artist has propelled me to become an international global educator in the true sense of the word.

REFERENCES

Cosse, I. (2014). Mafalda: Middle class, everyday life, and politics in Argentina (1964–1973). *Hispanic American Historical Review, 94*(1), 35–75.

Pérez-Prado, A. (1973). *Los gallegos y Buenos Aires.* Ediciones La Bastilla.

Pérez-Prado, A. (2023). *City feet.* Reycraft Publisher.

Pérez-Prado, A. (in press). *Mercedes Sosa: Voice of the people.*

Pujol, S. (2003). Rebeldes y modernos. Una cultura de los jóvenes. In *Nueva historia argentina: Violencia, proscripción y autoritarismo (1955–1976)* (pp. 283–327). Sudamericana.

Sims Bishop, R. (1990). Mirrors, windows, and sliding glass doors. *Perspectives, 6*(3).

EPILOGUE

How we treat each other in this world can either bring about healing, peace, development and sustainability, or the destruction of our world.

PLACES OF BIRTH AND GROWING-UP OF AUTHORS

The geographic spaces of participating scholars and artists' place of birth and growing up in this book have covered five continents—including the Caribbean region of North America, and ranging from capitals and major cities to townships and small villages. Five of fourteen scholars were born and lived their young lives in cosmopolitan cities including Buenos Aires, Istanbul, Kathmandu, Odessa, and Paris. Nine scholars were born and grew up in geographically smaller cities, towns, and villages. Two authors from Africa were born and raised in the southwestern part of rural Rhodesia and the southern part of rural Nigeria. One of three authors from China saw the light of day in a northeastern city on the Pacific coast in Shandong Province; the second scholar's hometown was a large city in the Xinjiang Uygur Autonomous Region located in the northwest of the country; whereas, our third Chinese scholar was born in a small township in the Liaoning Province in the northeastern part of the country on the border with North Korea and Mongolia. The birthplace of our author from the Caribbean region of North America is a small village near the capital of Havana, Cuba; and the two editors of this book began life in a small, picturesque village in

The Netherlands and Germany. The scholars' birthplaces clearly represent the diverse uniqueness of the global community.

IMMIGRATON STATUS OF AUTHORS

Significant commonalities and differences are reflected in our scholars and artists' immigration status in the United States. They arrived in the United States between 1958 and 2000. The authors left their homeland from the following countries: Argentina, Cuba, France, Germany, Nepal, Nigeria, the People's Republic of China, Rhodesia (Zimbabwe), the Soviet Union (Ukraine), The Netherlands, and Turkey. Their application for U.S. citizenship followed the regular tedious routine for Dr. Josiah Tlou from Rhodesia; Drs. Yali Zhao and Guichun Zong from China; Dr. Barbara Cruz from Cuba; Dr. Anatoli Rapoport from the former Soviet Union; Dr. Binaya Subedi from Nepal; and for composer Hayg Boyadjian from France and visual arts painter Varteni Mosdichian from Turkey.

All but two scholars became citizens of the United States retaining their native citizenship: Dr. Lin Lin from China retained her original citizenship due to the complexity during the COVID-19 pandemic of attaining visas to visit her family. Dr. Misato Yamaguchi retained her Japanese citizenship due, unfortunately, to a medical condition which required her to return to her native country for recovery, recuperation, and rehabilitation. Three scholars have dual citizenship: Dr. Omiunota Ukpokodu from Nigeria; Dr. Frans Doppen from The Netherlands; and Dr. Aixa Pérez-Prado from Argentina. Deciding to renounce her German citizenship as a result of her personal experiences during the Nazi era and uncertain future between the United States and the divided Germany at that time, Dr. Toni Fuss Kirkwood-Tucker was able to obtain her U.S. citizenship after 3 years of being married to an American citizen. Retaining his Dutch citizenship, Dr. Frans H. Doppen, at the urging of his spouse, decided to apply for U.S. citizenship after 37 years in the United States in order to be able to cast a progressive vote in U.S. elections.

AUTHORS' MEMORABLE EXPERIENCES IN THEIR HOME COUNTRY

One question to our participating authors was to share some of their memorable, joyous, sad, or unique experiences while growing up in their native country.

Both scholars from African nations, Drs. Omiunota Ukpokodu and Josiah Tlou, recall their loving close-knit extended families steeped in active community life. Dr. Omiunota Ukpokodu, born and raised in one of the largest nations of the African continent, Nigeria, dearly remembers her loving extended family; her informal schooling; her close-knit community; and her beloved grandmother, a supreme storyteller. These surroundings instilled in her a strong sense of interconnectedness and group-orientedness, self-discipline, and self-regulatory behavior. She feels strongly that the most profound value she cultivated through her ancestral family was service to humanity. Her informal schooling socialized her to the values of humanity, humility, respect, life's intrinsic value, personal and collective responsibility, integrity, honor, corporate living, compassion, and cooperation. She remembers particularly that everyone in her community knew each other because of the shared participation in common basic human activities, such as the gathering at the community water source, the Ukheghi river, where everyone fetched their drinking water, bathed, swam, and washed their clothes.

Dr. Josiah Tlou from today's Zimbabwe, felt deep solidarity with his people in their attempt to combat apartheid and a White ruling class governing Rhodesia. Nevertheless, he is proud of having been appointed the first African principal of the Masase Mission Lutheran Boarding School for Girls, performing functions formerly exclusively reserved for European missionaries. In his frequent contact with missionaries from Sweden and other European countries, he recalls a thrilling experience when the White superintendent of the Central Primary Boarding School addressed him in his mother tongue, Sesotho. A new world opened up to him seeing the missionaries not simply as Europeans or White people but also as human beings with whom he could form friendships.

Dr. Misato Yamaguchi fondly remembers her well-educated forward-thinking professional Japanese parents who always emphasized the importance of education, knowledge acquisition, international travel, and international friendships. She has a vivid memory of being inspired by a newspaper article about a powerful speech by Severn Suzuki—a Canadian preteen environmentalist addressing the United Nations Earth Summit in Rio de Janeiro, Brazil in 1992—and wanting to be like her. Her parents saw the potential benefits of her living in the West where women's rights were more effectively established. Dr. Yamaguchi's upbringing was relatively rare as most of her friends had homestay mothers which resulted in her growing up quickly, being independent, and aware of her surroundings while watching the daily news well into her teenage years. Two of her cogent childhood memories are the Chernobyl disaster in the Soviet Union in 1986 and her maternal grandmother's birthday, August 6, coinciding with the day the atomic bomb was dropped on Hiroshima.

Dr. Binaya Subedi grew up in the city of Kathmandu, Nepal, an urban area of multi-ethnic and multi-lingual communities. He felt privileged to be raised in a middle class family setting and being born into a "higher" caste background. He lovingly remembers his parents and how important it was to them that he be enrolled in a Jesuit school to ensure that their son would receive a reputable education. Since neither of his parents completed high school, they were determined that he have access to a college education. Encouraged by relatives who already lived in the United States, he left Nepal at age 18 to obtain a college degree in the United States.

Dr. Lin Lin grew up in Qingdao, a port city on the Yellow Sea in China. She remembers fondly that despite a severe time of scarcity of resources in her country, her family of teachers was never in short supply of books and the joy that came with reading. The library at her parents' school was open to all children of the teachers and staff and the palm-sized black-and-white picture books opened the door of literacy to children who were free from the pressure of cut-throat academic competition. One of Dr. Lin's most joyous memories was the restoration of the National College Entrance Examination in 1977 which opened the opportunity for her to take the exam since many young Chinese who were sent to the countryside during the Cultural Revolution were never able to pursue higher education. Her involvement in higher education provided her with the opportunity in the 1990s to learn about women's studies in China and led her in 1993 to be among the official translators at the Chinese version of the *United Nations Declaration on the Elimination of All Forms of Discrimination Against Women* (United Nations, 1967).

Dr. Yali Zhao comes from a remote and small oasis surrounded by the Gobi Desert in Xinjiang—an autonomous territory in northwest China. Although she resided in a primarily Han Chinese community, she especially enjoyed the diverse Uyghur culture in her young life. She distinctly remembers plowing and planting in spring, harvesting rice with sickles under the scorching sun during the summer, handpicking cotton during a chilly fall, collecting livestock manure, and digging deep drains during freezing cold winters. She remembers the happiness she felt when the end of the Cultural Revolution resulted in eliminating the practice of labeling people into social classes and discrimination based on birth origin which removed her family's stigma of belonging to one of the Seven Black Categories. She fondly remembers her undergraduate years of living in the ancient city of Xi'an where for the first time she experienced life in a big city full of interesting people and life. After completing her studies and being hired as a full-time faculty member at Xi'an Normal University, she was excited to be part of a dynamic period of radical change that embraced democracy which ultimately culminated in the government crackdown on the Tiananmen Square protests. During the fall following the crackdown, Dr. Zhao moved to Beijing to join her husband and pursue graduate studies at Beijing University of Science and Technology. Living in Beijing for 11 years she was proud to be part of a changing China and excited about its economic progress which moved millions of people out of poverty.

The birthplace of Dr. Guichun Zong was the small township of Yebaishou in Jianping County of the Liaoning Province in northeast China. She vividly remembers the shortage of books and closure of schools during the Cultural Revolution when her father copied ancient Chinese poems, page after page, on large pieces of paper and posted them on the wall for her to read and recite. Dr. Zong's early social studies learning experiences included listening to stories from her parents, particularly her father, watching revolutionary movies, and reciting poems written by Chairman Mao. She also recalls the significant influence of gender equity on her as from her father was a strong advocate for women and girls' education. Growing up in a highly impoverished environment in China made her more aware of the poverty existing in the Deep South of the United States and led to her commitment to teaching about the United Nations Education for Sustainable Development goals emphasizing community-based experiential learning pedagogy.

Dr. Bárbara Cruz lovingly remembers the warmth of her maternal grandparents she had to leave behind in Cuba when she boarded the *Vuelos de la Libertad* (Freedom Flights) offered by the United States government. Ultimately, nearly 300,000 Cuban exiles fleeing the Castro communist regime were transported to the United States between 1965 and 1973. She clearly remembers Castro's promises of bringing access to medical care and education to all inhabitants, eradicating poverty, hunger, and achieving equality for all citizens regardless of race, creed, or gender. Dr. Cruz distinctly recalls the night before she and her 22-year-old-mother left Cuba to board a one-way PanAm flight to the United States with one suitcase of clothing when some of their neighbors derogatorily called them *gusanos* (worms), a term Castro used to describe those leaving the island and, by extension, turning their backs on the revolution.

Dr. Anatoli Rapoport recalls the beautiful city of Odessa in today's Ukraine, then part of the Soviet Union, where he was born and grew up among loving family and friends in an embracing Jewish community. He distinctly recalls an unforgettable encounter with his landlady's antisemitic KGB son and an unerving interview with two KGB officers when attending the University of Tula. After having been married for almost 3 years, his wife Inna, an ethnic Russian, having adopted his surname, was unable to obtain a teaching position due to having a Jewish last name. After changing back to her maiden name, she obtained a teaching position. This negative experience led the couple to decide that their children should have her last name which has left Anatoli the only Rapoport in his family.

Hayg Boyadjian, composer of international music, recalls one of his best memories in France at the end of World War II when the American Allies liberated Paris and an American soldier gave him a "heavenly" whole loaf of bread, something he will never forget in his entire life. Being starved he could have devoured the entire loaf on his own, but he went home and shared it with his three hungry brothers. After immigrating to Argentina, one of Hayg's most catapulting memories was the time when he heard the exquisite operatic music of German composer Richard Wagner flowing from a Grundig radio his brother had bought. That event was the decisive moment he knew that music was his calling.

Varteni Mosdichian, the multi-lingual Armenian author of compelling art of injustices in the world, happily recalls living with her maternal grandparents in a beautiful old house on the sea in Istanbul; celebrating elaborate birthday parties; attending the prestigious Österreichisches Gymnasium; earning a prize for writing a poem about Turkey, the country that committed genocide against her people; and courageously telling her teachers that they were omitting Armenian history and culture in the curriculum, and that she did not care whether she would receive a zero for her final grade as she stomped out of the classroom.

Emigrating from Argentina, Dr. Aixa Pérez-Prado speaks lovingly of her extended family, especially her grandmothers and her special memories of her father Antonio, who fought against racism directed at the Gallegos (Galicians immigrants from Spain) living in Buenos Aires and debating the famous creator of the *Mafalda* comic strip, social satirist Quino. She recalls her "heroic deed" as a little girl when her father took her to the local theater and, without asking him or being prepped, she went on stage, took the microphone, and annnounced that the Cuban revolutionary Che Guevara, who she believed to be her uncle, had been murdered—hushed news she had overheard at her grandparents' home. Unforgettable to the author is the event when she observed her grandmother on the city square in Buenos Aires walking in a circle of wailing women carrying signs with the names of husbands, sons, and uncles who were abducted and disappeared by the Videla junta.

Horrendous memories of Dr. Toni Fuss Kirkwood-Tucker during her upbringing in a small Bavarian village in Germany were her mother's fears about the unpredictable Nazi presence in their community during World War II; the sudden appearance of the Gestapo (security police) forcefully entering into their house demanding to be searched; and her dissident father's irregular appearances, disappearances, and reappearances allegedly from Munich where he worked at the Messerschmittwerke (factory) engaged in sabotage activities. Her father forbade her to raise her right arm and say the mandatory three-times "Heil Hitler" greetings in school and in the street and did not allow her to join the Bund der Deutschen Mädchen (League of German Girls) of the formidable Hitler Youth. Dr. Toni Fuss Kirkwood-Tucker's glorious and unforgettable memories before her immigration at age 22 to the Deep South of the United States emanate from her hiking trips in the Bavarian and Austrian Alps under often extremely dangerous and changing weather conditions without proper equipment. Her steady companion was usually her girlfriend Gittl, who had moved with her family to her village during the war and who loved the mountains like she did. At age 17, when they were hiking the Zugspitze summit—the highest mountain in Germany at 2,964 meters or almost 10,000 feet—a handsome young hiker from another village had reached the top of the summit first. As it was customary among German hikers, the first young woman reaching the summit would have to kiss him. Toni did, and Helmut became her first love.

Dr. Frans Doppen grew up as the son of the local barber in a small village in The Netherlands, about 10 miles from the German border, which he did not cross until he was 15 years old. He remembers the excitement he felt when his family got its first television when he was in second grade. He spent most of his teenage years working in his neighbors' grocery store. He has especially fond memories of the car-free Sundays during the OPEC oil crisis in 1973. Unlike today, Marienvelde was a typical Dutch village that had multiple grocery stores and bakery shops and many other businesses. Each day Dr. Doppen walked back and forth to his elementary school and came home each day at noon to have a home-cooked meal prepared by his mother. Living across the street from the Catholic church, he often visited the pastor and his housekeeper. Growing up, Dr. Doppen heard many stories about World War II. During his 6 years at a Catholic high school, where he got to watch *Jesus Christ Superstar* in religion class, he biked 8 miles each day to and from school, rain or shine. Matriculating at the University of Utrecht as a history major, he felt liberated having left Marienvelde as freedom was calling from a beautiful medieval city.

AUTHORS' EDUCATION

Dr. Omiunota Ukpokodu began her education at the missionary affiliated primary St. James Anglican School. Although under-resourced, she believes the school helped her to lay the foundation for her future academic aspirations and successes. Since Nigeria was a British colony, she learned about Britain's history, its national anthem and sang morning songs, such as "London Bridge Is Falling Down" and "My Fair Lady." The most meaningful experience during her elementary school years was Nigeria's gaining independence and becoming a republic in 1963. She attended an all-girls boarding school where she read books by prominent African authors, such as Chinua Achebe, Wole Soyinka, and Ngugi Wa Thiong'o, and was exposed to global literature including authors such as William Shakespeare, Charles Dickens, Robert Louis Stevenson, Charlotte Bronte, Jane Austen, George Orwell, and Langston Hughes. Dr. Ukpokodu learned to see education as the great equalizer. She came to the United States to obtain her master's and doctoral degrees in social science education.

Dr. Josiah Tlou was educated in primary and secondary schools in the former Rhodesia, today's Zimbabwe. Established in 1949, the Goromonzi Government High School was the first government-funded high school in the country to admit African students where he joined the school's fourth cohort, representing the top 5% of students from across the country. His primary education was influenced by both the teachings of his parents and elders and the Swedish missionaries of the Lutheran church. After graduating from the high school in 1955, he enrolled as a teacher exchange student at Morgenster Mission, a Dutch Reformed teacher training college. Upon graduation, he became the first African principal of Masase Mission Boarding School where he performed functions formerly reserved for European missionaries and was exposed to continual contact with missionaries from Sweden and other European countries. Dr. Tlou was an active member of the Rhodesian African Teachers Association (RATA), openly opposing the colonial policies and practices of segregation in Rhodesia which made him a target for arrest. Thanks to the Lutheran World Federation he was able to come to the United States to study at Luther College in Iowa and obtained his doctorate in curriculum and instruction from the University of Illinois. He taught eighth grade social studies and civic education for 2 years in the Glencoe Public Schools before accepting a position in the College of Education at Virginia Polytechnic Institute and State University.

Dr. Misato Yamaguchi attended elementary school in Japan. She was determined to learn English at the highest possible level in order to better understand cross-cultural and global issues. At the young age of 17, she joined a year-long high school exchange program in Houston, Texas, at Bellaire High School, a prestigious national public school composed of a diversity of students of varying economic backgrounds and recent immigrants. She enrolled in classes for English speakers of other languages (ESOL) and enjoyed working with caring teachers such as Mr. Lawrence. She particularly remembers this teacher as they discussed how to best approach a lesson on the dropping of the atomic bomb on Hiroshima on August 6, 1945. After high school graduation, and interested in becoming a diplomat, Dr. Yamaguchi joined the International Relations bachelor's degree program at St. Mary's University in San Antonio, Texas, and later the Chaminade University in Honolulu, Hawaii. Inspired by witnessing a 4-day-long reconciliation event held in December 2001 in Waikiki, Hawaii, where American and Japanese war veterans gathered to meet and shake hands with old adversaries, she interned in the United Nations World Food Programme (WFP). Fascinated with education, she joined the International Training and Education Program (ITEP), a master's program at American University in Washington, D.C.; interned with Youth for Understanding; and worked on board the educational global voyage program, Peace Boat, before pursuing her doctorate in social studies and global education at The Ohio State University in 2006.

Dr. Binaya Subedi believes that he received a "miseducation" in Nepal's schools leading to being disconnected from local experiences, local histories, and local concerns and needs. Instead, during his studies, he became more familiar with global events in Europe and North America than with those in his own country. What he was studying in school was somewhat akin to what students were learning in privileged schools in New York, New Delhi, Seoul, or Johannesburg. Arriving in the United States at the age of 18 to attend college, his cultural and political identity went through serious transformation. Ultimately, having earned a PhD in multicultural and equity studies at The Ohio State University, he believes that the globalization of education has led to a standardized neo-liberal curriculum that fails to consider students' experiences or local needs in communities.

Dr. Lin Lin received her bachelor's and master's degrees from Beijing Foreign Studies University (BFSU) majoring in English language and literature. Having been accepted at BFSU brought her one step closer to her dream of studying and teaching in higher education where more than 70 foreign languages are taught and that specializes in training ambassadors and foreign service officers who represent China around the world. At BFSU, she met classmates from across China as well as foreign students from North Korea, Cambodia, Great Britain, the United States, Australia, and New Zealand. Upon graduation, she taught United States history courses for 9 years as an assistant and then associate professor at BFSU where the seeds of global education were planted that shaped her teaching and scholarly work towards international and cross-cultural global education. She felt overjoyed when she made progress in listening and reading comprehension as she slowly acquired English proficiency, studying hard to pass examinations, and feeling proud that she could now communicate in English with people from around the world leading to many opportunities. Dr. Lin served as an interpreter for nongovernment organizations such as the Ford Foundation and the Canadian International Development Association. While teaching at BFSU, she applied for a 1-year Chinese language scholar position in the Chinese Language and Culture Department at Reed College in Portland, Oregon, and left for the United States. The 1-year visiting scholarship helped her decide to return to the United States in 2000 to obtain her PhD in social science education from the University of Georgia in Athens which led to an assistant professorship at the State University of New York (SUNY) at Cortland.

Dr. Yali Zhao obtained her bachelor's and master's degrees in her native China and served as tenured associate professor of English and the social sciences at Beijing University of Science and Technology (BUST) for 10 years. She started school at the age of 8 as she and her country experienced the chaotic period of the Chinese Cultural Revolution (1966–1976) during which time society paid little attention to education. Physical labor was a typical theme of ordinary school life due to a severe labor force shortage. Adults and children alike were busy in factories and in the fields all year as the large rice and cotton fields required intensive labor. Dr. Zhao and her peers were child field laborers during all seasons of the year. The physical tasks were heavy and dull, and she often compared the blisters and calluses on her hands with those of her peers. She vividly remembers having an extremely sore waist after bending over for a long time to cut the waist-deep rice and her dying of thirst for water under the scorching sun. She never questioned her child labor as it was mandatory work and part of the school curriculum. She believed that her labor helped alleviate the labor shortage and improve the future of her homeland. Having taught English and social sciences subjects at Beijing University of Science and Technology for 10 years, in 2000, Dr. Zhao decided to apply and was admitted to the social science education doctoral program at the University of Georgia in Athens.

At age 18, Dr. Guichun Zong passed the rigorous national college entrance exam and was admitted to Beijing Normal University (BNU) where she earned her bachelor's and master's degrees between 1984 to 1991. After graduation, she was employed for 10 years by China's National Research Institute for curriculum and instructional resources—both as an editor and as a research associate. She participated in several national projects in the area of K–12 curriculum development and school-based reform research. This provided her with the unique opportunity to work with educators in many different parts of China as well as with educational leaders from Great Britain, Japan, North Korea, Russia, South Korea, and the United States. As one of the leading national universities in China, BNU provided Dr. Zong with her first richly constructed cross-cultural learning experiences. With a long history of active student participation in the China's social and political movements, several student leaders of the 1989 Tiananmen Square protest studied at BNU. An invitation by Dr. Jan L. Tucker, renowned global scholar, motivated her to migrate to the United States where she earned her EdD in social science education with emphasis on global perspectives at Florida International University.

Not wanting to leave the warmth of her family, Dr. Cruz clearly remembers how she vomited her breakfast on the first day of Kindergarten in Cuba. Together with her mother, in 1965, she left Cuba on a U.S. government sponsored Freedom Flight to join her father in Miami. Upon completing her high school education, Dr. Cruz attended the University of Miami (UM). Having earned her bachelor's degree and starting her teaching career in the Miami Public School district, a chance encounter with Dr. Jan L. Tucker in 1983 led her to pursue her master's and doctoral degree at Florida International University. After earning her EdD in 1991, Dr. Cruz was hired as an assistant professor at the University of South Florida (USF) in Tampa, Florida.

Dr. Anatoli Rapoport grew up in a Jewish family in Odessa in Ukraine in the former Soviet Union. When he was in eighth grade, half of the students in his class of 35–36 students were Jewish. However, by the time he graduated from high school, there were only 7 Jewish students left in his class as large numbers of Jewish families were leaving the country. Being Jewish, his chance of being admitted to Odessa State University (OSU) was next to zero. Seeking to avoid the military draft, he decided to attend the Pedagogical University in Tula in Central Russia where Jews made up less than 1% of the half-million residents of the city and where antisemitism was less the order of the day. Since pedagogical and liberal arts colleges did not have military departments, their male graduates had to serve in the army for a year and a half. After having served his time in the army, Dr. Rapoport began his teaching career in Leningrad where he became disillusioned with the ongoing pokzikha, or window dressing, in education. In 2000, he was admitted to the doctoral program at Purdue University where he earned his PhD in 2006 and was hired as an assistant professor.

In France, composer Hayg Boyadjian experienced half a year of elementary school during World War II. After immigrating to Argentina, he was required to attend elementary school. Although he wanted to continue his education, his family's financial situation did not allow it. Mostly, he wanted to study music and was able to attend the small inexpensive Conservatory of Music in Alsina in the suburbs of Buenos Aires where he was able to take piano lessons and study music theory and counterpoint with well-known pianist Beatriz Balzi. After immigrating to the United States in 1958, he enrolled in a class for English for foreigners in Arlington, Massachusetts. After taking extension courses at the Massachusetts Institute of Technology (MIT) in Cambridge, passing the High School Equivalency Test, and earning his high school diploma in 1960, he completed a bachelor's degree in economics at Northeastern University. After taking classes as a special student at the New England Conservatory in Boston, and later being accepted in the School of Music at Brandeis University in Waltham, Massachusetts, he began his career as a contemporary classical composer.

Global painter Varteni Mosdichian clearly remembers attending a Turkish elementary school and qualifying to study at the Österreichische Gymnasium (preparatory school) in Istanbul where all subjects were taught in German. Although being an Armenian, as a Turkish citizen she had to take history, geography, and civics classes in the Turkish language. She began to question the absence of the 3,000 year-old history and culture of the Armenian people in Turkish textbooks. None of the well-known Armenian actors, musicians, scientists, novelists, and poets who contributed to the shaping of Turkey's culture were discussed in her classes. Neither was the

Armenian composer Edgar Manas who composed the Turkish national anthem, nor the world-famous Armenian linguist Hagop Martayan, renamed Dilachar (meaning tongue-opener) by Ataturk who converted the Ottoman Arabic orthography into the modern Turkish alphabet. She strongly feels that the education system in Turkey had effective systematic brainwashing mechanisms—such as thanking the Turkish government for how great it was to be a Turk, how righteous and how great Turks were, for being able to speak the Turkish language, respect for elders and Turkish laws, and more. After immigrating to the United States, she obtained a Bachelor of Fine Arts degree from the University of Florida.

Dr. Aixa Pérez-Prado's childhood was one of goodbyes from her parents, her paternal and maternal grandparents, and Buenos Aires, her city. When she was only 3 years old her mother left her behind when she emigrated to the United States to settle in Buffalo, New York. Only her father knew that her mother was actually emigrating. Having turned 4 and starting pre-Kindergarten and never having imagined for a moment that she herself would leave her beloved Argentina, the final goodbye with her father came a year later when he took her to "visit" her mother in the United States and told her one morning that he was going to work—only to never return. In college, she chose the field of teaching English to speakers of other languages (TESOL) so she could live and work overseas. After teaching English in Costa Rica and Morocco, she earned her PhD in social science education at Florida State University. Since 1997 she serves as professor at Florida International University in Miami, Florida.

Dr. Toni Fuss Kirkwood-Tucker attended elementary school in her village. Upon completing her fifth year, her teacher advised her parents that she should attend the Gymnasium—a preparatory high school required in Germany of students to qualify for the university—located 20 kilometers north of her village which required taking the train every day. After graduation, she registered for her first semester at the University of Munich as her father wanted her to become a teacher. She fell in love with an American, and, instead, followed him to the United States. After her immigration at age 22 and her two children attending elementary school, she earned her BA degree in secondary social studies education at Florida Atlantic University; and her MA, EdS, and EdD degrees in curriculum and instruction with emphasis on global international education from Florida International University.

Dr. Frans Doppen fondly remembers walking back and forth to his elementary school in Marienvelde, The Netherlands, and coming home at noon each day for dinner as well as the bike rides to and from his high school. He earned his Kandidaat's (bachelor's) and Doctorandus (master's+) degree in history and a teaching certificate at the University of Utrecht and participated in a yearlong student exchange program at the University of Florida. After immigrating to the United States in 1984, he obtained his EdS in educational leadership and his PhD in curriculum and instruction at the University of Florida.

TRIALS AND TRIBULATIONS IN NATIVE COUNTRY

While growing up in their homeland, each participating author, at varying ages in their young lives, encountered, firsthand, unerasable historical tragedies that left in them a deep sadness throughout their lives.

Barely 11 years old, and in her last year of primary education, Dr. Omiunota Ukpokodu personally experienced the Biafran Nigerian Civil War (1967–1970)—the most devastating political event in her country's history. Historically, Nigeria has been a complex, multiethnic nation characterized by great diversity in ethnicity, culture, language, religion, and philosophical thought. At the time of the war, Nigeria was divided into four major regions. When the country was redivided into twelve states, the Eastern region seceded and established the Republic of Biafra. This affront was unacceptable to the federal government, and it declared war on the Republic of Biafra. In the process, the Biafran Army captured Dr. Ukpokodu's town. Roadblocks were erected at all entry points, all transportation services were halted, and soldiers were everywhere. Nigerian warplanes flew over the villages dropping bombs. Holes had been dug in the woods behind the family compound where her family could run for safety. When the federal army recaptured and liberated the village, Biafran refugees were hiding everywhere. One day, a Biafran boy fugitive ran past her compound with his hands across his head begging, "Please, please, don't kill me, I surrender!" as federal soldiers were chasing him into the woods and shot him—a memory the author is unable to forget. Even today when she hears news reports on television about war in other parts of the world, memories of the Biafran Nigerian Civil War still haunt her.

Dr. Josiah Tlou experienced the British colonization of Rhodesia imposing divisions among African nations as artificially created geographic boundaries forced ethnic groups into separate entities. His native land, which was ruled by King Lobengula of the Matebele nation, had been named Rhodesia in honor of Cecil John Rhodes who used missionaries to spread British influence and occupation. Rhodes assured King Lobengula that he was only interested in digging for minerals, not gaining political power and control, and that the king would be allowed to rule Matabeleland without interference from White settlers. In exchange for mining rights, Rhodes promised the king 100 pounds of sterling silver monthly, 1,000 rifles with 100 rounds of ammunition, and a steamboat to sail on the Zambezi River. However, in 1893, Rhodes and the British settlers broke the treaty and drove the king off his land. In 1965 Rhodesian Prime Minister Ian Smith launched a

Unilateral Declaration of Independence (UDI) from Britain and declared a state of emergency which prohibited any African from leaving or entering the country and allowed for the arbitrary imprisonment of anyone who opposed the government. Just prior to his impending arrest, friends in Rhodesia's security services alerted Dr. Tlou and helped him to escape to the United States with the assistance of Swedish missionaries.

Dr. Misato Yamaguchi from Japan distinctly remembers a trip to China with her grandparents visiting the Great Wall, the Forbidden City, Tiananmen Square, the Yellow River, and the very location in the Beijing area where her paternal grandfather was stationed as a telegram operator during World War II. She witnessed her grandfather's gratefulness for the warmth Chinese people extended to him as a Japanese soldier during the war and saw him firsthand thanking Chinese people for their kindness and apologizing to them for their hardships during the war. While fighting in China, her grandfather was captured by the Soviet army and made a prisoner of war. Upon his return home, he spent decades searching for the families of his military unit to give them mementos of their missing and fallen soldiers. After the war, he organized trips for the Japanese government searching for Japanese orphans left behind in China.

Dr. Lin Lin was one of thousands of university students marching to Tiananmen Square in 1989. At Beijing Foreign Studies University, one of her classmates became the leader and asked her to be a receptionist in a makeshift office answering phone calls, printing flyers by engraving words on a steel plate and helping her peers make copies on a mimeograph. When the Chinese government issued the "April 26 Editorial" describing the student movement a "riot," they marched for 16 hours on Tiananmen Square before returning to campus with hoarse voices and tired legs. The marches quickly escalated into nation-wide demonstrations demanding the government to address inflation, unemployment, corruption, increase media transparency, and freedom of the press. A student hunger strike in mid-May on Tiananmen Square motivated 400 Chinese cities across the country to respond with similar actions. When student leaders asked for a dialogue with the government, the hardliners in the Communist Party decided to forcefully crush the demonstrations. Martial law was declared as 300,000 troops were deployed in Beijing. None of the students thought that the government would use force against nonviolent student demonstrators.

Born in 1965, Dr. Zhao lived with her parents and two siblings in a Xinjiang Production and Construction Corps settlement. She started school at the age of 8 during the Cultural Revolution. As Chinese society paid little attention to education at this time and there was no college admission or academic pressure, physical labor was a typical theme of school life. Assigned to one the Seven Black Categories, her family was labeled as being from an unfavorable class background which included capitalists, landlords, wealthy farmers, reactionaries, and even intellectuals. People in these "bad categories" were socio-politically discriminated against, punished, and excluded from many privileges such as better jobs, the honor of joining the army, the Communist Party, promotion at work, and advanced education. Dr. Zhao dreaded having to write down her class identity on school registration forms at the start of each school year. Fortunately, this categorization system was eliminated when the Cultural Revolution ended. When the Tiananmen Square protests happened in June of 1989 she was still living in Xi'an, nearly 600 miles distant from Beijing.

Dr. Guichun Zong was born in Manchuria, a region in northeastern China, which was invaded and occupied by Japan in the 1930s. One of her sad memories growing up was listening to her father's stories about how he and his fellow soldiers were badly treated by the Japanese imperialists during World War II, stripped of their cultural symbols, forced to learn and speak only Japanese, converting their names from Chinese to Japanese, and resisting Japanese colonialism to maintain their identity and dignity during one of China's most difficult and turbulent times. Her parents were sent to the countryside for 10 years during the Cultural Revolution. Positive memories of Dr. Zong included the practice of gender equity in her home. Her mother, undereducated but experienced in life after having 10 children, encountered many hardships and obstacles with stoic tenacity. She rebelled in silence, yet used hard work, wit, and diplomacy to gain power in the community in support of her family. Her resourcefulness and problem-solving skills had a profound impact on Dr. Zong, both personally and professionally, as feminism was not about becoming "like a male" but about being an equal and shouldering the family's financial and economic needs.

When Dr. Bárbara C. Cruz entered Kindergarten, the Cuban Revolution was still in its infancy, flush with promises of bringing access to medical care and education, eradicating poverty, hunger, and achieving equality for all citizens regardless of race, creed, or gender. Schooling and literacy were hallmarks of the new government and the country's massive literacy campaign was being touted the world over. Castro and his army of revolutionaries had ousted the dictatorship of Fulgencio Batista on New Year's Day in 1959. Of humble peasant origins, Batista had risen quickly through the military ranks. He twice ruled Cuba between 1933–1944 and 1952–1959. It was during his second term that he emerged as a brutal dictator, incarcerating political opponents and enriching himself off the backs of the citizenry. As popular unrest grew on the island, and after the United States' withdrawal of support in 1958, Castro was able to wrestle power from Batista and establish a new revolutionary government.

It was in the dvorik, a community of Jewish people in Odessa in the Ukraine that Dr. Anatoli Rapoport's self-identification was first tested when he was called a "kike" by one of the boys playing on the street. He felt scared, disgusted, and humiliated. Antisemitism was an integral part of his life as a boy and growing into adulthood. When he turned sixteen his national ID card identified him in thick black ink as a Jew. Being Jewish led him to apply to college in Tula in central Russia, a city more than 1,000 kilometers (about 600 miles) from home where antisemitism was not as prevalent. He realized early that life around him was a lie as the state media deceivingly reported the unimaginable success of the economy and the social harmony among the Soviet people. Abiding by a perverse social contract everyone, from political leaders to school principals, lied.

Born in Paris of Armenian parents and immigrating to the United States via Argentina, classical composer Hayg Boyadjian is permanently scarred by the Armenian genocide. The systematic killing and deportation of Armenians by the Ottoman Empire, that began as early as 1894 and reached its peak in 1915, has occupied him all his life in the attempt to make sense how one and a half million Armenians, half of the Armenian population, were killed in the most barbaric way. He vividly recalls the painful story of his then teenage father in search of his mother and two sisters who were forced on a death march to Beirut, Lebanon, where his blind sister was left behind in an orphanage, where his father had to find a wife according to the passport given to him and, boarding a ship to Marseille to begin a new life in France. Experiencing the Allied bombing of Nazi-occupied Paris, a close brush with death from bombings, and fear for his wife and four young sons and their survival motivated his father to immigrate to Argentina after the war ended. As the third oldest son born in Paris, Hayg Boyadjian's deepest burden to this day is the Turkish government's blatant denial of the Armenian genocide.

The life of painter Varteni Mosdichian has been equally shaken by the Armenian genocide and forced Islamization of Armenian women and children who survived. Living in Turkey on the land that once belonged to the Armenians before it was annexed by the Ottoman Empire, she was forbidden to speak in her own tongue. While a century ago the government would have cut out one's tongue for not speaking Turkish, by the mid-20th century Turkey penalized Armenians with imprisonment, monetary fines, and closing professional career fields to them such as in science, medicine, law, teaching, or journalism. She was forbidden by her mother to call her "Mama" in public which would have identified her as an Armenian, which was a difficult thing for a little girl. Her life under the Turkish government consisted of constant fear for her safety overshadowed by pain and suffering. The genocide that took the lives of many of her family members is at the epicenter of her memories.

Dr. Aixa Pérez-Prado recalls the 1960s as a particularly turbulent time in the history of Argentina. Under the Perón administration there existed deep controversy about how to implement social reform and wealth distribution. While Perón was popular with the lower socioeconomic classes, many in the middle classes struggled to maintain their family businesses. As women demanded equality with men, Dr. Pérez-Prado's mother became a medical doctor against great odds. Young people started to explore and debate new ideas about love, sex, and family. A military coup by Videla in 1976 established a brutal grip on power, cracking down on anybody his junta believed might be a challenge to its authority. The regime was responsible for disappearing, torturing, and murdering thousands of Argentinians. Even pregnant women were kidnapped and kept imprisoned until their babies were born, then murdered. Their babies were then adopted out to military families or others and raised without knowledge of their origins. Although this was happening in Buenos Aires, most Argentinians were either unaware of or chose to turn a blind eye to the situation. Those aware of the atrocities lived in fear.

During World War II, Germany was terrorized by the Nazi regime. Dr. Toni Fuss Kirkwood-Tucker vividly remembers the village priest removing the wood-carved crucifix from the classroom wall replacing it with a framed portrait of Adolf Hitler, commanding her and her classmates to raise their arms three times shouting "Heil Hitler" from now on in lieu of saying their traditional prayers. She remembers her mother hiding three boy soldiers in her cellar with her father yelling that she would be shot by the Gestapo; retreating German soldiers hiding in the mountains being mowed down by the Waffen SS; thousands of refugees fleeing from bombed-out cities; and evicted Germans, living for centuries in former Czechoslovakia, begging for a place to stay in her village. She vividly recalls her dissident father telling her stories about the brutality of the concentration camps and warning her of unannounced house searches by the Gestapo and Waffen SS. With her father's irregular appearances, disappearances, and reappearances during his sabotage activities, she feared that one day he would be shot by the Gestapo.

AUTHORS' REASONS FOR IMMIGRATION

A major commonality among the immigrant scholars and artists was their desire to further their education and academic and artistic aspirations.

Dr. Omiunota Ukpokodu from Nigeria, who followed her husband already studying in the United States, came to the United States to pursue her dreams for higher education. Seeing the United States as a microcosm of the world, Dr. Misato Yamaguchi from Japan wanted to become a global citizen educated in the United States. Each of the three Chinese scholars who emigrated from the People's Republic of China already had bachelor's and master's degrees and pursued a PhD in social science education: Dr.

Lin Lin first applied for a 1-year Chinese language scholar position in the Chinese Language and Culture Department at Reed College in Portland, Oregon, which paved the way for her pursuit of a doctorate at the University of Georgia in Athens. Dr. Guichun Zong—after meeting Dr. Jan L. Tucker, professor of global education and social studies education, at an international conference in Beijing—decided to pursue an advanced degree at Florida International University in Miami, Florida, thanks to his sponsorship. Feeling the need to further advance her academic career and see the outside world, Dr. Yali Zhao decided to apply to the social science education doctoral program at the University of Georgia in Athens. After being offered a full-time graduate research assistantship, she left China for the United States. Dr. Binaya Subedi came to the United States at the age of 18, encouraged by relatives already residing there, to pursue higher education in America. Hayg Boyadjian's reasons for immigrating to the United States were motivated by his dislike of the climate of Argentina, his two older brothers having left the country, and an uncle living in the United States. Varteni Mosdichian, at the age of 16, came to the United States from Turkey to join her mother who had come to this country to work as a private nurse to a wealthy Armenian family.

The following scholars—also in the pursuit of higher education—however, had additional compelling reasons for immigrating to the United States. Dr. Josiah Tlou, to avoid arrest, had to flee from his birthplace and homeland in Rhodesia where scores of individuals and family members who participated in demonstrations against colonial policies and segregation laws were arrested and killed. Dr. Anatoli Rapoport, born in Odessa in the Ukraine, studied, and taught in the former Soviet Union for nearly 2 decades. Consistent, unrelentless, overt and covert forms of antisemitism—and the big lie pervading Soviet society—led him to immigrate to the United States to pursue his PhD. Dr. Barbara Cruz from Cuba, at Kindergarten age, left her country with her mother as a result of the communist revolution, taking advantage of freedom flights offered by the United States government. Argentine scholar Dr. Aixa Pérez-Prado who, at 4 years of age, was taken to the United States by her father, had no choice but to become an American citizen as demanded by her mother.

The editors of this book, however, immigrated to the United States for a very different reason: they fell in love with an American citizen. Dr. Toni Fuss Kirkwood-Tucker fell in love with a fluent German-speaking American lieutenant, who wore civilian clothes and was in charge of the security of the NATO and Special Weapons School in Oberammergau. This school was established at the end of World War II by the Allies in the village next door to her hometown. She met him at the American Express office where she worked to improve her English, married him, and followed him to New Orleans, Louisiana. Dr. Frans Doppen fell in love with a college student while on a student exchange program at the University of Florida. After she joined him the following year on the same exchange program at the University of Utrecht, they decided to get married, and he followed her to Florida.

PROFESSIONAL EDUCATION AND ACADEMIC ACHIEVEMENTS IN THE UNITED STATES

Astoundingly, the twelve global international scholars in this book earned their doctorate in education at various public universities in the United States. Each attained the rank of assistant professor, associate professor, teaching professor, or full professor in their respective fields of social studies education and/or teaching English to students of other languages (TESOL) and English language learners (ELLs) at prestigious U.S. public universities: Florida International University, University of Florida, University of Georgia, University of Illinois Champaign-Urbana, University of Kansas, University of South Florida, Purdue University, State University of New York, and The Ohio State University. The two global international artists of music and painting represented in our book received honorary memberships in prestigious professional associations. Moreover, the global scholars' research in global international education has contributed to new knowledge about the diversity of humanity, cross-cultural understanding and interaction, global interconnectedness, and development of empathy. Their seminal research presentations at state, national, and international conferences have made significant contributions to the global education literature and transformative pedagogy. Each has been honored with national and/or international professional awards.

Dr. Omiunota Ukpokodu earned her BEd, MA, MSEd, and PhD from the University of Kansas in Lawrence, Kansas. She has reached the highest rank in the academy as full professor. Her research areas include transformative pedagogy, social justice, culturally responsive pedagogy, critical global citizenship education, and African immigrant education.

Dr. Josiah Tlou earned his EdD in curriculum and instruction with a minor in comparative education from the University of Illinois in Champaign-Urbana; a master's degree from Illinois State University in history; a bachelor's degree in history from Luther College in Decorah, Iowa, and specialized in African Studies at the University of Wisconsin. He served as professor at Virginia Polytechnic Institute and State University for over 30 years. His research includes interdisciplinary global education projects, civic education, a train-the-trainer model in teacher education programs in Botswana and Malawi, and the integration of the African concept of ubuntu in teaching and learning.

Dr. Misato Yamaguchi received her PhD in social studies education, global education, and teaching English as a second or foreign language (TESOL/TEFL) at The Ohio State University. She was hired as assistant professor at the University of Georgia in Augusta, Georgia. Her research focuses on authentic cultural learning and global citizenship education. A medical emergency forced her to permanently return to Japan where she now serves as a workshop facilitator for the internationally recognized Disability Equality Training program while exploring how global education research should address issues related to disability and inclusion.

Dr. Binaya Subedi obtained his master's and PhD degree in social studies and global education at The Ohio State University in Columbus where he serves as a professor of multicultural and equity studies in education. His research examines issues of migration; social studies education; global citizenship; global education; race; visual culture; immigrant youth identities developing community-based leadership programs within marginalized communities that have faced trauma and violence; and the possibilities immigrant and refugee families create when they collectively migrate across national and international borders.

Dr. Lin Lin obtained her PhD in social science education at the University of Georgia and serves as an associate professor at the State University of New York (SUNY). She applied for a 1-year Chinese language scholar position in the Chinese Language and Culture Department at Reed College in Portland, Oregon. The 1-year visiting scholarship helped her decide to return to the United States in 2000 to obtain her PhD in social science education from the University of Georgia in Athens which led to an assistant professorship at the State University of New York (SUNY) at Cortland. Her research focuses on critical historiography, culturally sustainable pedagogy, and global awareness.

Dr. Yali Zhao serves as associate professor in the Department of Early Childhood and Elementary Education at Georgia State University. She graduated from the University of Georgia in 2004 with a PhD in social science education and a graduate certificate in interdisciplinary qualitative studies. She teaches undergraduate and doctoral students in social studies methods, cultural foundations, instruction and curriculum in contemporary urban settings, and cultural perspectives in education. She is actively involved in cross-cultural and international teaching, research, and service. She has been leading the China study abroad program and the educational exchange program with Chinese universities for the department for 16 years and also serves as a mentor for Georgia State's Faculty Learning Community on International Virtual Exchange.

Dr. Guichun Zong graduated from Florida International University with an EdD in social studies education with emphasis on global education. She taught at the University of Kentucky and Georgia State University prior to joining the College of Education at Kennesaw State University. She centers her teaching, research, and service around the theme of preparing sustainability-literate teachers committed to experiential learning and teaching about human diversity, cross-cultural understanding, and global interconnectedness.

Dr. Bárbara C. Cruz earned her bachelor's degree from the University of Miami, and her master's and EdD degree from Florida International University in Miami. She is a first-generation high school and college graduate. Her research interests include multicultural and global perspectives in education; Latin America and the Caribbean; LGBTQ+ inclusive social studies; teaching social studies to English language learners (ELLs); and InsideART, an innovative visual arts program that promotes the teaching and learning of critical global issues. Her collaborative Global Schools Project of many years brings together teachers from different countries around the world with local social studies teachers in her effort to globalize curriculum and instruction.

Dr. Anatoli Rapoport obtained his PhD in social science education at Purdue University in West Lafayette, Indiana, after teaching for nearly 2 decades in the former Soviet Union. His research interests include citizenship education, comparative international and global education, and constructivist theory.

Hayg Boyadjian enrolled in a class for English for foreigners at the local high school in Massachusetts since fluently speaking three foreign languages did not help him to learn English. He obtained his high school equivalency diploma (GED) and a bachelor's degree in economics from Northeastern University. He continued his musical studies as a special student at the New England Conservatory and at Brandeis University. He concentrates on composing chamber works, concertos, sonatas, oratorios, choral music, and symphonies using aspects of his diverse heritage to guide his musical form. His over 150 compositions have been performed in renowned music halls throughout the world, including Armenia, Argentina, Brazil, England, France, Japan, South Korea, Spain, and The Netherlands,

Varteni Mosdichian graduated from Lynn High School in Massachusetts and received her bachelor's degree at the University of Florida in Gainesville where she met her stimulating philosophical mentor Dr. Walter Gaudnek. Her admission to the prestigious Cité International des Arts Studio at Les Marais in Paris is one of great pride. Her full range of compelling art is dedicated to global issues such as genocides, refugees, universal grief, massacred minorities, and to a Turkish parliamentarian of Kurdish origin who was imprisoned upon her return from Sweden where she had dared to utter the word "hello" in Kurdish. To the editors' joy and gratefulness, Ms. Varteni Mosdichian agreed to create a special painting for our book to honor the suffering Ukrainian people whose country was invaded by the

Russian army on February 24, 2022, titled, *An Armenian Mother Longing for Peace in Ukraine.*

Dr. Aixa Pérez-Prado received her Bachelor of Arts in English/creative writing and a Master of Arts in teaching English to speakers of other languages (TESOL) from the Monterey Institute of International Studies in Mexico. She obtained her PhD in social science and education at Florida State University in Tallahassee, Florida, and now holds the position of teaching professor in foreign language education, TESOL track, at Florida International University in Miami. She has worked as a cross-cultural teacher educator in pedagogy for linguistic and cultural minority students in the United States, Costa Rica, and Morocco. Her research interests include multilingualism and identity, home learning, critical/creative pedagogy, peace, linguistics, diversity studies, and promoting empathy.

Dr. Toni Fuss Kirkwood-Tucker earned her AA degree from Miami Dade Junior College and her BA degree in secondary social studies education at Florida Atlantic University. Her first teaching position was at Ida Fisher Junior High School on Miami Beach, Florida, at the height of school integration in the 1960s when black students were bussed in from their segregated neighborhoods to all-White schools. While teaching full time in Miami's public schools, she attained her MA in secondary social studies education, her EdS and her EdD degrees in curriculum and instruction with emphasis on global international education from Florida International University. She is a first-generation university student. Her primary research centers on the integration of global perspectives in teacher education and schools, global pedagogy, curricular balance, human rights violations, implementation of the Model United Nations in schools, and minorities' issues such as the inequitable recruitment of minority students into the armed forces.

Dr. Frans Doppen earned his EdS in educational leadership and PhD in curriculum and instruction with a concentration on social studies education, at the University of Florida in Gainesville. His research interests focus on place-based education, service learning, and civic education, multicultural education, social studies education, and the intersection of local and global (glocal) contemporary issues in education.

AUTHORS' CHALLENGES AFTER IMMIGRATING TO THE UNITED STATES

Despite differences among authors' reasons for their immigration to the United States, it is evident from their stories that their lives in their newly adopted country of the United States have been exposed to numerous challenges ranging from prejudice, professional and personal discrimination, micro- and macroaggressions, and lack of leadership opportunities.

For Dr. Omiunota Ukpokodu, life in the United States has been a bittersweet experience. The opportunities to earn a PhD, become a professor, and attain U.S. citizenship surpassed her wildest dreams. However, her lived reality as an African Nigerian-born American has been one of unwelcomeness and outsider treatment due to her racialization, colorization, and Africanness. She has experienced double racialization in the form of vertical racism by Whites and horizontal racism by African Americans. She is not only subjected to White supremacy that affects all Black, Indigenous, and people of color (BIPOC) but also faces exclusion and hostility from native-born Black Americans who question her choice and preference to identify as an African American. Another major challenge she faces is the difficulty of straddling two oppositional cultures. Whereas Nigerian society places a premium on cultural collectivism, human dignity, reverence and deference to age and figures of authority, among others, American individualism places a premium on the individual, self-sufficiency, supremacy, competition, and exceptionalism. Dr. Omiunota Ukpokodu also sadly has experienced challenges from faculty at two universities where she worked for more than 2 decades that included hostility, differential and discriminatory treatment, and microaggressions. Colleagues felt she was unqualified, incompetent, and solely hired as a result of affirmative action. While supported by some colleagues, she has met strong departmental resistance denying her opportunities for leadership advancement.

Dr. Josiah Tlou recalls two incidents at Virginia Polytechnic Institute and State University which will always remain in his memory. When, in his efforts to introduce global and multicultural education to the teacher education program at this university, he invited Professor Geneva Gay from Purdue University, a renowned national specialist in the field, to offer a seminar for faculty and students on the merits of global and multicultural education—only his students attended. Dr. Tlou was deeply hurt by this blatant, overt rejection of his goals by faculty, and became acutely aware of the struggles he would encounter with his colleagues in the Department of Teacher Education. The second incident occurred with his application for promotion and tenure at the university. In his dossier, he emphasized the importance of global and multicultural teaching, community engagement, and student cross-cultural understanding in the classroom, and relevant research. The committee delivered a split decision. Dr. Tlou received tenure but not promotion based on the proposition that the College of Education was focused on K–12 programs, not on global or multicultural education. The rationale seemed weak, unconvincing, and discriminatory as, at that time, the university was actively encouraging colleges and departments to internationalize their curriculum.

Dr. Misato Yamaguchi felt isolated when she first arrived in the United States. Her feeling of being invisible frightened her when she entered the high school cafeteria at Bellaire High School in Houston, Texas, where students sat together by race, and she was subjected to name-calling. Not only the racial majority but various minorities called her "oriental, yellow monkey, Jap, fresh off of the boat," the latter referring to recent refugees with no status. They also called her "Yellow Cab" referring to an Asian woman seeking American men to obtain a Green Card. She was unaware of the hidden meaning behind the labeling at first, but once she became culturally aware, her double consciousness became a way of life and a survival skill. Dr. Yamaguchi also conformed with the Asian model minority notion of appearing easy-going even when she had strong disagreements. Only when she lived in Hawai'i did she feel comfortable and at ease.

Dr. Binaya Subedi has experienced a literal transformation of his cultural and political identity since his arrival in the United States at the age of 18. Because of his racial identity he has realized that he is both invisible and visible to dominant people in U.S. society. He strongly believes that people of Asian descent are seen as perpetual foreigners and not having any sort of legitimacy in the United States. He has been told that Asians are "good" minorities or "good" immigrants. He has also been told that he is fortunate to be "here" as if he has been "saved" by being in the United States. Three lived experiences demonstrate his challenges in being an immigrant: When walking home from a public event with family, a group of White youth yelled: "You fuc*%#@ Mexican; go back to where you came from." A second incident occurred with his father walking in a suburban area and a White person calling the police complaining that "a suspicious person is walking in the neighborhood." A third incident occurred with his son stating: "Dad, I don't know if I told you this, but my friends often call me a "bomber." Dr. Subedi concludes that the racial profanity he has encountered speaks to the anti-Mexican or anti-immigrant sentiment in our country, illustrating how White people feel entitled to racially harass people of color in public spaces.

Dr. Lin Lin is very concerned about the treatment of Asian Americans in the United States, especially about the violence that followed the 2021 Atlanta spa shootings that killed eight Asian Americans, noting that some hate crimes against Asian Americans are not always covered in the media. She had colleagues at her university who argued against hiring more qualified faculty with international backgrounds. Being tokenized, she realized that her tenure had become a potential block for other candidates with international backgrounds. She also speaks to the lack of representation of Asians and Asian Americans in the school curriculum and instructional materials in American public schools which undermines the self-confidence and identity of Asian American children. She strongly feels that

Asian Americans suffer greatly from the "model minority" myth that works against Asian Americans in that they are expected to be tough, self-sufficient, and self-reliant.

Dr. Yali Zhao recalls the historic systematic discrimination against Asians and Asian Americans in the United States, such as the Chinese Exclusion Acts of 1882 and 1943, and the Japanese Internment Camps during World War II. Moreover, due to COVID-19 and blaming the Chinese for the global pandemic, there has been a new surge of anti-Chinese and anti-Asian discrimination, hate crimes, and violence. The attacks against Asian Americans escalated dramatically when a gunman in Atlanta killed eight people. This brutality shocked, traumatized, and angered all communities. People across the country took to the street to grieve the victims. On March 20, 2021, Dr. Zhao joined thousands of people in the Anti-Asian Hate March in downtown Atlanta and was interviewed by Fox News. With the global pandemic still going on, anti-Asian discrimination and violence continue in the United States. Since 2020, many Asians, Dr. Zhao's own family included, have been physically or verbally attacked and often live in fear, distress, uncertainty, and isolation.

Dr. Guichun Zong is convinced that many Asian women faculty members serving in American universities today have to walk the extra mile to make up for their cultural and linguistic differences to construct their professional niche and win support from colleagues and students. Many feel isolated, lonely, and unsupported. Some experience rejection, exclusion, and stereotypes, and she feels that she traveled the same path as most women immigrant faculty from East Asia. She has adjusted her thinking, writing, and teaching style, struggling long and hard to find her footing to carve out a place for herself in the profession. As a scholar developing critical perspectives in the analysis of social and sustainability issues, she strongly advocates a constructive outlook on how educators need to communicate and collaborate to facilitate positive change.

Dr. Bárbara C. Cruz experienced blatant discrimination from a checkout clerk at her university library demanding that she prove her faculty status for reserved materials. In her classroom, a student seriously questioned her teaching style. She professes that the steep cultural/color "tax" minority faculty pay in academia can result in a number of negative outcomes, including stressors on personal and family life, not achieving tenure and promotion, and professional burnout. The ability to "live on the hyphen," living with one foot firmly planted in one's home culture while the other foot navigates life in America, can result in a "never fully here nor there" identity. On the one hand, one must acculturate and adopt the language and customs of the new home in order to not just survive, but ultimately be successful; on the other hand, at home the cultural practices are celebrated.

Life in between these two spaces, life on the hyphen, was a never-ending source of dissonance and conflict for her.

Although Dr. Anatoli Rapoport's transition to the United States was relatively easy, it took him a long time to overcome "the fear of authority." He also learned to appreciate that his identity as a Jewish person was no longer a matter of public concern but that, instead, he had been relabeled as a Russian. He has struggled with how to best make multicultural and citizenship education relevant to his young Midwestern students who, at times, have questioned whether he, as a White male, can really teach them about the importance of diversity and hearing the voices of the Other. This has led him to the realization that many individuals simply see him as a regular American and that he is no longer part of a minority deprived of its voice. He believes that people seldom give personal accounts of how power tears the human mind in pieces by forcing them to live simultaneously in two worlds, the world of reality and the made-up world of hypocrisy and lies. Having lived in two dramatically different worlds, he believes that he can explain to students and colleagues what it means to live surrounded by official hypocrisy and even participate in it.

The painter Varteni Mosdichian has confronted discrimination firsthand in America. When applying for a position as a tour guide at Disney World while attending the University of Florida, the interviewer informed her that she was not eligible for the position because she "did not fit the perfect image of the candidate as she was darker than average, had an accent, and her nose and teeth were uneven." The words of the interviewer scarred her permanently. She has also been confronted by friends challenging her why she has not sold more of her paintings; and she has encountered discrimination regarding her accent and her difficult Armenian name. She was told by art gallery directors that the problem is not her artwork but that she "does not fit their mold." Being an immigrant, according to Varteni, is a lonely life. For the sake of her family, she continues to endure all kinds of humiliations and degrading attitudes while living in the United States even when ridiculed by conventional so-called close relatives.

Dr. Aixa Pérez-Prado speaks of her childhood immigrant experience as a story about never really belonging anywhere. It is a story of balancing two cultures and languages that cannot be combined into one. It is a story of never quite finding oneself in books or movies, yet always searching for kindred spirits everywhere. Her personal story led to a love of language, diversity, and discovery, the field of TESOL, and a passion for writing and illustrating world culture books for children. One unforgettable event was at her American school when the teacher told the class that although the curriculum calls for learning about South America, they would not study about South America because it wasn't important. At that time Aixa felt as if her name, her family, and her country were ripped away from her, and that she was nobody. She strongly feels that the rigid and compulsory patriotic discourse that youth in the United States are socialized into exposes the operations of dominant power and control in society, and it is the hyper patriotic socialization, saturated with racism, that blocks meaningful learning about global communities.

For Dr. Toni Fuss Kirkwood-Tucker, settling in the Deep South of the United States with her strong Bavarian accent and making linguistic mistakes was very difficult at first. She often felt the double-consciousness expounded by African American scholar W. E. B. Du Bois, and the need to perform her academic responsibilities with 200% perfection. Prejudicial encounters were both subtle and overt but cruelly blatant when she was called a Nazi. One specific incident occurred in teaching high school when she invited the language arts teacher next door to her classroom, who was Jewish, to consider requiring her students to read *Anne Frank's Diary of a Young Girl* (1947/1997) while she was teaching about World War II and the Holocaust to which her colleague gladly agreed. Leaving her classroom, the language arts teacher called after her, "I love your soft French accent." When Toni replied that the accent was a German one, she let out a numbing shriek and never spoke to Toni again. Even after 60 years living in her adopted country, Toni believes that a degree of marginalization is an integral aspect of her life in America.

After first immigrating to the United States, Dr. Frans Doppen encountered several instances of racism in the public schools where he taught as well as in the community where he lived. The first return trip to The Netherlands planted the double-consciousness in him that he was no longer strictly Dutch but also partially American. His American students' evident lack of knowledge of the global world and a visit by Walter Dean Myers—an author of young adult literature focusing on the African American experience—prompted him to make teaching about cultural diversity an integral part of his curriculum. Even after nearly 40 years in the United States, Dr. Doppen continues to possess a sense of double-consciousness that, in many ways due to contemporary communications technology, has made it easy to keep up with news in his native country. Until recently, he has not felt compelled to seek American citizenship as he has wanted to be sure to keep the option open of being able to move back to and live in The Netherlands. He presently feels uneasy about living in a highly polarized United States that is in the process of rolling back the clock on decades of progress. He believes that his prospect of being able to vote for progressive candidates is not very encouraging as American democracy is on the edge of a deep abyss.

CONCLUSION

The storied oral history narratives of 14 scholars and artists from around the world presented in this book offer a unique window into unknown, untold stories experienced by witnesses of historical and contemporary events that will enhance the teaching of a globalized social studies curriculum in classrooms (Connelly & Clandinin, 2006). The authors of this book are committed to global education informed by their work that is deeply grounded in the philosophy that all members of humanity are created equal regardless of ability, age, class, creed, culture, ethnicity, gender, nationality, sexual orientation, socioeconomic status, and race (a human construct). The scholars have implemented the criticality of global pedagogy into curriculum and instruction at all levels of education in K–12 public schools and in teacher education programs across the United States and in other nations—a relatively new construct in education advanced by national and international global scholars in the 1960s in the United States and around the world (see Kirkwood-Tucker, 2018). The artists, with their visual and tactile appeal to the aesthetics are reaching students, lifelong learners, and the public at home and abroad.

To bring the storytelling methodology to an even higher level of teaching and learning, the editors of this book strongly believe that the philosophy of the concept of *ubuntu* implemented and advanced by African scholars Drs. Josiah Tlou and Omiunota Ukpokodu need significant more attention by educators who seek to promote global education. This African concept embraces a philosophy of cohesion, mutual understanding, solidarity, and peacebuilding to promote a common link among human beings that leads to the discovery of one's own humanity (Manda, 2009). In essence, people affirm their humanity when they acknowledge the humanity of others. Ubuntu acknowledges both our interconnectedness and shared responsibility that flows from these connections. The epic story of renowned civil rights activist Nelson Mandela is grounded in the concept of ubuntu. During his 27 years of incarceration on Robben Island, Mandela maintained his faith in human goodness and a culture of peace extending beyond hatred and vengeance.

We presently live in ominous times in the United States, an alleged nation of immigrants, as we are increasingly confronted with disinformation, racist hatred, and violence that is deeply concerning. Political divisions are the order of the day resulting in basic human rights violations such as the reversal of *Roe v. Wade*, assault on the LGTBQ+ community, blatant voter repression, anti-immigrant sentiments, endangered academic freedom, and much more that are testing the very values of our democracy. It is critical that in these auspicious times we must declare our moral responsibility to confront the ways in which we are complicit in the hatred and violence embedded in the United States and in other societies around the world today. Rather than remain silent, scholars and practitioners in international global educators must respond to the pressing need to produce a global minded citizenry that acknowledges multiple perspectives, is aware of the state of the planet, cognizant of cross-cultural phenomena, knowledgeable of the global dynamics affecting nations, and well informed about the criticality that individuals, groups, and entire nations make different choices based on pressing issues confronting humankind (Hanvey, 1976).

The field of global education has taken on a new urgency and necessitates a focus on teaching students and the general public about communication, conflict resolution, compromise, respect, joy, dreams, hope, and peacebuilding. We, the editors, believe that the integration of human experiential stories—as told by global scholars and artists from around the world—strengthened with the African concept of ubuntu, offers a powerful assemblage of knowledge, skills, and wisdom that will improve the art of teaching and deepen our understanding of humanity.

REFERENCES

Connelly, F. M., & Clandinin, D. J., (2006). Narrative inquiry. In J. Green, G. Camilli, & P. Elmore (Eds.), *Handbook of complementary methods in education research* (pp. 375–385). Lawrence Erlbaum.

Frank, A. (1947, 1997). *The diary of a young girl: The definitive edition.* Mass Market Paperback.

Hanvey, R. C. (1976). An attainable global perspective. *Theory Into Practice, 21*(3), 162–167. https://eric.ed.gov/?id=EJ269219

Kirkwood-Tucker, T. F. (2018). *The global education movement: Narratives of distinguished global scholars.* Information Age Publishing.

Manda, D. S. (2009). *Ubuntu philosophy as an African philosophy for peace.* https://www.benkhumalo-seegelken.de/wp-content/uploads/unconditional-humanness.pdf

United Nations. (1967). *Declaration on the Elimination of All Forms of Discrimination Against Women.* https://www.eods.eu/library/UNGA_Declaration%20Women_1967_en.pdf

ABOUT THE EDITORS

Toni Fuss Kirkwood-Tucker was born in Unterammergau in Bavaria, Germany and raised in her war-torn country during the Nazi era. At age 22, she immigrated to the United States. She obtained her BA degree from Florida Atlantic University and her MA, EdS, and EdD degrees from Florida International University. She served as associate professor at Florida Atlantic University from 1996 to 2004 and visiting professor and  program coordinator in the School of Teacher Education at Florida State University from 2006 to 2012. During her tenure at both institutions, she globalized the social studies curriculum and instruction in the social studies teacher education program and introduced new courses in the curriculum: Methods for Teaching Global Perspectives Across the Curriculum, Global Perspectives in Education, Global Perspectives of Curricular Trends and Issues Across Nations, Methods and Materials for Teaching the Holocaust and Other Genocides, and Teaching Global Issues: Simulating the United Nations. Prior to her appointment to Florida Atlantic University, she worked in the Miami Public Schools teaching secondary social studies until her promotion to social studies curriculum specialist. In the global education reform movement of the Miami Public Schools between 1984 to 1994, she became the principal global teacher-of-teachers in training leadership teams in two thirds of Miami's 274 public schools leading to her promotion to director of the Global International Education Program. In the democratic reform movement of Russian education after the fall of the Berlin

Wall, she participated between 1991 and 1997 as a member of the Florida International University-Indiana University delegation in the training of Russian administrators, teacher educators, and pre- and inservice teachers in global education.

Dr. Kirkwood-Tucker served as a Fulbright teacher to the People's Republic of China and Fulbright Scholar to Russia. She was honored twice as the Florida Global Teacher of the Year and twice as the Agnes Crabtree International Relations Teacher of the Year. She is a recipient of the Global Apple Award from the American Forum for Global Education and the Distinguished Global Scholar Award from the International Assembly of the National Council for the Social Studies. Her primary research centers on the integration of global perspectives in teacher education and schools, global pedagogy, curricular balance, and human rights. She has authored numerous chapters and articles including her two edited books, *Visions in Global Education: The Globalization of Curriculum and Pedagogy in Teacher Education and Schools* (Peter Lang, 2009) and *The Global Education Movement: Narratives of Distinguished Global Scholars* (Information Age Publishing, 2018). email: tonifusskirkwoodtucker@gmail.com

Frans H. Doppen was born in 1957 in Marienvelde, a small village in The Netherlands near the German border. He earned his bachelor's degree in modern history from Utrecht University. As part of his program of study, he joined a yearlong exchange program at the University of Florida in the United States in 1980. In 1984 he returned as an immigrant and began a 19-year career as a middle and high school teacher. After completing his PhD at the University of Florida, in 2003 he began his  career as a teacher educator at Ohio University Athens where, after serving as chair of the department for 8 years, he now serves as professor of social studies education and curriculum and instruction. Dr. Doppen has served as the executive editor of the *Ohio Social Studies Review*. He also served on the executive board of the International Assembly of the National Council for the Social Studies and was elected its president. He was twice awarded the Distinguished Faculty Research and Scholarship Award in his college and was honored for "The Belize Project," as the best annual research paper by the International Assembly which was published in the *Journal of International Social Studies*. He has authored 10 book chapters and 37 peer reviewed articles addressing global issues published in the *Journal of International Social Studies*, the *Ohio Social Studies Review*, *Social Education*, and *Citizenship and Social Justice*. He has authored a book, *Richard L. Davis and the Color Line in Ohio Coal: A Hocking Valley Mine Labor Organizer, 1862–1900* (McFarland & Company, 2016), which addresses an African American labor organizer rising to national prominence. As the program coordinator of the Consortium for Overseas Student Teaching at Ohio University (COST), he has sponsored more than 140 student teachers to complete their professional internship in 14 different countries. Dr. Doppen obtained his U.S. citizenship in 2022. email: doppen@ohio.edu

ABOUT THE CONTRIBUTORS

Hayg Boyadjian was born in 1938 in Paris, France. At the age of 10, he immigrated with his Armenian-born family to Argentina where he started his musical studies at the Liszt Conservatory in Buenos Aires. In 1958, he left for the United States and became an American citizen. He continued his musical studies as a special student at the New England Conservatory and later at Brandeis University. Among his teachers were re-  nowned Beatriz Balzi, Seymour Shifrin, Alvin Lucier, and Edward Cohen. He has composed over 150 compositions ranging from chamber music to symphonies. His first symphony for orchestra, *Of Life and Death: Genocide*, presenting genocide as a human tragedy occurring around the world, was premiered in Lviv, Ukraine in 1996, and also performed in Yerevan, Armenia. His proudest work is his second symphony, *Time of Silence*, a 1-hour oratorio on the Armenian Genocide referred to as *Esse Aeternam*, accompanied by his poem, *Genocide*. It is written for orchestra, choir, solo soprano, and speaker, and was premiered on April 21, 1986 in the Sanders Theatre at Harvard University, Cambridge, Massachusetts. His third symphony, *Black Lives Matter*, is composed of four movements. Each movement reflects the suffering of Black people and includes a funeral march and a last movement of apotheosis. The symphony is scheduled to premiere in 2023. His *Final Bell* CD recording that includes his third piano sonata was nominated for a Grammy Award in 2006. His compositions have been performed in

Argentina, Armenia, Belgium, Brazil, Germany, Norway, Ukraine, Russia, Scotland, and South Korea. He is a member of the following professional organizations: the American Composers Forum, Composers' Union of Armenia, The MacDowell Colony, Meet the Composer, and the Society of Composers. His name can be found in *Who's Who in American Music* and *Who's Who in International Music.* email: haygboya@rcn.com

Bárbara C. Cruz is professor of social science education at the University of South Florida. Her research and teaching interests include multicultural and global perspectives in education, English learners, Latin America, and the Caribbean, and the infusion of the arts across the curriculum. In addition to her scholarly work in the aforementioned areas, Dr. Cruz has published several young adult biographies of inspirational Hispanics, in-  cluding *César Chávez: A Voice for Farm Workers* and *Multiethnic Teens and Cultural Identity,* for which she has received the Carter G. Woodson Book Award. For her nationally recognized research, she has been honored with a Fulbright Scholar Award to Spain, the Outstanding Faculty Research Achievement Award, and the Faculty Excellence Award. Currently she co-directs the InsideART program, an innovative visual arts program that promotes the teaching and learning of critical global issues. Dr. Cruz was the director of the Global Schools Project, a collaborative program that prepares teachers and students for an increasingly globalized society. Under the auspices of this program, she has hosted dozens of teachers from abroad for concentrated study in the United States. This cross-cultural educational exchange also has resulted in significant benefits for the U.S.-based teachers and students who participated in the interchange. email: bcruz@usf.edu

Lin Lin was born in the city of Qingdao in the Shandong Province of China. In 2000, she came to study in the United States and is now a Chinese permanent resident. She joined the Department of Childhood and Early Childhood at SUNY Cortland in 2005 with a PhD in social science education from the University of Georgia. Prior to coming to the United States, she taught English and United States history courses for 9  years at Beijing Foreign Studies University in China as associate professor. From 1997 to 1998, she taught Mandarin language courses and facilitated cultural programs as a Chinese Language Scholar at Reed College, Portland, Oregon. Since 2005, her approaches to teaching elementary social studies pedagogical courses and peer-reviewed publications are informed by literature in critical historiography, culturally sustainable pedagogy, and global awareness studies. She advocates for increasing children's exposure to diverse narratives and enjoys being a lifelong learner as the global pandemic has challenges us to teach effectively in multiple delivery formats. In 2010, she was awarded the nontenure track award of Excellence in Teaching from SUNY and in 2016 she was honored with the Excellence in Teaching Award by the Cortland Chapter of the National Society of Leadership and Success. Dr. Lin served as a global education learning fellow with the South Asia Area Study Program at Cornell University in 2017 and again in 2021–2022. Moving forward with transformative research studies, culturally responsive teaching in undergraduate and graduate elementary social studies courses, she continues to provide services to her communities. email: linlin@cortland.edu

Varteni Mosdichian was born in the Armenian quarter of Istanbul, Turkey. Her people were under tremendous pressure to renounce their Armenian heritage and become Turks. She left Turkey as a teenager in the late 1960s settling in the Boston area with her mother and became a U.S. citizen in 1976. Her formal art education began at CalArts. She graduated from the University of Florida under the mentorship of Dr. Walter Gaudnek, a  Czech-born German artist who had experienced the brutalities of the Nazis just as her grandparents had experienced the pogroms during the Armenian Genocide of 1915. In the early 1970s, she began exhibiting her work in such diverse locations as California; Louisville, Kentucky; Boston, Massachusetts; New York City; Rhode Island; Washington, D.C.; and Florida as well as in Europe and Armenia. Ms. Mosdichian is a member of the Cité International des Arts, Paris; the Armenian Académie of Fine Arts, Yerevan; and the Amaras Arts Alliance, Boston. She comes from a disturbed world filled with intolerance and discrimination. She is a global artist who feels the pain of injustice from all directions and among all peoples. Her works carry the burden of millions who are being dehumanized today. She describes her paintings the following way: *Departure* (1992) is dedicated to Leyla Zana, a Turkish parliamentarian of Kurdish origin who was imprisoned upon her return from Sweden where she had dared to utter the word "hello" in Kurdish; *Moment* (1996) is dedicated to refugees of the world: refugees of Iranian exiles as well as from Europe, the Middle East, and Afghanistan who continue to be a part of her life since her college years; and *Threnody to Yezidi Women* (2018) is dedicated to the women of ethnic Yezidis living in eastern Turkey who were massacred by ISIS. She has confronted discrimination firsthand both in America and abroad. email: vartenim@gmail.com (Photo by Ditoma David).

Aixa Pérez-Prado is a native of Argentina who immigrated to the United States as a small child. She has a Bachelor of Arts degree in English/creative writing, and a Master of Arts in teaching English to speakers of other languages (TESOL). Dr. Pérez-Prado was a Title VII bilingual/bicultural fellow at Florida State University where she received her PhD in social science education and is currently a teaching professor at Florida  International University. She began her teaching career as a bilingual Kindergarten teacher in Salinas, California and has since worked as a cross-cultural trainer and teacher of teachers in pedagogy for linguistic and cultural minority students in the United States, Costa Rica, and Morocco. Her teaching and research interests include multilingualism and identity, home learning, critical/creative pedagogy, peace linguistics, and diversity studies. Dr. Pérez-Prado is a global learning faculty member who teaches pedagogy for language learners, cross-cultural communication, and diversity of meaning. Her latest book is *LAF with the Habits of Mind: Strategies and Activities for Diverse Language Learners* (The Institute for Habits of Mind, 2021). She also writes and illustrates books for children that highlight issues of identity, belonging, diversity, and communication across cultures. She has two picture books currently in production, *City Feet* (Reycraft Books, 2023) and *Mercedes Sosa: Voice of the People* (Lee & Low, 2024). She writes in Spanish and English, and translates in Spanish, English, and Portuguese. Her author/illustrator website is https://www.aixaperezprado.com. Twitter: @professoraixa; email: professoraixa@gmail.com

Anatoli Rapoport serves as professor of curriculum and instruction in the College of Education at Purdue University. He was born in Odessa, Ukraine, then part of the Soviet Union. He lived in St. Petersburg, Russia, until 2000 before immigrating to the United States. Before receiving his PhD in social studies education, he worked as classroom teacher and school administrator for 20 years. His research interests include citizenship  education; comparative, international, and global education; and the application of constructivist theory in education. He is a board member of the National Council for the Social Studies International Assembly and the editor of *Journal of International Social Studies*. Dr. Rapoport is the recipient of the Leadership in Globalization Award, the Curriculum and Instruction Discovery Award, and the Curriculum and Instruction Engagement Award. He holds an honorary doctorate (*honoris causa*) from the Academy of Science of Moldova. Since 2003, he has organized and coordinated several international programs for teachers and students at Purdue University and teaches social studies methods courses and graduate seminars on international and comparative education. He has published in several journals and served as guest editor of special issues publications of *Compare: A Journal of Comparative and International Education* (with Serhiy Kovalchuk); *Education, Citizenship and Social Justice* (with Miri Yemini), and *Research in Social Sciences and Technology*. He is the author of four books: *Fields Unknown: Russian and American Teachers on Their International Exchange Experiences* (VDM Verlag Dr. Mueller E K, 2007), *Civic Education in Contemporary Global Society* (with Andrey Borshevsky; Institute of Democracy, 2009), *Competing Frameworks: Global and National in Citizenship Education* (Information Age Publishing, 2018), and *Democratic Citizenship in Non-Western Contexts* (with Serhiy Kovalchuk; Routledge, 2019). email: rapoport@purdue.edu

Binaya Subedi is associate professor in multicultural and equity studies in education at The Ohio State University. He was born and educated in Nepal. His research examines issues of migration, social studies education, and global citizenship. His current research addresses the challenges that immigrants and refugee families face and the possibilities they create when they collectively migrate across national and international boundaries. Dr. Subedi has published numerous journal articles on topics such as global education, race, visual culture, immigrant youth identities, and served as co-editor of the journal *Educational Studies* from 2013–2018. His current work includes developing community-based leadership programs within marginalized communities that have faced trauma and violence. email: subedi.1@osu.edu

Josiah Tlou was born and raised in the southwestern part of rural Zimbabwe, Africa, under the colonial rule then called Rhodesia. He came to the United States in 1965 and is a U.S. citizen. As professor of social studies and international education, he taught over 30 years at Virginia Polytechnic Institute and State University (Virginia Tech). He earned his doctorate in education in curriculum and instruction with a minor in comparative education from the University of Illinois in Champaign-Urbana; a master's degree from Illinois State University in history; a bachelor's degree in history from Luther College in Decorah, Iowa; and specialized in African Studies at the University of Wisconsin. Before his arrival in the United States, he held diplomas qualifying him to teach students in secondary schools and served as principal in a Lutheran boarding school in Zimbabwe. During his professorship at Virginia Tech, he participated in the implementation of degree programs for teacher educators at the University of Botswana and Domasi College in Malawi, sponsored by USAID. In Malawi he also devel-

oped CIVIC education programs to be incorporated in the social studies curriculum for all primary schools. In Kenya and Malawi, he established Civitas chapters supported by the Center for Civic Education in Calabasas, California. Thanks to the International Assembly of the National Council for the Social Studies he was instrumental in providing backpacks for students and coordinating the drilling of a borehole to provide fresh water for the Mwanje primary school and community in Malawi. His research ranges from the development of teacher education programs in African nations to the integration of the ubuntu concept in teaching and learning. He was honored with the following awards: Certificate of Recognition for Public Service on Global Inter-Cultural Dialogue by the Cross-Cultural Dialogue Organization, Virginia Tech (1980); Dean's Excellence in Service Award College of Education, Virginia Tech (1986); Virginia Tech's Alumni Award for Excellence in International Programs (2002); Twenty-Four Years of International Effort, Virginia Tech (2002); an Honorary Degree for International Service: Doctor of Humane Letters from Luther College in Decorah, Iowa (2003); and the prestigious Distinguished Global Scholar Award from the International Assembly of the National Council for the Social Studies (2012). email: tlou@vt.edu

Omiunota Nelly Ukpokodu was born in Jattu, Nigeria, immigrated to the United States in 1982 and obtained her U.S. citizenship. She is a professor in the Division of Teacher Education and Curriculum Studies in the School of Education at the University of Missouri-Kansas City, Missouri. She teaches undergraduate and graduate courses that include, among others, a seminar in social science curriculum, social studies methods, multicultural perspectives in education, teaching for equity and social justice, and fundamentals of culturally responsive pedagogy. Her research studies include transformative pedagogy and learning, global education/global perspectives pedagogy, ubuntu pedagogy, global/multicultural citizenship education, and African immigrant education. She has been honored, amongst others, with the following awards: the 2019 Chancellor's Award for Embracing and Promoting Diversity; the 2019 Carlos J. Vallejo Memorial Award for Lifetime Scholarship, the 2019 Outstanding Contribution Award to the Field of Social Studies Research, the 2018 Outstanding Educator Service, the 2011 National Association for Multicultural Education Equity & Social Justice Advocacy Award, the Fulbright-Hays Scholarship Award to South Africa (2007), and the University of Missouri-South Africa Education Program Award at the University of Western Cape (2020). She is the founder and president of the International Association for African Educators and served as president of the International Assembly of the National

Council for the Social Studies. She is author/co-author of seven books and of numerous chapters and articles published in refereed professional journals. email: ukpokoduo@umkc.edu

Misato Yamaguchi was born in Yokohama City in the Kanagawa Prefecture of Greater Tokyo in Japan during the height of the 1980s economic bubble. Her forward-thinking parents raised her and her elder sister to be internationally minded, introducing them to different countries. In the 1990s, the end of the Cold War shifted world affairs capturing her attention. Eager to see the world beyond Japan, she completed a high school exchange year in Houston, Texas, as she saw her future in the United States.  In the 2000s, she earned a bachelor's degree in international relations from St. Mary's University in San Antonio, Texas; a master's degree in international education from American University in Washington, D.C.; and a PhD in social studies and global education from The Ohio State University in Columbus. She gained international experience interning for the United Nations World Food Program, the international exchange program of Youth for Understanding, and the educational global voyage program Peace Boat. In the 2010s, she served as assistant professor of multicultural and global education at Augusta University in Augusta, Georgia. Her research focused on authentic cultural learning and global citizenship. She has published in *The Journal of Social Studies Research, Social Education,* and *The Social Studies.* After teaching 4 years in higher education in the United States, a medical condition has led to her permanent return to Japan. In the 2020s, she now serves as a workshop facilitator for an internationally recognized Disability Equality Training program, exploring how global education addresses disability and inclusion. email: misatoy2000@gmail.com

Yali Zhao was born in China and grew up in the ethnic minority area of Xinjiang in the 1960s. She pursued her undergraduate and graduate study, respectively in the early 1980s and 1990s. She taught at two Chinese universities and served as an associate professor at the University of Science and Technology in Beijing before she came to the United States for doctoral study in 2000. She obtained her doctorate in social science education  at the University of Georgia in 2004 and, upon graduation, joined the faculty at Georgia State University (GSU). She is associate professor at GSU teaching courses to both undergraduate and doctoral students, including social studies methods, cultural foundations, instruction and curriculum in contemporary urban settings, and perspectives of culture and education. She has published in reputed journals such as *Social Education, International*

Journal of Social Education, Journal of Technology and Teacher Education, Social Studies and the Young Learners, Asia-Pacific Journal of Teacher Education, and *Innovations in Education and Teaching International.* She co-edited a book *Seeking the Common Dreams Between the Worlds: Stories of Chinese Immigrant Faculty in North American Higher Education* (Information Age Publishing, 2013). She has been actively involved in cross-cultural and international education teaching, research, and service in the past 17 years at GSU. She has been leading the GSU Faculty Learning Community on International Virtual Exchange for the past several years and received the College of Education and Human Development Innovation in International Education Faculty Award in 2021. email: yzhao@gsu.edu

Guichun Zong was born in Liaoning, China and moved to the United States in 1995. She is professor of curriculum and instruction at Kennesaw State University. Her research interests include examining policies, programs, and practices of global learning and sustainability education. Her publications have appeared in refereed journals such as *Teaching and Teacher Education, Social Education, Theory and Research in Social Education,*  *Social Studies Research and Practice, Teachers College Record,* and *Teacher Education Quarterly.* She has contributed to the following books: *The State of Global Education: Learning With the World and Its People* (Routledge, 2015), *Bridging Cultures: International Women Faculty Transforming the US Academy* (UPA, 2011), *Critical Global Perspectives: Rethinking Knowledge About Global Societies* (Information Age Publishing, 2010), and *Visions in Global Education: The Globalization of Curriculum and Pedagogy in Teacher Education and Schools* (Peter Lang, 2009). Dr. Zong has co-edited a volume with Dr. Elinor Brown, titled *Global Perspectives on Gender and Sexuality in Education: Raising Awareness, Fostering Equity, Advancing Justice* (Information Age Publishing, 2017). She has received her bachelor and master's degrees from Beijing Normal University, and her doctoral degree from Florida International University. She has taught courses in curriculum and instruction, social studies education, teacher education, multicultural education, and global education at Florida International University, University of Kentucky, Georgia State University, and Kennesaw State University. email: gzong@kennesaw.edu

SUBJECT INDEX

A

Accents, xxiv, 26–27, 179, 193, 249, 275, 310, 326, 333–334, 370
Anti-Asian Incidents, 65, 81, 103–104, 112, 129–130, 146
Antisemitism, xxiv, 181–189, 349, 355, 359–360, 362
Armenian Genocide, xxv, xxvii, 197–205, 220–222, 293–296, 303–308, 350, 360
Apartheid, 38, 60
Auerhahn Resistance Group, 240–241, 245–246
Awards, 20, 23–24, 26, 107–108, 169, 184, 283

B

Birthplace, xix–xxviii, 5, 22, 29, 35–36, 58, 75, 88, 115–117, 141, 179–181, 206, 226, 229, 293–294, 317, 345–351
Boy Soldiers, xxvi, 16, 232–234

C

Child Labor, 119, 210–211, 252, 354, 358
Citizenship, 4, 17–19, 21, 88, 191, 286, 324, 346, 367
Colonialism, xx, 6, 36–40, 52, 76, 83, 141, 304, 352, 357, 359
Communism, 91–93, 95–96, 117–119, 182, 190–191, 242–243, 254, 270, 274, 358–359, 362
COST (Consortium for Overseas Student Teaching), 282–284
Cultural Revolution, xxii–xxiii, 78, 90–91, 98, 115–116, 119–124, 140–142, 348–349, 354, 358–359

D

Decolonize, 82–84
Deng Xiaoping, xxiii, 155
Die Weisse Rose (The White Rose) Intellectual Resistance Group, 229
Discrimination, xix, xxi, xxiii–xxiv, xxvi, 19, 26, 41, 43, 47, 65, 79–82, 95, 116, 119–121, 129–130, 141, 145–146, 165, 173, 184–185, 188–189, 199, 247, 258, 285, 310, 336–338, 348, 367–372
Dissident, xxvi, 43–44, 172, 187, 225, 239, 241, 245–246, 253, 256, 258, 294, 358,
Distinguished Global Scholars, 280
Dvorik, 181, 187, 190, 359

E

Education in Native Country, xix–xx, xxii–xxiv, xxvi–xxvii, 7–13, 26, 29, 36, 38–41, 59, 76–79, 94–96, 118–123, 141–143, 157–158, 184–188, 212, 230–231, 237, 246, 264, 266, 268–271, 293–294, 300–302, 322–323, 347–348, 350–358, 361–362
Education in the United States, xx–xxii, xxiv–xxv, xxvii–xxviii, 17–18, 20, 44–46, 61–64, 82, 98–100, 125–126, 135, 144–145, 160–163, 191–192, 215–216, 250–251, 272, 276, 294, 304–305, 313, 325, 328–329, 335, 348, 351–357, 361–366
Exchange Programs, 24, 26, 40–42, 48–50, 61–62, 254, 270–273, 352
Experiences in Native Country, xix–xxviii, 5–17, 35–44, 58–60, 71–73, 75–79, 89–98, 116–125, 128–129, 131–133, 140–144, 157–159, 180–191, 206–209, 225–247, 262–270, 272–274, 293–304, 308, 319–323, 326–327, 329–333, 346–357, 357–361, 363

F

Freedom Flights, xxiv, 158, 354

G

Gestapo, 239, 350, 361

H

Hate Groups, 108, 130, 275
Historical Events in Native Country, xix–xxviii, 3, 9, 14–17, 36–40, 43–44, 58–59, 78, 89, 90, 92–93, 95–96, 117, 122–123, 143, 157–158, 172, 207–209, 226–246, 264–265, 267–268, 273–274, 293–297, 300, 307, 317–319, 329–333, 346–351, 357–361

I

Immigration, xix–xxi, xxiv–xxvi, xxviii, 4, 17, 43–44, 64–65, 71, 98–99, 110–111, 125–127, 135, 144, 146, 158–159, 166, 183, 198, 205–206, 209, 214, 247, 249, 258, 274, 284, 300, 304, 313, 320, 322–324, 326, 338, 346, 350, 355–356, 360–363, 366–371
Internment Camps, 72
Invasion of Ukraine, v, 17, 30, 88, 89, 110, 151, 194, 220, 237, 248, 294, 310, 366

J

Japanese Orphans, 62
Japanese Prison Camps, 94
Jyuken Senso, 59

K

Kike, 181, 185, 187, 359
Kintsugi, 74

L

Labeling, xxviii, 65, 105–106, 121, 165, 192, 307, 327, 334, 348, 358, 368, 370
Lived Experiences, 4, 47, 52, 115–116, 121, 133, 136, 139, 140.
LGBTQ+, 168, 170–171, 173, 286, 365, 372

M

Missionary Schools, 9, 11–12, 36–43, 351–352

N

National College Entrance Examination, 121, 143, 348
Nazis, xxvi, 207–209, 225–244, 245–246, 253, 258, 263, 266–267, 305, 346, 350, 361, 371
Nazi Genocide, 225, 228, 250
Nelson Mandela, 69
Nigerian Civil War (Biafra), xix, 3, 14–17, 357

O

Oral History, xx, xxiii, xxv, 8–9, 24, 62, 115–116, 118, 126, 141, 220, 225, 293, 308, 341, 343, 372

P

Pokazukha, 190–191
Prisoners of War, 61, 358
Professional Accomplishments, 22–26, 46, 48–50, 67–68, 72, 97, 108, 126, 137–138, 144, 148, 165–166, 168, 171–172, 216–218, 250–256, 277, 280–285, 343, 347–348, 352–353, 363–366
Propaganda, 78, 90, 119, 182–183, 187–189, 191

R

Racism, xxi, xxvi–xxviii, 19, 20, 38, 40–42, 52, 65, 79–82, 103–105, 130, 247–250, 252, 259, 274–275, 321, 367–372
Research, 22–26, 44, 47, 67–68, 83, 168, 172, 252–253, 276, 278, 282–284, 354, 362–366
Rice Fields, 119, 354
Rhodesian African Teacher Association (RATA), 77

S

Shanghai Communiqué, 94
Sino-Japanese War, 58
SS (Schutzstaffel), 229, 239–240, 243, 361

T

TESOL (Teaching English to Students of Other Languages), 70
Tiananmen Square, xx–xxii, 60, 93–96, 123, 143, 348, 354, 358

U

ubuntu, xx, 6, 23, 24, 30–31, 35–41, 43–46, 48, 50–52, 363, 372–373
Uyghur minority, 118

W

World War II, xx, xxv–xxvi, 58, 60–62, 67, 78, 94, 198, 207–209, 225–246, 250, 258, 263, 264–265, 266–268, 272, 286, 349–351, 355, 358–362, 371

Printed in the United States
by Baker & Taylor Publisher Services